THE UNIVERSITY OF CHICAGO
PUBLICATIONS IN ANTHROPOLOGY

SOCIAL ANTHROPOLOGY SERIES

THE FOLK CULTURE OF
YUCATAN

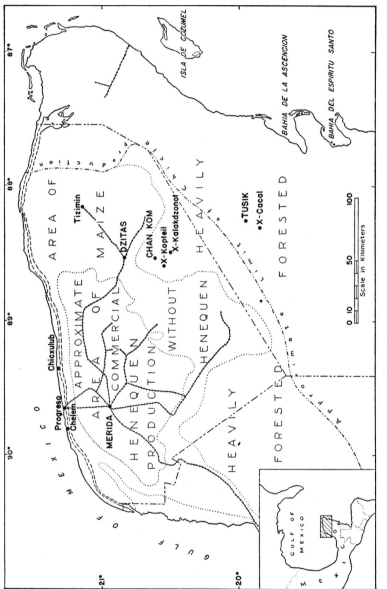

NORTHERN PART OF THE PENINSULA OF YUCATAN

The (necessarily approximate) limits of the area of commercial henequen production, of the area of maize-without-henequen, and of the heavily forested area are taken from the *Carta geográfica del estado de Yucatán* (Mexico City, D.F.: Secretaría de Agricultura y Fomento, Dirección de Estudios Geográficos y Climatológicos, 1931). The broken line showing the approximate northwestern limits of the area of commercial chicle exploitation was drawn for the author of this book by a representative of the chicle industry.

(See cartographic references given on Pl. I, Map 1, of George H. Shattuck *et al.*, *The Peninsula of Yucatan* [Carnegie Institution of Washington Pub. 431 (Washington, D.C., 1933)].)

THE FOLK CULTURE
OF YUCATAN

By

ROBERT REDFIELD

THE UNIVERSITY OF CHICAGO PRESS

CHICAGO & LONDON

This volume expresses results of research carried on under the auspices and at the expense of Carnegie Institution of Washington.

THE UNIVERSITY OF CHICAGO PRESS, CHICAGO 60637
The University of Chicago Press, Ltd., London W.C. 1

For R. E. P.

PREFACE

I HAVE here attempted to do two things at once: to summarize a great many particular facts about a particular people at a certain time and also to declare or to suggest some general notions about the nature of society and culture. This volume renders an account of field work done in which the facts gathered are grouped and filed for reference. It also contains some ideas of more general application. One might say that the volume tries to be both a report and a book. The former is something you look up facts in; the latter is something you read.

It may be that these two are incompatible and that one cannot read for its general value a written product that also does its duty by new facts that have been assembled in the survey of an area of interest. I have made the attempt because I think that every plausible means should be tried in strengthening our shaky bridges between general propositions as to society and culture and as to the nature of social change, on the one hand, and such special knowledge as we have of particular societies, on the other. So while I have in these pages now and again used language which is more comprehensive than is needed to report some facts from Yucatan, I have (except briefly in the last chapter) stayed strictly with the facts from Yucatan in giving substance to the generalizations. Or, to put it the other way, I have reported on the facts we gathered in Yucatan in terms considerably larger than would be needed if this volume were only a report. In these pages the reader will frequently encounter the words "disorganization," "secularization," and "individualization." They are words that seem to me applicable to some differences among communities in Yucatan. As they are also big enough to describe facts in other places and times, the use of them here is designed to favor the comparison of these facts from Yucatan with other facts gathered elsewhere.

It is not that the few general ideas that occur in these pages are new. The reader of Durkheim will recognize the influence of his contrasts between the social segment and the social organ and between the sacred and the profane. There is a strong flavor of Henry Maine about the transition implied in the following pages from a familial society to one emphasizing individual action and formal political controls. Lewis H. Morgan's opposition of *societas* to *civitas* finds a response in these pages. Tönnies' antithesis between the *Gemeinschaft* and the *Gesellschaft* has contributed to the general conceptions which helped to formulate questions asked of the materials in Yucatan. And there have been other influences.

The contribution of the book, as a book and not as a report, seems to me to lie in the degree to which it demonstrates a connection between some general ideas and a single large body of considered and sifted facts. The concepts of cultural disorganization, of secularization, and of individualization are given some new content. The new content takes the form not of some additional citations of scattered examples but of an account of one society, or of closely related societies, in terms of these concepts. By reason of the review of the same facts several times in terms of these concepts successively, some concomitance if not interdependence of the general phenomena represented by these terms is indicated. I am not discovering anything very new about society, but I am trying to make some old discoveries carry more weight and more usefulness for further research by working out in some detail the existence of the general ideas in a segregated body of particular fact.

Of course "the facts," the full facts, about Yucatan are not contained in this volume. Necessarily a summary such as this must deal with something that is already summarized. We studied four communities in Yucatan, and each study involved collection and elimination and abstraction and generalization. So in the following pages what is picked up and handled in a

single sentence may go back to a great many particular observations and many concrete instances. If this were not the procedure, the volume of materials and facts would weigh the
reader and the publisher down.

I do regret that there are not now available published descriptive accounts of all four of the communities. One is available (*Chan Kom: A Maya Village* [Carnegie Institution of Washington Pub. 448 (Washington, 1934)]), and a second (*The Maya
of East Central Quintana Roo* [Washington: Carnegie Institution
of Washington, 1942]) will appear not long after the publication of this volume. References to these two reports are made
on many of the pages following and will give the reader access
to some of the more detailed facts that underlie the present
study.[1] Dr. Hansen's study of Merida has been delayed, and is
likely to be still further delayed, so that it seemed best to issue
this comparative volume now. I am responsible for the fact
that there is no book about Dzitas, the fourth of the communities studied. The materials there collected overlapped so much
with those collected on one side in Chan Kom and on the other
in Merida that I decided there was no need to issue a fourth
monograph on Dzitas. Perhaps this decision was a mistake.
Two long papers on special aspects of the life of that town have
been published.[2] In recognition of the absence of a general
monograph on Dzitas, this present volume includes more citations of particular facts and cases from Dzitas than from any
of the other three communities.

The field work of which I have taken advantage was done by
a group of associates in collaboration. Merida was studied by
Dr. Asael Hansen, with the assistance of Mrs. Hansen. He

[1] In the following pages the two Carnegie Institution publications just mentioned are cited briefly as "CK" and "QR," respectively.

[2] Margaret Park Redfield, *The Folk Literature of a Yucatecan Town* ("Contributions to American Archaeology," No. 13 [Washington, D.C.: Carnegie Institution of Washington, 1935]), and Robert and Margaret Park Redfield, *Disease
and Its Treatment in Dzitas, Yucatan* ("Contributions to American Anthropology
and History," No. 32 [Washington, D.C.: Carnegie Institution of Washington,
1940]). The latter is briefly referred to as "DDZ" in the present publication.

spent all but five months of the three and a third years from
August, 1931, to December, 1934, in that city. I have used
the as yet incompleted manuscript of his monograph on Merida; I have gone over his abundant notes; I have spent
many days in discussion with him; I myself lived in Merida
during half of the period between January and May, 1931.
Mrs. Redfield and I collected the materials bearing on Dzitas
during the winter and spring of 1933. These materials I have
talked over with both Dr. Hansen and Mr. Villa; both of
them spent time with me in Dzitas during the period of study.
The study of Chan Kom was the result of residence in that
village by Mr. Villa (then teacher in the Chan Kom school)
from 1927 to 1931, with periods of absence, and of about four
months which I spent with Villa in the village in 1933. We
worked together very closely and went over each other's notes
as they were prepared. After making brief visits to villages in
east central Quintana Roo in 1931, 1932, and 1933, Villa
spent seven weeks with these Indians in 1935, and six months,
chiefly in Tusik, from January to July, in 1936. Thereafter
groups of the Indians visited Villa in Merida and gave him
further information. All the materials Villa secured there he
sent me; I translated them into English, and we corresponded
extensively about them. Later I was of assistance to him in the
preparation of his account of these communities. Throughout
the entire project Hansen, Villa, and I have exchanged with
one another information, suggestions, and doubts. The manuscript of this volume has been read by Villa and Hansen, and
each has made careful corrections especially with reference to
the community each knows best. So, all in all, I have made
myself familiar with a very large amount of case material and
other particular fact, and I have had the benefit of a great deal
of criticism.

All the field work was done under the auspices and at the
expense of Carnegie Institution of Washington. Besides the
suggestions for improvement made by Hansen and Villa, valuable comment and criticism have been received from Dr. A. V.

Kidder, Dr. Sol Tax, Mr. Arch Cooper, Dr. Leo Srole, and Mr. William Lessa, all of whom read part or all of the manuscript and to whom I am, therefore, grateful. Mr. Ralph L. Roys was helpful in matters of early history of Yucatan. Appreciative acknowledgment is also made to Miss Celia Levering, who made the manuscript ready for the press. I am grateful to Frances Rhoads Morley for permission to publish portrait photographs which she made in Yucatan and Quintana Roo.

The reader should be prepared for one characteristic of the exposition which he will encounter in the following pages. Because I have tried in this book to improve the connections between some general ideas and some particular facts, I have not formally separated the materials from the theoretical discussion. The reader will not meet first with a part of the book giving the facts and then with a part commenting upon or analyzing them. The more general ideas are introduced as the facts are set forth; an idea appears only after some facts seem to the writer to demand the presentation of the idea. And, furthermore, the more general inferences or hypotheses appear in many cases quite casually and without any announcement of their advent. Such general ideas as the book contains are woven into the texture of the argument, a thread at a time. I have followed this manner of writing because I hoped that by its means the reader might repeat much of my own experience of interaction between general conception and new material.

There is one other remark I should like to make in the direction of those people who like matters to come out either "Yes" or "No." I shall certainly disappoint them, for the differences among the communities of Yucatan are not of that unequivocal character. The differences are not like those that have been reported, for example, from parts of New Guinea, where we are told that you pass from one valley to another and, so doing, pass from one thing to quite another thing. In Yucatan, where Spanish control and its successors have rested for four centuries, and where one people, the Maya, held the land before the Spaniards came, institutions and customs are pretty generally distributed everywhere. In Yucatan, as you pass from village to town, or from town to city, you find the same elements of living that you left behind. Only they are differently accented, differently worked into the whole of the local life. So the differences are not like those among the paint tablets in a paint box; they are like the colors of a spectrum. The concepts—culture, disorganization, secularization, etc.— are similarly represented in the materials not by absolute instances and their opposites but by shades of difference that are in some cases very small. The attempt in this book is to clarify some general language by showing how the language is *more* applicable here and *less* applicable there. If one were to find a formula for the book, it would be "to the extent that" or "in so far as." I have been curious to find out how finely some tools given me by wiser men might cut.

ROBERT REDFIELD

UNIVERSITY OF CHICAGO
April 1941

TABLE OF CONTENTS

The outstanding cultural contrast in Yucatan is that between the Spanish-modern area of the populous northwest, including the one large city of Merida, and the more Indian and rustic hinterland in the sparsely populated southeast. This book reports the results of a comparative study of four communities chosen to represent points along the line of this contrast: a village of tribal Indians, a peasant village, a town, and the city. The four communities are in this order less isolated and less homogeneous. They are also in this order progressively characterized by less organization of the customary ways of life, by more individualization of behavior, and by more secularization. The book will present materials in support of this proposition and in support of the conclusion that the disorganization, individualization, and secularization have not simply been conveyed by example from the city but are, in ways to be investigated, causally interrelated with mobility and heterogeneity and with one another.

The city (Merida) is the single large urban community, the center of commercial activity and of political and social influence and of a society extremely heterogeneous as to degrees of education and participation in local or in cosmopolitan life. The town (Dzitas), a center of trade situated on important lines of communication and including people of all degrees of Spanish and Indian admixture, is a meeting place of urban and rural ways of life. The peasant village (Chan Kom) and the tribal village (Tusik) are both composed of independent agriculturalists of largely Maya descent. They differ in that the people of the former community accept the government of the modern state and seek to follow city ways so far as they know them, while the people of Tusik not only are more independent of the city economically but are hostile to the national government and seek to keep free of the city man and his ways.

xv

A consideration of the terms used in the four communities for ethnic or for status groups leads to a conclusion that in each community there are definitions of such groups which are local variants of more general definitions characteristic of all four communities. The definitions given in any one community resemble most closely those given in the next community to it. Further, some definitions of ethnic or status groups that prevailed in earlier years in a less isolated community are still emphasized in a community that is more isolated. Considered with reference to the life of the one community, the categories emphasized in each constitute a partial definition of the social system of that community. Presented in an order of degree of remoteness from the city, the four sets of social definitions appear to represent steps in that historic process whereby two ethnically separate societies (the one Spanish and the other Indian) have moved toward the formation of a single society, composed of classes, in which the original racial and cultural differences disappear.

Both Spanish and Indian influence have pervaded Yucatan to such a degree that village, town, and city hold many customs and tools in common. A comparison of the four communities as to the presence or absence of Indian or of Spanish elements leads to emphasis on the fact that elements of Catholic ritual are most abundantly present, as a matter of popular practice, in the villages remote from the city. It is in these villages, moreover, that these elements of European origin have undergone the greatest modification from the original models. There the Catholic cult has been brought into close association and congruence with the pagan religion. This fact illustrates the more general conclusion that the interaction of Spanish and of Maya religious custom has resulted, in the peripheral communities more than in the town, in the development of a single body of interrelated ritual and belief in which one part is consistent with and expressive of another and which is meaningful to all members of the community.

Consistent with the conclusion stated in the last chapter with reference to the integration of the pagan and Christian cults in the more isolated communities, the more general proposition may be asserted that it is in the villages that the native's entire view of life has this quality of organization and inner consistency. The point is concretely made by an extended account of the conceptions held by conservative persons in the peasant village. It is not simply that members of the peripheral communities tend to think and act alike; the quality of human social life here emphasized which is more plainly to be recognized in the villages is the organized character of the elements which make up the view of life of any one member.

The organization of conventional understandings that is the old culture of the peasant village is not complete in that it shows imperfect juncture between elements of Spanish origin and those which are native. This absence of integration appears chiefly in the area of religious ideas and practices. In the tribal village elements that are separate in the peasant village are more closely interrelated. Moreover, the less isolated community rather than the more isolated provides examples of actual disconformities or inconsistencies in elements of culture. A comparison of the communities indicates the manner in which, under conditions of isolation, the trend of change in the conventional understandings is in the direction of greater harmony and interdependence of parts. The opposing processes of reorganization and disorganization of culture are also suggested by changes noted over a period of years in the peasant village. In the town, as compared with the villages, the meanings attached to acts and objects are relatively few and are less completely connected with one another, and inconsistencies and uncertainties are present in the experiences of members of the community. If organization of elements be emphasized in speaking of culture, it may be said that, while assimilation of Indian and Spanish, of urban and rural ways, has progressed in the town, culture has there become less well organized.

A comparison of the four communities in their spatial order, beginning with the tribal village and ending with the city, exposes two approximated contrasting conditions: one in which commercial dealings within the local group are lacking and one in which they are general. In the tribal village maize is not a

money crop, and its value does not respond to prices established in outside markets; in the peasant village the reverse is
true. Yet it is notable that in the latter community maize has
both a religious and a commercial aspect: The role of wealth
in determining status increases as one goes from the remote village toward the city. Compared in the same order, the four
communities show increasing degree of individual freedom with
reference to the control of wealth and the undertaking of commercial ventures. It is in the villages that family estates are to
the greatest degree preserved. Individual ownership of land,
while known everywhere, becomes usual as one approaches the
city. Associated with these progressive differences in commercialization are progressive differences among the communities with respect to the division of labor: (1) it becomes more
complex; (2) as between the sexes it becomes somewhat less
rigidly defined; (3) collective effort becomes rarer and individual effort commoner; and (4) the discharge of special function, from being predominantly sacred, becomes secular.

In the villages actions assume a more nearly joint or collective form, but in the town, in connection with the same or corresponding institutions, the individual acts relatively independent
of the group. This general difference, already noted in the
preceding chapter, is especially apparent in the progressively
weaker character of the familial organization as one goes from
the tribal village to the city. The changes include a lessening
of the stability of the elementary family; a decline in patriarchal or matriarchal authority; a disappearance of customs or
institutions (especially family worship and familial religious
symbols) which express cohesion in the great family; a reduction in the strength and importance of conventionalized relationships of respect; an increasing vagueness of the conventional
outlines of behavior appropriate toward relatives; and a progressive restriction of the application of kinship terms to smaller
and nearer groups of kindred. The general point appears also
from consideration of the materials with regard to marriage
and baptism. In the villages restrictions on choice of spouse are
greatest, marriage is an arrangement by parents for the adult
security of their children and in order to establish relationships
between the two bodies of kindred of which the spouses are
representatives, and nuptials are most strongly sacramental.

Similarly, the customs of baptism and of *hetzmek* (a ritual whereby the future sound development of the child is supposedly secured) tend in the villages rather than in the town or the city emphatically to express the linkage of two adult couples and also in the villages have a more seriously binding and moral character. Thus the materials of this chapter illustrate not merely the greater individualization of town and city but also the relative secularization of life there.

In the villages, as compared with the town and the city, socially approved behavior has greater moral value, and attitudes find expression in sacred symbols. The cult of the pagan agricultural deities declines in religious value and becomes magic and then a superstition. Its decline is associated with the separation of the shaman-priest from the local settlement and with the abandonment of agriculture by some members of the community. The secularization of urban life occurs, however, not only in respect to pagan elements of religion but also in connection with Christian elements. The symbols of saints and of God are most venerated in the remotest community. The secularization of the *santos* that occurs in town and city appears to be associated with their change from symbols predominately of groups to symbols predominately of the religious faith of individuals. The secularization of the Catholic cult is also to be observed in connection with the corresponding ceremonies, especially the novena organized by laymen. The materials suggest that the disorganization of culture is itself one cause of secularization. Related to the secularization of life appears to be the emergence, in the city, of Catholicism as a formal church, self-consciously organized and maintaining itself in competition with other interest groups.

The trend toward secularization appears from a comparison of the festivals of the patron saint as they occur in several communities of Yucatan and from consideration of information as to changes over the years in certain of these communities taken separately. From being a collective act of homage rendered by the community to its supernatural guardian, the festival becomes more nearly a commercial undertaking for the profit of individuals. In the peripheral community the festival is most closely integrated with the political and social organization of the group, and here also it is the sacred aspects of the ritual that are emphasized. In Tizimín, where the patron saint has wide sacred prestige, the festival has retained a religious meaning for the genuinely pious while becoming otherwise a business enterprise. In still another community, Chicxulub, the festival has lost most of its traditional content and its sacred nature and is now a secular entertainment deliberately managed to attract paying customers from the city.

Similar ideas and practices with regard to disease and its treatment occur in all the four communities studied; nevertheless, considered in relation to other aspects of the social life, this group of customs and conventions differ notably as the villages are compared with the town and the city. In the villages the ideas as to disease are closely interdependent with moral and religious conceptions; in the city they are much less so. In the villages these ideas and the corresponding practices form a relatively simple and stable body of interrelated parts, but in the town and the city the conceptions are less consistently and less stably related to one another. The secularization of the folk medicine is significantly associated with the transfer of the healing functions from the male shaman-priest to curers who are women. The secularization of medicine converts it from a semireligious exercise to magic and is accompanied by the commercialization of the healing art. As a special aspect of the importance of secular magic in the city is to be recognized the greater frequence of acts or allegations of sorcery: black magic is more believed to occur in the town and the city than in the village. A part of the explanation for this difference lies, it is argued, in the greater sense of insecurity of the individual members of the more disorganized urban community.

The general conclusion is that the same relative order, corresponding to their spatial order, serves to range the four communities as to the progressively increasing or decreasing extent to which several general social or cultural characters are present. The less isolated and more heterogeneous societies are the more secular and individualistic and are the more characterized by disorganization of culture. The significance of this method of comparison of four contemporary communities so ranged is probably small for historical research. As a contribution to generalizing scientific knowledge of society and its changes its importance depends on clarification of terms and more precise testing of the generalizations implied with reference to particular fact and on the extension of the comparisons. The concepts of disorganization of culture, of secularization, and of individualization are re-examined in the light of these materials. Questions then arise as to the interrelation of the phenomena observed: are these causally connected in the case of Yucatan and are such connections to be expected to recur in other like situations of social change? The questions are considered in reference to material briefly reported from Guatemala, and in conclusion some general hypotheses are offered as promising for further study in this field.

LIST OF ILLUSTRATIONS

The photographic portraits of Maya Indians included in this book were made by Frances Rhoads Morley. That which appears opposite page 157 was taken in Chan Kom. The others were taken in X-Cacal, Quintana Roo.

xxiii

CHAPTER I

THE PENINSULA OF YUCATAN

TO THE student of Hispano-Indian culture the peninsula of Yucatan offers a situation less complex than is
ordinarily encountered. The essential social facts in
Yucatan are few, and they are simply and consistently distributed in space. They so present themselves to the visitor's
first inspection that if he is interested in learning something
further about the nature of society, and if his mind runs to
the employment of a comparative method, he will soon see
what may be profitably studied and compared. This volume
presents the results of a study of four communities. The reader
should at once know what there is about Yucatan and about
the author that caused the investigation to be formed as it
was, and why these particular four communities were chosen
for study.

The facts as to the geography, history, and population of
Yucatan are to be presented in the book about Merida which
A. T. Hansen is preparing. His book contains references to
the chief sources on these matters. In the following pages only
such of these facts will be reviewed as are necessary to explain
the formulation of the project that is the subject of the present
work. When Hansen's book appears, the reader will have a
more extended and balanced general description of the peninsula than is contained here. That book will contain references
on the geography and population of Yucatan and to the chief
secondary sources for its history.

The relative simplicity of Yucatan arises both from the nature of the land and from the events that have taken place
upon it. In the first place, in everything but literal truth it is
an island. A rectangle of low, stony land projecting north-

1

ward into the Gulf of Mexico, it is inaccessible except by boat or airplane. Its landward connection to the south with the rest of Mexico and with Guatemala is blocked by a dense tropical forest penetrated by no road or railroad. Almost everyone who enters the peninsula, and almost all the goods imported into it, arrive by sea. And Yucatan is relatively isolated even by sea. It lies on no important trade route. Furthermore, access to the eastern shore is barred by tropical forests, and ships may not approach most of the northern coast because of almost continuous sandbar and lagoon. For these reasons almost all entries and departures are by the single important port of Progreso in the northwestern corner of the peninsula.

Yucatan is insular politically and sentimentally. Sharing no borderlands with people of marginal culture, withdrawn physically from immediate contact with others, and characterized by a distinctive regional culture, the inhabitants think of themselves as different from the other people of Mexico. Much more commonly do they call themselves "Yucatecans" than "Mexicans." Movements for political separation from the republic of Mexico flourished at various times in the history of the peninsula.

Early in these pages should be emphasized the importance of the Yucatec Maya heritage in the ethnic distinctness of Yucatan. Whereas in other parts of Middle America of comparable size many Indian languages and cultures have merged with the Spanish, in Yucatan, an area geographically segregated, only one Indian language and tradition is present and that one is vigorously persistent. By this circumstance a certain nationalistic character is given to the group consciousness of the Yucatecans. Although the Indian language is in no way official, and although it is not spoken by the sophisticated people of the city, nevertheless Yucatec Maya is the most-used language of the peninsula and one of which everyone has some knowledge and awareness. Especially since the Revolution of 1910–21 the stories of the Maya chieftains who fought against the Spanish conquerors have played a role in political propaganda and mythology. To this insularity and consciousness of national character, based on Maya themes, recent literary men and artists of Yucatan have made their contribution. "Mayab," this land calls itself, or, quoting poetically the ancient aboriginal chronicler, *u luum ceh yetel cutz*, "the land of the deer and the pheasant (curassow)."

Yucatan was no exception to the general fact that during the Colonial period practically no Europeans entered Latin America except Spaniards, and other ethnic elements acquired since independence have in Yucatan been few and unimportant. During the last forty years a considerable number of Orientals, chiefly Chinese, and a smaller number of Syrians and Levantines, have entered Yucatan. The few negro slaves disappeared by amalgamation before independence; more recently a small number of Cuban negroes have been added to the population. The Yaqui sent to Yucatan in the Diaz period soon died or were absorbed into the population. In general, except for the Spaniards, a few North Americans, the Germans, and the Orientals in Merida, the capital, and except for the few Syrians and an occasional Chinese or Korean to be found in towns in the peninsula, no account need be taken, in describing the ethnic composition of Yucatan, of any but the two stocks and heritages overwhelmingly dominant: the Spanish and the Maya.

With respect to topography and climate Yucatan is exceedingly simple. The peninsula is a shelf of porous limestone, barely elevated above the level of the sea, and covered patchily with a scanty soil. The land rises imperceptibly from the coast to the interior. In the basal portion of the peninsula there are ranges of low hills; the highest of these, running northwestward and southeastward in the southwest corner, attains an elevation of 270 meters. Except for these hills, Yucatan is without any noticeable eminence of land; it is a country of extraordinary flatness; from any point in the north the horizon appears as an even and unbroken circle. Yet the land is not level; the unequal decomposition of the limestone has broken the surface into innumerable small knolls and hollows. The foot traveler in Yucatan rarely mounts an eminence from which he may have a view of the country before or behind him; nevertheless, his footsteps do not move along a level; they are forever adjusting themselves to brief changes in grade.

Because the topography is so uniform and because the limestone is so porous, northern and central Yucatan is entirely without rivers or streams. The rain water passes quickly into the limestone. In the eastern and southern parts of the peninsula there are shallow lakes and water holes, but in the northwest, where most of the people live, little water stands on the surface, and then only just after rains, in an occasional tiny pool accumulated in a hollow eroded in some piece of harder rock.

The outstanding topographic feature, characteristic of northern Yucatan, and the essential source of water supply for the population, is the *cenote*. The cenote, in its typical form, is a deep, circular, vertical-walled hole in the limestone. In it the ground water stands from nine to forty meters below the surface of the land. The surface rock is harder than that below; therefore, the rain water passes through the upper rock, causing comparatively little solution; below, it dissolves out caverns. When the roof of such a cavern is at last eroded through, a cenote results.

The ancient Maya built reservoirs, but it is not clear that they could dig wells. Upon the cenotes, therefore, chiefly depended human settlement. Knowledge of well-digging was either introduced or greatly improved by the Spaniards; the windmill and the motor appeared in recent times. Nevertheless, most of the settlements of Yucatan are still to be found where there are cenotes. To the village dweller, as will appear in subsequent pages of this book, the significances of the cenote provide a principal thread for the web of social institutions and religious ideas by which he lives.

With one important exception—rainfall—the climate of Yucatan is as uniform as the topography. In general, the cli-

mate is warm and fairly moist. The prevailing winds are east-
erly. All months of the year are characterized by high tem-
perature, but the coolest nights occur in January and Febru-
ary, and the highest temperatures in May, June, July, and
August. Between the two climatological stations which have
reported the coldest and the warmest temperatures, respectively, there is only 2° Fahrenheit difference in respect to
January temperatures, and 2°.1 with respect to July. There is
throughout the peninsula a marked seasonal contrast: the
summers are characterized by plentiful rainfall; there is much
cloudiness and there are many thunderstorms. During the
winters, on the other hand, little rain falls; there are many
clear days and no thunderstorms. While this seasonal alterna-
tion is marked and regular, the total amount of annual rainfall is subject to great fluctuation. During some years three or
four times as much rain falls as in other years. Thus, although
the agriculturalist may count upon the coming of the rains, he
may not count upon the coming of enough rain. The piling-up
of the clouds in the spring, the first thunder, and the first
downpour remind the Indian of the reality of his rain-gods;
but the uncertainty as to whether enough rain will fall to enable him to raise a crop suggests their worship and propitiation.

The one great locally varying environmental factor is the
amount of rainfall. The amount of rainfall increases as one
goes inland from the coast, and as one goes southeastward from
the northwest. About eighteen inches of rainfall a year occur
at Progreso, about thirty-five at Merida, about forty-eight at
Valladolid (the eastern terminus of the railroad and a town
not far from the village of Chan Kom, later described), and
about eighty-three at Belize in British Honduras in the southeast corner of the peninsula. Furthermore, the concentration
of rainfall in the summer months is less marked in the eastern
part of the peninsula than in the western part.

This rainfall gradient, running from the northwest to the
southeast, brings about corresponding local differences with

respect to the natural flora, to the crops grown, and to the human population. The gradients of life in Yucatan, natural and social, run from the coast to the interior, from the north to the south, and especially from the northwest to the southeast. In the northwest the long, dry winter and the scanty annual rainfall allow the development of only small bushes, chiefly xerophytic. As one travels inland and southeastward the size of the trees increases; the scrubby jungle gives way to a taller, denser growth, and then—east of Valladolid and south of Peto —to a true tropical rain forest, where the trees may be fifty or sixty feet high, and where many remain green all year. Of course, no line can be sharply drawn between dry-land jungle and tropical rain forest, but the political boundary between the state of Yucatan and the territory of Quintana Roo might also serve as such a boundary. What is to be emphasized here is that, except where cut away for crops, the entire peninsula is covered with trees ("bush"; *monte*), that practically all this flora is regrowth, and that its height, density, and verdure increase proportionate to the distance from the northern coast.

Where man has cut away the bush, it has been for two chief purposes: maize or the growing of henequen. These two crops, by far the most important produced in Yucatan, may be contrasted in several respects. Maize is the great subsistence crop, grown by small independent agriculturalists, by techniques that originated with the Indian. Henequen, the agave which gives the sisal fiber made into twine and bags, is the money crop of Yucatan; it is (or was) grown chiefly on large estates; its techniques of production involve modern machinery; and its sale abroad results chiefly from the demand for a cheap twine for binders and reapers. Maize determines the local economy of Yucatecan communities; henequen determines the role of Yucatan in the world-economy.

It is the local differences in rainfall that fix the areas within which these two crops may profitably be grown and that in turn accounts for the distribution of population. While maize may be grown almost everywhere in the peninsula, it may be grown best in the northern part, and especially in the northwestern part, with the exception of the coastal region where insufficient rain falls. Maize is grown by the "milpa system": the bush is felled, dried, and burned; after one, two, or three crops have been grown on a plot of land, it is allowed to revert to bush for a period of years before it is again cleared and planted. In the south and southeast, where the bush gives way to rain forest, the labor of felling trees to make the cornfield is much increased, and the greater moisture causes second growth to appear while the felled trees have not yet dried sufficiently for burning. Therefore, not more than 2 or 3 per cent of the population of the peninsula live in the southeastern forests of Quintana Roo, and these few live there because they prefer the isolation and accompanying independence. It is probable that northern Yucatan, with the present agricultural techniques, could support a considerably larger population at the present level of subsistence.

The accounts of the early Spaniards indicate that at the time of the Conquest, as today, the population was heavily concentrated in the northwestern part of the peninsula. But there is some reason to suppose that this concentration is more marked today than it was then. Apparently the population of Quintana Roo declined rapidly immediately after the Conquest. The important change in the economic life of Yucatan since the Conquest occurred in the second half of the nineteenth century, when henequen became a commercially important crop. This circumstance further emphasized the economic importance of the northwestern part of the peninsula and thus increased the tendency of population to center there. Henequen, to be commercially useful, must be grown in a region where there is not too much rainfall. If there is too much moisture, the fiber is too soft. This fact, together with the greater cost of production and transportation the farther the crop is grown from the port of Progreso, has made the northwestern corner of Yucatan the area of henequen production.

Henequen is grown in small quantities throughout the peninsula, and extensive plantations, since abandoned or put to other uses, existed at one time as far east as Valladolid; but the area of effective henequen production may be drawn by means of a radius a hundred kilometers long swung from Progreso in an arc from coast to coast, omitting a strip along the coast.

These geographical and agricultural facts may be summarized by pointing out that if the traveler begins a journey at the port of Progreso, and travels southeastward, he will pass through four or five zones of human occupation and will pass through them transversely, that is, on a line drawn at right angles to the boundaries which might be taken to indicate the approximate limits of the zones. First he will pass through the narrow coastal strip, a region of little agriculture, small population, and no henequen exploitation. He will then enter the wide zone of commercial henequen exploitation. Here a large part of the bush has been removed. Great areas are under cultivation for henequen. Interspersed with these plantations are patches of corn. So dense is the population here and so much of the land is given over to henequen that the area does not produce enough maize for its support but must buy maize from elsewhere in the peninsula or even from central Mexico or—in the earlier years—from the United States. Within this area—not more than an eighth or a tenth of the entire peninsula—are concentrated most of the population, the commerce, and the social and political leadership of the peninsula. A little northwest of its center lies Merida, the capital of the state of Yucatan and the only large city in the peninsula.

Outside of the area of commercial henequen production occurs a zone of somewhat less dense population, within which maize is produced in quantities to make it both a subsistence and a money crop. This area helps to feed the territory northwest of it. As there are practically no henequen plantations, much more of the land is covered with bush. Cattle are produced in this area, but the bush is not felled in the tracts where they are pastured. The railroads of Yucatan are, in Hansen's words, like "threads of varying lengths held together at Merida and tossed outward carelessly"; the threads are longer to the east and south of the capital. The railroad lines penetrate only the three zones already mentioned; the termini of the eastern and southern lines—Tizimín, Valladolid, Sotuta, and Peto—lie within the area of much maize production and little or no henequen. The rail lines end where the population declines in the middle of the third zone.

Between the third and fourth zones the dry bush changes to tall rain forest. An account of human habitation in these areas also requires reference to the fact that ever since the Conquest the forests to the south have constituted a hiding-place and base of operations for Indians unreconciled to the domination of the Spanish and the Mexican government. Shortly after the Conquest a large area in east central Quintana Roo became almost depopulated. The most important Indian rebellion, the "War of the Castes," began in the forties of the last century. Peace was not made until 1904. Recalcitrant Indians withdrew again to the southeast and have maintained there until the present day a semi-independence, a tribal government, and a hostile or suspicious disposition toward outsiders.[1]* The towns that the Spaniards had built along the highway they had constructed from Peto to Santa Cruz del Bravo were abandoned at the beginning of this war; a gap developed, a sort of no-man's land, between northwest Yucatan, committed to modern civilization, and the unreconciled tribal Indians, an inconsiderable fragment of the population, established to the south. These Indians, like all the other people of the peninsula, during Colonial times had been subjected to the influence of Spanish missionary and administrator; missions and garrisons had been established all the way down to Chetumal Bay. We may suppose, however, that the influence of the Spaniards was never so strong here as toward the northwest, where their capital was established at

* See pp. 370–87 for "Notes."

Merida and where the population and activity centered. At any rate, the War of the Castes, emphasizing the results of earlier and lesser rebellions, produced a cleavage and interrupted the continuous distribution of settlement and civilizational influence by bringing about a totally uninhabited zone beginning approximately on the political boundary between the state of Yucatan and the territory of Quintana Roo.

The third zone, of maize-without-henequen, is the outermost within the area of effective governmental control. Within it lie some towns, such as Valladolid, that were early established by the Spaniards upon the sites of Indian villages already there, and it includes many old-established Indian villages. It includes, on its eastern and southern edges, communities, such as Chan Kom, established within the last few score years by settlers from the north and west. But, old or new, all the towns and villages within this area, like those northwest of them, are integral parts of the state of Yucatan and the republic of Mexico. The local authorities form a part of the modern hierarchy of political authority. The people pay taxes, they vote, and their children attend local schools supervised by central governmental control. But, in contrast to the situation in the second zone, the towns are shipping-points for maize and cattle rather than for henequen; and the villagers do not work as laborers on henequen plantations but as independent small farmers grow maize for sale and export as well as for domestic consumption.

The uninhabited area that begins approximately where one enters the territory of Quintana Roo may be distinguished as a fourth zone. At the time when these studies were made it was a horseback ride of two days from the last occupied settlement in the third zone to the first settlements of the tribal Indians of Quintana Roo. The path through the forest follows in part the old Colonial road of the Spaniards, and the traveler's camp is made in the shells of the stone churches and other buildings abandoned to the forest almost a century ago. The course of travel, still southeastward, enters a territory of such heavy rainfall that human settlement is difficult: it involves much labor to clear a plot for a cornfield or to keep a path open for communication and transportation. The trees, much taller and thicker, include the sapodilla, from which chicle is extracted. The outsiders who enter this area are chiefly merchants on their way to deal with the Indians beyond, or chicle gatherers. It is with these two sorts of persons, then, that the tribal Indians of Quintana Roo are accustomed to deal.

These Indians, whose settlements may be taken to constitute the last zone to be distinguished in the area under consideration, occupy a region which may be delimited by drawing a line from the south end of Bacalar lagoon to a point on the Quintana Roo–Yucatan boundary just south of Peto; another from the last point to Tuluum, which is situated on the east coast approximately opposite the south end of Cozumel Island; and a third line from the north end of Bacalar lagoon to the south end of Espíritu Santo Bay. This area, east central Quintana Roo, includes the villages of the *sublevados*, descendants of the insurrectionaries of the War of the Castes and of earlier rebellions.[2] The Indians here have the same small admixture of white blood as have those who live in villages of the second and third zones, and they speak the same Maya language. But for almost a century, and at other times during the Colonial period, they, or some of them, have maintained their political independence. They do not pay taxes or vote, and only in recent years have the occupants of some of these villages accepted schools instituted by the Mexican government. If by "town" we mean a larger settlement, characterized by commerce and the presence of mixed-bloods and of authorities of the national government, then there are no towns in this area except the territorial capital, Santa Cruz del Bravo.

The simplicity of Yucatan which was urged upon the reader in the first paragraph of this chapter is to be found in three chief circumstances. First, the natural environment of the peninsula is nearly uniform, except for the local differences in rainfall. These, however, are so regular as to bring about a concentration of population in the northwest and a rough zoning of land use and types of human settlement as one goes southeastward. Second, there is and has been only one important center of cultural and political influence—Merida. With its attendant seaport it constitutes the focus for all social change. In Colonial times it was the chief center of Spanish influence upon the Indians. Secondary centers of such influence were, of course, established in other towns, but the capital dominated then, too; and, as already suggested, it is probable that Spanish influence was least effective in the heavily forested area most remote from Merida. Today, as one leaves Merida and passes through towns located on the railroad, and from them to villages in the third and fifth zones, there is an apparent increase in the amount of Indian blood in the population, in the amount of the Maya language spoken relative to Spanish, and in the notorious existence of such obviously Indian customs and institutions as the performance of agricultural ceremonies to pagan deities under the direction of Maya-appearing, Maya-speaking shaman-priests. The hinterland is more rustic and more Indian.

In the third place, the contrast between a Spanish-modern center of influence in the northwest and a Maya-rustic (or primitive) hinterland to the southeast, especially that hinterland which lies distant from the railroad and deep in the bush, is the only outstanding cultural contrast in the peninsula.[3] The underlying Indian culture is practically uniform. In Yucatan one cannot study the difference between one aboriginal Indian culture and another, because there is only one. And no other center of cultural influences impinges with any sharpness upon the people of Yucatan. Cuban negro culture probably has influenced the popular customs of Merida to some degree; its influence is, in comparison with the culture changes dealt with in this book, of almost no consequence. Soon after the Conquest there existed in Yucatan the cultural difference between the man with Spanish ways and the man with mixed Indian-Spanish ways. In terms of communities, then, there was, no doubt, a contrast between the relatively Spanish mode of life in Merida and a few large towns and the much more Indian mode of life of villages remote from the capital. This difference has continued, except that, while the fusion of Spanish and Maya elements of culture has everywhere been going on, new elements of culture have entered the peninsula. So, while the Spaniard has been modifying the Maya, and the Maya the Spaniard, to make the Yucatecan, the Colonial Spaniard has been becoming the modern urban Westerner. Thus a difference that began as that between Spanish and Maya cultures has become, gradually and not completely, a difference between modern Western urban life and the life of the Yucatecan peasant. But though the descriptive character of the interacting cultures has changed as the interaction has proceeded, the routes of diffusion and the spatial distribution of communities representing stages in the transformation have remained the same.

In short, Yucatan, considered as one moves from Merida southeastward into the forest hinterland, presents a sort of social gradient in which the Spanish, modern, and urban gives way to the Maya, archaic, and primitive. This volume results from a study of four communities chosen to represent points, not too unevenly distributed, along this gradient. These four are: Merida, the only large city; Dzitas, a town situated on the railroad; Chan Kom, a peasant village; and Tusik, a tribal village of semi-independent Maya in Quintana Roo. The selection of Merida was almost inevitable, as it is by far the largest city in the peninsula and the center of modern and urban influence. The Indians of Quintana Roo, in their special circumstances of isolation induced by the War of the Castes, provided an equally obvious opposite extreme: they plainly occupy the other terminus of the southeastward gradient. The Indians of this region are divided into three sub-tribal groupings. Of these three, the central group has most successfully resisted the attempts of the government to impose schools and other forms of control; therefore, the central group was chosen for study. Of the nine settlements making up this group, Tusik appeared, after survey, to be a typical village of moderate size.

Dzitas and Chan Kom, the other two communities studied, lie between these two extremes. Dzitas is a town situated on the railroad in the zone of maize-production-without-hene-quen. Chan Kom is a peasant village located in the bush a day's walk from the railroad in the same zone. The selection of these two intermediate communities was made, within the general limits set by the problem, following considerations of convenience. The association in the field work of Alfonso Villa, rural schoolteacher in Chan Kom, and the early friendly contacts established with the natives of that village by members of the Carnegie Institution staff at the archeological site of Chichen Itza, not far from the village, made Chan Kom a favorable place of study.[4] Similar considerations brought about the selection of the town of Dzitas, at that time the point of the railroad through which passed persons and goods destined for Chichen Itza or for Chan Kom.

Dzitas, Chan Kom, and Tusik are in that order increasingly distant from Merida, where social change, for Yucatan, origi-nates and from which social and political influence emanates. Merida is the hub of the railways, the terminus of all modern lines of communication; Dzitas is located at a junction on one of the radial rail lines; Chan Kom is connected with other communities only by paths through the bush, but its people not infrequently visit the towns; the Quintana Roo villages lie in deep forest, cut off from northwest Yucatan by a wide unin-habited zone. Merida publishes the newspapers of Yucatan and reads most of them; Dzitas receives about one copy for every hundred inhabitants; Chan Kom occasionally sees a single copy of a newspaper which only two or three in the vil-lage can read; no one in Tusik ever reads a newspaper. The people of Merida are well aware of their leadership and look down on rustics outside the capital; the more educated people of Dzitas seek consciously to be like the city dwellers and are much like them; the people of Chan Kom, understanding far less of the ways of the city and town, strive nevertheless to take over the techniques and practical advantages of the town; the Quintana Roo Indians are suspicious of outside influence and seek to maintain their independence and to be allowed to follow their old ways. The people of Merida exhibit a wide range of education, class, and some variety of ethnic origin; Dzitas includes city-trained people of largely Spanish culture as well as Indians from villages in the bush; the people of Chan Kom are all of Maya Indian race and are derived from similar villages, but recent differences in education and in response to influences from the towns have brought about notable differences among the natives; while Tusik, left alone for many generations, exhibits in its population the highest degree of uniformity.

Resemblances and differences among these four communities may be stated in general terms so as to make possible the definition of the scientific problems which are to concern the reader. A social relation may be said to exist wherever the investigator finds it appropriate to describe the behavior of two or more individuals as undergoing reciprocal modification with reference to the interests of each.[5] A society may be recognized in any aggregate of individuals among whom there are social relations. The four societies which have been studied in Yucatan have already been denoted communities because, like most human societies which become the object of special study, they are made up of individuals occupying a common territory, possessing a habitat. The societies which are here considered are like other human societies in that the social relations which define them exist in terms of those conventional understandings we call "culture." Special differences among the societies studied with regard to particular aspects of this common quality—culture—are discussed in later pages. In so far as any defined human aggregate is characterized by social relations, it is a society; in so far as it is characterized by conventional understandings, it exhibits a culture; and, in so far as it may also be said to occupy a territory, it is a community. Therefore, the three terms may be applied to small human aggregates and as well to large ones, even to those which are world-wide. Accordingly, in this book the words will be applied, as the context suggests, to the particular four aggregates that have been studied or to Yucatan as a whole.

The obvious differences among the four Yucatecan communities may be described in common speech by saying that they are, as compared with one another, more or less primitive. But "primitive," though useful as a pointer to designate roughly certain societies rather than others, or certain characters of society rather than others, may be set aside in favor of more denotative terms. The facts just summarized about Merida, Dzitas, Chan Kom, and Tusik, and those to be given in the next chapter, should support the statement that in that order each is less homogeneous or more homogeneous and is less isolated or more mobile than the next. A homogeneous society is one composed of the same kind of people doing the same kind of things.[6] In it the habits of any individual tend to conform to the customs of the group; or, in other terms, the organized mental life of any individual tends to coincide at many points with the organized mental life of other individuals. A society is isolated to the extent that contacts among members of the local society (community) are many and intimate and characterized by a high degree of mutual understanding of much of the habitual mental life of one another, while contacts between members of the local society and outsiders are few, not intimate, and characterized by a lower degree of mutual understanding. The "isolation" here in view is that which has persisted over considerable time: the isolation of the primitive tribe, not that of recent castaways.

The "literacy" or "preliteracy" of a society is a special aspect of its isolation. In the next chapter facts will be given as to the extent and nature of the use of reading and writing in the four communities. In all four some of the people can read, but differences in the degree to which literacy is effective in determining the character of the society depend not so much on the technical literacy rate as on the role of books and reading and writing in the society. In Tusik writing and reading are esoteric arts cultivated by special functionaries for the benefit of the entire group, and the uses of the art are to consult sacred books and to prepare and read messages emanating from the supernaturals. In this society literacy is, along with oral tradition, an agent for the preservation of the society in its present state and for the perpetuation of a sacred lore. Chan Kom is more literate than Tusik, and Dzitas than Chan Kom, in that reading and writing are to a greater extent used to enable the society to come into communication with other societies or to record and to consider critically its own past experiences.

The four societies also differ obviously with respect to the complexity of the division of labor and with regard to the elaboration and specialization of much of the technology. In these respects, also, it may be felt that the more peripheral community is more "primitive" than those nearer the city. The changes in technology are not examined in this volume, and indeed in this respect there are very few differences between Tusik and Chan Kom. In fact the basic technology of maize agriculture is substantially the same in all four communities. Differences in the division of labor do receive consideration in subsequent pages. But the characterization of these four societies as progressively less isolated and more heterogeneous, as one goes from tribe to city, is not further examined, although the proposition is given further factual support in the next chapter. These differences are the plane from which other differences are determined. They are the more or less controlled variables.[7]

The chief objective of this investigation is, then, to define differences in the nature of isolated homogeneous society, on the one hand, and mobile heterogeneous society, on the other, so far as these kinds of societies are represented in Yucatan.

Although the discussion centers in a description of differences as represented in these particular Yucatecan communities, the account of the contrasts is made in general terms. It is hoped that questions of more general interest will arise out of consideration of these materials. Are some of the differences among these four communities instances of what often happens when an isolated homogeneous society comes in contact with other societies? Stated as though the comparison represented a process illustrated at four stages of its course, the chief of these general differences, as they will be developed in following pages, are the disorganization of the culture, the secularization of the society, and the individualization of the society. So stated, the comparison may be converted into a hypothetical description of any contrasting isolated-homogeneous and mobile-heterogeneous pairs of societies. It may then be asked to what extent this description applies to other societies. The formulation makes it possible to ask a number of general questions which the analysis of new facts and the further analysis of the facts from Yucatan might answer, or perhaps reformulate. The important question may be asked whether, if regular changes of the kind noted result from the contact of the isolated-homogeneous society with another society, the changes would result from contact with any other society or only from contact with a more heterogeneous, less isolated, society, or perhaps only from contact with some recent Western society. In the concluding chapter this and related questions as to the existence and nature of the interrelationship among changes in the societies in the course of contact and communication with other societies will receive attention.

CHAPTER II

CITY, TOWN, VILLAGE, AND TRIBE[1]

MERIDA is the one real city of Yucatan. It is located in the northwestern part of the peninsula, twenty-four miles inland from the port of Progreso and within the area of capitalistic agriculture based on the production of sisal fiber (henequen). In size the city completely overshadows all other communities. Its 96,660 inhabitants account for one-fourth of the total population of the state of Yucatan and for one-fifth of the combined population of Yucatan, Campeche, and Quintana Roo. The next largest communities, Campeche (city) and Progreso, have some 20,000 and 11,000 residents, respectively. Excepting these two seaports, the next largest town, Ticul, contains a little over 7,000 people, less than one-thirteenth of the number in Merida.[3]

This concentration of population is indicative of the dominant position of the city in the economic, political, and social life of Yucatan. It functions as the unchallenged metropolis. All lines of communication, both with the hinterland and with the outside world, converge upon it. It is the hub of trade and finance. Here are found banks, importers and exporters, large wholesale houses, insurance agencies, department stores, automobile dealers, modern hotels, and various other specialized kinds of business. There is not much machine industry anywhere in Yucatan, but Merida has most of what there is. The leading examples are the railway shops, several cordage mills, an electric-power plant, a brewery, and many smaller shops and factories for making decorticating machines,

19

furniture, cigarettes, soap, vegetable oil, soda water, matches, and tiles. Even much of the agriculture of the region is controlled directly from the city. The owners and managers of about 80 per cent of the sisal haciendas live in Merida,[4] and the proportion is probably about the same in the case of other large rural enterprises. Moreover, the government-sponsored Co-operative of Sisal Producers, with headquarters in the city, regulates many details of the growing and marketing of the fiber.

This last fact is just one expression of the great political dominance of Merida. It is the seat of a highly centralized state government. The only administrative subdivisions are a large number of *municipios* (ninety-six in 1930), all directly dependent on the capital. They are restricted to handling purely local affairs, and even in such matters their freedom is distinctly limited. It is unwise for them to take any important step without first getting the approval of the state officials, since these officials do not hesitate to interfere whenever they are dissatisfied with the way things are going in a municipio. Political control is rendered more complete by means of a party organization that is closely allied to the government. Most of the voters are affiliated with the Socialist Party of the Southeast through either local or occupational unions known as *ligas de resistencia*. The central offices of both the party and the ligas are situated in the capital, and it is here that discussion takes place and decisions are made. The activities of party members elsewhere consist mainly of receiving orders and carrying out predetermined programs. In addition, the agencies of national authority are centered in Merida and operate out from there.[5]

Another aspect of the dominance of Merida is its position as the center of "culture" and enligntenment. It has all the institutions of higher learning—a normal school, a preparatory school for pre-university training, and a university giving degrees in law, medicine, and pharmacy. Facilities for study of the fine arts are offered by an art school and by numerous teachers of music. There is a press and a body of writers and a pretentious theater where local and imported talent performs. Organizations for cultivating "culture" and conducting "social" affairs abound. It should be noted further that Merida takes the lead in adopting new and modern ways from Euro-American civilization, which are then passed on to the hinterland. The function of the city in this process is important. By adopting these innovations, the city, in effect, gives them its stamp of approval and endows them with added prestige. It may also modify them somewhat in terms of the local culture so that they become more readily transmissible. Merida, therefore, serves as a focus of social change, as a source of what most people feel is "progress."

A final indication of the pre-eminence of the community and, in turn, a factor which contributes to its prestige is the extreme concentration of the élite, the wealthy, and the educated in the city. More than three-fourths of the doctors in the state of Yucatan live in the capital,[6] and about the same proportion of hacienda owners, as has been pointed out already. These are the only numerical measures of the degree of concentration that could be found. But the facts are so clear that they require little formal demonstration. Merida has always been the particular home of the established aristocracy. During the sisal boom it boasted of the number of its millionaires, and there are still a few of them. Not many really rich individuals, according to city standards, reside anywhere else in the state. A large part of these people have country origins. For generations there has been a tendency for ambitious young men to go to the capital to seek their fortunes and for successful merchants and planters to follow the same path in order to enjoy their wealth or to launch their children into Merida "society." This movement has had the effect of accentuating the prestige of the city and of weakening the comparative position of communities in the hinterland.

The urban character of Merida is manifest in many ways. Scarcely any of its inhabitants till the soil. A few men in the semirural, lower-class suburbs have milpas in the surrounding country, and a slightly larger number work on near-by haciendas. But in most cases these occupations appear to be the last resort of persons who have been unable to find employment in the city itself. The owners and managers of haciendas derive their income from agriculture, but they are not really agriculturists. Rather they are capitalists whose investments happen to be in rural properties, or business administrators whose concern happens to be with enterprises located in the country. The great majority of people do not have even this much connection with growing things. They live by buying and selling commodities already produced, by manufacturing or processing goods, by furnishing credit, and by providing services, professional and governmental. Their places of work are shops, factories, stores, and offices.

Since the city produces little of what it consumes, most of its supplies must be brought in. The size of the community and the varied tastes of its inhabitants make it dependent on other parts of Mexico and on the world beyond Mexico as well as on its own hinterland. The only important products furnished by the hinterland in significant quantities are some of the more common foods. The staples—corn and beans— come from the region of maize agriculture in the south and east; cattle and hogs from here and there throughout the peninsula; sugar from a small section in the south; and fish from Progreso. Except in the case of the last item, it is necessary to supplement the local supply with purchases in the Mexican market outside the peninsula, and most of the sugar is obtained from that source. There are other common foods, used regularly by everybody, which are derived entirely from areas of Mexico outside of Yucatan. These include cocoa beans, coffee, rice, wheat, and wheat flour. The diet of the well-to-do and of people in more moderate circumstances on special occasions contains such articles as apples, wine, cheese, ham, and canned goods of all kinds which are imported from Europe and the United States.

The population of Merida is heterogeneous. The city directory lists almost a hundred different occupations, ranging from the professions to casual day labor, just for persons whose surnames begin with "A."[7] Many of the inhabitants of the city were not born there. People from the towns and villages of the hinterland constitute probably one-fourth of the population,[8] and there are individuals from every Mexican state and fifty-six foreign countries.[9] This last group is very small, composing only 2 per cent of the total residents of Merida municipio.[10] But the figure represents 64 per cent of the foreign-born in the whole state of Yucatan. The city has enough immigrants to give it a slight cosmopolitan air. One reason for this is that two of the largest groups are Syrians and Orientals, both of whom are conspicuously different in appearance.

Racially the majority of the people are mixed white and Indian in varying proportions, but there are some almost pure Indians among persons of recent rural origin. The number of pure or nearly pure whites is larger. The old aristocracy managed to keep itself fairly free of Indian admixture, and newcomers from Europe during the last several decades have augmented the white element considerably. Then there are the Orientals already mentioned and a few negroes from the West Indies.

Spanish is the chief and the favored language of the city. It derives prestige both from the fact that it functions in communication with the world beyond Yucatan and from the fact of its association with the historically dominant class. Nevertheless, Maya remains an important secondary language. The census of 1930 reported 6 per cent of the population as entirely dependent on Maya and 24 per cent as bilingual.[11] These figures, of course, do not present a full picture of the linguistic variety. To the educated, Spanish is an efficient tool for practical communication and a means of artistic expression as well. Many of the lower class, on the other hand, learned Maya first and are not really "at home" in Spanish. It serves them with sufficient effectiveness in ordinary discourse, but they often lapse into Maya in emotional situations. People in Merida are also aware of foreign languages. One can hear Arabic or Chinese in the market place, and some contact with English is a part of the experience of almost everyone. Much of the technical jargon of sport, especially of baseball, is English, and it is used in the dialogue of the great majority of motion pictures—a very popular form of entertainment in the city. Probably a thousand individuals speak English fluently,[12] having acquired the language during study or residence in the United States.

Compared with the rest of the state, Merida has a high literacy ratio. If the municipio in which the capital is located is omitted, 38 per cent of the population of Yucatan ten years of age and over is literate. The corresponding figure for Merida municipio is 73 per cent.[13] But, among the persons the census-taker sets down as literate, great differences exist in the degree of literacy and in the use to which it is put. At the time today's adult generation of the masses was being educated it was usual for those who did go to school to stop after two or three years, and the practice is still common. This means that the most "ordinary" people read and write little and laboriously. At the opposite extreme are the few individuals who support themselves or express their personalities through writing for publication. A larger number have learned to depend on the printed work as a way of participating in the world. It is to these people that the leading local newspaper distributes some 6,500 copies daily during the week and 9,000 on Sundays.[14] Also for them a local dealer carries 112 different magazines, published in Mexico and in four foreign countries.

These differences of occupation, origin, race, language, and literacy, coupled with a few other factors, provide the bases for a wide range of social status in the city. At the top of the scale are the descendants of the old aristocracy who have maintained their incomes at a fairly high level and persons of acceptable though less distinguished lineage who have achieved outstanding success in business or the professions. This upper class is characterized by predominantly white ancestry, by superior economic advantages, by an approved amount and kind of education, and by a way of life expressive of its income and its long-established position as the élite. The other end of the social scale is occupied by those descendants of the traditional lower class who have not been able or willing to climb above the position of their ancestors. The members of this class were formerly clearly marked by a distinctive local costume. By cultural definition the wearers of this costume were mixed white and Indian and were, accordingly, called *mestizos*. A minority possessed Maya surnames as well, which meant that they might be referred to as Indians in keeping with the accepted fiction that an Indian was a person with an Indian name. Today, Maya surnames have lost much of their status meaning, and only the more conservative continue to wear mestizo clothes. Consequently, the lower class must be described in other terms. It is composed of those who work at the manual trades, who have small incomes, and who have had little formal schooling. Generally, though there are many exceptions, members of the lower class show more evidence of Indian admixture than do persons of higher status. Between these two classes there is a confused and ill-defined middle class. It is made up of people of "good family" who are rather unsuccessful economically, people who have recently raised themselves from the lower class through wealth or professional achievement, and people whose background is mixed or just so-so and who barely manage to hold their position. The presence of foreigners serves to complicate the status situation further. Orientals tend to form a special category outside the system, while Syrians are in the uncertain position of being partially accepted and yet excluded in many ways. Other immigrants appear to find places which are more or less satisfying to themselves and to the native population.

The size of Merida, the variety of its institutions, and the heterogeneity of its population have given rise to a fairly complex ecological organization.[15] One of the first things that becomes apparent when this organization is examined is that the present situation is the result of the operation of new and modern influences on a traditional pattern of long standing. More than three centuries of building in accordance with conditions embodied in the stable local culture produced a physical structure that has been modified but not destroyed by recent developments. A brief sketch of the older pattern as it was some seventy-five years ago will make the description of the city today more understandable. The geographical and social center of the community was an open square, flanked on three sides by the city hall, the state government building, and the cathedral. The municipal market and such stores and offices as existed at that time were concentrated at a short distance to the southeast. In every other direction, to the depth of a few blocks, were the dwellings of the upper class. In general, persons of highest social and economic status lived closest to the square, with those of lesser status farther out. The whole area of upper-class residence was called the "center." At points five to ten blocks from the central square were five other squares, each one with a church. These were centers of lower-class communities called *barrios*, named in every case after the church. The distribution of people in the barrios tended to reproduce roughly the arrangement in the center. The houses of the more successful members of the lower class were located near the barrio squares, while poorer families occupied more distant streets. It may be noted that the barrio squares were centers only in a social sense, since they were situated on the inner edge of the barrios.

This division between the center and the barrios was the basic feature of the traditional pattern. The two areas differed sharply from each other in ways expressive of their spatial positions in the community and of the social positions of their inhabitants. In the center were the institutions, already noted, which served the whole city and certain others—a theater, a fashionable promenade, social clubs, and schools beyond the primary grades—which pertained chiefly or exclusively to the upper class. All over the central area the streets, though not paved, were sufficiently smooth to permit the easy transit of horse-drawn vehicles. Here the houses were flat-roofed, box-like structures built of masonry. One-story buildings predominated, and five to eight rooms was the most common size. But the homes of the wealthy were often immense. A few had two floors, and those with just one floor spread over enough ground to provide ample space for a household composed of a usually large parental family, perhaps a number of more distant relatives, and a dozen or more servants. The front walls of all the houses were set on the margin of the street, and each house touched the next, with the result that continuous walls bounded the streets on both sides.

In contrast, the streets of the barrios, with the exception of a few main thoroughfares which connected with roads leading out of the city, had been improved little beyond clearing away the vegetation. In view of the rocky terrain of Yucatan, this meant that they were hardly usable for wheeled vehicles. On and near the barrio squares and on the main thoroughfares there were some masonry houses, generally smaller than those of the center. Elsewhere, oval, thatch-roofed dwellings prevailed. These consisted of a single room, but frequently a lot had two such buildings, the second serving as a kitchen. The houses were ordinarily placed back from the street behind dry stone walls four to six feet high.

The kind of streets, houses, and institutions found in the center conformed to the ideas most people held as to how a city should be. In fact, the center was frequently referred to as the city in contradistinction to the barrios, as if the latter were thought of, in some senses at least, as lying outside of the city. Historically this was literally true. The barrios began as Indian settlements clustered about the area of Spanish residence, and for a long time they carried on a semi-autonomous existence politically and socially. But by seventy-five years ago the distinction between Spaniards and Indians had become a distinction between upper- and lower-class Yucatecans. A parallel change had tended to integrate the barrios into the city. The process, however, was still incomplete, and they remained separate communities to a considerable degree. In each barrio square there was a public building in which a set of barrio officials exercised limited powers of local government under the direction of the municipal authorities. The other visible symbol of the community was the church. It seems to have been the chief object of collective loyalty. It housed the patron saint whose fiesta constituted the outstanding common enterprise. The barrios were somewhat isolated from one another. Families that moved from one to another had to expect to be treated as outsiders. Several years were required for them to be fully accepted by their new neighbors. Inter-barrio rivalry expressed itself in periodic clashes between gangs representing the different barrios. To most of the inhabitants of all the barrios the center was socially· distant. It was another world occupied by a superior class. Barrio residents had quite frequent contacts with it through working, buying, selling, and participating in religious and patriotic celebrations, but their real home was their own local community.

During the last three-quarters of a century the population of Merida has trebled.[16] There has been great improvement in intracity transportation. The streets over all of the old center and a fair number in the barrio area have been paved. The masses, who formerly walked, may now ride in the motor buses that connect the center with the periphery along ten different routes. About two thousand automobiles operate in the city,[17] a large proportion of which are for hire; and these are supplemented by many one-horse cabs. The growth of population and the fact that people buy more of what they consume than they used to have increased trade and commerce. A few factories and the railroad with its shops and terminal have been added to the community. The established class system has been disintegrating. As a consequence the location of people comes about more through competition and less through birth-determined status than in the past. These are perhaps the chief modern developments that have tended to transform the older organization.

Today the central business district surrounds the central square on all sides. Its axes run about six blocks east and west and five blocks north and south. The business section is the heart of the whole city to a much greater degree than in the past. Seventy-eight buses arrive and leave hourly. During the morning, when most of the marketing is done, the streets are full of people. Again in the evening crowds gather to attend the movies, to patronize the coffee shops and bars, or to sit in the square and visit. Here there are bright lights, movement, and noise. Or, as Yucatecans say, the place is *alegre*, that is, gay or happy. Most of the buildings are old upper-class residences that have been taken over for commercial purposes. But two or three dozen have been erected specifically for business use. Several of these have three stories and one has five. This tendency to go in for increased height in modern construction is noteworthy in view of local conditions. Well-informed persons agree that floors above the second are economically unjustified and that it is not easy to utilize even the second floor efficiently. The men responsible for the higher buildings seem to have been motivated by a desire to give the market area a more metropolitan appearance rather than by the prospect of profits arising from a demand for space.

Subsidiary centers of business are found here and there in the rest of the city. Of particular interest are those which have developed in the barrio squares. They differ from one another widely in size and importance—differences expressive of time-distance relations with the main business section, of the direction of population growth, and of the spatial distribution of income in present-day Merida. The greatest expansion during recent years has occurred in the square of Santa Ana barrio. It is located toward the north, five blocks from the edge of the central business district, on the street that connects with the highway to Progreso. Surrounding it is the most popular new residential area of the middle and upper classes. In this barrio square there are some thirty business establishments. A partial list includes two motion-picture theaters, two garages, a service station, two restaurants, three drug stores, two general stores, and a market building housing venders of all the common foods. About the same number and variety of commercial services are available in the square of the barrio of Santiago, situated toward the west. It is nearer the main business district than is Santa Ana, but this appears to be counterbalanced by economic position of the inhabitants of its trade area. Many middle- and upper-class families settled in the vicinity before the movement to the north began, and it is still looked upon as a suitable place for such families to live. In contrast, San Sebastian has only a half-dozen establishments. This square is farthest from the center, but it lies toward the southwest in the poorest part of Merida and the part that has experienced the least amount of population increase. The remaining two, San Cristobal to the southeast and the Mejorada to the northeast, are of distinctly minor importance, though they offer more services than San Sebastian. Both squares are quite close to the main business district in areas not so poor as San Sebastian but much less prosperous than Santa Ana or Santiago. A further working-out of the same factors that have produced these differences have given rise to three small secondary centers in sections not effectively served by any of the barrio squares. One is four blocks south of the main business district on the street that forms the north-south axis of the city, another is four blocks beyond the Mejorada toward the east, and the third is in the square of Itzimna, formerly a village outside of Merida at the north, now a rapidly developing residential suburb.

There is no very well-defined industrial area. The railroad station, yards, and shops are located in the northeastern part of the city, and most of the larger factories are in the same general region. Altogether they provide employment for about two thousand persons. But the region over which they are distributed is so extensive that, except in the immediate vicinity of the railway terminal, it has the appearance of a working-class residential area, which most of it is. Moreover, smaller plants and shops are scattered over much of the rest of the community.

Although the barrio area is still occupied predominantly by the lower class, it is less homogeneous than it used to be. The most obvious evidence of this is the invasion of Santa Ana by upper-class persons from the center. There is a similar intrusion into Santiago along one street. In addition, throughout the barrios the more successful people, many of whom have achieved middle-class or near-middle-class status, tend to find homes on the paved streets. The houses on these streets are better, and more of them are masonry than are those elsewhere. The extensive sections between the paved streets, where the poorer people live, present a situation suggestive of the old barrios. But here, too, some variation is observable. In general, status declines with distance from the center. As the periphery of the city is approached the ratio of thatched houses becomes higher, rents are lower, and individuals wearing the traditional costume of the lower class are seen more frequently. The location of the railway terminal and larger factories in a part of the barrio area introduces another diversifying influence. Industrial workers, Merida's emerging proletariat, are more numerous in that vicinity than anywhere else.

The social and spatial mobility that has blurred the center-barrio division has practically destroyed the barrio communities. Politically they are undifferentiated segments of the city. The local church seems to be little more than the most convenient place to attend mass. Patron fiestas, formerly expressions of community solidarity, have disappeared in some of the barrios and are moribund in the others. Santa Ana and Santiago correspond roughly to the trade areas of the important secondary business centers situated in the squares of these two barrios. The remaining three can hardly even be called trade areas. This contrast should not be taken to mean that Santa Ana and Santiago retain more of their community characteristics. On the contrary, they are more heterogeneous and mobile than the others. The barrio names are still popularly used to designate certain sections of the city, but they have come to have an almost purely territorial connotation.

One new type of community has grown up as a result of immigration. Syrians are concentrated in a small area adjoining the main business district on the east. There is evidence that for a number of years this side of the business section has been considered the least desirable for residence and that it has undergone some deterioration. This circumstance and the fact that Syrians are engaged primarily in trade probably accounts for the location of the settlement. Two clubs constitute the social centers of the community. No other newcomers to Merida have formed similar localized colonies. Apparently only Syrians are both sufficiently different and sufficiently numerous to give rise to one.

The changes in the organization of Merida suggested in the foregoing discussion are but a part of the transformation that is affecting every aspect of its life. This situation presents a marked contrast to the time, more remote in the case of Merida than of other communities in Yucatan, when the city was relatively stable and when its ways conformed to a well-established local culture. This does not mean that it was ever homogeneous. At its founding in 1542 it was designated the capital and was, therefore, the chief place of residence of the invading Spaniards. Indians settled in the community, a few negroes were added, and mixed-bloods soon appeared in increasing numbers. Merida had all the elements of population and two distinct culture groups. But during the Colonial period these differences of race and culture and the status differences associated with them were fitted together into an orderly pattern that persisted without any apparent basic alteration for generations. By the eighteenth century the Spaniards had become a provincial upper class, socially accepted as whites though some successful mixed-bloods had achieved admission. Culturally defined categories of Indians and mixed-bloods had evolved. The categories, based on the possession of Maya or Spanish surname, represented racial realities less accurately as the years passed. The significance of the distinctions between them tended to fade, and they came to constitute, for most purposes, a single lower class. The negroes can be ignored since they gradually disappeared through miscegenation. The two main status groups, the upper class and the lower class, provided the basic framework on which the society and culture of Colonial Merida was organized. They were distinguished from each other by costume, an obvious sign, that announced the social position of every individual. Each class had an established location in the city, a distinctive social role, and a characteristic way of life.

Yucatan at this period was extremely isolated. Even members of the upper class appear to have had no great interest in the outside world and seem to have been content to carry on their lives mostly within the local society and culture. There was literacy, maintained as an adornment appropriate for upper-class males and as a tool for keeping routine records, but there was little writing. Almost nothing survives to suggest questioning or dissatisfaction with the status quo. Early nineteenth-century writers, separated from the Merida here referred to by only a few years, decry its provincial narrowness, its ignorance, and its backwardness. These condemnations, made at the time modern changes were beginning, state in other words that the city previously was more stable and that it had a more distinctively local culture which its inhabitants showed little inclination to modify.

After 1800 this picture of stability and isolation changed, at first slowly and superficially and then more rapidly and deeply. The basic developments were political innovations, starting with Independence and culminating in the Revolution of 1915; economic expansion, especially that of the sisal industry subsequent to 1870; and contacts with the outside world that increased in frequency and intensity throughout the period.

The following chronology of events, taken from many different fields, will perhaps show the broad sweep of the changes that have taken place. They are not always the most significant events, since the necessity of dating them limited the choice.

1813   The first press was established.
1815   The Masonic Order was introduced, then, as now, anti-Catholic. (Approximate date.)
1833   The school of medicine was founded.
1841   The first literary magazine was started.
1857   The first upper-class social club was formed.
1865   The first system of numbering the streets and houses was instituted.
1868   The normal school opened for the first time.
1870   The barrios ceased to have their own local officials. (Approximate date.)
1873   A conservatory of music and declamation opened.
1876   A telegraph line connecting Merida with Mexico was completed. A magazine devoted to spiritualism began publication.
1879   The first Protestant missionary arrived in the city.
1880   Service began on the first streetcar line, using horse-drawn cars.
1881   The first railway, Merida to Progreso, was inaugurated.
1882   The first daily newspaper started publication.
1887   The first lower-class social club was organized.
1888   The first effort to found an upper-class suburb was made. It failed.
1892   The first electric-power plant began operation, furnishing current for lights in and near the central square.
1898   The first real estate boom began, following a sharp rise in the price of sisal.
1901   The first large cordage mill was established.
1902   Paving the streets was started and was carried out vigorously. A modern police system was organized. Motor power was substituted for horses on the streetcar lines.
1904   The fashionable boulevard in the barrio of Santa Ana was inaugurated.
1906   The most successful of the upper-class suburbs was laid out.
1908   The first motion-picture theater opened.
1910   The first permanent, voluntary, civic organization was founded to work for reform and progress.
1911   The first important strike of industrial workers took place.
1914   A lodge of the International Theosophical Society was organized. The Country Club was established.
1915   The first student strike occurred.

1916   Public schools were made coeducational for the first time; later abandoned and then re-established.

The Cathedral was sacked by an anti-Catholic mob.

1918   The first feminist congress convened.

1923   An easy divorce law was passed, making Merida a minor "divorce capital."

1924   A Rotary Club was organized.

1927   Mothers' Day was instituted.

1928   The highway to Progreso was opened.

Air service to Mexico City was started.

1930   Secondary schools were founded, providing opportunity, never available before, for education beyond the sixth grade, which was not pre-professional.

The first local communist organization was established.

The first woman physician was graduated.

1932   There was a mild "epidemic" of elopements involving children of upper-class families, very rare occurrences in this class before.

1933   The fashion of permanent waving of women's hair reached, and began to be accepted by, the lower class.

Here we see material improvements, increased indirect communication, expansion of formal education, formal organizations for carrying on recreation, reflections of international fashion even among the lower class, weakening of familial controls, and conflict in religion, industry, and political ideology. These and many other things are characteristic of the mobile and heterogeneous city Merida has become. It stands out among the communities of Yucatan as the place where the old culture has suffered the greatest amount of disorganization and where new ways of life, borrowed from other urban societies or developed under the stimulus of its own urban conditions, are most in evidence.

II. DZITAS

Of the dozen largest towns in Yucatan, only three lie in the eastern half of the state. The railroad line which serves these three divides at Dzitas, one branch going to Valladolid and the other to Espita and Tizimín. Dzitas lies almost in the middle of the state and slightly to the south of the latitude of

Merida. But, because of the unequal distribution of population in the peninsula, most of the people of Yucatan are to be found west of Dzitas, while not many kilometers to the east and to the south begin the almost empty rain forests and the area of chicle exploitation.

Dzitas is far from one of the largest towns; about forty others in Yucatan have larger populations. There are about twelve hundred people in Dzitas itself; the smaller villages and hamlets which also form parts of the municipio have together about as many.[18] It is the third town in size in the (once-existing) *partido* (administrative division) of Espita.

Like other towns in this part of Yucatan, it is a center of production and a shipping-point of maize. Maize accounts for about nineteen-twentieths, by value, of exports from Dzitas. Cattle production, once important, is in recent years undergoing a revival; several haciendas are beginning to raise cattle for market. Nevertheless, monthly shipments include very few hides. A few chickens and pigs are exported; and very little lumber and palm leaves. There has been no sugar produced for export since the Revolution, and no henequen for a much longer time than that.

Maize is sent out during all the months of the year, but especially from September to March; in summer the agriculturalists are likely to hold their surplus maize until assured that the next year's crop will be a success. About eight thousand sacks of maize are exported annually. The *milpero* sells his maize to any one of the storekeepers and merchants; these men put it in bags and sell it to buyers in towns to the west. Because Merida can secure maize from nearer regions to the south, west, and immediate east of it, the largest part of the maize exported from Dzitas is bought in Motul and Cansahcab, the two largest near-by towns in the henequen area.

The *ejidos* (land, title to which, as recognized by the national government, vests in the village or town as a whole) of Dzitas consist of 8,132 hectares of land lying about the town. But because most agriculturalists prefer to go farther to better land, where the bush is high, most of the maize is produced on land owned by large estate owners, none of whom are resident in Dzitas. In most such cases the milpero pays the landowner one-tenth of his crop as land rent. It is common for an agriculturalist to have a small milpa within the ejido and a larger tract on more distant rented land.

Most of the transportation occurring between Dzitas and other communities is by rail. There is one passenger train a day each way and several freight trains each week. A few people and a small amount of goods enter or leave Dzitas by the automobile road to Chichen Itza or by the poor cart roads and trails to various small towns and to haciendas. Until 1934 tourists coming to visit the Maya ruins at Chichen Itza passed through Dzitas; in 1934 an automobile road was opened up from Merida to Chichen; and in 1937 a road from Piste (near Chichen) to Valladolid. Therefore (but since the period represented by these studies), the commercial life of Dzitas has suffered: business has been deflected to Piste or to Valladolid.

Dzitas is the *cabecera* (seat of municipal government) of its municipio. It is the seat of the judicial district; a court of first resort, both civil and criminal, is maintained here. During the first part of the period covered by these studies a regional administrative center of the federal school system was located in Dzitas. There is a public school employing three teachers. The census of 1930 reported that 41.8 per cent of the people of the municipio of Dzitas could read and write, as compared with an average of 36 per cent for other rural municipios and 49 per cent for the state as a whole. Both Merida newspapers maintain, somewhat irregularly, local correspondents in Dzitas; once or twice a week these papers publish news from the town. About twenty copies of one or another newspaper are distributed each day in Dzitas. The post office handles about two thousand pieces of mail a month, including both mail received and mail sent and including governmental communications. The telegraph office transmits chiefly messages on behalf of branches of the government.

Although Dzitas is predominantly agricultural, it is not completely so. About two-thirds of the men of Dzitas make milpa by their own labor and for their own benefit. Most of these have no other gainful occupation, but some are also woodcutters, carters, and, in a very few cases, trackworkers, mechanics, or other artisans. About a score of heads of families, too busy with specialized occupations to work in the fields or disinclined to do so and with the means to avoid it, employ others to make milpa for them (as do many widows). And about one-quarter of the men carry on no agriculture at all, either directly or indirectly. The officials sent down from the city, the teachers, the storekeepers and the saloonkeepers, the butchers, carpenters, and most of the other skilled artisans, as well as the principal railroad employees, live on what they earn by performing their specialized services. All these know the life of the milpa, familiar and close at hand as it is to everyone, but they themselves participate in it little or not at all. If the milperos perform a ceremony for rain out in some distant group of fields, these others, who are more definitely townsmen, hear of it, but they are not likely to take part.

The men who follow specialized occupations without recourse to supplementary agriculture may be mentioned somewhat in descending order of social importance. Near the apex of the pyramid of status are the district judge, the secretary of the municipal government, and the director of the school. Near the top also are the two innkeepers, the leading storekeepers—some of whom are also grain dealers or operators of transportation by truck—certain of the five saloonkeepers, the postal and telegraph agent, and the station agent. To be mentioned with these last are the five butchers and the two or three men who travel about buying and selling livestock. The artisans occupy a status slightly lower; these include two stonemasons, seven carpenters, a smith, one shoemaker, four mechanics (who help maintain the steam gristmill, the engine and generator of the electric-light plant, and the few automobiles), four brakemen, and one tinsmith. Some of those mentioned toward the end of this list are humbler people, and some of them work also in the milpa. This is true also of the two soft-drink sellers and of the four tailors. Downward, in terms of status, the list ends with the three or four carters and freight handlers, the trackworkers, and the many woodcutters and few charcoal-burners, many of whom are otherwise indistinguishable from the other poor milperos who live also on the outskirts of town.

During the time of these observations no city-trained doctor lived in Dzitas, although for periods before and after that time one such did. A doctor from Merida, or one from Espita, occasionally pays the town a brief visit, as does a curer with herbal medicine and magic who enjoys a great reputation throughout Yucatan. Dzitas has also its native healers. There is a *curandera*, a woman who treats the sick with herbs and spells and exorcises evil from afflicted bodies.[19] There are also two or three midwives, whose practices follow tradition and who have learned their art from women like themselves; and there is another woman (*x-kax-baac*) who treats sprains and dislocations. All these live in side streets some distance from the plaza and belong to the humble agriculturalist families whose houses merge with the milpas on the outskirts of town and who have their roots and the sources of their ways in the isolated villages of the bush.

Over two-thirds of the tradespeople and professionals are not natives of Dzitas. Most of these have come from larger places where the economic development is greater; they have come to make a living here where the competition in their fields is less. Espita, Valladolid, and Merida have provided the largest number, but there are tradespeople from Cenotillo, Hekelchakan, and Campeche. None of the principal merchants has come from small villages, but several of the small tradespeople—barbers, bakers, and carpenters, as well as a teacher and a political leader—were brought up in little villages. The immigrant merchants' families have intermarried with the native Dzitas families of highest social and economic

status: other merchants and tradespeople quite like themselves. Two of the storekeepers (and one of the saloonkeepers)
are Syrians. One of these married a woman of Dzitas, amassed
a considerable property in land, houses, and stock in trade, and
became a social leader in Dzitas before moving, very recently,
to Merida for new business opportunities. The one tinsmith
is a Korean. Perhaps half-a-dozen people have come from
that part of Mexico outside the peninsula.

The distribution of buildings, residences, and types of people and activities is characterized, as is usual with Latin-
American towns, by the dominance of the central plaza; but
this familiar pattern is modified by the presence of the railroad
station at the northern edge of the community.[20] The railroad
station and its sheds, sidings, water tank, and stacks of wood
fuel form a cluster of heterogeneous structures strikingly conspicuous among the huts and cornfields that are so close and
intimate a part of the landscape. The railroad is a center of
activities very different from those of the milpa. It is an approximation to an industrial development, and the only one
in Dzitas. It employs the station attendants and watchmen,
several brakemen, an engineer for the steam pump that fills
the water tank, a gang of trackworkers, and a large gang of
woodcutters who spend several days each week away from
Dzitas cutting wood and hauling it to the cars waiting on a
siding. Many of the people who live in the little houses near
the station are employed in one or another of these ways;
people refer to "the railroad workers near the tracks."

Ten minutes' walk from the railroad station brings one to
the plaza. There is the usual little park with its bandstand
and benches; the usual church and civic public buildings occupy three sides of the square. There is no market, although
occasionally a traveling vendor of hats, sandals, or hammocks
takes his temporary stand in the plaza. Nearly all the buying
and selling is done in the stores. Seven general stores, a
butcher shop, three bakeries, and five saloons make up the business center of the town. All the stores offer much the same

general assortment of goods imported by the local merchants from Merida, from Mexico, or from further abroad. All these do business not merely with the people of Dzitas but also, and especially on Sunday, with the people of the villages and rural settlements of the region. Dzitas is a trading center for a population about twice its own size.

In connection with two of the saloons there are poolrooms. Just as these are meeting places for men in the evenings, so the steam gristmill, also on the plaza, draws to it during the day the women who come to have their corn ground and to exchange gossip while waiting with other customers. Near the gristmill is the moving-picture theater, where pictures are shown—during periods when the promoter's capital is sufficient to maintain the enterprise—once or twice a week. The building that houses the gristmill provides also for the steam engine and generator which, also through private enterprise, supplies electric light to the principal streets and to a very few of the houses of Dzitas. In the plaza are concentrated almost all the public life and the commercial activity of the community: the trials before the judge and the discussions of matters of municipal administration in the town hall, the prisoners in the jail which this building includes, the movements of the military garrison, the three schoolrooms of school children, the arrival or departure of a truck or automobile once or twice a day, the performances in the roofed shelter which serves as a cinema theater, the rarer amateur theatrical performances in the more pretentious little theater behind the school, the still more exceptional use of the church for festal purposes, and the daily rounds of miller, artisan, storekeeper, and the customers of these—all center in or converge upon the plaza.

A walk from the plaza toward the outskirts of the town is a walk from the world of the commercial townsman to that of the agricultural villager. The houses around the plaza, many of them also stores, situated where come the city people and the visitors to Dzitas, are nearly all of masonry, built in

Spanish style; most have windows, and some of the windows have iron grilles. Most of the electricity consumed in town is used on these street corners and in some of these houses and stores. They have built-in charcoal cooking-stoves, tables, and chairs, and a few have shower baths. But toward the outskirts the houses are thatched huts with plastered or wattled walls, and the furniture is hardly more than hammocks, mats, and a few simple cooking utensils. With these differences in housing and economic condition go parallel differences in costume and in language. The people who live near the plaza tend to wear the clothes of the city: dark trousers, shirt, and shoes in the case of the man; dress and shoes in the case of the woman. Toward the outskirts these become rare; the men are clothed in the sandals and straw hat of the rural villager; and the women wear the *huipil* and go barefoot or wear soft, heelless slippers (*chancletas*). Around the plaza Spanish is spoken in many of the homes, but Maya, which is the language spoken by almost everybody on some occasion and is the only language for many people, is the domestic tongue in almost all the little huts on the outskirts of town. Our survey indicates that Spanish is ordinarily spoken in 29 per cent of the homes of Dzitas, and Maya in the rest. But even in the homes where Spanish is usually spoken it is common for people to drop into Maya, and not merely when Maya-speaking visitors are present but also among members of the family. The dwellers in the little huts on the outskirts are practically all Maya-speaking. They live by the same primitive agriculture practiced in the more remote villages; their labor grows the corn which feeds Dzitas and contributes to the support of the henequen-producing areas to the west.

Dzitas had its beginning before the Conquest as an Indian village in the territory controlled by the Cupul family.[21] Spaniards probably settled here very early. Nothing is known by the author as to the history of the community in Colonial times. About 1875 the population of Dzitas could not have exceeded 700. In 1895, according to the federal census, it held

737 people. There have been schools in Dzitas for at least fifty years. Maya was more generally spoken fifty years ago than now (at that time it was spoken in most of the houses), and much instruction in the school and many sermons were given in that language. The growth of population and the development of commerce were accelerated after the railroad reached Dzitas in 1902; they were further accelerated after 1910, owing to the Revolution. Then, with the abolition of peonage and with the mobility occasioned by warfare and social changes, many hacienda peons and other villagers came to the towns, including Dzitas. About 1880 there was only one store in Dzitas. By 1934 there were seven. About 1905 the first handmills appeared, and people began to give up the grinding of corn on the *metate*. The first machine mill was set up in (about) 1908. The first moving picture was shown in (about) 1924. The road to Chichen, which brought tourists in numbers, was opened in 1926.

Dzitas is typical of towns of Yucatan in that it is larger than most of the villages, in that it is a center of trade, in that it is an axis of important lines of communication, in that it contains organs of the national and state governments, and in that its population includes people of every degree of Indian and Spanish racial intermixture.[22] It is further typical of the towns in that it lies on the frontier between the urban and rural ways of life. From what has been said it should appear that in Dzitas two worlds meet and mingle so that there is no line between them but rather a mixing and a gradual transition: the world of the villages and the little settlements out on the haciendas or situated by themselves in the bush and represented in Dzitas by the milperos, who are only milperos and live, chiefly, in the small huts on the periphery of the town; and the world of Merida, maintained, in some degree, by the more mobile, educated, and economically advantaged families who live chiefly in the center of town and maintain connections with the other towns and with the city.

III. CHAN KOM

About thirty kilometers south of the town of Dzitas lies the village of Chan Kom. It is situated in the same maize-producing zone as is Dzitas, but a day's walk from the railroad, in the deep bush. In the middle of the nineteenth century this area had been practically depopulated by the War of the Castes; the region a day's walk to the southeast of Chan Kom is still uninhabited from the same cause. About sixty years ago people began to return to the Chan Kom area to resettle on ancient sites. As is the case in most of the other villages of the immediate region, the young men and women of Chan Kom are the first generation in modern times to have been born there; their parents came from communities north and west of Chan Kom and not far from it. These communities were villages much like Chan Kom; Chan Kom is a village settled by neighboring villagers. In size (two hundred and fifty people) it is not far from the average for villages in this area of maize-without-henequen.[23]

Without exception the men of Chan Kom grow maize with their own hands and for their own benefit. Some of the older men before the Revolution worked as peons on cattle estates; this is now only a remote memory. Chan Kom is and always has been since its settlement a village of independent farmers. The amount of maize a man may grow depends on the ambitions and abilities of the milpero; but, though a man may accumulate enough corn to go for a year without planting milpa, or may in one year plant only enough to supply his domestic wants, over periods of years a man must grow twice as much as his family consumes, so as to convert half his crop into textiles, soap, gunpowder, sugar, salt, and other necessaries. There is almost no other source of livelihood. The maize is sold to traveling merchants or is carried to the towns (Valladolid in most cases) and there sold. Some hogs, cattle, and poultry are raised for profit; the collection and the sale of these products are unorganized and are carried on by the individual as opportunity offers itself in a trip to the town or in the visit of an ambulant trader. The lesser crops—chile, beans, fruit, and a little tobacco and sugar—are consumed, with small exception, locally.[24]

The 2,400 hectares of land which constitute the ejidos of the pueblo are not large enough to provided enough good land for the people. Therefore, most milpas are made on lands of the federal government; with small restriction these are available to anyone. People make long trips to their milpas, the average distance to a milpa being nine kilometers. As only a few pieces of land are owned individually, as no contract with a landowner is necessary to cultivate a tract in the federal domain, and as the surrounding bush is high and little of it is cleared away at any one time, nothing stands between the woods and the milpero; he deals, so to speak, directly with nature.[25]

All transportation and communication to any place is on foot or by horse or mule. During the latter part of the period of this study the people opened a road wide enough for a wagon, but it was not leveled; it remains a path for foot travel. One of the principal paths runs northeastward to Valladolid; another runs northward to Chichen, where it meets the highway to Merida and the road to Dzitas. These are the two roads that connect Chan Kom with the outside road; they are roads by which outside influences are received. Lesser trails to the dozen little hamlets politically subordinate to Chan Kom, and to villages farther from the towns lying, principally, to the south, are the routes by which influence extends out from Chan Kom to more backward communities. Every week a few people, other than local villagers, pass through Chan Kom. Most of these are traveling merchants from the towns; a few are schoolteachers or governmental officials, or, more rarely, a North American visitor from Chichen Itza, or a Protestant missionary.[26]

During the period of this study Chan Kom, having received its ejidos in 1926, claimed that with increase in population it should no longer be called *ranchería* but be recognized as a *pueblo*, a representative of the next higher category in the hierarchy of municipal organization. It was then subordinate to Cuncunul, the seat of the municipal government to which Chan Kom belonged. (After the period of study, Chan Kom became the cabecera, or seat of municipal government, of its own municipio.) Connection with the state and federal governments is maintained by the *comisario*, locally elected, and his assisting officers, through the local liga, a unit in the national political party which controls Mexican government, and through the agrarian committee, also organized by representatives of the national government. At national and state elections the people of Chan Kom cast votes within the limits set by the operations of the controlling party; but for the people of the village this is a formal and unimportant act. In short, the only governmental agencies in Chan Kom are maintained by the natives to serve strictly local interests.[27] Except for the schoolteacher, there are no outsiders in Chan Kom.[28]

There has been a school in Chan Kom since 1910. Most of the men and some of the women of the older generation had some schooling in the villages from which they emigrated. Much of the instruction in the Chan Kom school is given in Maya. With the exception of a single household, where the parents have made an effort to see that their children learned Spanish in the home, the language of the village is Maya. It is used in practically all conversations among villagers. Yet one out of every five men, and about one of twelve women, can speak Spanish. One woman was born in Merida, and her husband lived there for a number of years; these people, and perhaps a dozen others, speak Spanish with fluency. The census reported one-fourth of the people over eighteen as literate. It is doubtful if five people can read a Spanish newspaper with understanding. Chiefly through the teachers, newspapers are occasionally brought to Chan Kom, and on such occasions one of the literate leaders may read something in it. School readers are found in most homes; almanacs in not a few; a few have Bibles; more have printed texts of Catholic prayers. Most of the men have been to Merida; practically everyone has been to Valladolid. A very few people have seen a moving-picture performance. None has been outside of the peninsula of Yucatan. During the period of study, mail was brought irregularly from Chichen Itza and consisted almost entirely of governmental communications for the comisario or the officers of the liga.[29]

Everyone is an agriculturalist, and such specialized occupations as occur either are performed without pecuniary return or are carried on for a gain that is incidental to the yield of the milpa. The one or two keepers of little stores, the man who has an oven and occasionally bakes bread, the man who learned the art of the mason in Merida, and those who do a little carpentering or a little barbering—all carry on these occupations as mere incidents to their lives as farmers. The same is true of those specialists whose arts are more traditional, more esoteric, and more weighted with prestige: the shaman-priests (*h-mens*), who are charged with performance of agricultural ceremonies, with divination and the healing of the sick; the reciters of Catholic prayers (*maestros cantores*); the marriage negotiator (*casamentero*); the midwife; and the bone-setter. The growing of maize is the main task and preoccupation of all; these other occupations are subordinate.[30]

All the people are similar in the apparent relative purity of Indian blood. In some individuals white admixture is apparent. With hardly an exception all are derived from the same rural village, agricultural Maya-speaking population of the Valladolid region. But some can better deal with the new ways of the city than others: some speak Spanish and can read; some know how to meet and negotiate with officials from the towns and the city. Chan Kom has set its face forward with progress; its leaders have listened to the voices of the Revolution. Therefore, those who have these abilities are accorded prestige and become leaders of the community. But the old leaders, who transmit the sacred tradition and embody it in their own conduct, are also accorded recognition: the men who know the Catholic prayers and who can give moral instruction to the young; also the h-mens, those exponents of a parallel and no less sacred lore, centering in the milpa, the rain, and the bees. When this study was begun, these two kinds of leaders, old and new, were evenly balanced in authority, and each group enjoyed the confidence of the other; but during recent years the modern group has become ascendant. The old ways have waned, and with them the influence of the men who best preserve them. But the men of both groups are, essentially, Indian farmers and represent the same body of folkways; and all have arisen, leaders and led, from the same homogeneous local village population.[31]

Before the Revolution the houses of the hamlet were scattered about the cenote without order or plan. The determination of the inhabitants to make their settlement a pueblo caused them to delimit a plaza, to mark off streets, and to move their houses down on the streets at right angles to them. Now the village begins to have some of the physical outlines of a town. Most of the houses on the plaza are of masonry; these are occupied by the leaders, the "principal people." A school, a municipal building, and a small open-air theater, operated in connection with the school, were built, during or just after the period of this study, on one side of the plaza. But, although the building of a new church has been more than once proposed, a thatched edifice or poles and mud plaster still houses the village saint, and nearly all the houses off the plaza are built in the same primitive manner characteristic of the smaller bush settlements. Throughout the village the same simple kitchen equipment and furniture is used; all the women build their fires on the floor and support the clay griddle on three stones; all the people sleep in hammocks and use, chiefly, little wooden benches to sit upon. When Chan Kom was studied, all the people wore the folk costume, but in recent years some changes have taken place in this regard.[32]

The municipal building is used for formal gatherings. Women find the cenote, at one side of the plaza, a place to meet and gossip. The men gather more casually in the little store or more often sit or squat in little groups outside the houses on the plaza. Except for one or two gasoline lamps, there is no illumination but candles and little kerosene flares. At nightfall the plaza is dark, and, if there is no moon or no fiesta, the people are soon asleep. The crowing of cocks, the occasional cries of children, or the rumble of cattle coming into the village for water are the most noticeable sounds to be heard.

The first settlers of modern times built their houses around the cenote in the 1880's. The first school was opened in 1910. In the 1920's a few masonry houses were built. In 1923 the people petitioned the government to grant them communal lands. In 1929, under the influence of Alfonso Villa, the people entered into friendly relations with the Americans at Chichen Itza. In 1930 a young girl and a boy went to the town to look for jobs. In 1932 the people laid out a road to connect them more directly with Chichen and the railroad. In 1933 the first Protestant missionaries arrived. In the next year—after the period of this study—some of the men acquired watches and began to use them, and the first baseball game was played. In 1935 the village became the capital (cabecera) of the municipio, and a post office and a civil registry were opened.[33]

Chan Kom is typical of villages of the maize area and different from most of the towns in that its population is composed of Maya born in this or similar villages and is overwhelmingly agricultural, in that commerce is little in quantity and local in importance, in that the village lies on no railroad or important road, and in that it is the seat of no governmental institution except those of purely local consequence. It is further typical not only of villages in this area but of peasant villages in many places, and in these respects different from the community to be described in the next section, in that the villagers are dependent upon the store and peddler of the towns, in that grain constitutes an important money crop, in that trade within the community is important, and especially in that the villagers, though centered upon very local interests, accept a part in the government of the modern state and are disposed to follow suggestion and leadership emanating from the towns and the city and to change its ways so as to make them more nearly conform with what is done in the towns and the city.

On the other hand, Chan Kom, along with many other villages established on this frontier of resettlement, differs from most of the villages of the Valladolid area in that it is a community of relatively recent colonists. Because its people are colonists, the average age of the population is unusually low.[34] It is further exceptional, and in this respect even among its neighbors, in the great enthusiasm its people have shown for progress and in the rapidity in which social changes have taken place within it in recent years. So far as can be determined, no other village in the eastern part of the state has modified its ways so rapidly and consistently since the Revolution. It has a reputation in Yucatan for industry, determination, and ambition. In fifteen years from an inconspicuous bush village it has become (since the study ended) the governmental seat of a municipio. The rapidity of these changes makes unusually difficult the reporting of the ways of life of Chan Kom as if those ways had been static during the observations. On the other hand, the fact that the village is extreme in this respect accentuates the contrast that it is desired to make between the peasant village of Chan Kom and the tribal village of Tusik.

IV. TUSIK

Three days' ride on a horse or a mule from Chan Kom across the uninhabited fourth zone to the southeast, within the quadrangle previously delimited (chap. i), lie the villages of the Maya of central Quintana Roo. The natives of this area fall into three groups, which may with reason be called subtribes (*cacicazgoes*). All share the same culture and regard themselves as a single people, but each group has its own political organization. This organization is both military and theocratic: a military chieftain shares ultimate authority with a supreme priest (who is also a native); authority is distributed through a hierarchy of subordinate chiefs but, in the case of each subtribe, is exercised centrally in one village of the group which includes a shrine housing a cross of great sacredness. This village is the capital of the subtribe; subtribal councils are held here and religious ceremonies of greatest importance and especially those affecting the whole subtribe.

One subtribe has for its capital the village of Chunpom, southwest of Tuluum; another centers at Chancah, southeast of Santa Cruz del Bravo; and the third, the western or middle group, with which this study is particularly concerned, recognizes X-Cacal as its shrine village. X-Cacal lies approximately at latitude 19°85″, longitude 88°30″, about eighty-five kilometers a little west of south of Valladolid. Nine settlements compose the X-Cacal subtribe; the northernmost, adjacent to X-Cacal, is Tusik. Of all the natives of Quintana Roo those of the X-Cacal subtribe are the most seclusive and the most resistant to modernizing ways. Tusik is one of the villages of this group. With a population of one hundred and six persons, it is the third largest of the villages of the subtribe. Altogether the nine settlements include 723 persons. Forty years ago this area was uninhabited. The settlements were formed when Mexican troops entered the region of Chan Santa Cruz in 1901; thereupon the villages then existing on the road by which the soldiers entered were abandoned, and the people found new homes to the westward.[35]

Like the people of Chan Kom, those of Tusik and surrounding settlements are independent growers of maize; but, unlike the former, the people of the Quintana Roo villages do not grow maize as a money crop. Here chicle is the important marketed commodity.[36] The sale of this gum is seasonal; therefore, commerce with the traveling merchants is much greater at one time of year than at another. Furthermore, the market for chicle fluctuates sharply from one year to the next, and in some years chicle has no market. Rarely does the native of Tusik go outside his territory to the towns, and therefore the traveling merchant is almost the sole outlet for chicle and the only source for manufactured goods. As in Chan Kom, hogs and poultry are sold to these merchants, but the Quintana Roo people have almost no cattle or horses.[37]

As the Indians have not accepted the Mexican government and have no ejidos (or had none at the time of this study), the native is limited in selecting a site for his milpa only by customary law. All the milpas made by members of the group lie within the area, a rough square about twenty-five miles on a side, which the people of the subtribe regard as their territory. Encroachments upon this area by other Indians are resented. Within this area the native makes his cornfield almost where he will. As elsewhere in the peninsula, the milpas tend to concentrate in the small areas of relatively rich land, forming clusters of cornfields (*milperíos*). Each village asserts a vague sphere of influence in the territory nearest to it; thus a milperío very near one village is likely to be exploited exclusively by the inhabitants of that village, while one distant, and approximately equally distant, from two villages is shared by the inhabitants of both. From this situation land disputes commonly arise within the subtribe.

The relative scarcity of population, the great size of the trees of the forest, and the total absence of outside governmental regulation of land use and of commerce in land (at the time of the study) are circumstances tending to emphasize for the native the nearness and importance of the bush and to favor the development of a mystical attitude toward it.

The policy of the natives with regard to communication with the world of the towns is the reverse of that prevailing in Chan Kom. Chan Kom sought to build a highway to Chichen: "We must make a road to the light," the people said. Tusik hides itself in the bush; none of the nine villages are built on the roads that connect Santa Cruz del Bravo with Valladolid and Peto, and the paths that lead to Tusik are deliberately concealed. The advent of a visitor is a cause for alarm, and

Photograph by Frances Rhoads Morley

the news of the appearance of a stranger within the territory
of the group is an occasion to send out a party to reconnoiter.
Especially is the shrine village, X-Cacal, secluded in the forest.
Two narrow paths enter Tusik from the north; by one of these
come the merchants from Peto and by the other those who
come down from Valladolid. Similar paths to the south lead
to the neighboring villages of Señor and X-Cacal. Merchants
of established trustworthiness are allowed to stay briefly in the
settlement to transact business; other outsiders are rarely permitted to remain, and their entrance into the village is discouraged. In the absence of newspapers, of a school, and of
every organ of the Mexican or Yucatecan government, the
merchants are the sole bearers of news.

The natives regard the territory of Quintana Roo as theirs;
they sometimes call it "the land of the Indians" (*u luum
mazehualob*). The central region, within which lie the three
subtribes already spoken of, is the area with which the native
has familiarity; the shrine villages of the other two subtribes
are recognized as places of importance. Religious pilgrimages
take the native to Tuluum, thirty-six leagues to the northeast.
Because of the hostility felt for the Mexican and the townsman,
visits to Valladolid and Peto are rare. On the other hand, relationships with the British have been friendly, and visits to
Corozal, in British Honduras, used to be not uncommon.
Very recently sympathetic interest has shifted from the British
toward the Americans, first met at Chichen.

The political organization[38] is entirely different from that of
Chan Kom. In the latter community municipal officers are
elected annually as provided by state law; through these and
other functionaries the local government is articulated with
that of the state and the nation. The subtribe of Quintana Roo
to which Tusik belongs is governed by a body of chieftains
who serve for life. The tribal government exists not only for
purposes of internal control but also to maintain the group in
perpetual armed defense against feared aggression from the
Mexicans. The subtribe is divided into five companies. Each

(with one exception) is ruled by three officers of descending rank. The paramount chief of one of the companies is recognized as supreme chief of the subtribe, but he shares this authority with a religious functionary, the *Nohoch Tata*. In each village the members of one company predominate, but members of other companies are also present. Membership in a company is transmitted by a father to his children. Upon marriage a woman joins the company of her husband. At subtribal meetings, which usually take place at X-Cacal, all the members of one company camp together.[39]

For brief periods the small settlement of Chan-chen, of the nine villages the one most exposed to outside influence, allowed the presence of a governmental teacher and school; but with this exception the villages have been and are without schools. The only literate persons in the subtribe are two special functionaries, called "secretaries" or "scribes"; these read names and dates from a Spanish almanac, the Maya texts of certain religious writings, and occasional messages also set down in Maya. Reading and writing are closely identified with esoteric and religious matters, and the few practitioners of the art have a quasi-priestly role. Except for one man who speaks broken Spanish, no one in the subtribe has any command of that language. As the speech of the enemy and oppressor, Spanish is depreciated. On the other hand, English, although not spoken by the natives, as the language of the friendly neighbors of British Honduras and of the Americans, is well regarded.

Racially the population is about as homogeneous as is that of Chan Kom. Maya blood overwhelmingly predominates, but not a few individuals exhibit white admixtures. Eight per cent of the surnames found in the entire subtribe are Spanish, but only one such name is present in Tusik itself. A similar situation prevails at Chan Kom. A very few individuals of the Quintana Roo village are recognized descendants of Chinese who came from British Honduras in the 1880's and settled among the Maya. As the people of Chan Kom are drawn from villages in the region, so the people of Tusik came from villages like it situated to the east. But while a few of the Chan Kom people come from places more remote, and one was born in Merida itself, the cultural antecedents of the Tusik people are more completely homogeneous.

The only man in the community who is not an agricultural-ist is the priestly leader, the Nohoch Tata; he is supported by the people as is appropriate to his august office. The few half-specialists, in commerce or in craft, to be found in Chan Kom are absent here: there are no storekeepers, no masons, and no carpenters. One resident of Tusik who repairs guns and sewing machines provides an exception. In another village one family makes baskets to sell.[40]

Prestige is accorded to the military and religious leaders. No other member of the community approaches the Nohoch Tata in prestige. Next come the principal chiefs, then the lesser chiefs and the scribes or secretaries (functionaries who have in their keeping certain sacred books); after these the maestros cantores, who assist the Nohoch Tata in religious exercises, and the h-mens. The h-mens have functions similar to those carried on in Chan Kom, but their prestige, relative to that of the other leaders, is less than it is in Chan Kom. What is to be stressed in summarizing the facts in connection with status in Tusik is that, as the community faces outward toward a hostile world, ability to speak Spanish or to deal with the townsman, let alone the practice of the townsman's way of life, carries no prestige. The leaders in Tusik and neighboring villages are those who express and maintain the old and local way of life and only those.

The physical appearance of Tusik is like that which Chan Kom must have exhibited twenty years ago. The thatched houses, fowl pens, elevated vegetable gardens (caanche), and beehives are almost identical to what then prevailed in Chan Kom and are still largely to be found there. As in Chan Kom, the cenote provides a central point around which the houses are built. But although the space around the cenote in Tusik is kept clear of weeds, forming a rude public park, no attempt has been made to lay off a square plaza, to establish streets, to build masonry structures, or to arrange the houses in any regular order. These are distributed haphazard among the overshadowing trees. Near the cenote stands the village church, a large structure of poles and thatch. Scattered among the twenty-three houses are five smaller buildings used as familial oratories. These oratories are lacking in Chan Kom, where the religious worship of the family is carried on in the house itself. Another difference arises from the fact that, while in Chan Kom the dead are interred in a cemetery set apart from the village, in Tusik they are buried beside the houses right in the village; the graves are outlined with small stones. There is, as has been stated, no school, and the concentration of government in the subtribal institutions which operate at the capital, X-Cacal, obviates the necessity of any municipal building. The household furnishings in Tusik are like those of Chan Kom, except that such modern improvements as chairs, gasoline lamps, and sewing machines are scarcer or absent entirely.

The village of X-Cacal, as shrine center of the nine settlements, exhibits a special civic design which reflects the political and social organization of the subtribe. The church is a large pole-and-thatch structure with cement floor and whitened walls. Here religious ceremonies are held daily, and here marriages and tribal ceremonies are celebrated. Beside the church stands another structure (*corredor*), even larger, in which all secular gatherings of the group take place. These two structures express the dual leadership, religious and military, of X-Cacal. These centers of group activities are protected from invasion by danger or evil by four wooden crosses set in four mounds of stones which bound the area of the two public buildings in the intercardinal points of the compass. Outside this sanctified precinct, but adjacent to it, and arranged to suggest a circle around it, are five buildings constructed as is the corredor but smaller. These represent the five companies into which the subtribe is divided. When the people assemble in X-Cacal, the members of each company are housed in the one building of these five associated with the company. The house of the Nohoch Tata, priestly leader, stands near by and completes the civic center.

In 1847 the War of the Castes broke out, interrupting the control of Mexico over the central Quintana Roo Maya for three generations. In 1901 General Bravo reasserted governmental control by occupying Chan Santa Cruz; the natives fled into the bush to the west, and Tusik and the other villages of the group were founded. In 1915–16 an epidemic of smallpox destroyed a large part of the population. In the years that followed, chicle exploitation developed in the territory, bringing money and new wants to the natives. By 1935, when chicle production had declined, the phonographs and sewing machines bought in the period of affluence had fallen into disrepair. In (about) 1928 Chan-chen accepted a school, which was later withdrawn. In 1935 the natives sought the aid of the Americans at Chichen. In 1936 negotiations were opened between the people of the X-Cacal subtribe and the Mexican government for a grant of ejidos and acceptance of the federal government; an agreement on these points was later reached.

In its greater industry, cleanliness, and village solidarity Tusik is distinguished among villages of the X-Cacal group. In these respects it bears the same relation to its neighbors that Chan Kom does to other villages in its area. But Tusik also exhibits the typical characters which distinguish the X-Cacal group from Chan Kom and other villages of that zone. These characters are the existence of strong in-group sentiments within the society made up of the nine villages with corresponding feelings of political distinctness from the other subtribes and of great hostility toward the Mexicans; the maintenance of a tribal political organization closely associated with religious institutions and sacred sanctions; and the much greater economic independence of the local community (the community is almost self-sustaining on maize and other products locally produced and consumed, the sale of chicle providing for occasional luxuries). The Tusik people are not peasants but a people economically, politically, and socially independent of the towns.

CHAPTER III

RACE AND CLASS[1]

IT REQUIRES little special knowledge to assert that the contact of the Spanish with the Maya, as is generally the case with long-continuing interaction between diverse ethnic groups, began with the existence of two separate societies, each with its own racial and cultural characteristics, and has moved toward the formation of a single society in which the original racial and cultural differences disappear. At the time of the Conquest there were two groups that looked across at each other, both aware of the marked ethnic differences that attended their sense of distinctness one from the other. As the two groups came to participate in a common life and to interbreed, the ethnic differences became blurred, so that other criteria of difference, such as occupation, costume, or place of residence, came to be relatively more significant signs of social distinctness than was race or general culture. At the same time customs, institutions, and ideals came to be generally shared; and the people of the peninsula, whatever their ethnic origin, came to feel themselves all members of a single society—that of Yucatan. Such social distinctness as now existed could not be simply a sense of difference, because the single society was brought about by the conquest of one of the original groups by the other. One was the dominator; the other, the dominated. The groups, converted into a single society, accepted the situation and came to look up and down at each other. At first there were two separate societies, ethnically distinct. At last there is a single society with classes, ethnically indistinct.[2]

The objective of this chapter is to establish three related facts about ethnic and status groups in Yucatan as contributions to more special knowledge of what is generally stated

58

above. The conclusions are reached by comparison of the phenomena of "race" and class as they appear in the four communities of the study. Each of these may be considered a small society by itself, inclosed within the larger society of Yucatan. The first conclusion from this comparison, here announced in advance, is that there are general definitions of ethnic and status groups that are common to all the four communities. In other words, throughout Yucatan, as represented by the four communities studied, there is conventional recognition of the same broad categories of people—of people who are thought to belong together in that they have the same features of race, genealogy, or custom, or in that they are to be looked up to or to be looked down upon, or in both circumstances in combination. The second conclusion is that, in spite of what has just been said, each of the four communities exhibits a special variant of the general Yucatecan understandings as to ethnic and status groups; each of the four societies is notably different as to the ethnic and status groups which go to make it up. The third conclusion is that, when the four sets of social definitions of ethnic and status groups are arranged in an order corresponding with degrees of remoteness from the city of the four communities in which they occur, they appear to represent steps in the historical process described in the first paragraph of this chapter. Tusik provides us with an approximation of the situation that existed just after the Conquest, when the Indians were racially and culturally distinct and for the most part contemplated their conquerors from a distance. Merida, at the other extreme, represents the result of four centuries of interaction: a single society, with social classes, racially indistinct. In Chan Kom a distinct ethnic group has also some of the characteristics of a lower class. In Dzitas the materials show that the two ethnic groups were at one time converted into classes in a single local society. Today, however, these classes have largely disappeared. The situation in Dzitas provides, therefore, material as to two successive periods in the ethnic history of that community which may be distinguished and compared with the contemporary conditions in the other communities. Dzitas will receive the most attention in the following pages. But the comparison will begin with Tusik.

The Indians of the Quintana Roo villages call themselves *mazehualob*.[3] By this term they refer to all who have their customs, their costume, their language, and—in most cases—their physical appearance. The territory is their homeland; all who dwell upon it by right are mazehualob. It does not matter that some who share their lives with them have physical features markedly like those of the townspeople of European descent. Common culture, costume, and view of life overbalance the effect of a thin nose and a light complexion. It is remembered that during the War of the Castes some mixed-bloods voluntarily joined the rebels and that some white prisoners were spared and lived to have children in Quintana Roo. Their descendants are all equally mazehualob now. Nor is it a matter of consequence that some mazehualob have Spanish names. The priestly leader himself looks white and has a Spanish surname; yet he is a mazehual. The natives hesitated when Villa put the case of this man to them, saying, finally, that if he had been brought up in Yucatan he would not have been a mazehual, "but as he was born here he is one of us."

Those who are not mazehualob are *dzulob*.[4] This term[5] is applied to the people who live in the city and towns, speak a different language, have different customs, and exhibit a different physical appearance. As these characteristics of distinction are not always sharp, or are not all present in the same individual, the phrase *kaz-dzul* (half-dzul) is available for such persons as *chicleros* and labor agents who exhibit marginal characteristics. (The word "mestizo" is not used.) Such persons are outside the in-group of the mazehualob but are recognized as somewhat akin to the mazehualob.

The dzulob are regarded as the natural enemies of the mazehualob. The organization of the tribe exists to defend the mazehualob from the dzulob. Particularized among dzulob are the *huachob*, the Mexicans, and members of the federal forces. These are regarded as men of cruelty and wickedness. They are associated with the devil and witchcraft. Some say that it is they who bring evil winds after them. No epithet is too strong for them.

The essential distinction recognized by these terms is therefore that between Us, the in-group, an ethnic unity, and Them, the outsiders, Our enemies, a different ethnic group or groups. Nevertheless, the natives are not ignorant of the fact that the dzulob look down upon them. They have heard the word "indio" used as a term of contempt; therefore, such friends as they make among the dzulob are careful not to use the term in talking to the natives, but to use "mazehual" instead. Furthermore, the word "dzul" in the native's own language, although meaning primarily "foreigner," is recognized as having appreciative connotations. Therefore, although the mazehualob may use it in its neutral sense when speaking among themselves of the white outsider, they will use *uinic*, a half-contemptuous term meaning literally "man," in speaking directly to an outsider with whom they have not established personal friendly relations. This they do to make plain that they are not treating the outsider with respect. Once friendly relations are established, they will use the term "dzul," now willing that the word be understood as one that recognizes the superior status of the other, and they may even augment it to "*nohoch* dzul" (great dzul). But the context will show whether the term is used as one of respect; and, if it is, it is because the respect is felt for that particular individual, not for his group. They are aware that the dzulob, as a group, would accord them inferior status, but they do not accept it.

In Chan Kom, on the contrary, the inferior status is accepted. The same principal terms for ethnic and status groups are used as in Tusik, but with variations of meaning and differences of emphasis which accord with the fact that the people of Chan Kom recognize themselves to participate with the white man of the city in a single society. All, no matter

whether urban or rural, white or Indian, share the same interests and essential objectives. It is understood that leadership in
the larger society will come from the dzulob. The prestige expressed by that term is accorded as natural to those who are
educated, have familiarity with the ways of the city, speak
Spanish, and exhibit Caucasian racial traits. As in Tusik,
"kaz dzul" is used for marginal individuals, with lessened
respect, mingled perhaps with a tinge of contempt for a mixed
people.

In Chan Kom, as contrasted with Tusik, the stranger who
exhibits the external characteristics of the dzul is immediately
addressed and referred to by that term; to speak of him as
"uinic" would be to offer him insult. Furthermore, the
woman corresponding to the dzul is addressed and referred to
in Chan Kom as *xunan*, but the woman of the village is not so
addressed, no matter how much respected, whereas in Tusik
the married woman of the dzul and the married woman of the
mazehual are addressed indifferently by that term. In Tusik
the term is merely descriptive, or, if it implies respect, it is
that due any woman of married status; in Chan Kom, on the
other hand, it implies the respect accorded the ethnic group of
superior status. Finally, although the people of Chan Kom
more frequently speak of themselves as "mazehualob," the
word "indio" may be used for the natives there with little fear
that offense will be given.

It has already been stated that in the Quintana Roo villages
the word "mazehual" is applied to every member of the in-
group, even to those whose physical features are not characteristically Indian or whose surnames are not Maya. This,
it may be emphasized, is consistent with the solidarity of the
tribe and the strong sentiments of hostility maintained toward
outsiders, the dzulob. In Chan Kom, on the other hand, there
is no sharp line between Us and Them; relations with the
dzulob are friendly, frequent, and more intimate. Persons with
marginal characteristics are more easily recognized and admitted to the local group. A man who lives the life of the vil-

lage but who has a Spanish surname is in Tusik a mazehual. But in Chan Kom he is "half-dzul" (kaz dzul). Such persons are not, the Chan Kom people will say, "genuine Indians," but they are treated no differently from other members of the local community. Tusik calls such a person a mazehual; being one of Us, he is so categorized.

In the Tusik region the village and the tribally organized group of villages are composed (with the unimportant exception of Villa, the ethnologist, and of visiting traders) exclusively of mazehualob. In Chan Kom the village is one of mazehualob with the occasional addition of a few dzulob in special roles (teacher, resident merchant, governmental officer), but many other dzulob are to be found in other villages and especially in towns with which the people of Chan Kom have frequent economic, political, and social connection. Thus, though the ethnic distinction between Indian and white is plainly recognized, but with room for marginal or transitional instances, the two groups interact in ways that involve recognition by the people of Chan Kom that each group occupies its own status level, even though the recognition is ill defined and unformalized. For a Yucatecan society in which the status relations between the two groups is (or was) sharply defined and supported by appropriate conventions, one may, it appears, turn to the Dzitas of a hundred years ago. In the following discussion some understanding of what prevailed in Dzitas then will be reached through a consideration of the situation in Dzitas today.

Before going on to give the facts for present-day Dzitas, the essential differences among the three communities in the respects under consideration may be stated with oversimplification as follows: Tusik is a local community of Indians who do not recognize a fixed status inferior to whites. Chan Kom is a local community of Indians who to a notable extent do recognize a status position inferior to whites. Dzitas is a local community composed of both Indians and whites; a well-defined status (class) relation did once exist between these two groups, but it is now very much broken down. Of the three communities, Dzitas is the only one in which whites and Indians met and mingled in not very unequal proportions to form one single local society.

It will be remembered that the twelve hundred people of Dzitas represent every degree of apparent racial admixture, that their occupational range runs from judge to simple agriculturalist, and that with respect to culture they span the gap between the world of Merida and that of the villages of the bush. They are, furthermore, to be distinguished as to whether the language commonly used in the home is Maya or Spanish. In a still further respect they fall into one of two groups as to whether they wear the folk costume or wear the clothes of the city. In Dzitas, as in Merida, the word *mestizo* is used for persons of the former sort, and *de vestido* (occasionally *catrin*) for persons of the second sort.

The various social characters (and others immediately to be mentioned) contribute to establishing the social positions of the individuals in whom they are to be found. They are symbols of status. Furthermore, they tend to occur with a considerable degree of consistency. Thus, on the whole, but with many exceptions to be noted below, specialized trades or professions, higher standard of living, education and habitual communication with the city, the costume of the city, the use of the Spanish language, residence near the plaza, and superior social position tend to coincide in the same individuals and families. To these elements may be added, again with important qualifications, European ancestry and Caucasian physical traits. The opposites of these occur together in other individuals and families.

A detailed investigation of these facts was made as they are encountered in 225 households (nearly all) of Dzitas. In 60 per cent of the households the language of the home is Maya, the costume of both man and wife (where both are present) is that of the folk, and the occupation of the man is either simple agriculture or woodcutting or equivalent simple manual toil or a combination of agriculture with such simple labor. These people (Group I) represent, with consistency as to the characters mentioned, the one social extreme and the lowest social position.

On the other hand, in 16 per cent of the households the language spoken is Spanish, both man and woman wear the city costume, and the man conducts, in a few cases supplemented by a little agriculture, a specialized occupation. These people (Group III) represent the other social extreme and the highest status in the community. They are prevailingly European in blood, as those of the former group are prevailingly Indian.

In another 16 per cent of the households (in all the remaining households for which data were obtained) the social factors listed do not occur consistently; that is to say, the individuals have some characteristics identifying them with the inferior group and some associating them with the superior group. This group (Group II) may be subdivided into three: the households of Maya-speaking mestizos who have specialized occupations; those, some simple agriculturalists and some specialized workers, where the language is Maya but where the man wears the city costume; and those, where likewise the occupation is various, where the women wear folk costume (the men having in most cases taken to wearing some of the garments of the city),[6] but where the language of the home is Spanish.[7]

It is plain that the people of Group II are marginal to the other two groups. It is also true that, on the whole, they occupy intermediate positions of status. Persons of Group I are sometimes mentioned in local news items sent to the Merida newspaper (by a correspondent belonging to Group III) as "members of our working class." Members of Group III are, generally speaking, secure in their superior social position. But the heterogeneous people brought together here as "Group II" are not easily to be regarded as the same as those of Group III; neither are they to be readily recognized as equivalent of Group I; they present something of a problem, and indeed, in the thinking of the old conservative people of Dzitas, they ought not to be there at all—there should be only the two extreme groups.

It becomes apparent that an older social system remains—a vestige, especially in the minds of old people in Dzitas. This older system is inconsistent with the facts and the social theory of contemporary Yucatan. The present social doctrine in Mexico requires that no man be disadvantaged because he is an Indian or the descendant of an Indian. The Revolution accepts the Indian and seeks his education and full incorporation into the state. The newspaper may refer to "the working class of Dzitas" but not to "the Indians of Dzitas." Rapid social changes break down old class lines. But once it was otherwise, and the old system persists in Dzitas, its outlines, now shadowy, conflicting with the mobile and democratic society which is coming about.

So far in this discussion of status in Dzitas no mention has been made of that criterion of status which to the old conservative people is the most important of all: ethnic ancestry as attested by surname. The great degree of racial intermixture in Dzitas makes impossible any social stratification based upon determined degrees of biological intermixture or upon skin color. It is probable that there is no one without Indian ancestry,[8] and there is certainly more Indian than European blood in the population as a whole. The classification that does exist and that is strongly emphasized in the oldest generation is that between the Leals, Arceos, and Aguilars, on the one hand, and the Peches, Poots, and Nahs, on the other. All those with Spanish surname are denoted *vecinos*[9] and accorded superior status; all those with Indian surname are termed indios and accorded inferior status. Any indio is theoretically inferior to any vecino. It does not matter how poor or how dark skinned such a man or woman may be or how humble his occupation; if he has a Spanish surname, it is proof that he is not an Indian, that his heritage goes back to the Spaniards, and that he is entitled to some recognition from mere indios of the fact that he is better than they. A man—especially an old man—may have a very dark skin, speak only the Maya language, live on the outskirts of Dzitas in a poor hut, wear the white drawers and apron of the rural folk, and yet, by reason of his Spanish surname, look down upon his neighbors with Maya names.[10]

For reasons already indicated the distinction between indio and vecino is not one that is recognized in the newspaper or in any other official or public connection. It is not recognized in the census or civil registry. But the terms are frequently used, and especially by older vecinos, still more especially by those who occupy a social position on the margins of the two old classes or by those who have come down in the world. A person with three indio grandparents and one—the father's father—vecino grandparent clings to the prestige attached to the Spanish surname. A woman, impoverished to beggary, with four vecino grandparents, does her best to look down upon her well-to-do indio neighbors.[11] Marriages between indios and vecinos are fairly common, and informal unions are even commoner. The old classes are broken down; a successful Indian may marry a vecina; many vecinos have lost economic and cultural advantage, and as a class they have no longer political control of the community. So the distinction between indio and vecino is little bar to interbreeding. Nevertheless, when an india becomes the wife of a member of a vecino family that maintains some cohesiveness and class pride, she is not readily accepted, and the marriage may be a matter of some embarrassment.[12]

It has been said that in the viewpoint of the older people only the two kinds of people ought to be found in Dzitas represented by Groups I and III, as the population was classified in the foregoing discussion (pp. 64–66). It may now be added that to the old people Group III should all be vecinos and Group I should be indios. It is clear that these elders recall a time when Dzitas was more isolated and less mobile than it is today, when the society of Dzitas consisted of two distinct social classes, indio and vecino. Their accounts indicate some of the characteristics of that older society.

At that time, fifty years ago or more, only vecinos lived near the plaza, and all the indios lived on the outskirts of the town. The posts in the local government were filled, with only the rarest exceptions, by vecinos. The indios had their own separate place of public meeting, called *audiencia*, and the decisions and orders of the vecino government were transmitted to them through their own chieftain (*batab* or *alcalde*) whom they themselves selected. Only a vecino might be a soldier; in military activities the indios were permitted to be watchmen and messengers. In short, the vecinos were politically dominant; they were the real citizens of Dzitas; the indios maintained a separate government for matters concerning exclusively indios; and the vecinos ruled the indios, making use of the indio officers.

The indios occupied positions of less dignity and acknowledged their inferior position in name, costume, occupation, and place of residence. An older indio was addressed with a term of respect, recognizing his years, but the term (*yum*) was not the same as that by which a vecino was addressed; only vecinos were called *don*. By the manner of salutation the indio expressed deference, while the vecino received it. In domestic life both classes wore the folk costume (i.e., were mestizo, not de vestido), but there were many small differences in costume associated with the difference in status. The huipils (blouses) of the indias had little or very simple embroidery, while the huipils of the vecinas (*ternos*) had cross-stitch embroidery.[13] "If an india had worn a terno, it would have been taken from her and burned at the door of the church." The vecinas wore petticoats, coral hairpins, fine combs, and head scarves of fine cloth; the indias had to content themselves with hairpins of native tortoise shell, wooden combs, and head scarves of crude cotton cloth. It was the vecinas who responded to the fashions. They went to mass in the costume of the city (de vestido), and as each novelty in dress or display reached Dzitas—gold chains, good shoes, new embroidery designs—it was the vecinas who took it up, and public opinion allowed the indias to assume these modes only when they had been abandoned by the class above them.

It is probable that the separateness of the two classes was supported by a greater disposition than is now the case to limit the choice of spouse to one's own class. Old people say that the church discouraged intermarriage by charging a higher fee for performing such marriages.[14] The definiteness with which role in the community was associated with the classes is attested by the fact reported that, when on occasions an indio was allowed to be a soldier, his surname was changed to some Spanish form.

The essential difference between indio and vecino was (and is) one of status rather than of custom and belief. In the times "before the railroad" indio and vecino carried on domestic lives that were similar and a public life that was common. Both were baptized and went to mass, and both participated in the beliefs and rituals attendant upon agriculture. Both were required to perform public service; the laws bore equally, or almost equally, upon both groups. Yet at that time there were some differences in the customs of the two groups that have now disappeared. The older people in Dzitas say that they remember being told that the present patron saint of all Dzitas (Santa Inez) was once only the patron of the indios, that the vecinos then had a patron, Nuestra Señora de la Concepción, and that the indios and vecinos accordingly celebrated different annual fiestas. In the youth of these older people this separate patronage had, apparently, already disappeared, and only Santa Inez received a fiesta; nevertheless, at that time only the indios carried on the ritual of transfer of sacred vow from one group of votaries to their successors the following year (carga, chap. x), while the vecinos stood somewhat aside or participated in the more orthodox Catholic rituals and in the secular entertainment of the fiesta. But this difference did not go to matters of basic custom and belief; it too, probably, expressed public recognition of the existence of two social groups.

It may now be repeated that three generations ago the Dzitas society was composed of two groups, the one occupying an inferior and the other a superior social position. The two groups had very similar customs and beliefs[15] and shared most institutions and organizations. We may suppose that, in general, those of the inferior group were Indian in blood, whereas those of the superior group exhibited some traits of European ancestry. But they were already much mixed and assorted racially, and the emphasized indicium of status was the surname.[16]

Today the indios to a large extent occupy the lowly stations in life which they accepted under the old regime, and thus far that regime is perpetuated. The indios are very predominately Maya-speaking, all-mestizo milperos. The nonagricultural, specialized, Spanish-speaking, citified people who live near the plaza are, with hardly an exception, vecinos. As yet the indios have not risen far in the occupational scale, and it is only this generation of indios that is giving up the folk costume.[17]

On the other hand, to a considerable and to an ever increasing extent, the indios have "got out of their place," and this fact is an important element in the disorganization of the old society and in causing the older vecinos the distress incident to loss of status. The Revolution has taken the municipal government out of the hands of the vecinos and placed it in the control of indios.[18] Indios are entering specialized occupations, while vecinos work as simple milperos. Indios put on clothing of the city, while some vecinos, too poor to keep a suit of city clothes, have taken to wearing the folk costume only. Indios get employment on the railroad, or become barbers or bakers, while many vecinos scrape a living by doing the work of the common milpero. And indios no longer, by gesture and manner of speech, indicate that respect for vecinos which old vecinos regard as their due.

This blurring of class distinctions results as much from the social decline of vecinos as from the social rise of indios. While occasional indios, since the Revolution, have put on the costume, entered the occupations, and come to have the independence and assurance of the city man, many vecinos have encountered economic adversity and have failed to maintain the symbols of their prestige. While india neighbors are putting on vestido attire, poverty-stricken vecina women still wear the house dress usual to their class fifty years ago—the huipil—but cannot afford the modern costume and have, perhaps, been forced to sell their gold chains. So they find themselves left behind in the march of social advance, and, without any of the symbols of the status which traditionally they should have save the Spanish surname, they emphasize the worth of this and resent the chemises, dark dresses, and good shoes of women whose Maya surnames show what their proper social level should be.[19]

It has already been indicated that, as the distinction between the social classes has become blurred, the few differences in custom and belief between the two groups have tended to disappear. For at least a generation both indio and vecino have served as votaries for the annual fiesta. Both indios and vecinos participate in the attendant religious guilds (gremios). When the rain ceremonies are held in the milpas, under the guidance of a shaman-priest from a village, milperos with Spanish surnames as well as those with indio names take part, although, of course, the citified commercial vecinos, who have no milpas, are not likely to be present. Yet even some of these, in years not long gone, have eaten the sacred maize cakes offered to the rain-gods and the pagan protectors of the corn. Today over one-third of the vecinos live, work, appear, and, so far as was determined, think as do the great body of agricultural indios.

It does not follow from this that in recent years Dzitas has been becoming culturally more homogeneous. The reverse is the case. While Maya and Spaniard, as represented by indio and vecino, have tended to approach a cultural identity, on the other hand, at least in the last two generations, Dzitas has become culturally more heterogeneous, for there are now not two kinds of people but many kinds. It will be remembered that many of the peripheral hut dwellers are recent immigrants from villages in the bush and that many of the upper class have come to Dzitas from the city or from other towns. There are also great differences between one household and another as to the closeness and frequence of present-day contact with Merida. With the railroad and the newspaper it is possible to maintain friends and intimate interests in the city while living physically in Dzitas. At the same time the disruption of the social stratification makes it no longer necessary that these differences in sophistication correspond exactly with genealogy or race. Thus it has come about that the people who are the most citified in Dzitas differ perhaps more than ever from the most rustic residents and yet, in respect to social derivation, differ more than ever among themselves. The *Sociedad cultural y de beneficiencia* "Aurelio Rosado E" brings together in its directive membership the most sophisticated people in Dzitas for activities including the accomplishment of public works, provision for mutual death benefits, and programs of dramatics and sports. These social and cultural leaders are, of course, chiefly vecinos. Some are natives of Dzitas and some are temporary residents. But the daughters and sons of the most advanced indio families also participate in the amateur theatricals and other activities, and the leading spirit has been one of the Syrian shopkeepers. This group of diverse origins is made up chiefly of younger persons. Their generation has lost contact with the stabilized, class-bound, and strongly religious life of the times "before the railroad" and is now very remote from the primitive, rain-god-worshiping milperos—indios and vecinos alike—who live on the outskirts of Dzitas.

The situation in Merida, with regard to race and class, both as to the Colonial period and as to the present, will be fully set forth by Hansen. It is here to be only briefly summarized. In the Colonial period the society of Merida involved the recognition of a primary distinction between the upper class and all the people below it. The upper class was composed of the Spanish *encomenderos* (grantees of land or of Indian villages) and Spanish recipients of important administrative posts, including those families recognized in Spain as aristocratic, and lesser, but "good" families, and also embraced families with Indian as well as Spanish blood whose mode of life and fortunes were closely identified with the conquerors. These, the *gente decente*, the *gente de categoría*, or, simply, "the whites," together were the rulers; below them were the ruled—the lower class. The gente decente were chiefly European in ancestry, while Indian blood predominated in the lower class. The lower class was within itself divided into two groups, one being lower in status than the other. The upper was composed of those who had Spanish surnames; the lower included those who had Maya surnames. By the middle of the nineteenth century, if not before, occupational, costume, and residence differences between these two groups had disappeared, so that there remained only the distinction of surname, with its implication of racial difference, and certain legal or customary discriminations. The reader will recognize in these two groups that together made up the lower class of old-time Merida the vecinos and indios of Dzitas, and indeed, when they still existed in Merida, these same terms were applied to them. As the vecinos did not play the intermediate role in the society which the modern middle class plays and did not constitute a social frontier within which social change took place but were, in fact, as conservative as the indios or as the ruling aristocrats, there is justification for regarding the old society in Merida as constituting essentially a two-class system. In Dzitas the upper-class aristocrats never appeared, or perhaps appeared and disappeared, so that the significant class difference within that local community was that between vecinos and indios.

With political independence from Spain, with economic development allowing individuals to attain prestige by individual effort, and with the shift in social doctrine attendant upon the Revolution, the old, rigid class system of Merida, with its connotations of racial difference, has broken down and nearly disappeared. Status has become less a matter of belonging to a recognized social category and more a matter of the circumstances that happen to attend the individual. It is less definitely assigned at birth and is more dependent upon competition. As is also true in present-day Dzitas, a number of characters—ancestry, wealth, occupation, education and sophistication, language, place of birth and residence, and race—join with the character and personal charms of the individual to fix his status. The difference between Maya and Spanish surnames is of little or no importance; many born with Maya surnames have taken Spanish surnames; there are persons with surnames of each sort in every class.

Three social classes, no longer emphasizing ethnic characters, are recognized, but their boundaries are exceedingly vague. Recognition of the upper class now tends to emphasize wealth—the simplest phrase for these people is "the rich" —but old elements of pedigree and new elements of personal success help to bring about admission to it. There is a new middle class, composed of people cast off from the old upper class and of new arrivals from the lower class. This group is, in general, identified with the occupations of moderate status —it is a "white-collar group." Its members are on the frontiers of changing status; they tend to be strugglers, and they are less conservative than the people at the other social extremes. Finally, the present-day lower class is composed of those with the humblest occupations. Although it is recognized that some who wear modern clothes belong to this class, those Meridanos who wear the folk costume are by that fact identified with inferior status. The huipil and the *rebozo* (shawl) of the woman, the white cotton trousers and the sandals of the man, symbolize the lower class. This group is breaking down, but it is still characterized by self-respect and an acceptance of the subordinate status position. It is to be pointed out that as the members of the original lower class, whether vecinos or indios, all wore this folk costume, and as they were characterized by mixture of white and Indian blood and of European and Maya customs, the word "mestizo," originally referring to the mixing of blood and culture in the group, came to refer particularly to the special costume by which alone members of the class could be recognized. The only obvious social difference that remains in Merida today—a difference so plain that every individual[20] must be either the one thing or the other—is that between one who is, in this sense, mestizo and one who is de vestido. The role of race in defining the classes has diminished almost to the vanishing-point. From the point of view of the people of Merida the indios are to be found out in the villages; there are none in Merida, except as the term becomes an epithet addressed to any low-class person, especially if dark in complexion or rude in behavior.

The foregoing accounts have been composed to bring out the differences in the definitions of ethnic and status groups in the four communities. Before summarizing these differences it is well to declare that there are also resemblances. In some sense all the four small societies belong to one large society and represent one culture. Merida and Tusik, the social extremes, share fundamental common understandings. In its broadest outlines the same conception of race and class is held throughout Yucatan. Everywhere it is understood that there is a dominant or socially superior urban group of people tending to be light in color, associated with the Spanish language and Spanish surnames, and a subordinated or socially inferior rural or peripheral group of people with darker skins, associated with the Maya language and Maya surnames. Everywhere it is recognized that these groups are not sharply distinct and that there are intermediate individuals. Some of the principal terms used to describe these groups enter into the vocabularies of people in all four communities, and each of these terms carries some of the same principal elements of meaning everywhere. Where "dzul" is used—and even in Merida some people occasionally use it—it connotes the former of the two groups of people mentioned a few lines above, and where "indio" is used—and that is everywhere—it connotes the other group. Wherever the term "mestizo" is used, it carries a double connotation, of mixture of blood or of custom or of both and of the wearing of the folk costume, although in many contexts only one of these elements of meaning is present.

For the differences between the four communities in the matters under consideration in this chapter, like those to be considered in later chapters, are gradual. The definitions emphasized in one community grade into those emphasized in the next. The situation in one community overlaps with the situations in the communities to the one side and to the other of it. In Tusik a dzul is, predominately, an outsider, a foreigner of different customs and appearance. In Chan Kom a dzul is such a person with clear recognition of his superior status. But there the dzul is not so much of a foreigner; there are dzulob in the local community who are welcomed there. In Dzitas "dzul" is a word sometimes used by members of the inferior indio class with reference to the superior vecino class above them who are not foreigners at all; the word is approximately equivalent to vecino. The use of the word in Chan Kom is intermediate between the use emphasizing "foreigner" in Tusik and that emphasizing "superior status" in Dzitas. The word "vecino" is, so far as was determined, not used by the all-Maya-speaking people of Tusik. In Chan Kom the word is little used, but it is understood as referring to a person with a Spanish surname who lives the life of town or village but who is not a "great dzul." And in Dzitas the term is of importance in denoting the old socially superior class characterized by possession of a Spanish surname. In Merida the term is in disuse, but it is probable that older people in Merida would understand it in the sense in which older people in Dzitas now use it, and it is sure that formerly the term was used in Merida as it is still, but diminishingly, used in Dzitas.

In Tusik, the possession of a Spanish surname is of small importance; one may be identified with the in-group nevertheless. In Chan Kom more account is taken of the surname, while in Dzitas it is of still greater importance.

Similarly, a gradual increase in importance attached to the difference in costume may be noted as one goes from the periphery to the city. In Tusik the word "mestizo" is not used at all, and, although the natives are perfectly aware that other people dress and act differently from the way they do, there are no terms to denote groups distinguished by costume. In Chan Kom the word "mestizo" is sometimes used for the man or woman who wears the folk costume, but the term is infrequent. In Dzitas the term and its complement "de vestido" are much used, while in Merida, as we have seen, these words stand for costume and class differences of first importance.

Thus it appears that the peripheral communities tend to use these terms in senses once recognized more widely in the peninsula and to recognize social categories that were once but are no longer recognized in the central communities. In Merida the surname was once of great importance. Today that importance has almost entirely been lost in Merida but persists in Dzitas, where, in turn, it was once more important than it is now. Similarly, Dzitas preserves a meaning of vecino which, on the whole, has been lost in Merida. A third example is probably present in the changes that have taken place in the word "dzul." Whether the word was originally a generic term for foreigner as used by the ancient Maya, or whether it was first applied to a special people, probably in that case the Nahua-speaking peoples, and so transferred to the Spaniards because they too were invading foreigners, in any case it is clear from references to the early chronicles[21] that before the Conquest it was used to mean simply "foreigner." In Tusik it means approximately that now, although with special references to whites. The general meaning it has come to have, however, is "member of the ruling class who is ethnically distinct from us, the mazehualob."

The definitions of ethnic and status groups recognized in the four communities are, then, local variants of more general definitions shared by all. Further, the local variants occur in continua between extremes, and the differences tend to be less between any two of the four communities that are spatially adjacent than they are between any two that are spatially separate. And, still further, some definitions of ethnic or status groups that prevailed at one time in one of the less isolated communities are still made in some of the more isolated communities. In short, these definitions of ethnic and status groups have characteristics of distribution such as are more frequently demonstrated in connection with such elements of culture as stone implements or forms of ritual.

At the same time each set of definitions of ethnic and status groups may be regarded as a separate and independent system, expressive of and appropriate to the particular local society which it helps to define. Out of the range of category and term represented in the four communities taken together, certain special emphases are made in each of the four. In Tusik the important terms are "dzul" and "mazehual." These denote the two groups, in-group and out-group, which for Tusik it is important to distinguish sharply. These terms distinguish between Us, the Indians, and Them, our enemies, the whites. The question of status relations between these two groups is unresolved. Neither within the local community nor between the members of the local community and outsiders are there established any mutually acknowledged relations of superiority and inferiority. In Chan Kom the same pair of terms is important, but their connotations differ, and other terms are used to take account of other differences also recognized as important. "Dzul" and "mazehual" refer to ethnic groups, one largely outside the local community and the other inside it; one has superior, and the other inferior, status. In old Dzitas the important terms were indio and vecino, to denote the two well-defined social classes, each connected by pedigree with antecedent ethnic groups, of which the local society was composed. In the Dzitas of the present day these terms are still important, but they share importance with others, such as mestizo versus de vestido, which denote status differences independent of and even inconsistent with those of race and pedigree. Old Merida was made up substantially of the Spanish conqueror and the natives and half-castes he ruled; then the important difference was between gente de categoría (or equivalent term), on the one hand, and the indios and vecinos, on the other, and the terms denotative of these classes, that rose to first importance, were de vestido and mestizo. In present-day Merida, as in Dzitas, but to an even greater degree, there are many roads to status, and these roads are open to many; accordingly, there are many terms that tend to deal with status by individuals rather than by groups; further, there are new terms to refer to those who are outside of or between the traditional categories.

Attention may now revert to the supposition expressed at the beginning of this chapter that the general historical trend in Yucatan initiated by the conquest of Maya by Spaniard has been from a situation in which there were two separate societies, ethnically distinct, to a situation in which there is a single society with classes, ethnically indistinct. From the foregoing comparion it should appear that Tusik furnishes an approximation of the former of these two situations, and present-day Merida an approximation of the latter. The people of Tusik, the dzulob and mazehualob, constitute two almost separate and independent societies; the ethnic distinctness of these two is emphasized by the Tusik people; status relations between the two are ill defined, and essentially the Quintana Roo natives look across, hostilely, at the dzulob. It is true that the Meridano is aware of "Indians" somewhere out in the remote villages and may on occasion refer to countrified, Maya-speaking persons as "Indians," but the difference between Indian and non-Indian is unimportant; for him, both inside the local community and in Yucatan generally, ethnic differences are subordinated to class differences.

The ethnic and status definitions may be once more summarized with reference to these contrasting situations. The summary can be made in the form of diagrams. The diagrams can be made to express three of the differences involved in the foregoing discussion. Each difference may be stated in the form of a question and then assigned an appropriate symbol. The first question is, "Does the local community include a single society, or more than one?" By "a society" is here meant a recognizable system of human relations characterizing a group the members of which are aware of their unity and of their difference from others. A society may be represented by a circle; two or more societies, by two or more circles.

The second question is, "To what extent are ethnic differences recognized by members of the local community, either within the local community or between members of the local community and outsiders?" By ethnic difference is meant recognized difference as to biological race (real or supposed), or as to culture, or as to both. In this discussion only the difference between Maya and Spaniard is involved. Within any large circle representing a society may be drawn small circles representing the individuals that compose it; these circles representing individuals ethnically Maya (or some similar or derived ethnic category) will be blacked in; those representing individuals ethnically Spanish (or some similar or derived ethnic category) will be left in outline.

The third question is, "To what extent are there fixed status differences as to superiority and inferiority between social groups, either within the local community or between the people of the local community and outsiders? Such fixed status differences exist when the members of one group look up to those of the other group who look down on those of the former, the attitudes being reciprocal and the understandings as to relative vertical social position being common to all. In the diagrams the existence of such fixed understandings as to status may be indicated by the spatial position of the circles representing the societies and the individuals equivalent to or composing the status groups. Vertical relation of the circles implies status differences. Such status differences may exist as between groups regarded as ethnically distinct from each other, or between groups that are not defined in ethnic terms. Where the difference is between two groups that together form a single society, and to the extent that differences between the two groups are matters of status alone and not of ethnic difference, we may speak of the group as classes.

In Tusik the local community (together with other villages of the subtribe not shown in the diagram [Fig. 1]) approxi-

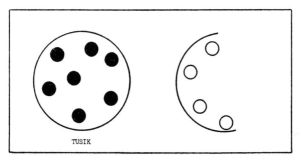

TUSIK

FIG. 1

mates an independent society, ethnically distinct from outsiders; status relationships with the outsiders are not fixed, and there are no social classes within the local society.

In Chan Kom the local community is less of an independent society (this difference is not included in the diagram [Fig. 2]); the ethnic difference between members of the local community and outsiders is not so marked, so that ethnically intermediate individuals are recognized; some of these ethnically different individuals are in, although not fully of, the local society; the indios make some recognition of the inferior position assigned them by the dzulob.

Relations between old (and present-day) Dzitas and Merida with groups outside the local community are too complex to lend themselves to expression by these simple diagrams. The diagrams for Dzitas and Merida will deal only with the situation within the local community.

In old Dzitas the local society was composed of two groups, with fixed status relations between them. Differences between the two groups as to race and culture were not great, yet such as remained were stressed and were (especially the surname) indicia of class membership. The two groups had both ethnic and status characteristics. They shared to a very large degree

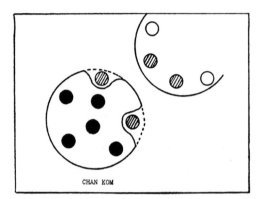

FIG. 2

the same customs and institutions and approximated a single system of social relations. Yet this was only an approximation; it was probably possible (in the audiencia of the indios and in other political and social institutions) to recognize, in some features of living, a vecino society and also an indio society. The diagram can be drawn so as to take account of this (Fig. 3).

In Dzitas, as it is today, there are many exceptions to the old rule of status, and status is much more a result of the achievements of the individual. There are not two kinds of people but many kinds. Two separate societies, one indio and one vecino, are not distinguishable. The old social classes, however, based on ethnic indicia are still present. But there is also a definition of class that makes little use of ethnic difference but rather emphasizes achievement, occupation, and education. The people who perform unskilled manual labor, especially the poor farmers, are referred to not infrequently as "the workers," in contrast to the gente decente (a phrase that might be freely translated as "the better people"). This new social stratification (*obreros* versus gente decente) may be indicated in the diagram (Fig. 4) by horizontal broken lines.

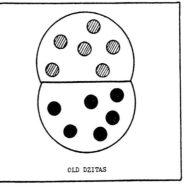

The situation in old Merida is not well enough known to the writer to allow the making of a diagram. It is clear, however, that in Merida of the present day the ethnic differences are reduced still more in importance as indicia of status, so that a status

OLD DZITAS

Fig. 3

classification based on ethnic considerations is not to be seen. Ethnic differences are elements in the definition of the individual's position in fairly loose classes (Fig. 5).

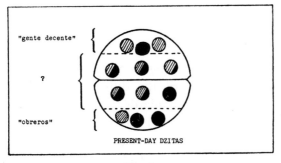

"gente decente"

?

"obreros"

PRESENT-DAY DZITAS

Fig. 4

It is not implied that the situations in each of the four communities necessarily represent stages in the course of social change through which the entire peninsular society has actually passed. The comparison is offered rather to clarify problems of the classification of societies in which ethnic differences play a part. That the five or six situations appear to represent steps in an actual historical process may be only appearance. The making of the diagrams merely suggests the possibility that a history of Yucatan might—assuming the materials to be available—be written so as to describe the changing course of ethnic and status relationships, in Merida alone, perhaps, or in Yucatan as a whole. That changing course was certainly not a simple movement from one kind of situation to its logical opposite. The interrelations of factors in social change are too complicated, even in relatively simple Yucatan, for such a

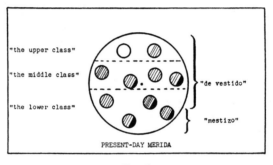

Fig. 5

result to follow. For one thing, the introduction of new techniques and new ideas into Yucatan tended to disturb whatever equilibriums were developing in Yucatan's relative isolation. While, on the one hand, the difference between Us, the Indians, and You, the Spaniards, was being changed into a difference between upper and lower class or caste in a single society, other circumstances were tending to break down fixed social classes and to make the individual mobile with respect to status.

The conclusion here reached—that, while this method of comparison of contemporary communities may offer suggestive hypotheses for more strictly historical research, the usefulness of the method for history is limited—will be reconsidered in the last chapter of the book. The substance of the chapter just concluded may inform the reader more fully as to the resemblances and differences among the four communities and so contribute to his understanding of the comparisons which follow. Otherwise the materials of the chapter lie somewhat apart from the main theme of the work. The comparison of ethnic groups and classes does not greatly contribute to the discussion of differences in organization of culture, of secularization, and of individualization. But the shift in interest, expressed in this chapter, from considerations of historical event true for Yucatan alone, to inquiry as to the interrelations of ethnic definitions with other characteristics of the society in which the definitions occur, suggests the more generalizing inquiries which chiefly concern the writer. In the next chapter a quite different summary of materials will be given—one in which the contributions to Yucatecan society from Spain and from aboriginal heritage will be distinguished. In this following chapter, as in that just concluded, conclusions which are essentially historical lead, nevertheless, into one of the problems of the general nature of society which are central to the book.

CHAPTER IV

SPANISH AND INDIAN: THE
TWO HERITAGES

I

THE people of Yucatan, even including those of Merida, carry on many ways of life that are derived from native Maya tradition. The Indian far outnumbered the Spaniard; also, he was the established occupant with a manner of livelihood adjusted to the habitat. Therefore, many of his ancient ways have persisted into modern times. On the other hand, the Spaniard was the conqueror; some of his tools and customs announced their own advantages, and many of his ways, especially those of religion, he imposed upon the Indians by force and persuasion. Therefore, even the Quintana Roo Indians carry on a mode of life that is in great part Spanish in origin.

The discussion contained in this chapter involves the assumption that it is possible to identify certain elements of present-day Yucatecan culture with the Spanish tradition and other elements with the Indian tradition. The difficulties of doing so have been elsewhere[1] emphasized. Some arise from our lack of knowledge of the early Indian cultures and of the cultures of sixteenth- and seventeenth-century Spain. And some of the difficulties are inherent in the problem, no matter how well we may assemble the available information. These latter difficulties are chiefly two: the fact that the Spanish culture of the invaders and the Indian culture of the natives had so many elements in common that the present-day custom may with likelihood be assigned to either heritage or to both and the further fact that the changes in Spanish-American folk life

during the course of four centuries of interaction have tended
to bring about what may be regarded as new inventions and
the development of a new culture.

Dr. Parsons has shown the degree to which these difficulties
may be overcome in her analysis of the culture of the present-
day Zapotec town of Mitla, Oaxaca.[2] She has attempted to determine in what parts of the contemporary culture the Indian
influence is paramount and in what parts the Spanish influence. Knowledge of the Indian cultures of the North American Southwest, acquaintance with the literature of Middle
American ethnology, and interest in Spanish folklore contribute to her success. Her conclusions are the reasonable
judgments of an informed and careful student. They take the
form of a reconstruction of pre-Columbian Mitla culture and
of some guided speculations as to the factors making for the
retention of some aboriginal features, the loss of others, and
the modification of still others. Of necessity some of her judgments as to specific matters are based on remote and circum-
stantial evidence. For many of the traits analyzed, information is lacking as to what the ancient Zapotecs did, and re-
liance must be placed on the fact that such behavior is or was
characteristic of other Indians. It is probable that our ignorance of sixteenth-century Spanish folk culture causes us to
underestimate the number and importance of the parallels between what was characteristic of the Spanish village or town
and what was characteristic of an Indian village of the same
period.

In this book no attempt is made to analyze the culture of any
one of the four communities into the details of its historical
components. In reaching the conclusions summarized at the
end of the chapter as to the varying roles of Spanish and
Indian influence in the four communities and as to the relation of these elements to one another in the modes of living
that have evolved, the analysis deals with elements that are
relatively easily recognized and that can, in most instances, be
assigned to the one or the other heritage with some degree of

assurance. Excluded are elements known to have had parallels in both Spanish and Indian cultures: use of flowers with images, pilgrimages to sacred shrines, incensing, notions of lucky and unlucky days. Also excluded are elements uncertain as to origin because parallels, or partial parallels, may have existed, or because the element is so ill defined that it is difficult to deal with it: reading omens from nature, compulsory labor for public benefit, the separation of the sexes and the lack of open courtship, the marriage go-between (although attested by Landa in his chap. xxv), carrying on the head, measuring on the hand or arm, giving a name from the name of the saint or god appropriate to the birthday in the calendar, disinclination to bodily contact, reluctance to be concerned with another's personal affairs, witchcraft, salt in exorcism, the *mayordomía*, flagellation.

Certain it is that exchanges between Spanish and Indian heritages have resulted in a body of common understandings over the entire peninsula of Yucatan. In city, town, peasant village, and tribal village there is a great deal of customary life which the inhabitant of any one of them would find understandable and even commonplace in any one of the others. As in dealing with the local differences in definitions of ethnic group and class, so in taking up a comparison of the four communities with respect to the contributions of Maya and European heritages to the customs represented in each, it is necessary first to speak of the resemblances.

Although the city dweller[3] is rarely a farmer, he is likely to be familiar with the essential agricultural techniques practiced almost universally throughout the peninsula: the felling and burning of the bush, the sowing with the aid of a pointed stick, the clearing of the second growth, the bending-down of the maize, and the manner in which the ears are taken from the stalks and stored in granaries of certain form. Many of the methods for preparing maize, beans, and chile for eating are the same from the rude fireplace in the hut in the forest to the kitchen of the sophisticated Meridano. The corn must be boiled, softened, and then ground, either on a metal mill or on a grinding-stone. The *tortilla* is cooked on a flat griddle. Some of the principal other ways of cooking maize are also general throughout. The *tamal* has festal connotations everywhere. Chocolate is beaten up in wooden jugs with wood beaters. Turkeys are raised, and turkey meat is associated with festal occasions.

Beside the modern house of the well-to-do city dweller stands the same sort of hut of poles with rounded ends and a thatched roof (apsidal house)[4] that one finds, with small differences, in Quintana Roo. Many of the lesser elements of architecture are widespread, although they may be rare in the city: the fowl pen, the raised vegetable bed, the beehive made of a hollow log. Much of the domestic equipment, including not only the griddle and mealing stone mentioned above but the principal pots and baskets and gourd dishes, is found everywhere. Even in Merida most people sleep in hammocks, and it is known how to make hammocks of henequen fiber. Men carry burdens on the back, supported by tumplines. Certain men wear sandals (if they do not wear shoes or go barefoot), and certain women wear the loose blouse known as huipil.

All the elements of custom and artifact mentioned so far (with the exception of the use of the metal mill) are almost certainly elements of pre-Columbian Maya life.[5] The Indian elements which characterize the mode of life not only of the villages but also of the urban population with much white blood are, most strikingly, the agricultural and culinary techniques centering around corn and beans. Others are certain objects and techniques for which, it must be supposed, no superior Spanish substitutes were offered: sandal, huipil, hammocks, chocolate beaters and pots, thatched houses.

In addition, there are elements of custom, certainly or probably of aboriginal Indian origin, which penetrate even the city and help to make for common understandings among all the people of Yucatan. They are of a sort which causes one to suppose that it was the women, originally the Indian women, through whom they were introduced into Spanish homes and through whom they persist today even in Merida among certain groups. One such is the custom of carrying a small child astride the hip, and the little ritual that is performed with the child the first time he is so carried.[6] Another is the notion that dangerous or uncanny spirits, the Lords of the Bush, exist out where the trees are tall, and still another is the belief in a long-haired female spirit (*x-tabai*),[7] dangerous to men and associated with the ceiba tree.[8] A careful study of the behavior of the lower-class city dweller would probably multiply this list several times, especially in little matters of domestic practice and of popular belief. The custom of rinsing the mouth after eating is probably a derivative from aboriginal custom.[9] The widespread belief in sickness and danger associated with evil wind[10] may have Indian origins.[11] An examination of the herbal and other medicinal lore current in Merida today would probably reveal a considerable number of contributions from the Indian tradition.

The contributions from European tradition to the world of understandings in which all the local groups of Yucatan participate are much more numerous. The Spanish influence has percolated downward more than the Maya influence has worked its way up. The mode of life of Merida, except for its agricultural base, many of its culinary techniques, and a sprinkling of little customs and beliefs, is Spanish, except where one has to say that it is modern Western rather than Spanish. The mode of life of Chan Kom and Tusik is, roughly speaking, about half-Spanish and half-Maya in origin.

The influence of Spain is stronger upon social organization and religion than it is upon tools and techniques. Yet there are many elements of technique and artifact that Spanish influence has made universal in Yucatan. These supplement the many Indian elements that have remained. The techniques of animal husbandry (hogs, cattle, and fowl), including the trappings of pack animals, are generally understood. The growing of citrus fruits is a part of the practical knowledge of all four communities, as is understanding of sugar-cane culture and of the manufacture of brown sugar. Money is used everywhere, counting is done by the use of Spanish terms, and simple arithmetical operations are performed. The essential metal tools are used everywhere and for the same or similar purposes: knives, axes, machetes, handmills, pans, and kerosene lamps. Even the Quintana Roo natives depend on factory-made textiles. Even these natives add rice, coffee, sugar, wheat bread, and spices to the comestibles of Indian origin. Everywhere men wear shirts, trousers, and hats, and women wear shawls (rebozos) as well a huipils. Candles are used everywhere, and nearly everywhere there is the same knowledge as to how to make them. Firearms are in general use, to mention articles of more recent invention; a few sewing machines and phonographs are known even to the natives of Quintana Roo.

A second large group of elements were provided to the common life by Catholic Christianity. Everywhere in Yucatan there is recognition of the names and some of the same personal and religious qualities of a Supreme God, of the Virgin, of Christ, and of the saints. Everywhere the principal Catholic prayers are recited, and there is some idea of vespers, octave, novena, and low and high mass. Everywhere it is understood that a special priest, of sanctity due his office, should be in charge of the ceremonies with these elements and that certain specialized chanters are required to sing or recite the prayers. Everywhere the cross is regarded as a powerful supernatural or religious symbol, and it is understood that one may take an oath by kissing the cross. To these elements of Catholic Christianity may be added the devil, punishment after death, a celestial heaven and a subterranean hell, the Last Judgment, elements of the story of the birth of Christ and of the Passion, bell-ringing in religious rites, a notion of communion, kneeling as a sign of respect, and the position of the hands appropriate to prayer. Closely associated with these elements of ritual and belief are other elements that were presumably taught along with the Christian faith as essential to it or as associated with the celebration of its rituals in the tradition of the Spaniards: the Christian calendar, with its week, its Sabbath, and its saints' days; alphabetic writing; the folk dance known as *jarana;* certain Spanish music, some secular and some religious; certain customs in connection with these folk dances; the festal bullfight; and festal fireworks.

A third group of elements in the common body of customs have to do with the forms and meanings of social organization and with the ritual attending the life-cycle. Most of these common elements are probably Spanish in origin, the priests having inculcated them; but aboriginal Maya parallels probably existed for certain of these features, and to this extent the heritage in this group is double. The Indian of Tusik and the man of Merida share the same general conception of the family: the individual parental family with a slight tendency to form compound families;[12] bilineal descent, with some stress on the paternal line through patrilocal residence (hardly recognizable in the city) and the transmission of the surname through males. Common to all is the institution of godparenthood; in general, the Meridano and the tribal Indian recognize the same attitudes between *compadres* and between godparent and godchild. The restrictions on the choice of spouse, based partly on blood kinship, partly on affinity, and partly on the godparental relationship, are substantially the same throughout. Everywhere (except among city people who have left Catholicism) great importance is accorded to baptism, and the form of the rite is substantially the same. Throughout it is customary (with the same exception for some city people) to give a child a saint's name. The marriage ritual performed in X-Cacal by the Nohoch Tata of the Quintana Roo Maya[13] includes many of the elements of Catholic practice which are employed in church marriages in the city. From the city to the tribal village the preparation of the dead for burial and the customs of disposing of the body of the dead are similar: the laying-out of the body on a table; the distinction between the funerals of children, who become at once "angels," and those of adults, whose sins must be judged; the recitation of the prayers for the dead; inhumation in a wooden coffin;[14] and a strong distaste for the idea of cremation.

In addition to the elements that have been briefly reviewed under three heads, there are other conceptions and practices which help to make up the common understandings of Yucatan. One of these, the complex of beliefs having to do with the evil eye, including the special susceptibility of children, treatment with rue or by contact with the person of the individual who caused the ailment, is certainly an introduction from the Old World. These beliefs and practices flourish in all four of the communities studied. Other elements common to all four cannot with assurance be assigned to Spanish or to Maya tradition but should be mentioned here. The notion that dangerous winds may invest or attach themselves to persons or things is one of these that has already been mentioned. Throughout it is understood that many foods, medicines, and plants are to be classified as "cold" or "hot" and that the beneficial or harmless effects of taking one of these depends upon the condition of the taker with respect also to his being "hot" or "cold." Another widespread element is the belief in witchcraft and certain of the practices attributed to witches.[15] The great local differences with respect to the role of witchcraft will be discussed later.

II

The conventions of living in Merida, Dzitas, Chan Kom, and Tusik are, then, all derived from a mixing of Spanish and Indian heritages, but the mixtures are different in the four cases. It may now be asked in what respects are these mixtures different. One would expect to find the Maya tradition strongest in Tusik and weakest in Merida, to find the situation reversed with respect to the relative importance of the European heritage, and to find Dzitas and Chan Kom occupying intermediate positions in these regards. These expectations are in general met by the facts. But there are important qualifications.

The comparison may begin with a consideration of the distribution of elements traceable to the native Indian tradition. As Tusik is compared with Chan Kom in this regard, one encounters many aboriginal elements which are present in Quintana Roo but absent in Chan Kom. Many of these (marked with an asterisk in the following list) are remembered to have existed in the customs of the Chan Kom people a generation or two ago. The tribal organization, with its patrilineal "companies," its dual government of priest and chief, and its architectural expression in temple, community house, and five company houses, must be in some important degree a heritage from pre-Columbian times, however much its character has changed in response to later events. In kinship terminology, while Chan Kom[16] keeps only the three brother-sister terms and a tendency to classificatory use of certain of these, Tusik[17] not only extends the classificatory use of these but uses the same term for mother and mother's sister and the same term for a woman's child and her sister's child and employs reciprocal terms for uncle-aunt and niece-nephew relationships. In Tusik the boy earns his bride by living with her parents and working for them;* some degree of brother-sister avoidance is practiced; the sacred images are housed not in the dwelling but in separate shrines;* the dead are not buried in cemeteries but in the village itself; earrings are worn as symbols of authority; the intercardinal directions are recognized in the four crosses guarding the public buildings at X-Cacal, and, when food is carried in a procession at ceremonies and offered, it is first deposited at each of these intercardinal points; cotton is still raised and spun;* copal is burned;* a special vessel, equipped with arched branches, is used for certain ritual food;* articles of personal use are buried with the dead. It is possible that the custom of selecting the godparents before the child is born,* practiced at Tusik but no longer generally at Chan Kom, may go back to some Indian custom of selecting sponsors.

The largest group of clearly native elements is provided by

the body of beliefs and practices attending the deities of the rain, cornfield, bush, and village.[18] While a few of the elements that have been noted are apparently Christian (communion with a special liquor in a chalice marked with a cross; the use of candles and the cross; the names of God, the Virgin, and certain saints; perhaps table altars and kneeling), nevertheless so much of this complex corresponds with what is known from other Indian groups, and is so opposed to the spirit and practices of Christianity, that the complex can as a whole and in much detail be recognized as pagan and Maya in origin. Taken as a whole the complex is strongly present in both Chan Kom and Tusik. Both have an important communal rain ceremony (*cha-chaac* in Chan Kom, *okot-batam* in Tusik); both have an individual first-fruit ceremony (*primicia* or *hol-che*), a periodic individual ceremony to assure the agriculturalist good crops (*u-hanli-col*), and minor ceremonies at planting and burning. Chan Kom has a special ceremony (*x-thup-nal*) for quick-maturing maize which is not present in Tusik; on the other hand, in Tusik there is a special annual ceremony (*tup-kak*) which is lacking in Chan Kom. There is some reason for saying that the pagan agricultural ceremonies are more strongly present in Tusik than in Chan Kom: in Tusik both the communal rain ceremony and the individual u-hanli-col are performed annually, whereas in Chan Kom they are performed more rarely as conscience or fear dictates.

The core of ideas and practices represented in the agricultural ceremonies is the same in Tusik and in Chan Kom. It includes the following elements: spiritual beings associated with the rain, the cornfield, the bush, and the cenotes, and protectors of these, occasionally seen in the form of old men; the notion that these beings are hierarchically organized; rain deities (that ride on horseback) pouring rain from an inexhaustible calabash; the notion of waters that meet under the earth; a quadrilaterally conceived cosmos with deities, associated with colors, at the four corners, and therefore protecting crosses at the four corners of the village; the east as the direction from where the deities arise; ceremonies involving invocation of the deities, preparation and dedication of special breads of maize and squash seeds cooked in an earth oven, of broth of fowl, and of special sacred liquor; use of oriented altars for these offerings; use of certain ritual plants; corn meal prepared without lime (*zaca*) as a ritual offering; invocatory and dedicatory prayers; purification of domestic fowl before offering; divination by looking into a crystal; supernatural protectors of the deer (*zip*). The expected conservatism of Quintana Roo, as compared with Chan Kom, is in fact represented by certain Maya elements present there but absent in Chan Kom: the dance with a gourd rattle, around a table at the annual fiesta of X-Cacal; the occasional lustrative retreat (*loh*) of the shaman-priest; performance of a ritual symbolic of fructification by a coati-impersonator perched in a ceiba tree; the ceremonial kindling of new fire with a fire drill.[19]

On the other hand, the ceremonies and beliefs at Chan Kom include many pagan elements which those of Tusik and X-Cacal lack, and in these respects the expected intermediate position of Chan Kom with respect to indigenous features is not realized. The entire group of ceremonies attendant upon the bees and the beehives[20] is lacking at Tusik. So also are the exorcistic and curative ceremonies known as *kex* and *santiguar* (although these ceremonies are known in certain other villages of Quintana Roo).[21] The agricultural rituals lack the following elements, assuredly pagan, which those of Chan Kom possess: the impersonation of lightning- or rain-gods and of animals associated with the rain;[22] the bringing of "virgin water" for use in the ceremony; the construction of a roadside earth oven for cooking the first ripe new ears; the use of bark beer (*balche*) and the sacrifice of fowl by pouring balche down their throats; the naming of four men (who are called by the name of the rain-gods) to hold a fowl as it is sacrificed; the special ceremony for early ripening maize; and probably ceremonial continence.[23] The practices at Chan Kom, as they were carried on during the years of the investigation, provide as much material for a reconstruction of the aboriginal village ceremonies of the field and the hives as do those of Tusik and X-Cacal.

Why should so many elements of indigeneous religious practice be present in the progressive village of Chan Kom and yet be absent in conservative Tusik and X-Cacal? The principal answer lies in the fact that these ceremonies depend upon the particular shaman-priest who is available to carry them on. If there is no h-men to use them, they are lost. These elements are not "present in Chan Kom" so much as they are present in the h-mens who are used by the Chan Kom people. The knowledge possessed by any two h-mens is likely to differ considerably. A h-men does not teach his special knowledge to everyone, but to a disciple only. The Tusik people lack the elements enumerated because the Tusik h-mens do not know them. The people of the Chan Kom area feel free to call in renowned h-mens from distant villages to function in the local ceremonies. The very isolation and self-sufficiency of the X-Cacal subtribe tends to simplify the pagan rituals through obsolescence. There are only two h-mens in the entire subtribe. Warfare and the serious smallpox epidemic of 1915 may have removed h-mens and interrupted the ceremonial tradition.[24] A third reason for the absence of many elements in the pagan rituals of the X-Cacal group may exist in the great importance attained by the Nohoch Tata. The h-men actually has a more subordinate role in Quintana Roo than in villages of the Chan Kom area. The two X-Cacal h-mens would be mere apprentices in Chan Kom. This in turn is an aspect of the fact, to be emphasized at the close of this chapter, that Catholic and pagan elements are more closely united in the peripheral communities.

At any rate, it is the details of ceremonial practice that are lacking in Tusik, not the spirit which lies behind them. Each beekeeper makes an offering at the opening of the beehives; if the h-men knew the full rituals, they would no doubt be performed. Divination with maize grains is not practiced at

Tusik, but the h-men has some knowledge of the technique. When the Tusik h-men found out that Villa knew the kex and santiguar rituals (as he had learned them at Chan Kom), he arranged to have Villa instruct him in the manner in which these are conducted, so that his repertory might be enlarged.[25]

It is difficult to carry the comparison with reference to the presence of indigenous elements into the materials from Dzitas, because in that town there is such a range of interest and practice. Among the least sophisticated mestizo milperos, especially those who have moved into Dzitas from hacienda settlements, there is no doubt present much of what is characteristic of Chan Kom, at least in knowledge and memory. In the field investigations no search was made for such extremely marginal individuals, but instead materials were collected solely from people born in Dzitas, with attention to the range of conservatism or progressiveness among these native townsmen. These materials indicate a great diminution of the indigenous elements of custom and belief and a great reduction of their importance, as compared with Tusik and Chan Kom. The relation of this dwindling of the pagan beliefs and practices to the secularization of life in the town will be dealt with in a later chapter. Here it may be said briefly that the communal rain ceremony in Dzitas becomes an occasional ritual performed for a group of milperos by an imported shaman-priest rather than by the milperos; most of the special individual rituals disappear; bee ceremonies are entirely unknown; the pagan deities are confused with one another and treated with skepticism; the ideas as to the protectors of the deer and of the cattle[26] are gone; the exorcistic ceremonies are still practiced but more rarely; and the system of cosmological and religious ideas which support and invest the pagan rituals practically disappears. And in Merida, as is more fully discussed in chapter ix, only a very few of the semirural inhabitants on the edges of the city ever have occasion to be concerned with the pagan ceremonies; the pagan deities and rituals are vaguely known and are associated with a rustic life which the city man looks down upon as inferior to his own.

III

Attention may now turn to the distribution of elements of European origin in the four communities. It has already been indicated that the Spanish conquest spread many tools and customs over the entire peninsula. A few, that must have been introduced in the first years by the Spaniards, have not yet become a part of life in the outer periphery. Thus, the custom of riddling (in the Maya language) is known in Chan Kom (and, of course, in Dzitas and in Merida). But no riddles were collected in Tusik.[27] Rabbit stories, and other folk tales of Spanish type, flourish in Dzitas, are more moderately represented in Chan Kom, and form only a trifling part of the folklore collected in Tusik. The first Spanish missionaries required the Indians to bury their dead in walled cemeteries; today this is the general practice, except in Quintana Roo, where the dead are buried in the villages among the houses. The system of divining the weather for the year by observing the weather prevailing during January is probably European in origin.[28] It is used in Dzitas and Chan Kom but plays no role in Tusik. The distribution of such elements of culture as these represents the converse of that which on the whole characterizes elements of Indian origin. Similarly, many elements of recent invention or development fall off as one goes from Merida out to the periphery, as one would expect. Dzitas is familiar with baseball and moving pictures; Chan Kom with the former but not the latter; Tusik has no familiarity with either. Examples of this obvious situation could be multiplied.

What does strike the attention, as one compares the customs of the four communities with reference to the relative importance in each of elements of European origin, is the presence in Quintana Roo of so many features of Catholic ritual which are absent from the popular customs of the other three communities. The comparison here is with reference to the popular beliefs and practices only. It is, of course, true that in the city, and to a less degree in the town, there are educated, orthodox Roman Catholics, who are directly responsive to the teachings of the church as expressed by the priest and in written works. Such persons are excluded from this comparison. With the decline of the influence of the church in recent years, and with the restrictions laid upon her activities by government, the number of these, even among the urban sophisticates, has been much reduced. At any rate, the point to be made here is that it is in the peripheral communities, to some degree in Chan Kom, and to a much greater degree in Tusik, that elements of Catholic ritual are incorporated into the popular practices, so as to characterize the conventional behavior of everyone, or nearly everyone, in the community. The contribution of Catholicism to popular religious practice, as it appears today, is greatest, not least, in Tusik.

The natives of the Quintana Roo villages, and they alone of the four communities studied, observe daily recitation of Catholic prayers.[29] Only there is it required that every adult be able to recite six certain prayers constituting "the doctrine." Independent of control by the church, these natives celebrate masses on festal occasions, recognizing a distinction between high and low mass and making appropriate charges for each. Special communion bread is used, and also a communion liquor (of honey and water); and Spanish names used for these in Roman churches ("*oxdias*" = *hostia; caliz*) are applied to them. These people recognize not only the more frequently observed days of the church calendar but also less important saints' days—St. Mark, St. Bernard, St. John the Baptist—which, on the whole, pass unregarded by popular custom in the other communities. They preserve, furthermore, an observation of Lent and Holy Week in accordance with the uses of the church that cannot be matched in Chan Kom or Dzitas. These observances include Palm Sunday, Ash Wednesday, abstinence on the last days of Holy Week, especially Good Friday, and the kindling of new fire on Saturday of Glory. Only in this community is the ritual distinction between white and black candles fully recognized in practice. Only here is it customary, at certain festivals, to perform a devotionary act by approaching the shrine on one's knees.

The tenor of this comparison—that elements of Catholic ritual are best represented on the periphery—is supported by a consideration of the situation in Chan Kom. As compared with Tusik, Chan Kom carries on much less Catholic ritual. The elements mentioned in the preceding paragraph are absent in Chan Kom or very weakly represented. Yet, as compared with Dzitas, there is more of Catholic practice that has been incorporated into popular custom and is still maintained there: the professional male chanters with their knowledge of Catholic prayers, the frequent recitation of rosaries, and the ringing of the Angelus.

The conclusion is that Quintana Roo villages are not only the most pagan, with respect to their religious practices, but are also the most Catholic.[30] It seems plain that this situation results in large part from the retention on the periphery of elements received by instruction from priests of the church—elements which have been lost in the other communities. Older people in Chan Kom remember the observance there in former days of Catholic practice now obsolete, and similar memories exist in Dzitas. The isolation of Quintana Roo has favored the retention of sixteenth- and seventeenth-century modes of life, including both elements which the missionaries taught the natives and those elements of indigenous practice which the missionaries were unable to destroy or which they did not know existed. While modern influences have reduced the hold of religion and the authority of the church in city and town, these influences have failed to penetrate the extreme hinterland. Out in Quintana Roo the sacred images are paraded in processions through the streets; the Mexican law prohibiting such processions does not reach that far, any more than do skepticism and disbelief.

It may be repeated that the comparison here is with reference to popular custom. The orthodox practices of the church described for Quintana Roo are, of course, also to be found in town and city when the priest is present and his immediate influence is felt. But in Quintana Roo there has been no direct contact with the church for at least three generations. Yet it turns out that Catholic practices are more fully and popularly represented there than they are in Dzitas, where the priest comes several times a year, or in Chan Kom, where many of the older people have attended mass celebrated by an ordained priest. It is only out among the primitive pagans of the hinterland that Catholicism has been thoroughly naturalized. There the practices belong to all the people—all know the principal prayers, all participate in the rituals, all in turn prepare the sacred breads, and all together consume them. Only in Quintana Roo has the liturgy of the church been taken over completely by popular administration, so that masses and marriages are celebrated by a native functionary unconsecrated by the church. The leader in these rituals and teacher of moral doctrine is a native. The Nohoch Tata, at once priest and pope, local leader and supreme authority, grew up among and out of the people themselves, is one of them, and is maintained by them in his holiness and prestige. He had his esoteric knowledge from his father and his grandfather. He is no member of the Roman hierarchy. Quintana Roo Catholicism is independent of the Church of Rome, as the entire little local society is (largely) independent of the great society outside.

It is the "naturalization" of Catholic practice out in the periphery that is to be emphasized rather than the mere presence there of recognizably Christian ritual forms. Elements of European origin do not merely exist or persist out there; they invest the whole body of popular custom and belief so that each part is consistent with other parts and with the whole. The whole is made up of aboriginal elements, of elements taught by the Spanish priests, and of elements of popular secular Spanish lore. What impresses the investigator of the parts played by the two heritages in Yucatecan custom and belief is that the interweaving of Spanish and Indian threads to form a single web is most complete in the isolated peripheral communities. Catholic ritual elements are present in greatest number in Quintana Roo, but these elements are also most altered there from what must have been their original natures, and the alterations have been such as to present the investigator with a single system of conceptions and practices. If an investigator with no knowledge of either Indian or European Catholic customs were to be confronted with the religious ritual of the Quintana Roo villages, it is doubtful if it would occur to him that this ritual had been derived from two very different heritages. If the investigator should begin his investigations with the situation in Chan Kom, or with Dzitas, the idea would be more readily suggested to him.

The extent and character of the alterations which Catholic elements have undergone in Quintana Roo can be appreciated from a study of the materials as they have been presented by Villa.[31] An illustration is provided by the practices and beliefs attending Holy Week in Tusik and X-Cacal. The mass held on Palm Sunday is called "perfect offering" (*matan dzoc*). The Nohoch Tata blesses twelve palm leaves and places them on the altar. On the following day these are distributed to the worshipers, who make small crosses of them and place these over the doorways of their houses to keep out evil. Seven leaves are kept on the altar, to be burned on Ash Wednesday the following year, when crosses with these ashes are marked on the foreheads of the celebrants. No meanings in connection with the Christian epic attach to these acts. For the native the significance of the ritual lies in the opportunity to be purified through application of the ashes. On Holy Thursday the inner altar of the church at X-Cacal is covered with a leafy curtain made of the boughs of certain trees. This is called "shade" (*booy*); it represents the woods that covered the Teacher (Most Holy Lord; *Cichcelem Yum*) when he sought shelter during his pursuit and persecution by the Jews. Prayers are recited in the morning, and again at noon, the hour when the Cichcelem Yum was struck in the side by a sword, during the time he was on the cross, and at the moment when he died. At this time seven dishes of corn meal, made without lime (zaca), are placed on the altar in commemoration of the zaca given the

Cichcelem Yum by a generous milpero who stopped his maize-planting to help the fleeing Lord. A story is told of the punishments experienced by the first two milperos who ungenerously refused the Lord their aid. In the evening boiled beans and tortillas are offered and eaten. On Holy Friday (when other prayers are said) the women take off their earrings and gold chains lest the jingling of their jewels should identify them with the metal-loving Jews, enemies of God. On Saturday a ceremony called "Virgin Fire" is held: new fire is kindled with a fire drill by men who are supposed to have a special power or "fluid." All domestic fires are first extinguished; and, after the new fire has been lit, each householder strives to keep his fire until the next year. The fire is made in commemoration of the ascent of the Cichcelem Yum to Glory, when, after dying on Thursday, he was born again on Saturday, at which time the Jews were condemned to live forever underground in hell. The road to Glory was long and the way was cold, and the Lord stopped from time to time to light a fire with a fire drill to warm himself; therefore, the new fire is made each year on Holy Saturday in commemoration of these events.

The modification of Christian teaching in the course of the centuries is apparent here, as is the contribution made to this body of ritual and belief from native sources[32] and probably from Spanish folklore. What is more to be emphasized, as the situation in Quintana Roo is compared with that in Chan Kom or in Dzitas, is that ritual and belief are present, are deeply established in popular custom, and are so related to each other that the ritual expresses the belief and the belief is made manifest in the ritual. In Chan Kom Holy Week rituals are not performed. In Dzitas popular custom recognizes Holy Week much more simply. If the priest is there to celebrate masses, only part of the people participate, and few understand fully the relation of the church ritual to the Christian epic. But in X-Cacal everybody takes part in acts which for everybody are expressive of sacred stories about a principal symbol of the moral order. It is not so much that Catholic—

Photograph by Frances Rhoads Morley

or that indigenous—elements are present in the rituals and beliefs in X-Cacal as that elements from all sources have been modified and woven together into a consistent structure of idea and practice. It is the peripheral communities that provide us with interrelated bodies of ritual and belief. This is the fact to be stressed. It may be illustrated equally well from rituals prevailingly European in origin or from those rituals, chiefly pagan, attending the agricultural deities.

It is only in the Quintana Roo villages that the distinction between two cults—one carried on by a Christian priest for the God of heaven and the other by a shaman-priest for the beings of the rain and the cenotes—almost disappears. But there it does almost disappear. In Merida the pagan cult is something very distinct from the rituals of the church with their popular concomitants. The latter alone is found in the city; the cult carried on by the h-men is known about, but it is something uncanny, a little diabolic, carried on somewhere outside of the city on the cornfields of the ignorant and countrified. In Dzitas the pagan rituals are carried on with the participation of members of the community. The same man who takes part in the festival of the patron saint, and whose wife marches in the processions of the religious sisterhoods to escort the candles to be burned before the saint, may also go, upon occasion, out to the fields to kneel beside the h-men and eat the sacred maize breads of the *chaacs* and *balamob*. But the h-men is not a townsman, and the cult he maintains is not a part of the public life of the town. It is seclusive and surreptitious, while the cult of the saints is open and official. In the worship of the individual agriculturalists the two bodies of thought meet: he kneels and offers his prayers and his zaca to the Lord God and to the *yuntzilob*, the protectors of the fields and the woods. But the cults, as cults, in Dzitas do not confront each other and are never publicly joined.

In Chan Kom, however, the two cults are equally part of public worship. They are complementary ways of dealing with the supernatural. They are separate aspects of what the native feels to be a single body of pietistic practices. No priest of the church reaches Chan Kom; the prayers of the church are recited by native chanters. The chanter and the h-men are equally respected; each participates in the rituals led by the other; and the same congregation follows each. Each cult is as respectable, and as powerful, as the other. But they are separate cults. The chanter (maestro cantor) has his repertory of prayers, all derived from Catholic liturgy. In reciting these prayers he may use a rosary. He performs his rites indoors, either in a private house or in the church. Women take the lead in preparing the altar. *Atole* is the suitable food to place on the altar, and the appropriate flowers are *Plumeria* and *Caesalpinia*. The prayers of the h-men, on the other hand, are in Maya and, although they include mention of saints, are addressed to the pagan deities. His rites are performed out of doors and certainly never in the church. No image of a saint is present (although a cross is always used). Men prepare the offerings and the altars (except as women assist by cooking food in the houses to be carried to the field), and the offerings are different: zaca, breads of maize and squash seeds, bark beer, sacrificed fowl. A different group of plants is used to adorn the altar. An emergency may occasion the celebration of a ceremony, first from the one cult and then from the other. The same people participate in both, but there is no doubt when the chanter is through and the h-men, at a different place, takes over.

In Quintana Roo the two bodies of ritual are so intimately associated that it is almost true that a single cult results. At several points the two cults co-operate in what is felt by the natives to be a single ceremony, and there are occasions upon which the h-men and the chanter (or the Nohoch Tata) perform simultaneously, at the same place, as coleaders of the same congregation. The annual ceremony held to assure the coming of rain (okot-batam) provides such a situation. In X-Cacal the ceremony called "oxdias" corresponds with the *novena* of Chan Kom and, like it, involves the recitation of Catholic prayers, led by a chanter, with laymen participating, and concludes with the distribution of special foods that have first been placed on the altar of a *santo*. In Chan Kom nine (or fewer) such evenings of prayer may be held, before the patron saint, to ask for rain. As such they are independent of the pagan rain ceremony (cha-chaac). But in X-Cacal and in Tusik the corresponding okot-batam is characteristically held as the ultimate night of a series of seven prayers of which the first six are oxdias and the seventh is the okot-batam. The entire series is felt to be one whole. On the last day the h-men sets up the altar to the pagan deities inside the church itself. Entirely contrary to the practice in Chan Kom and in Dzitas, this is the usual practice in Quintana Roo. Meanwhile the Nohoch Tata (in X-Cacal) or the civil leader ("Corporal"—as representative of the Nohoch Tata—in Tusik) attends to the altar at the back of the church on which the santo (a wooden cross) is kept. The breads of maize and squash seeds are made in an earth oven, not outside the village, but within it, near the church. When they have been cooked, some are placed on the altar made by the h-men, and some—again contrary to practice in Chan Kom—are placed on the altar of the santo. A ritual drink, a mixture of honey and water, substituting for the older bark beer, is sometimes offered to the pagan deities and is sometimes placed on the Christian altar. Women are admitted to the church and kneel on one side, while the men kneel on the other. Then two sets of prayers rise simultaneously: the h-men, beside his altar, addresses the pagan deities, while the Nohoch Tata, or the civil leader, kneeling beside the other altar at the back of the church, recites Catholic prayers. At their conclusion, both religious leaders participate in the distribution of food and drink; the h-men passes out the holy sweetened water (caliz), while the other leader distributes the concentrated breads (oxdias). The worshipers attend a single ceremony with dual leadership.

IV

The conclusions expressed in this chapter may be summarized.

1. The people of Yucatan, as represented in the four communities studied, have in common a large body of tools, customs, and beliefs. The basic techniques of maintenance (maize agriculture), the essential outlines of family organization, many of the rituals of the life-cycle, and some principal religious beliefs and rites are present throughout, from city to tribal village.

2. The principal contributions to these common understandings from the native Indian heritage are the agricultural techniques, the procedures involved in the building of the thatched house, domestic equipment and culinary techniques centering around maize, beans, and chile, and some varied elements of folk belief and popular domestic ritual and practice.

3. The influence of the European heritage has penetrated more extensively into the ways of living of the hinterland than has the influence of the Indian heritage entered into the ways of living of the modern urban Yucatecan.

4. On the whole the Spanish influence is more considerable in the spheres of social organization and religion than it is with respect to tools and techniques, yet Spanish influence has carried everywhere a large number of practical practices involving European useful plants and domesticated animals, simple European tools, and money, Spanish numerals, and the European calendar.

5. The essential ritual elements, and many of the beliefs and myths, of Catholic Christianity have been incorporated into the ways of life of all four communities, as have also European notions with regard to family organization and the appropriate treatment of birth, childhood, marriage, and death. Some other European elements, not necessarily connected with the teachings of the church, such as the notion of evil eye, have

also been universally disseminated and incorporated into local bodies of custom.

6. In general, European influence is strongest in the city and weakest in the peripheral communities, with the distribution of elements of Indian origin reversed; European elements fall off as one goes toward the periphery, while Indian elements increase. But there are important exceptions.

7. Some elements of native Maya origin are present in Chan Kom but absent in Tusik. Most of these are elements of pagan ritual and belief depending for continuance upon the h-men or shaman-priest. The abnormal distribution of these elements is to be chiefly ascribed to special events by which the Quintana Roo people have lost continuity with the specialized esoteric tradition necessary to perpetuate these features.

8. Elements of Catholic ritual are most abundantly present, as parts of popular practice, in the peripheral communities rather than in the city or town. This is in large part due, it may be supposed, to the fact that the Quintana Roo people retain the effects of instruction received generations ago from the priests, while the people of other communities have fallen away from religious practices to which they once subscribed.

9. In the peripheral communities the elements of European origin have suffered the greatest modification from the original models. This modification has been such as to separate Catholic ritual from any dependence upon authority or officer outside of the local community and to bring the Catholic cult into close association and greater congruence with the pagan cult.

10. The interaction of Spanish and of Maya customs of religious ritual has resulted, in the peripheral communities more nearly than in the city and in the town, in the development of a single body of interrelated ritual and belief in which one part is consistent with and expressive of another and which all members of the community comprehend and in which they participate.

CHAPTER V

THE VILLAGER'S VIEW OF LIFE

THE historical analysis made in the last chapter concluded with the observation that it is in the peripheral communities that Spanish and native elements of religious ritual are most closely articulated into a single whole. This observation may be extended to the entire conventional life represented in the four communities. It is in the more isolated villages that the ways of living exhibit to the greatest degree an interrelation of parts and inner consistency. The mode of life of Tusik rather than of Chan Kom, and of Chan Kom rather than of Dzitas, can, therefore, be described as an organized body of conventional understandings. The reference here is not, essentially, to the fact that in the peripheral communities the habits of individual men conform most closely to the customs of the community. This is, of course, also true. In Tusik the outlook on life which one man has is very like that of any other, making allowances for temperamental differences. Even in Chan Kom this may still be said, in spite of the differing degrees to which influences from the city have modified the ideas and practices of individuals. In Dzitas the heterogeneity of mental worlds and of corresponding overt behavior is much greater, while in Merida the range of interest, knowledge, belief, and general sophistication is so wide that in describing the life of the city it is necessary to deal with one social class or interest group at a time, and even then general statements as to the thoughts and behavior of any one of these are more approximate than are corresponding statements for the entire subtribe in Quintana Roo. This progressive difference as to the heterogeneity among the mental worlds of individuals in the same community is, of course, to be anticipated

from such general information as to the four communities as
has already been presented. To demonstrate its truth is probably unnecessary. The ethnologist quickly perceives the differences. If, for example, he inquires as to the meaning of the
word "balamob" among members of the Quintana Roo settlements, he will find that to everyone he approaches the word
connotes those incorporeal guardians of men, villages, and
cornfield, awesome beings, beneficent but also dangerous, who
enter into many repeated situations involving the safety of man
and of his crops and who are to be propitiated and appealed to
in well-defined and well-understood ways. In Dzitas, on the
contrary, appeal to a corresponding number of individuals will
yield not one but several varying views. To one man the balamob are the awesome beings just described; to another, they
are recognized, intellectually, as the guardians of the fields but
are not appealed to, propitiated, or genuinely feared; while, to
a third, their very existence is a matter of doubt or denial. One
man has lived in the city; another has not. The run of experience varies so much in Dzitas and so little in Tusik.

Students of the primitive peoples have used the phrase "design for living" in connection with the cultures of these peoples. The quality suggested, to the writer, at least, by this
phrase is to be found not in the extent to which the modes of
living of members of the community are alike but in the organized character of the elements which make up the view of life
of any one of them. If one considers the people of the city and
even of the town, this quality of organization and consistency
is much less notable. And this is true even if one considers a
single class, a neighborhood, or a single individual. In comparison with the isolated villager, two observations may be
made as to the life-view of the lower-class Meridano studied
by Hansen. In the first place, instead of a single significant
connotation for an act or an object, in many cases several are
possible. In Linton's terms, there are more "alternatives" in
the case of the mode of life of the city man.[1] If a conservatively
thinking native of Chan Kom falls ill and does not soon re-

cover, he calls the shaman-priest. A Meridano of the working class in similar circumstances may call an herbalist, buy a patent medicine, see a spiritualist, or visit a doctor. These are all well-known ways of dealing with the practical problem of illness. In the second place, the ideas of the city man, in comparison with those of the villager, are more discrete. Each connotation tends shortly to end. If one is sick, then one should do one thing or another to be cured. The experience has few further connotations. To the villager, however, sickness suggests that he has offended against the gods or the souls of the dead by some omission of ritual or pious duty; the diagnosis of the shaman-priest is likely to remind him of this conventional connection between sickness and religion; the religious connotations in turn depend upon the agricultural or beekeeping practices of the native. Thus, approaching the complex of ideas from the other end, when he cares for his bees or plants his corn, he will perform the customary rituals with a thought to the preservation of his health and that of his family.

In referring to this quality of organization and inner consistency which one apprehends in entering into the mental world of the participant in the life of a well-established isolated community, it is difficult to avoid the use of terms referring properly to physical qualities. The system of ideas and practices is a "structure." It is a "web" or a "network." The villager's view on life has "depth," while that of the urbanite is relatively "shallow." Such terms do not denote qualities which may be precisely limited and compared; they merely suggest them. It will be useful to devise ways by which the conventional modes of living of two communities can be more objectively and exactly compared with reference to this quality of organization. The present pages merely record the insight obtained by students of four communities felt to differ significantly in this regard. The differences are clearly felt as the student proceeds to organize his impressions and his notes. In the case of the town, or still more the city, the customs, beliefs, and institutions remain an aggregation; they must be presented topically, almost one by one. In the case of the isolated community the knowledge obtained by the student proceeds to fall together so that one subject becomes closely linked with others and so that a consistency or even symmetry becomes apparent. In this case it is easy, or even necessary, to see the life-view of the native as a whole; and a presentation of materials in terms of separate topics, while convenient, seems, to one enjoying a close acquaintance with the community, to do violence to reality.

Such a violence is done by the monographs on Chan Kom and the cacicazgo of X-Cacal. They are convenient compromises among a number of claims upon the authors. These include the responsibilities to report the presence or absence of elements of custom, to present specialized knowledge, such as that of the shaman-priests, and to take account of individual differences among contemporary natives. Furthermore, these monographs include much matter outside the life-view of the native, such as data on population and historical information. These assorted data are exhibited in chapters and section heads involving categories in part suggested by consideration of the particular societies studied and in part by traditions of ethnographic reporting. Volumes result which present in an orderly way many facts about the communities involved but which obscure the outlines of that design for living which controls and stimulates the native's conduct. The facts in the monograph cannot be fitted back upon the mind of any native, or upon that of an "average" native, with any success.

In this chapter an attempt is made to indicate some of the outlines of the design for living which is to be recognized in the thought and action of the native of Chan Kom. Most of the facts to be involved have appeared in the Chan Kom monograph; they are here stated with different connections and emphases. In order to make clear the qualities of organization and internal consistency with which this chapter deals, the materials used are those drawn from the older people, and particularly from those older people who appeared to have the most thoughtful and penetrating view of the world around them. The attempt is, therefore, to present part of the conception of the world and of life held by the more reflective members of the older generation in Chan Kom at the time just before the recent period of expansion, increasing mobility, and education—in, let us say, 1928. The sample of life-view that appears in the following pages has been selected with a view toward showing its organization and consistency. Points at which the organization is not apparent are neglected; some of these are specially considered in chapter vi. None knows better than the author how incomplete is this presentation and how much it would be corrected through more intimate knowledge of the people. The view of life of the Quintana Roo native would offer a better opportunity to draw a design for living except that the author has much less direct knowledge of the southern communities.

As the view of life of the older native is a whole, there is no single appropriate point of beginning. Adopting the figure of a network for the organized conceptions and practices, one may say that one may lay a finger upon the fabric at any point and find an entrance. Any one thread leads to other threads, and some threads wind their way through most of the texture. Such a thread, in the network of ideas governing the native of Chan Kom, is the milpa. An account of village life must recur often to the milpa; the connections of the milpa with other elements in the design are manifold.

Four chief terms define the terrestrial world within which man moves: the bush, the cenote, the village, and the milpa. The first two are of nature, that is to say, of the gods, while the village and the milpa are what man has made out of nature with the permission and protection of the gods. The bush covers almost everything; it is the background within which lie all other special features of earth's surface. It is never reduced permanently to man's use; the milpas are but temporary claims made by men upon the good will of the deities who animate and inhabit the bush; after a few years each planted field returns to its wild state and becomes again an undifferentiated part of the forest. Therefore, each new invasion of the tall bush must be accomplished with prudent and respectful attention to the gods of the bush, the *kuilob-kaaxob*. For the same reason—that it is only when the gods grant to man the use of a piece of bush that is then wild, that is theirs— a man makes the ceremony of recompense ("dinner of the milpa") and makes the offering of first fruits only in respect to the first crop grown on land he has cleared.

The milpero marks off only so much bush for felling as will correspond with the future milpa. Thus an understanding is reached between the kuilob-kaaxob and the milpero: the milpero respects the bush, making use of only so much as he needs and wasting none; in return the gods of the bush will refrain from deflecting the swung ax against the milpero's foot. All relations with the gods have this character of a contract or, rather, of mutual expressions of good faith. The ceremonies that attend the fields and the beehives are essentially renewed pledges of pious respect and temporary discharges of a persisting obligation that is reciprocal between gods and men. Whenever a man takes from the fields or from the hives their yield, it is felt that he owes an appropriate return to the deities for what they have granted him. The first-fruit ceremonies and the rituals called "dinner of the milpa" and "dinner of the hives" formally return to the gods what they have granted. If the return is not at once made, the agriculturalist recognizes the existence of a debt that must be discharged. For each yield a certain return is due. Thus a large fowl and a small one should be offered for each springtime yield of honey. But the return need not be made at once; the debt may accumulate. But, when at last the appropriate ceremony is performed, the fowls sacrificed equal in number and kind the amount of the total obligation. So man keeps an account with the gods. Yet it is not simply a matter of arithmetical accounting. Good will must be present too. A man who scrimps against the deities is "haggling"; his health will suffer and his crops will fail. So one does not too long accumulate a debt to the deities. As another year passes without the performance of the proper ceremony, as the harmonious adjustment between man and the gods is by that much more disturbed, so increases the danger of sickness and crop failure, misfortunes by means of which the gods punish.

The obligation not to fell more bush than one needs is a part of the more general obligation never to take from the gods all the yield that is available. When the honey is taken from the hives, a little is left. When the ripe corn is taken from the field, some ears must be offered to the gods before man eats of them. When a deer is slain, certain parts must first be given to the spiritual protectors of the deer before the hunter eats his venison. For all the yield of bush and field is the gods', because the bush and the animals therein belong to the gods. These offerings return in part and in symbol what is essentially the property of the gods and which is by them ceded to men of pious conduct.

The bush is, then, the principal lodging-place of the supernatural beings. All aspects of nature have their spiritual aspect; each tree or knoll or cave may hold an invisible being and should therefore be approached with circumspection and without irreverence; and some natural features are more particularly associated with supernatural beings. The silk-cotton tree is the haunt of the x-tabai, the being in woman's form who may entice men to their death. The mounds of red earth made by the leaf-cutter ant are the abiding-place of the devil and are therefore likewise to be avoided. And throughout the bush and especially along the roads may pass the balamob, the invisible protectors of the cornfield and of the village. In certain places the bush is taller; there grow wine palms, and there the milpero finds mounds built by the ancients. Here especially lurk the aluxob, little mischievous beings, who are not the owners of wood or field, as are the gods, but who must on some occasions be propitiated. The bush teems with unseen inhabitants. Especially at night does the native hear a multitude of rustlings, murmurings, and whistlings that make known the presence of the many beings who people the bush. And each of these is disposed, well or ill, toward man, and of them man must take account.

Of all natural features, that attended by the most important considerations is the cenote—the natural well perforated by erosion through the limestone upon which grows the bush. The bush, even in the rainy season, is tough and thorny and after months without rainfall is a sere and dusty tangle of brittle branches and vines. But the cenote, a shaft down to the distant water, is ringed with fresh verdure. From its mouth emerges air, moist and cool; swallows twitter about its sides. The plants about the cenote are green and soft and luxuriant; they are, therefore, the plants used in the ceremonies to the rain-gods. Similarly the frogs, toads, and tortoises that are found near the cenotes are the animals of the rain-gods. The cenotes are the places of the rain-gods, the chaacs. These, residing behind a doorway in the eastern sky, come to earth and are also thought of as dwellers in these natural wells. The land is known largely by the cenotes; they are the points by which are located other features of the bush. In the prayers uttered by the shaman-priest in the agricultural ceremonies all the cenotes in the region in which the native moves and makes his milpas are mentioned by name; thus the priest calls, one by one, upon the chaacs associated with the cenotes. For the chaacs have within their power the granting or the withholding of the rain upon which the maize and, therefore, the life of the people depends. Of all the gods of nature, the chaacs come first in importance.

The chaacob, the balamob, and the kuilob-kaaxob are guardians, respectively, of the rain, the village and the milpa, and the bush. Lesser features of nature have also their protectors. The deer are watched over by spiritual beings called "zip," who have the form of deer; and the cattle have their guardian who is himself in form a great steer. Certain birds who frequent the milpa but appear not to eat the grain are the *alakob* of the balamob, as the frogs are the alakob of the rain-gods. The principal wild animals are the domestic animals of their protectors; they are yielded to man only under appropriate conditions, as crops are yielded and the honey which the bees make. The bees, too, are under the tutelage of special deities. All these wild animals are, therefore, referred to in prayers as alakob, "domestic animals"; and, when man makes an offering to the gods, he offers his own alakob, hens or turkeys.

All these supernatural beings are not of the substance of which this world is made. They are, the native says, "of wind." The wind that blows suggests these beings and may, in fact, be them. The wind that blows from the cenotes, or from dry caves, comes from the sea to which all winds return. The winds, as they blow to refresh the land or to fan the flames at burning time, are beneficent; but there abound innumerable winds, often not felt at all—winds only in the sense of incorporeal spirits—that are evil, actually or potentially. These winds may go about of themselves, but also they attend all supernatural beings and all critical, dangerous, or morally wrong situations and human beings involved in such situations. Together the gods of bush, milpa, rain, and village are "the Lords," the yuntzilob. Wherever the yuntzilob go, the winds go too. So the gods are a source of danger to men; their sacred quality involves a peril. Also the Lords may send the evil winds to punish the impious or those careless of their obligations to the deities. So the ceremonies, besides propitiating the deities, ward off the evil winds or, in certain cases, clear from the bodies of the afflicted the evil winds that have attacked them.

The cenotes are particularly the sources of the winds. As the water makes its cycle, carried by the rain-gods from the cenotes up into the sky to fall as fertilizing rain upon the milpa, so the winds have their sources in the sea and pass up through the cenotes. Therefore, in certain ceremonies offerings are thrown into the cenotes to propitiate the winds. The cenotes are also the openings to the underworld; the suicide, worst of sinners, hurls himself into the cenote to pass directly into hell.

Except for rainfall, the cenotes are the only source of water. They determine the position of human settlements. Each cluster of milpas that has any permanency of settlement, each established village, centers about a cenote. The cenotes in the uninhabited bush retain more of their sacred quality; some, indeed, may not be approached by women and are visited by men only when water of that high degree of sacredness is to be fetched for use in the most important ceremony. But the cenote of the village becomes a part of the mundane and human life. To it the women and girls come for water; there they exchange gossip and talk, and there the cattle are driven to water.

The village, like the world itself, is a square with its corners in the four cardinal directions. The cenote is its center. So five crosses should be set up in each village: one at each corner and one at the cenote. Each village has its five (some say four) protecting balamob. Four hover above the four entrances to pounce upon noxious beast or evil wind that might attempt to enter. The fifth stations himself above the center point. The milpa also is square, and similarly oriented, and provided with its five balamob. Five rain-gods occupy, respectively, the cardinal points of the sky and the center of the heavens. In all these sets of five the smallest of the five occupies the position either at the east or at the center. Though he is the smallest, he is the most powerful. The word for him (*thup*) suggests to the native the smallest and the most powerful of a series; by the same adjective is known the kind of corn that produces small ears early in the season; for this corn, because of its special virtue in ripening before other corn, a special ceremony must be made.

Of the four cardinal directions, the east is dominant. From the east blow the principal winds, out of the east arise sun, moon, and planets; and from the east, in springtime, the first clouds and rains, carried by the chaacs, emerge. In the dense forests to the east dwell the bee-gods and a number of lesser supernatural beings; and inconceivably far, somewhere to the east, lies Jerusalem, where Jesus Christ lived. When a man prays, therefore, he faces east; and every altar, from the little table of poles set up by a milpero in his field, when he makes an offering at the time of sowing, to the altar elaborately laid out by the shaman-priest for the rain ceremony, is oriented to the points of the compass and so arranged that the worshiper kneels before it to face the east. At the rain ceremony the rain-gods of the cardinal directions are impersonated by men placed at the four corners of the altar, and four boys, impersonating frogs, alakob of the rain-gods, sit at the four supports of the altar.

The milpa, also, is thought of as square, and its four corners are protected by four balamob; a fifth, the thup, is sometimes conceived as occupying the central point. When the agriculturalist makes an offering in the milpa, he sets one bowl of cornmeal-in-water in each corner of the milpa and may add a fifth in the center. In the center of the field he builds his granary, and here he leaves his corn for months, it may be, coming there after the harvest only from time to time to supply the needs of his household. There the maize is safe, for who would take it from under the eyes of the unseen gods who have set a watch upon it? The milpa is, indeed, not only a work place but a place of worship. It is a place that must not be sullied. One works, eats, talks, and prays in a milpa. But one should not act boisterously in a milpa. Though one may take one's wife to a milpa, one should not have sexual intercourse under the sky out in a milpa but only within a house or shelter.

That the milpa, like the cenote and the bush, is set aside from the ordinary life of the village is indicated when the native says that the milpa is *zuhuy*. Everything that is protected from or is not exposed to the contamination of the ordinary, the earthly, the profane, is zuhuy. What is held from contaminating experiences is zuhuy: a girl who does not go about with other people, especially with men; a fowl penned by itself to make it ready for offering to the gods; a tablecloth that has never been used; water in a cenote to which women have not had access. What is appropriate to or associated with the gods is zuhuy: balche, the bark beer offered to the gods at the rain ceremony; the piece of ground upon which the ceremony has just been held; a milpa. The maize is zuhuy, especially as long as it is growing in the milpa. One does not rudely grasp a growing maize plant; one does not wantonly throw kernels of maize on the ground or crack them between the teeth. The Virgin herself is one of the guardians of the maize; by such a term she is addressed in the prayers used in agricultural ceremonies. So long as the maize is in the milpa it is not referred to by the word used for maize as it is prepared for eating or as it is sold in the market (*ixim*) but by the same word (*gracia*) used to denote the spiritual essence of offerings made to the gods.

Not only have the gods their special functions and their special positions in the quadrilaterals of village, milpa, earth, and sky but they have also their positions in a hierarchy of power and authority. When the offerings are laid out on the altar of the agricultural ceremonies, this relative order of power and importance is expressed in the placing of the offerings: the largest breads are committed to the highest beings and are closest to the candle that marks the central point of the eastern side of the table altar, while the smaller breads, for the lesser gods, are placed farther away from the candle. There are, the native recognizes, two hierarchies, but the two interlock, and there is one supreme head to them both. This is the *Hahal Dios*, the Great God, who sits in a place, called Glory, very remote, beyond the sky. Nothing happens but that he has it so; yet he is too remote to deal directly with men. The great saints sit high, but below him, and below them are the lesser saints and the souls of the virtuous and baptized dead. Some of the saints are protectors of the animals of the forest and are to be propitiated along with the windlike supernatural deer who watch their corporeal kinds. The saints have their embodiment in their effigies, but these are also saints, with personalities and powers in their own right, especially those of miraculous origin. Each family may have a saint of this sort, but every village must have one. This saint is the protector of the entire community and the intermediary between the people and the Hahal Dios, as the balamob of the village protect it from terrestial invasion by evil winds and marauding animals. One of the great saints, St. Michael, is chief of the chaacs. Through him the Hahal Dios controls the rain. Captain of the chaacs when they ride across the sky is the *Kunku-Chaac*, the great rain-god. Under orders from St. Michael, he leads the other rain-gods, who are subordinated to him down to the least chaac, the thup, who, being the least, has special powers to produce rain in torrents.

As it is with the gods, so it is the proper condition of men that they respect their proper order of duty and responsibility. One must be chief and father, expecting and receiving respect and obedience, while he gives protection and dispenses justice. So it is with the family, where the father is the head; so with the village where the comisario (chosen by the people more frequently than was the old batab who held his office for life) leads his people, composes their disputes, and determines punishments; and so it is with the state, where the governor has this role. Under each such leader come others who are next in authority. Everyone in a post of authority has supporters—his *noox*. When one stick is set up to support another, it is a noox. So the comisario has his *suplente*, and so the *cargador*, who is in principal charge of the annual festival of the patron saint, has his *nakulob* to help him. The municipal officers are a hierarchy, and so are the men composing the organization that maintains the festival of the patron; in each case there is one head and a distribution of authority and responsibility downward. In the case of the organization maintaining the festival this hierarchy is expressed in the ritual wherein certain festal foods are solemnly and publicly transferred from the outgoing cargador to his successor and are then distributed among the supporters of the new cargador, first to the three next responsible, and then among the lesser followers and votaries.

In the natural order of authority men are above women, and the old above the young. So, when a married couple leave the church, the bride walks ahead of her husband to show that he is to command; and so they walk afterward on the trail. A woman's activities center around the hearth; her usual path is from the house to the cenote. The path of men leads to the milpa and to the town; men and not women are concerned with public affairs. At all gatherings for the discussion of affairs outside the large family only men are present, or, if women are present, they do not take part. When the ceremony of *hetzmek* is performed to assure that an infant will develop as it should, the objects placed in its hand to symbolize its future capacities include a needle if it be a girl, an ax if a boy.

Among one's kinsmen one occupies, at every age, a well understood position in an order of respect, authority, and responsibility. To one's father one owes the greatest obedience and also respect; while he cares for you, his commands are to be obeyed. To one's father's or mother's brothers, but especially to the former, respect and obedience, but less, are due. One's older brother is distinguished from one younger than one's self by a different term which implies the obedience due him. If the father dies, the oldest brother will take his place at the head of the family. To an older brother (*zucuun*) one may go for help and advice as one would to a father or an uncle. But these kinsmen by blood are not the only members of this constellation of duty and obligation. By baptism and by hetzmek ceremony the parents provide *padrinos* for the child, older persons who stand ready to aid, to advise, and, if necessary, to chide their godchild. To these persons one shows the greatest respect, and this respect is expressed, throughout life, in gestures of greeting and in the making of gifts. Upon marriage one's parents-in-law become still another pair of these older persons to whom respect is due. So the younger person is inclosed, so to speak, within pairs of older persons. And the older persons, linked with one another through the sponsorship involved in baptism or hetzmek, and in the marrying of their respective offspring, are linked with one another in bonds of mutual respect and trust. After one marries and has children, one arranges, for each, the padrinos of the baptism and of the hetzmek and later sees to it that one's son finds a wife. And each of these undertakings to complete the social position of that child for whom one is responsible creates a new tie between one's self and one's wife and the person or the couple chosen to sponsor one's child or with the parents of the child's spouse. Or, at the least, it solemnizes and sanctifies a relation of intimacy and trust that has already come into existence through kinship or friendship.

Each of these relationships is created in ritual and sanctioned by tradition; some are renewed or later recognized in other rituals. When parents come to ask a couple to sponsor their child at baptism, they express their solemn petition through formal speech expressed through an intermediary, and the unbreakable relation established is signalized by the offering and acceptance of certain traditional foods and by eating and drinking together. The petitioner kisses the hand of the man he seeks as compadre, for, though the respect is to be mutual, the gratitude moves from the child's parents to the godparents. This gratitude later receives formal recognition in a special ceremony when the parents kneel before their compadres and wash their hands and in which the tie between the child and his godparents is expressed by placing the child in the godparents' arms. The responsibility assumed by the godparents of the baptism is paralleled by that assumed by the person who "makes hetzmek" with the child, first placing it astride the hip, where it will therefore be carried until it learns to walk; and a short domestic ceremony expresses this relationship and the assurance which performance of the ritual gives of the future sound development of the child. The relationships established by marriage are likewise signalized in procedures that are formal, solemn, traditional, and appropriate. Marriage is not only an arrangement for the adult condition of two young people; it is also the forging of a new relationship between two groups of kindred. As men take the leadership, so the parents of the boy come to the parents of the girl to ask for the girl's hand. As formal matters should be expressed through third persons, it is well to engage one specializing in the negotiation of marriages to express the petition and prosecute the negotiations. As every petitioner brings a gift, those coming with the petition bring rum, chocolate, cigarettes, and bread. And as the matter under consideration is important and concerns relatives on both sides, as well as the boy and girl, four visits are made and negotiations are extended. In the determination of the amount and nature of the gift to be made to the girl by the boy's parents and in the settlement of the details of the marriage arrangements, grandparents and perhaps godparents have an appropriate place, as well, it may be, as have uncles on both sides or elder brothers. If the old-style marriage is followed, a ceremony will be held in which the boy's parents are hosts. In this, by an order of kneeling and of offering rum, by the formal speeches made by the sponsor of the marriage, and finally by the offering of cooked turkeys by the boy's father to the girl's father and by the boy's father to the sponsor of the marriage, all the new relationships of obligation and respect are expressed and appropriately sealed.

So each new tie in the web of social relationships is fastened with rituals meaningful of the character and importance of the relationships. As ties are broken by death, new ones are formed. The new ties bring in new individuals, but they merely repeat the old patterns so that the design in the texture is always the same.

Death does not quite break the old ties. After the soul has been released from the body it does not go directly to its destination (whether *metnal* in the underworld, Purgatory, or Glory above). The behavior of the living, after a death, is such as to conduce the soul, by appropriate stages, to its ultimate destination in the other-world, where it will no longer trouble the living. If dying is difficult, chants will be sung to loosen the soul from the body. An opening must be left in the roof for the soul to pass through. The soul will return once to visit its home before it sets off on the road to the other-world. To make sure that it will not lose the way, in the event that the death takes place away from home at some settlement in the bush, corn may be scattered along the path to the village that the soul may not go astray in the woods. The soul may be addressed in speech and charged to come to the place of burial. Of the nine days of prayer which follow a death, that held on the third day tells the soul that it has left the body and must take the road away from earth; on this day the soul returns to its home to collect its sins, which it must carry to judgment. Therefore, the house must not then be swept; nothing must be done to make it difficult for the soul to collect the sins. The prayers on the seventh day commend the soul to God and start it on its journey. The living should not cry; this might wet the road of the dead and delay its passage.

Thereafter the souls of the baptized will no longer remain near their old homes. At certain times after the death, and at last on the anniversary of the death, prayers must be held for the repose of the souls of the recently dead. But only on All Souls' Day do the dead return; on this day food is to be set out for them, their names are to be called, and prayers are to be said for them. This the souls ask, and, if it is denied, they will visit the living with sickness and misfortune. Cases are known, and stories are told, of people who have neglected these obligations and who have been punished accordingly. To make sure that no soul is overlooked, a special offering is set out on All Souls' Day for "the nameless souls." The relation between the presence of the souls of the dead and danger to the living is apparent in the fact that, when, two or three years after interment, the bones of the dead are removed from the cemetery to make room for other interments, the people feel free to express their sorrow and mourning. To have done so earlier when the soul was about would have been to induce the soul to remain.

The proper course of man is set by piety and a prudent application of practical knowledge. The first need of man is to plant maize that one may eat. So, beginning as a small boy, one learns how this may best be done. In choosing the place in which to make milpa, one learns to seek the wine palm and the *uaxin* tree and to avoid the aloe. In felling the bush, one learns to leave certain trees and how to cut the others. In burning the felled trees, one comes to judge the signs of coming rain and to make use of the weather prognostications of the h-men. So each activity by which a livelihood is gained or by which life and health are kept involves much knowledge as to how to act if certain results are to follow. A fruit tree had best be planted just after a full moon; one should drive two cross-shaped sticks through a papaya tree to cause it to bear; the proper part of the plastron of a tortoise, tied around a child's neck, will protect it from whooping-cough. But many of these courses of action, felt to be in themselves direct and practical, lie within a context of piety. There are many things one should do if one is wise; there are more important things one must do because it is virtuous. Yet virtue and prudence are so closely intertwined in thought and action that they can hardly be separated. The good man is the fortunate man. The man whose soul is at peace can expect his body to be in good health. The maize must be cared for, and the gods of the maize must be attended. To fail in the latter is to sin; one's fellows will condemn one, and, furthermore, misfortune will visit one. The milpa is a working-place; it is also a place in which approach is made to the powerful unseen beings. To make milpa is also to participate in those acts by which one establishes good relations with the gods. Not to make milpa is to put one's self outside that round of action, partly individual, partly communal, by which, in prayer and offering, the good will of the yuntzi-lob and of the saints is kept. A man who has enough maize to last him for a year or more will make at least a little milpa so as to maintain his part in these acts of virtue and of responsibility to the gods. A man personally incapacitated to make milpa will make milpa by employing the labor of others, even at economic loss. To give up making milpa entirely is to take a step serious for the soul as well as for its practical consequences.

Health of body and peace of soul depend upon the mainte-nance of conditions of balance. Extremes, and the meeting of extremes, are to be avoided. The relationships with the saints and with the yuntzilob rests, as already stated, upon preserva-tion of a balance expressed in offering and ritual performance, on the one hand, and in protection and favor, on the other. To let the account go too long unpaid is to court misfortune. One's body, too, is best off if equable conditions are main-tained. Excessive exercise or the excitement attendant upon association with the other sex, as at dances, carries with it the danger of sickness. "The evil winds come at such times." A menstruating woman, or even a person with a wound, carries the danger to others of the contagion inherent in such ab-normal conditions. The shaman-priest who leads a ceremony in which are invoked the yuntzilob exposes himself to the winds the nearness of deity involves; he must be appropriately puri-fied. When the men come back from lassoing the bulls at a festal bullfight, their lassos are loaded with these winds, and a ceremony is performed to cleanse them. To sick persons, es-pecially to newborn infants, these dangers of attack from winds are greatest; and from such persons everyone who has been ex-posed to winds, even the man who has walked in the bush where a balam may have passed, will prudently keep away.

Good health involves also the maintenance of that median condition which the native expresses in terms of heat and cold. Some persons are naturally hot, others cold. Two persons repre-senting the extremes of such natural conditions should not marry; the outcome will not be fortunate. Nor should a man whose blood is "hot" attempt to raise kinds of domestic animals known to be characteristically "cold." The foods one eats and the beverages one drinks are known to have their characters in terms of these opposites. Something that is a little too "hot," as beef, may be made safer for consumption by adding a little lime juice, which is "cold." But it is dangerous to bring the greatest extremes together: honey is very "hot," and it should not be followed by water, which is "cold." If a man has a fever, he is hot, and he may be treated with moderate amounts of herbs or foods which are cold. On the other hand, a person who is weak is "cold" and should be given "hot" things to eat and drink. The plants that are "cold" are, in some cases, the plants that grow near the cenote and that are used in the rain ceremony. For drought is the fever of the milpa. As man's fever may be treated with cold plants, so it is appropriate to use "cold" plants in seeking an end to drought.

The word "taman" expresses for the conservative native those appreciated qualities which may be roughly identified with our "piety." A man who is taman maintains faithfully the ceremonies of the field and of the hive. He is respectful of the maize, and in his milpa his behavior is decent and circumspect. Such a man takes his part when the offerings are made to the patron saint. He does not forget his dead and makes for them occasional novenas and sets out for them the dinner of the souls on All Souls' Day. When his harvest has been good, when his beans are ripe, or when the new ears of maize are ready to eat, he sees to it that cooked beans or new ears are hung in his yard for the yuntzilob to partake of. He participates in the new-corn ceremony over which the shaman-priest presides; and, if his harvest is good, he makes a novena in his house for the patron saint and the Hahal Dios. When he takes the honey from his hives, he is careful not to injure any bee, and, if he moves his hives, he secures permission of the bee-gods by making the proper ceremony. A man who is taman does not throw maize grains on the ground or throw water onto a dog. He does not quarrel or raise his voice against children.

The kind of valued behavior implied by the word "taman" represents an ideal which few attain but with which everyone feels his own conduct should in some degree correspond. Some of the norms of virtue are more compelling than others. Industry, for example, and obedience to authority, whether that of the comisario or of one's father, are expected of everyone, and a serious failure in these respects is not compatible with continued residence in the community. A man may be slow to set out the offerings for the yuntzilob, but he will certainly work in his milpa, and he will certainly not omit entirely his ritual obligations. Nor is the virtue implied by "taman" inclusive of all conduct which the society applauds. One may seek to lead his fellows in public office, provided always one works for the good of the entire community. One may seek recognition at festivals, as a leader of the dancing, or by providing fierce bulls for the festal bullfights. Certainly it is good to acquire corn and cattle, provided one is generous. If one is so inclined, a man may learn to play a cornet, and a woman may distinguish herself at embroidery. But none of these achievements will be attended with the approval of one's fellows if it involves significant departure from the normal ways of life. The success of the bullfighter or the wealth of the fortunate agriculturalist must be regarded as attained through piety and right conduct, and indeed too much success in any line of endeavor is likely to arouse the suspicion that the conduct of the successful one has not always been right.

The pattern of meanings and standards that has here been sketched is a background, a mold of conduct, within which individual interests and enterprise must work themselves out. The conceptions here presented as the view of life of the villager are not, of course, present in the form here offered with any degree of entirety at most times, or even, probably, at any time. Men and women go about as they do elsewhere, attending to immediate concerns. They solve the present difficulty. They do the day's work; they plan to sow or to harvest; they laugh at something that amuses them, or they worry over illness or misfortune. Yet the scheme of ideas is there, nevertheless. It is forever implicit in their conduct. It provides the goals of their action. It gives a reason, a moral worth, to the choices they make. It says: "Yes, this is right" and "This is why." With such a charter they may be unhappy because unfortunate, but they cannot feel themselves lost.

CHAPTER VI

CULTURE ORGANIZATION AND DISORGANIZATION

I N SPEAKING of "culture" we have reference to the conventional understandings, manifest in act and artifact, that characterize societies. The "understandings" are the meanings attached to acts and objects. The meanings are conventional, and therefore cultural, in so far as they have become typical for the members of that society by reason of intercommunication among the members. A culture is, then, an abstraction: it is the type toward which the meanings that the same act or object has for the different members of the society tend to conform. The meanings are expressed in action and in the results of action, from which we infer them; so we may as well identify "culture" with the extent to which the conventionalized behavior of members of the society is for all the same. Still more concretely we speak of culture, as did Tylor, as knowledge, belief, art, law, and custom.

For we find it natural and convenient to deal with the culture of any particular society in terms of separably denotable entities: this form of calendar, that marriage custom, this belief as to life after death. At the same time, in attending to the whole of those conveniently separable elements which taken together characterize that society, we feel it to be not simply an aggregation but an organization. There is no society the conventional life of which may be described realistically in terms of a series of accounts of customs and beliefs taken one by one so that each is completely reported without reference to any one of the others. The items into which we separate the whole are not, we feel, really separate. In describing one we find it necessary to describe others.

So the quality of organization among the conveniently separable elements of the whole of a culture is probably a universal feature of culture and may be added to the definition: culture is an organization of conventional understandings manifest in act and artifact. The point here explored through consideration of the materials from Yucatan is the question whether cultures differ as to degree to which the quality of organization is present and as to the nature of the connections among the elements which make the whole an organization rather than an aggregation. In the first paragraph of the immediately preceding chapter it was asserted that it is in the more isolated communities that the ways of living exhibit to greatest degree an interrelation of parts and inner consistency. That chapter was devoted to a description of the culture of the conservative people of Chan Kom so as to show some of the interconnections of meaning and action in that particular society. It was suggested, but not demonstrated, that the conventional ways of life of the town and the city differ, in this regard, from those of the villages in that more possible meanings are present to the individual in connection with many objects or situations and that hence (it was implied) there is less consistency, less stability, as to the connections of meaning which make up the organization characterizing the people of that town as compared with that characterizing the village. It was also asserted that the ideas of the city man, as compared with those of the villager, are more "discrete," that is, that connotations of acts and objects end more quickly, whereas in the village the significance of such a situation as sickness, for example, extends farther and into other elements of the social life.

The present chapter takes up in some detail differences among the communities as to the extent to which this quality of organization exists among the elements of convention which make up the culture, attempts to distinguish one kind of relative absence of organization from another, and urges the general proposition that under conditions of isolation there is a tendency for the quality of organization to increase, whereas contact and communication with other societies tend to diminish the degree of organization.

The materials from the communities studied help toward the recognition of antithetical processes whereby the organization of culture increases or decreases. The existence of such opposing tendencies is probably a commonplace. If a community be left alone, at least under certain favorable circumstances of maintenance of life, culture, considered now with special emphasis on the quality of organization, seems to grow of itself. Communication with other societies characterized by different common understandings tends toward a disorganization of the conventional understandings; and a serious invasion of new ideas or compulsive change with regard to the old may result in great disorganization. On the other hand, there is a disposition of culture after such occurrences to repair its losses in organization. To recur to the figure used in earlier pages, we may say that the torn ends of the broken web of meanings knit themselves together again and include in the knitting threads provided from the culture of the communicating society or threads new-spun out of the exigencies of the occurrence. Culture is an organization with regenerative powers.

Something as to how this takes place appears from a consideration of the culture of Chan Kom alone. It has been stated how the "view of life" given in the previous chapter represents the conservative and more pious native only and that it disregards changes occurring in Chan Kom just before and at the time when this view of life was nevertheless current to a considerable degree. Yet even this emphatic presentation of a system of ideas bears on its face the record of the great violence done the culture of the communities ancestral to Chan Kom by the Spanish Conquest. One cannot with justice present the view of life of even the conservative native as an evenly woven, perfectly integrated system of ideas. There is a sort of seam across the fabric that marks the incomplete junc-

ture made between the Spanish conceptions and those which
were aboriginal. This is in spite of the fact that there is now a
single texture, a single culture. It is a seam, not a tear; there
is one fabric now with threads that bind the whole together;
but one can see the place where the repair occurred.

The seam appears chiefly in the area of religious ideas and
practices. The religious practices and ideas are dual: those
in which the maestro cantor is leader and in which Spanish
and Latin prayers to the saints and the Virgin are involved
and those led by the shaman-priest involving Maya prayers
addressed to the yuntzilob. The native does not think of their
different historical origins, but he does recognize their distinctness. One comes after the other. Or one is appropriate
to one situation and the other to another. They are separate,
furthermore, because the two sets of conceptions are imper-
fectly connected with common or linking ideas. The native
cannot give any clear account of the relation of *Gloria*, where
are God and the saints and the souls of the happy dead, to
those heavens across which ride the chaacs when the rains
fall. The yuntzilob are nearer men; they are, in general,
terrestrial; God and the great saints are very far away in some
remote height. The notion of a Christian heaven has not been
closely interwoven into the earlier quadrilateral cosmogony;
it is, with some exceptions to be noted, something simply added
on. The persisting discreteness of the two systems of ideas is
also apparent in the existence of double definitions of good
conduct. If a native is asked to say of what right conduct consists, and the context is that of the maize plants and the milpa,
he will speak in terms of that "taman" mentioned in the
previous chapter; but, if the subject is raised in connection
with the fate of the soul after death, he is likely to give an ab-
breviated version of the Ten Commandments as the standard
of virtue.[1] The whole complex of practices and ideas concerning death, interment, and the afterlife[2] is apparently Christian in origin and has little or nothing to do with the yuntzilob. On the other hand, to pick something that will serve as

contrast, the usages and conceptions centering around the care of the hives and the cult of the bee deities remain pagan in nature.[3] (This is to a large degree true, but less, of the milpa rituals.) No saint enters into the conceptions, nor does any saint's name appear in the prayers used; except for the cross and candle used in almost every ceremony, there is nothing in the ritual of the hives which might easily be attributed to European influence. One may imagine that the cult of the apiaries was something which escaped the missionaries or which did not so strongly concern them, whereas the treatment of the dead, with its essential connections with Catholic sacrament, was a matter with which they dealt vigorously. But apart from speculations as to how present conditions came about, what is here to be pointed out is that there are, so to speak, compartments in the view of life that until recently prevailed in Chan Kom. Certain areas of thought and practice are weakly interconnected with others, and where such absences of interconnection occur it is frequently between one cluster of ideas of European origin and another that is of pagan origin.

It is not that these discrete groups of ideas are inconsistent with one another. It is merely that they are not closely connected with one another. Though it is a repetition, it may be said that the native does not feel any conflict between the cult of the bee-gods and the cult whereby he assures the well-being and the good will of the souls of the dead. There is no problem of making a choice; both are to be maintained. One is engaged in one sphere of activity and thought, or in the other, but not in both at the same time. It is merely that the cult of the bee-gods does not provide reasons for the cult of the dead, or vice versa. This is to be compared with the interconnections which do exist between the work of the milpa and the cult of the yuntzilob and between each of these and the health and fortune of the agriculturalist. To work in the milpa is to involve one's self in relationships with the yuntzilob which call for ritual expression; the rituals express the wishes of the agriculturalist for a good harvest and personal well-being; the occurrence of sickness suggests to the agriculturalist that he has committed some indiscretion in the milpa or has failed to comply with his commitments in the form of offering and ceremony.

The old view of life in Chan Kom does provide a few examples of inconsistencies between elements of European origin and those of native origin. The inconsistencies here in mind are not those which are simply of a logical character, such as the simultaneous notions to be found in Europe and America that the spirits of the dead are in heaven and also in their graves in the cemetery. It may be that there are such cases of inconsistency in the conceptions held in Chan Kom; indeed, this same pair is substantially present.[4] It may be that many such logical inconsistencies can occur in well-organized systems of ideas and practices provided that each notion has its supporting and explaining elements and provided that their presence does not involve the individual in the necessity to refuse one and accept the other. Of more significance in considering the effect upon culture of new communications from outside the community are those inconsistencies which do present a dilemma with regard to attitude or overt behavior. The native of Chan Kom *is* confronted with a disconformity if not actually with a problem of choice when he repeats the well-known and traditional belief that the souls of men who have married, or had sexual intercourse with their deceased wife's sisters, become little whirlwinds or pass through the cenotes into hell. In fact, many men do marry their deceased wife's sisters (one lives with such a sister-in-law although the wife is living), and there is no feeling against it and no priest of the church is present to speak against it. Men must either disbelieve the story or feel uncomfortable in the presence of such a mating. The ethnologist, seeing no signs of embarrassment when the belief is told by or to men toward whom the belief apparently points, concludes that it is not a belief but a mere saying. He concludes, in other words, that the choice has now been made, the statement as to what happens to the souls of such men remaining only because it is intrinsically interesting or is felt vaguely to have the support of tradition. Are not such disconformities some part of what Tylor called "survivals"? How well and how long can such an element persist if in form, at least, if not in substance, it flies in the face of the prevailing conventional understandings? The statement may in Chan Kom be evoked by the appearance of whirlwinds blowing across the milpa or the path. But the connection the declaration had at the other end with marriage customs is broken, and indeed the declaration runs against the customs. Villa tells us[5] that in Quintana Roo the injunction against marriage with the deceased wife's sister has full moral force. The interpretation of the whirlwinds is present there also, and it is interesting to note that the explanations are there more fully given than in Chan Kom: the punishment applies also to those who have had sexual connection with their compadres; the whirlwinds that fan the flames at burning of the milpa are particularly held in mind; and in the Quintana Roo version it is more explicitly stated that the Hahal Dios condemns such men for their sins to spend their afterlife surrounded by the flames that then arise. The interconnection of these elements is complete and consistent in Quintana Roo; in Chan Kom it is incomplete and inconsistent. As we know that the segregation of the Quintana Roo people occurred about ninety years ago, we know that this disconformity is relatively recent. Apparently the Chan Kom people have ceased to disapprove the sororal marriage, while retaining the saying about it.

One may at least distinguish the situation in which mutually compatible clusters of ideas and practices exist together in the same view of life, but without interconnections, from the situation in which a view of life includes ideas which are incompatible in terms of the conduct which they recommend or justify. Calling them, for brevity, the separates and the incompatibles, one may say that the views of life prevailing in Quintana Roo and in Chan Kom (among the older people) are much alike, but that of Quintana Roo lacks the few incompatibles to be found in that of Chan Kom, while the separates, though present in the same areas of religious thought and practice as in Chan Kom, are somewhat less evident. The pagan and the Christian complexes are to a greater extent tied together: the bee cult is under the care of the Virgin; the patronage of certain saints over certain animals is more explicit;[6] the rituals led by the shaman-priest and by the maestro cantor, respectively, tend to form a single cult.[7] In Quintana Roo a man may acquire both esoteric acts and so come to discharge both the functions of the h-men and those of the maestro cantor; in Chan Kom this is hardly possible. The greater degree to which a culture is present in Quintana Roo, as compared with Chan Kom, is to be found in the absence of incompatibles, in the lesser degree to which clusters of ideas exist separately without interconnection with others, and, more generally, in the greater number of associations and interconnections which many acts and ideas have for the natives. Examples of the last, some of which will be taken up in detail in later pages, are the elaborateness and meaningfulness of the baptismal rituals; the closer correspondence of the mundane hierarchy of authority with that of the gods; and the presence of a Holy Week ritual with a closely corresponding myth. But the differences between these two views of life are small compared with the difference which exists between either one of these and the situation in Dzitas or Merida.

Before considering Dzitas, reference is made once more to the relations between the pagan and the Christian conceptions in Chan Kom. In the immediately foregoing paragraph three examples were given of respects in which the pagan and Christian conceptions are linked in Quintana Roo, although they are not so linked in Chan Kom. It should be made explicit that interconnections between the two complexes are not lacking in the thinking of Chan Kom. The gap between what the Spanish priests taught and what survived of pagan religion has been in part bridged. Lines of mutual dependency have developed to relate the one set of conceptions with the other. St. Michael, acting under the direction of God, is chief of the rain-gods; and thus is the hierarchy of Gloria connected with the yuntzilob. The Virgin is appealed to as a special protector of the maize plants. The two kinds of rituals share the symbol and sanctification of the cross, the use of candles, and the taking of the names of the Trinity as a concluding formula in prayer.[8] In the practice of certain shaman-priests a ritual apparently modeled after the Catholic communion has been incorporated into the ceremonies addressed to the yuntzilob.[9] It may be that the ceremony of blessing of the new house which the shaman-priest carries on by the use of ritual elements derived from the pagan complex[10] is a development induced by observation of the Catholic ritual by which a new house is blessed. From the instance reported of a special ceremony held to rid Chan Kom of an epidemic,[11] it appears that the welding of pagan and Christian elements may be favored by special circumstances, such as the emergency of this epidemic. In this case the h-men had the image of the patron saint carried out of the oratory in the manner done for a Catholic rogation ritual. The table-altar usual in pagan ceremonies was erected, and the procedure was in other details like the pagan rituals of exorcism, but the image of the saint was placed on the altar and the Lord's Prayer was recited. The festival in honor of the patron saint—in general, European in form—is attended, in the more conservative settlements around Chan Kom, by two ceremonies which represent the penetration of pagan conceptions and practices into this festival.[12] The young men who "fight" the bulls in the festal bullfight are secluded the night before the event and remain under the care of the shaman-priest, who requires them to maintain vigil "because the yuntzilob are present" and because the evil winds that attend them enter the lassos to be used in the critical situation of the bullfight. After the performance of the last (Spanish) folk dance of the fiesta the girls who exposed themselves to evil winds by dancing all night with the young men are purified of these winds by the h-men through acts which characterize the pagan rituals, and the shaman-priest thereafter makes an offering to the yuntzilob.

These instances (and no doubt many others) represent that phenomenon which Sumner referred to as the "strain of consistency" of the folkways "with each other."[13] Left undisturbed, the trend of change in the conventional understandings in terms of which a community persists is in the direction of greater harmony and interdependence of parts. A conception capable of general application is extended to new objects and experiences which then become consistent with the old. So must *X-Juan-Thul* have come about: the supernatural patron of the cattle, in the form of a bull, of the same pattern as the intangible animal-form patrons of the native wild animals.

In the same way, in seeking to locate Jerusalem, the native has looked naturally to the east, associated with so much in the pagan thinking; this is more important than the fact that Jerusalem *does* lie to the east. It is not certain whether the notion of the evil winds[14] has its roots in Spanish or in Indian history; but, whichever may be the case, the conception helps powerfully to integrate the two heritages into a single organization. The winds are present wherever men come close to the yuntzilob, or they are present when men are heated from exertion or are closely associated with women; they attack cattle as well as men; they bring most sicknesses, and these sicknesses may be cured by prayer to the santo or by lustrative ceremony performed by the shaman-priest; etc. The attitudes and practices attending the relationships between the sponsor of a child at a rite of passage, the child, and the parents of the child are probably largely Spanish in origin, although it may very well be that aboriginal elements have contributed to the present conceptions. Now the same consistent pattern applies in quite the same manner to the Christian rite of baptism and to the pagan ceremony of hetzmek. By the operation of this strain of consistency the blow to village culture occasioned by the Conquest and the work of the missionary has been in large part repaired. The old culture of the villages of modern times is a single organization, a single culture. The two webs have been woven together into a single web, although across a seam which still shows between the two.

The complementary processes of culture disorganization and organization—the tear and the repair—could be observed in such a situation as Chan Kom presented during the course of the field studies. The old culture sketched in the previous chapter suffered disorganization from new ideas entering since the Revolution and especially in the years just preceding and during the observations. A principal new idea was that which we call "progress": the notion that the ways of the city should be imitated, that these ways are better than the old ways, and that a prime objective should be the practical improvement of living conditions. Although piety remained as a highly appreciated way of life, efficiency appeared as a rival virtue. So long as the leaders of the old ways of life participated in the approval of these new values and took part in the reforms and the labor for public improvements, they retained much of their old prestige, and the cults they led continued to have the support of the people. The leading maestro cantor, exemplifier of the old piety, and the local shaman-priest who maintained the ceremonies for the yuntzilob, worked with the newer secular leaders for the betterment of the village. Nevertheless, situations arose involving conflicts between the old systems of ideas and the new. The cult of the yuntzilob suffered particularly from the development of what was earlier in this chapter referred to as "incompatibles." The city man, it was learned, as a result of schooling, travel, and propaganda, looked with disfavor or contempt upon the shaman-priest. The older view regarded him as a leader of the religious life. One of the reforms adopted was the prohibition of the drinking of rum. According to the older system of ideas, rum was a necessary component of ritual offerings, and the drunkenness of the h-men was essential to the success of certain of the rituals. So in one context, when the drying cornfields seemed to call for rain, the h-men was to be approached with respect as the mediator between the people and their gods; in another, when the people thought of themselves in the terms defined for them by leaders of reform from the towns and city, he was "the exploiter of the working man."[15] The ambiguous and inconsistent conduct of a Chan Kom native with reference to the h-men during this period appears in the account of his life written by this native and published in the description of Chan Kom.[16] In this instance the disconformity was in part solved by the withdrawal of one of the local h-mens and by the death of the other. Yet the people continued to make the ceremonies and to bring shaman-priests from other villages. On the other hand, the absence of any resident h-men brought it about that the special knowledge of the h-men was no longer transmitted directly to members of the community. This fact, and the fact that the townsmen, whose opinion was now respected, looked down upon the cult of the yuntzilob, as well, probably, as other factors, were working at the time the materials from Chan Kom were collected to reduce the completeness and consistency of this group of ideas and practices in the life-view of the natives, especially the young. Similar incompatible viewpoints were appearing in other sectors of the old life-view. The traditional way of life required that a woman or a girl remain always in a home under the authority of a man. The newer applauded individual enterprise and the earning of a living even by women. The old view identified the mestizo costume with the indios who exclusively made up the population of the community. Taking over the values of the town involved appreciating the vestido costume, by the old view inappropriate to one leading the life of the village. At the time the observations concluded, one young girl had gone to the town to look for employment, and two or three men had bought at least parts of the vestido costume.

These observations are few and casual. A considered investigation of the course of change in Chan Kom would be helpful to the understanding of matters dealt with in this comparative report. It will appear, it is safe to say, that, at the time when the culture of the village was being disorganized as a result of exposure to conflicting ideas and of events hindering the continuity of tradition, the opposing tendency of culture to repair itself was also present. A trivial example illustrates the point. There exists in the old life-view the notion that certain supernatural beings exist in groups of three: three saints protect the deer; three little beings bring whooping-cough; the evil winds known as *ojo-ik* are composed of a similar triad. A year after an American doctor had given a lecture, translated into Maya as he delivered it to the people of Chan Kom on the subject of vitamins, it was being said in the village that the *vitaminas* are three little beings who inhabit the body, one to make flesh, another bones, and the third blood. A more significant interpretation of a new experience in conformity with an old pattern of thought occurred with the revival of an old myth to the effect that once a long time ago there dwelt a race of blond men ("red men") who had been akin to the Maya of the present day. The revival occurred with the construction that the Americans at the archeological site, with whom friendly and helpful relations were established, were probably the descendants of these red men, and so an alliance between them and the Maya was to be explained and justified.

The double effects of the invasion of new ideas in bringing about the disorganization of culture and also its reorganization appear from the brief history of Protestantism in Chan Kom. The conversion of six or seven families to Protestantism in the winter of 1931–32 brought about the first important break in the cultural organization of the community. A large minority excluded the santos and the cult of the santos from their way of life. This meant that ten men and their families ceased to carry on novenas and ceased to participate in the annual festival for the patron saint. These people constituted a sect: they spoke against the saint-worshiping ways of their neighbors and carried on an independent cult, consisting chiefly of meetings three evenings a week at which the Bible was read and strange hymns were sung. At first the converts accepted the teaching of the missionaries that drinking and smoking were wrong. One of the storekeepers was a convert; he gave up selling liquor, cigarettes, and wax candles. As the division between the two groups followed in part the separation between the two largest and most influential great-families of the village, the new cult served to bring into the open a schismatic division of the population which had long been latent. The community no longer acted as a unit in its religious life, and the principal leaders, who remained Catholic, felt the weakness and often expressed their sorrow and chagrin.

With the lapse of a little time the behavior of the Protestants underwent modification in a direction which to some degree restored a cultural homogeneity and which reduced the separatist character of the new cult. While maintaining their separate prayer-meeting, the Protestants began to attend novenas of their neighbors. Some of the Catholics accepted invitations to come to the prayer-meetings. While the Protestants did not resume full participation as votaries in the fiestas of the santos, some of them came to the fiestas and danced in the jaranas, while others contributed bulls to the bullfights. The Protestant storekeeper resumed the sale of liquor, cigarettes, and wax candles. When All Souls' Day came around, the Protestants held a prayer-meeting with a table decorated much as they had decorated tables on such occasions before conversion; and, while they did not set out food for the dead or call upon them by name, their prayer-meeting was felt to have the same ghost-averting function as its more traditional predecessor. The change to Protestantism made little or no difference in the participation in pagan rituals. The converts continued to make *hanli-col*, and, when drought caused the community to make the rain ceremony, everyone took part as usual. So the community remained a single community, although with alternate cults for certain classes of occasions and with an unresolved conflict as to the sanctity and value of the santos.

The brief comparison of conditions in Tusik, of the old situation in Chan Kom and of the new, leads to some understanding as to what may be meant by culture as an organization, as a "design for living." Involved are at least two related but distinguishable characters: the consistency of the ideas and understandings with one another, and their interrelation and interdependence. The former is essential to the latter, but, as in the case of parts of the pagan cult and parts of the Christian cult, there may be consistency without interrelation. Consistency is essential if the individual is not to experience some conflict or need to choose between two courses of attitude or action. If there are no "incompatibles," then at least there is only a single course of action for the members of the community to follow. In so far as the elements of the design are interdependent upon one another, a ritual receiving interpretation from a myth or the work in the cornfield constituting a part of the religious activities, the reasons for action and the sanctions of conduct are multiplied and the efficacy of the design as a guide for conduct is by so much increased. Or so it seems to an observer of the four communities in Yucatan.

Moreover, it appears that in the reorganization of culture the elimination of "incompatibles" takes place relatively early. Or, at least, judging from the old view of life in the villages, "separates" can persist long after most or all "incompatibles" have been eliminated by the regenerative tendency of culture. Correlatively, the presence of "incompatibles" indicates a relatively recent disorganization of the culture. Yet the process whereby culture is made again after some disorganizing occurrence involves at the same time the elimination of incompatibles and also of separates. Both are present in Tusik, Chan Kom, and Dzitas in degrees roughly proportionate inversely to the isolation of the community during the last few centuries. Presumably the culture of, let us say, Zuni just before the white men came was highly organized and self-consistent; the accounts of contemporary ethnologists indicate that, at least until quite recently, it still was. The culture of Tusik approaches this condition; and that culture, the old view of life of Chan Kom, and the present life-view characterizing Chan Kom since the reform have in that order less organization of parts and progressively more "incompatibles." Yet even in the case of recent Chan Kom the observer does not have difficulty in tracing the outlines of a design for living. When, however, after experiencing the village life, he makes acquaintance with Dzitas, the transition is abrupt. In Dzitas the relationships of one course of thought or action with another are so uncertain or ambiguous, and the possible courses of action so many and inconsistent, that it is difficult to speak of a design for living in that town. As the people of Dzitas have no single conventional garb that characterizes them but wear many combinations of the mestizo and the vestido dress, so they have, to speak figuratively, no psychic costume. Correspondingly, the objectives of conduct are less well defined for the individual by convention; the springs of action have been weakened.

In chapter ii some facts were given as to the sources of the population of Dzitas. The statements that follow have reference to that large majority of the people who were born and brought up in Dzitas. The few recent comers from larger towns and from Merida, and the recent comers from small villages, of course increase the heterogeneity of the town, but they are not included in the portrayal of the view of life of the native.

Chapter ii also includes facts as to the variety of occupations represented in Dzitas. The railroad offers employment to a large group; the stores and offices provide livelihood for others. The making of milpa is therefore not inevitable. If one chooses another course of action and does not make milpa, one is cut off from participation in the rituals which attend the making of milpa. Then one does not encounter those situations which by tradition call for expressions of piety, nor does one so often hear the older men explain the need for performance of the ceremonies or hear the telling of myths which justify piety. So for the man who does not make milpa this group of meanings is diminished or lost. On the other hand, the man who continues to make milpa encounters the man who does not, and the latter does not respect the ceremonies as does the former, nor does he make offerings. On his part the milpero encounters two inconsistent attitudes toward the milpa and the attendant ceremonies: the old pious viewpoint and the ignorant and even skeptical attitude of the storekeeper or other nonagricultural town dweller. When the time comes to make an offering at sowing, he must, in his own actions and attitudes, choose between the inconsistent views or make some compromise between them. In general, it may be said that the outlines of the ideas as to the yuntzilob, as presented in the previous chapter for Chan Kom, are far less clear in the minds of agriculturalists native to Dzitas from whom materials were obtained. The cosmological ideas are vague; the quadrilateral, oriented conception of the village is entirely lost; as to the milpa the idea is very uncertain. The various kinds of yuntzilob, distinguished in Chan Kom, are confused with one another, and all of them are confused with the alux, who are properly not gods at all. Few natives can follow the prayers uttered by the h-men (who does not live in Dzitas), and the explanations of ritual contained in these prayers are therefore lost, the rituals tending to be simply the uncanny acts of a specialist with powers not understood. The symbolic connection between certain classes of plants and the need for rain is not understood. The cult of the bee deities is almost absent in Dzitas; this activity is thus disengaged from the fundamental body of religious conceptions.

For a generation there has been no resident priest in Dzitas. A small minority of people attends mass on those uncommon occasions when mass is held. The patron saint is respected, but many people take no part in the worship of St. Inez. Moreover, the individual who is faithful in his devotion to the patron is confronted with the fact that certain of his neighbors and even members of his family have, through travel, formed attachments to saints of other communities which they regard as more miraculous. There are few spontaneous novenas offered for thankfulness or as petitions to which friends and neighbors are invited, as in Chan Kom. There is a vigorous congregation of about forty evangelical Protestants who, of course, take no part in the cult of the saints and who speak out openly against it. There are a number of households in which one parent is a Protestant and the other has not given up Catholicism.

Compound domestic families with patriarchal control are entirely or almost entirely lacking. There are a good many compound families with separate financial arrangements; that is, related couples live under the same roof but have separate purses. Married children commonly neglect their parents. A considerable number of spouses come from without the community; especially are such daughters-in-law indifferent to the traditional standard of respect and obedience owed parents-in-law. The mobility of the population and the weakness of familial controls make it possible for men to maintain mistresses in separate establishments, usually in some other community.

The rituals of birth, marriage, and death are, as will be made clear in detail later, much simpler, and they are more lightly regarded. Furthermore, the rituals are not infrequently incongruous with the practices, as in instances where the godparent, being wealthy and powerful, furnishes the baptismal feast. The relationship between compadres is sometimes in disconformity with the underlying patterns of respect relationship, as in those cases where a parent selects a person much younger than himself to act as his child's godparent because the person selected belongs to the superior social class or is wealthy. Marriage, and its rituals, to a much less degree than is true in the villages, involves the union of two familial groups. Not infrequently two young people begin to live together without the performance of any rituals to express the system of relationships which, under an older culture, a marriage redeclared. The place of the souls of the dead in the scheme of social relations is uncertain, vague, and variable:

the prayers held after a death are not clearly understood to transfer the dead person to the afterworld.

In chapter iii the situation in Dzitas with regard to social classes has been summarized. There is a conflict between the conceptions involved in an old two-class system and the more mobile and individualistic situation that actually prevails. An indio, a person with a Maya surname, according to these conceptions, should wear the mestizo dress at all times, practice agriculture and other rude labor, live on the outskirts of the town, take no leading part in government, and show respect toward a vecino, a person whose surname shows his Spanish descent. Actually, many indios violate all these rules implied by the old system. There are many who regard the new practices as right; there are others who experience the difficulty of making a choice between conflicting attitudes both of which have some sanction and some attachment to other practices or conceptions. The Revolution, in putting town government largely into the hands of the Indians, brought about a serious discrepancy between the present institutions and patterns of subordination and superordination which were consistent with the old culture. A few vecinos joined the political party which represented the reform and which came later to control local government. To conservative vecinos these men betrayed their class. Most vecinos that participate in the government are no longer fully members of the vecino group. (A vecino, personally distinguished, may, however, help the indios with governmental matters without criticism from conservatives if he is not active in politics and if he indicates that he is merely lending his ability to the needs of local government.)

Characteristic of the situation in Dzitas is the presence of several kinds of persons whose behavior does not conform to any recognized social category but rather lies between or just outside such categories. In their modes of life they constitute social ambiguities. The indios who have assumed specialized occupations and are de vestido are such persons with reference to the old scheme of social classes which older vecinos would like to preserve. So is the vecino who seeks political leadership among indios. The persons who have entered Dzitas from the outside are in many cases peripheral: the Korean, who lives in part like a native and has a native wife but whose ways are nevertheless alien; the woman from Guadalajara who is the sole exponent of spiritualism in Dzitas and who is looked on by many of her neighbors as a dabbler in witchcraft. The roles which men and women may occupy in a system of family relationships are not always clearly categorized. When so many unions take place casually and may gradually become better defined and more public, it is not at all clear whether a man has a mistress or a wife. When a man maintains one household in Dzitas and another in Merida, the wife in Dzitas is a mistress to the people who hear about it from the woman in Merida. Especially is the role of consort doubtful if the woman be a mestiza india living with a de vestido vecino, and if she be, in addition, of small education and little sophistication. Such a woman was referred to by the man's sister as her "halfway sister-in-law" (*media cuñada*); the sister expressed her ambiguous or compromising attitude by offering her half the standard rate of pay for a midwifery treatment she gave her daughter. Had she been fully her sister-in-law, she would have offered her no money.

The observer who also knows the life of the village is impressed in Dzitas with the relatively greater indications of feelings of personal insecurity. Men raise questions as to the importance or the worth of making offerings in the milpa or ask the outsider to pass judgment on the conduct of their Protestant neighbors. The older generation frequently lament the changes that have occurred in their lives and criticize their neighbors and their children for their impiety and mannerlessness. There are relatively more open quarrels and disputes; vituperation, abuse, and even violence occur in public in Dzitas not uncommonly. In Chan Kom such occurrences are much less common, and they quickly become the subject of family settlement or of the administration of justice by the comisario. One is also impressed with a difference in the attitudes toward sickness as the village is compared with the town. In Chan Kom a man who is not very sick does not, openly at least, complain very much about his condition or express great alarm at the outcome. When a man has made up his mind that he is seriously ill, he may decide that he is going to die and express this conviction definitely. In Dzitas, on the other hand, small ailments are much discussed; people awake in the morning and complain of the bad nights they have passed; there is frequent expression of worry over ailments that appear to an outsider as minor.

The insecurity as to livelihood has this difference, broadly speaking: in Dzitas there are not a few men who do not consider the milpa as a field for their activities, partly because they have not been brought up to learn its techniques, partly because the religious sanctions for work in the milpa are weak, and partly because the standards of the city which they have come in part to share depreciate such common toil and suggest obtaining more interesting and remunerative employment. Such men are in search of jobs, and, if they are without a livelihood, it is because there are few jobs and they have had the bad luck not to obtain one. To the older native of Chan Kom, on the other hand, if one fails in a livelihood, it is because the milpa has not yielded a harvest, and this is because the gods willed it so and probably because one has done wrong. The latter interpretation of the situation conduces toward renewed industry and piety; the former, toward uncertainty and unrest.

The city, indeed, plays an important part in the view upon life prevailing in Dzitas. Meridanos come down to Dzitas to visit or to take positions; and people of Dzitas not infrequently go to Merida. The old resident of the state capital has a patronizing attitude for the person who rusticates in some small town or village; to be a *poblano* is to be something less worthy. The native of Dzitas is quite aware of this. The city is, therefore, looked up to; it is a place to which to escape, although few do escape. Even the United States has come to stand for a land into which one might, had one the money and the courage, pass from the troubles and uncertainties of life in Dzitas. To speak in personal terms, Chan Kom is a restful place in which to be, except as one may tire of monotony. But Dzitas is irksome because people are self-conscious and restless and frequently in evident distress.

The writer will agree that these statements are little more than a record of impressions. He will agree further, if restlessness, self-consciousness, and sense of insecurity characterize Dzitas as compared with Chan Kom, that he has not given full demonstration as to how these characteristics are connected with the relative disorganization in culture. The manner of their connection has been suggested in foregoing paragraphs where the inconsistencies and vagaries of the conventional life of the town are indicated, and the reader is invited to imagine the state of mind of a person presented with a situation so loosely and ambiguously defined for him by tradition and by his neighbors. So establishment of the connection rests in these pages upon an appeal to common knowledge of human nature.

The central objective of this chapter is the presentation of facts in support of the proposition that there is less organization of culture in Dzitas than in Chan Kom. In Dzitas, as compared with Chan Kom, the meanings attached to acts and objects are less highly standardized by convention, the meanings are relatively few and are less completely connected with one another, and inconsistencies and uncertainties are present among them in the experiences of any and all members of the community.

It may be reported also that information given as to the changes that have taken place in the last fifty years in Dzitas indicates that, while the culture has been breaking down, at the same time the process has continued whereby the old Spanish heritage and the Indian tradition have merged into a single body of ways. It has been already said in chapter iii that in the last third of the nineteenth century the vecinos and the indios of Dzitas were not only clearly separated social classes but also were groups still characterized in certain respects by differences of custom. The indios maintained their own government, apart from but subordinated to that of vecinos; the name of their chief officer (batab) persisted from pre-Hispanic days, and it is likely that some of the governmental notions and procedures were also survivals from pagan times. We know that the elaborate ritual of the patron saint, called "carga," was then maintained only by indios; some of the old people remember when the first vecino took part in these ceremonies. In those days apparently the important rain ceremonies were carried on by indios; now many vecinos take part (while some indios do not). Similarly, the wearing of mourning is becoming general. So it is less true than it was that there are two culture groups in Dzitas. But the culture, whether one recognizes one or two cultures, is less organized in Dzitas. Meanings do not ramify as far into the customs and institutions, and the elements of conventional life are not so closely and consistently related to one another. The practice of wearing mourning is more generally distributed among the people than it was before, but mourning means less to people, and is less completely observed, than it used to be. Each of the old groups has continued to borrow the ways of the other, while the ways have become disorganized.

The recent history of Dzitas represents, it appears, a transition from one type of society to another. The situation in old Dzitas more nearly approximated the situation probably characteristic of isolated homogeneous societies in which the elements of convention are closely and consistently related to one another. Later Dzitas is approaching the situation probably prevailing in cities and in mobile and heterogeneous societies: there is an increase in the range of knowledge and choice of conduct presented to the individual, there is an increase in the extent and complexity of the organization based on the division of labor which in part constitutes the society, but there is a decrease in the degree of organization of the customs and institutions and in all the elements of conventional understanding. In Dzitas assimilation (or diffusion) between two culture groups has been going on simultaneously with cultural disorganization.

CHAPTER VII

MONEY, LAND, AND WORK[1]

A LL the communities of Yucatan, even those of the independent and hostile Maya of Quintana Roo, participate in one pecuniary economy in the sense that every community exports some products and imports others and that the same national money is used as a medium of exchange in such transactions and as a measure of many values. Tusik is not self-sustaining; many necessities, such as cotton cloth, gunpowder, and soap, as well as luxuries, are regularly purchased with Mexican pesos from merchants from the towns. The situation approximated in some primitive communities, where distribution of goods occurs without money and solely as a concomitant of ceremony or as an expression of mutual good will or of the personal relations existing between individuals, is not represented anywhere in Yucatan.

On the other hand, the large relative differences among the four communities studied as to the degree of commercial development and as to the extent of pecuniary valuation are obvious. In the season when chicle is not exploited, commerce in Tusik is almost confined to the sales made to and by the occasional traveling merchants and to occasional employment by an agriculturalist of someone to assist him in the work of the field. There are no stores, and a family may go for many days without buying or selling anything, although each is living intimately with scores of others. In Chan Kom there are stores, and there is greater production of maize, hogs, poultry, and eggs for market. Dzitas may be characterized as a commercial town: the production and the sale of maize are much more highly organized and involve resident corn dealers; there

155

are many stores and more products are regularly bought rather than made by the consumer himself; and there are many specialized professional workers and producers. Merida, of course, provides a highly commercial and pecuniary economy in which people are dependent upon large permanent markets; even maize is regularly bought and not produced by the consumer, and banking and other elements of modern economic systems are present. These differences provide an opportunity for the consideration of some particular matters relative to the extension of commerce and the development of the use of money.

In this respect, as in so many others, the important influence in determining differences between one community and another in Yucatan is that emanating from the city and ultimately from the modern industrial and commercial world. Chan Kom is more commercial than Tusik in so far as it has become a market for factory-made goods and in so far as it has developed products which can be sold to the towns or the city. The Quintana Roo communities have only one significant commerce: that in chicle, which is entirely a development due to expansion of modern international commerce. Among the Maya peoples of the highlands of Guatemala there is an important regional specialization of production and an extensive interchange of native products in large fixed markets, all this apparently ancient and independent, in large part, of factory manufacture and of international commerce. In Yucatan, on the other hand, local agricultural products are few; native markets as distinguished from stores are almost nonexistent; and most of the manufactured products bought and sold have been manufactured in Merida or in Mexico or in the United States. Although it must have been different in pre-Hispanic times,[2] the Maya villagers have little commercial heritage. In the Guatemala highlands the trader is omnipresent—indeed, almost everyone is a trader—and the native market is central to the mode of life. This is not at all true among the Maya of Yucatan, where the city makes the trade.[3]

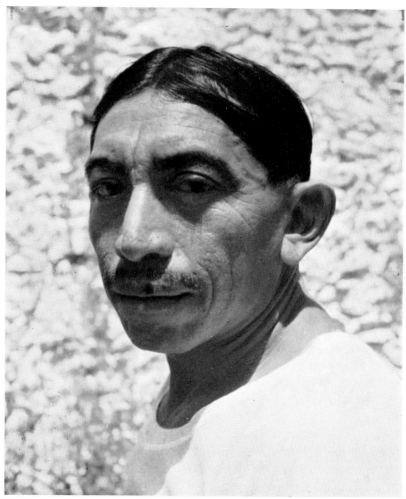

Photograph by Frances Rhoads Morley

Under these circumstances it is not surprising to find differences among the communities as to the extent to which commercial dealings between members of the same community are tolerated or defined. Tusik has no store, and its inhabitants will not allow any of the traveling merchants to set up a store. A merchant may stay just long enough to do his business; then he is required to leave. Chan Kom almost from its founding had stores operated by natives but for long resisted attempts of outsiders to set up a store; this permission was finally given during the time these studies were made. In Dzitas it is a matter of course that anyone, native or outsider, may set up a store when he wishes. The general attitude in Tusik is that members of the same community do not trade with one another. The attitude does not amount to a rule, for occasionally one native will buy some eggs or a hog or a little maize from another, and for one native to work for another in the milpa for hire is not uncommon. But commercial activity is not usual or favored. The attitudes are reflected in the way prices of small commodities such as eggs or hens are made. If a man needs an egg and applies to his neighbor for it, he will be asked to pay a small sum, much lower than the value of the egg in the market; an outsider will be asked to pay whatever the native chooses to ask, and the price may be ten or twenty times what a neighbor would be asked. In such a commercial culture as the Guatemalan highlands illustrate, this behavior would not occur. The relatively noncommercial attitude toward fellow-members of the in-group is further represented by the fact Villa reports[4] that one native does not borrow money from another, yet will ask merchants or other outsiders for loans. The same discrimination between dealings with a neighbor and dealings with an outsider may appear also in the circumstance that it is customary to remunerate a helper in the hard work of the milpa with a share of the resulting crop, except the helper be an outsider come into the territory to find work, in which case the remuneration is generally in cash. The outsider does not share the conventional understandings of the native as to the recompense proper for such work. Obviously it may also be that the outsider prefers cash to maize or beans as more transportable and of less variable value. Villa says that the particular relationship between individuals who exchange goods or services makes no difference in Tusik in the fixing of the consideration. One makes no discrimination between a brother or a compadre and any other neighbor in fixing a price.

The experience had in Chan Kom leads to the conclusion that in that village there is greater familiarity with trade and the fixing of a fair price, and correspondingly there is greater readiness to deal commercially with a fellow-villager. People go not infrequently to the stores in the town and are used to buying necessaries at the stores maintained by neighbors. It is common for a native to slaughter a hog and sell the meat to his neighbors. In Tusik this is not done. If a man cuts a neighbor's hair in Chan Kom, he is usually paid; in Tusik, he is not. The villagers, friendly toward outsiders, do not charge such persons exorbitant prices and their neighbors merely nominal prices, as often happens in Tusik. They sell eggs and hens and maize to traveling merchants, or in the towns or at Chichen Itza, and they are familiar with market prices and more disposed generally to expect a fair return for such goods as they have to sell, whether sold to outsiders or to insiders. On the other hand, in the case provided by the first offer of embroideries for sale in Chan Kom, where the makers knew nothing of the market price of their product, these women had only vague ideas as to how much should be asked and were unable to fix a fair price without guidance from Villa. In Chan Kom it does occasionally occur that one native borrows from another, but always without interest. The Chan Kom people exhibit a reluctance to treat a visitor as a paying guest. The occasional visitor, if respected, is commonly supplied, without charge, lodging and such food as is produced by the labor of the people; hospitality is offered. But for such contributions to his diet as must be bought at the village store he is expected to pay.

In Tusik, and to a less extent in Chan Kom, distribution of goods and services within the community takes place characteristically in connection with festivities and ceremonies and as a part of collective enterprise. Before a festival everyone participates in the work (according to age and sex): the gathering of firewood, the building of the shelter for the dancing, the preparation of festal foods. And after such ceremonies as represent an entire settlement the food prepared is distributed among all. Of course, such distribution is entirely noncommercial. What is observed in Chan Kom, in addition, is that commercial activity among villagers takes on not infrequently something of this character of a periodic enthusiasm. Trade among members of the Chan Kom community is not steady but rather occurs in bursts of interest, stimulated, perhaps, by the visit of a cattle dealer. Then for a few days many people will undertake to barter one thing for another, and the onlooker feels that the exchanges are made in large part just for the pleasure of the activity.

In Dzitas and in the city, of course, commercial activity is a part of the routine of living. Much of what is consumed must be bought, and little of what a man consumes he produces himself. In Dzitas no reluctance was observed to deal commercially with a neighbor; the prices of most commodities are well known, and it is expected that they will be realized no matter with whom one is dealing. (This statement does not, of course, deny the practice of bargaining and the fact that one always hopes to do a little better than one probably does.) The borrowing of money is not uncommon. A woman badly in need of money may pawn her gold chain with a neighbor. There is no feeling that the community should entertain the visitor who is not taken in by relatives or friends; he can go to one of two little hostelries. Except for the annual festival of the patron (which is in decline), there are no important occasions when goods are collectively produced and generally distributed and consumed as a part of tradition and ceremony. Within families, too, commercial dealings are common, and in compound families it is not unusual for one member to pay another for a service, although this conflicts with the expectations of traditional family life.

The materials from Merida indicate some of the respects in which commercial and pecuniary habits of mind are still further extended and also suggest limitations on the spread of commercialism. The family remains a group within which secular and pecuniary considerations do not fully prevail. Even among the most commercially minded groups of the city it is taken for granted, as it is with similar people in other parts of the world, that one does not drive a hard bargain with a close kinsman, that the taking of legal action to enforce a claim against a close relative is to be condemned, and that, in lending money to a semidependent or less fortunate close kinsman, one does not charge interest. The relations between parents and children, much more than those between siblings, resist the development of commercialism. There are cases among the lower classes of Merida in which artisans or small businessmen take over the earnings of grown sons who work in the parental enterprise and give these sons whatever spending money the fathers think they need.

On the whole the attitudes in Merida are such as to approve many sorts of business dealings within the extended family and even within the parental family, with the understanding that such dealings are more friendly, personal, and informal than are such dealings with persons who are not relatives. A conflict between the claims of kinship and the expectancies of business enterprise is recognized by people of the lower class. Hansen's materials include utterances condemning categorically business dealings with relatives. This condemnation is uttered either on the ground that business dealings are likely to give rise to quarrels, and that quarreling between relatives is to be avoided, or else on the ground that business transactions cannot be efficiently carried on between relatives because business dealings must be kept impersonal and must be guided by self-interest and because such a viewpoint is difficult to maintain in dealing with relatives. In the situation approximated by Tusik the conflict of motives recognized in such statements does not so easily arise because there is one recognized system of implict rules for dealing with the local settlement, including kindred, and another for outsiders.

One observation with reference to bargaining, made by Hansen with reference to Merida, is worth noting here. The practice of bargaining is a sort of ritualization of commercial dealings. It is a conventional way in which buyer and seller reach a sale through a stylized parley. Bargaining is a series of reciprocal concessions based on often-purported good will. It is an interchange that in form has some resemblance to a greeting custom, but in substance it is a way of making a price. It is not the quickest way to make a price, however, and it leaves uncertain and unstandardized the pecuniary value of many goods. It is in the city of Merida that bargaining is obviously on the decline. In Dzitas you may expect to bargain for most commodities sold in the stores as well as by traveling merchants, but in Merida in recent years there has developed a conscious movement in favor of fixed prices. The movement is probably partly a direct reflection of foreign standards and partly a response to local conditions: stores have become so large in Merida that many clerks are employed and economic relations within them are as a result more impersonal.

It is also to be noted that the collective production and distribution of goods in connection with religious celebration, which is so large a part of the system of distribution of the remote villages and which survives as a significant feature once a year in Dzitas in connection with the annual festival, is practically extinct in Merida. Only persons who have made money contributions are invited to the meetings of the groups (gremios) that maintain the festival, and there is a definite feeling that such contributions are payments for the refreshment and music provided. In the villages the contribution to the saint is a pious offering made as one of the necessary aspects of participation in the community; in Merida it has become almost the equivalent of the purchase of a ticket of admission to

a party. The general distribution of food to all comers, in connection with the fiesta of Santiago in the barrio of that name in
Merida, where the practice longest endured, apparently
ceased to be practiced about the year 1900.

With two important exceptions (Merida and Progreso,
which maintain themselves in the one case by performing
services and by manufacture and in the case of the latter
chiefly by performing services), the communities of Yucatan,
large and small, depend upon sending an agricultural product
to market. In the zone of henequen, sisal is the product, and
maize is raised chiefly in small quantities for local consumption. In that region in which Chan Kom and Dzitas lie, the
reader will recall, practically no henequen is grown for market, and maize is the money crop. Throughout all this area
the price of maize is made in Merida, either directly or indirectly after reflection of prices abroad. And in this area,
whether maize be the staple commodity for market or whether
it be a crop for domestic sustenance, the local price is responsive to the market price. In Chan Kom, as in Dzitas, when
maize is sold to someone within the community or to an outsider, the local price is responsive to the market price. A man
returning to Chan Kom from the town is at once asked what
he found to be the prevailing price of maize. The remuneration paid in Chan Kom to a laborer in the cornfield is usually
paid in maize, but the amount paid varies with the market
value of maize. In Chan Kom, as in Dzitas, men hold their
crops for a rise in the market, if they can.

In the Quintana Roo communities studied by Villa, however, maize is not a money crop. Its place as such is taken by
chicle. Chicle is exploited solely to sell to the outside world,
and, with the exception of small quantities of hogs, it is the
only exported product. Before chicle exploitation began, hog-
raising was more extensively carried on; so far as information
was secured, in those days maize was no more a money crop
than it is now. Maize is not exported from the Quintana Roo
villages for the chief reason that it is relatively more costly to

buy and transport maize to the town markets from these communities than from the communities near the railroad in the Chan Kom region. Chicle, of course, can only be obtained in the rain forests of the south. Furthermore, the natives are accustomed to getting money by selling hogs and chicle; they do not think of maize as something to sell. Consequently, when it is sold (to an outsider), the price varies considerably, according to the whim of the seller. The amounts of maize which one pays for help given in the milpa, on the other hand, have been standardized by custom and vary little.

As we might expect, the exploitation of chicle takes place in an entirely matter-of-fact manner, without any religious connotations or ritual requirements, while the growing of maize, as we know already, is deeply and closely involved in the religious life. Furthermore, while the growing of maize involves co-operative endeavor and the common sharing in religious ceremonies to secure abundant rains, in the case of chicle each man works strictly for himself and by himself. So in the case of Tusik we have the not unfamiliar contrast between a secular market product and a subsistence crop involved in the religious and moral life. One might then expect that in Chan Kom, where maize is valued in terms of a distant and variable market, and is held or sold on speculation, so to speak, its role in the religious and moral life might be small, or at least less than is the case in Tusik. Yet this appears not to be the case. The religious consequences of making a milpa, the respect in which are held the young maize plants and the milpa, and the importance of the agricultural ceremonies are as great, or nearly as great, in the one community as in the other. For the Chan Kom native maize is both a "grace" granted by the yuntzilob and the Virgin and a commodity to be sold when the market provides an advantageous opportunity. Separated from the milpa and placed into commerce, it changes its name correspondingly (gracia to ixim). The people of Chan Kom and of Tusik have been raising maize for market for generations, and for generations the shaman-priests have been leading them in the performance of the agricultural ceremonies. Tusik and Chan Kom, similar in piety, differ in that the central object of the cult is in the one case outside of commerce and pecuniary valuation, while in the latter case it is very much within that sphere. On the other hand, Dzitas and Chan Kom, which are alike in their marketing of maize, differ largely in the completeness and importance of the agricultural cult. Certainly in this case the mere habitual marketing of the principal sustaining product is not the determining factor in secularizing it. It is rather the direct acquisition of the skepticism of the townsman and of his critical attitude toward the shaman-priests that has had in Chan Kom in recent years some adverse influence on the agricultural cult.

In all the rural communities, the town as well as the villages, barter, as might be expected, plays a considerable part in the exchange of goods, but is rare in Merida. As might be expected, the use of money, while general, is less common in the peripheral villages than it is in the town. One curious difference has been noted in the use of money in Tusik as compared with Chan Kom. In the former community money serves chiefly as a medium of exchange in transactions involving small values, whereas in Chan Kom it is more usual for lesser transactions to take place through the medium of eggs or maize. This is in part due to the fact that eggs and maize, varying as they do in value with the market price, are the equivalents of money with the advantage that they can be directly produced by the person who spends them, while in Tusik, as stated above, these commodities are not valued as the outside market values them.

The natives of Tusik prefer either United States dollars or pounds sterling to Mexican money. Coins of the United States are obtained from Mexican traders, and British currency is obtained from Belize. These coins are kept as a form of saving; they are not in general use as currency. The natives are in total ignorance of the values of these currencies upon international exchange, and their preference is to be explained by a transfer of their dislike of the Mexicans to the money of the Mexicans and by an additional distrust of the currency produced by the fact that the form of Mexican coinage has changed several times in their experience.

In all the communities, among those families and groups where the women wear mestiza costume, wealth is conspicuously stored in the gold chains possessed by women of means. This chain forms a part of the bride-gift (*muhul*); its value is important in setting the economic position and so to a considerable degree the social position of the new family. These chains may be added to from time to time by a prosperous husband, and in bad times they may be sold. The de vestido person of Dzitas or Merida does not have this form of savings. On the other hand, in the Quintana Roo villages there are almost no ways in which sudden wealth can be invested, except in the form of these chains. The proceeds of chicle sales in Quintana Roo are therefore in large part expended for such luxuries as fine shirts and sewing machines, while in Chan Kom, and still more in Dzitas, such wealth is invested in cattle, good houses, or land. In Chan Kom and in Tusik, where the principal resources (land and chicle) are open, and a man with energy may make gains much beyond his idler or less efficient fellows, nevertheless it results from the differences just stated as to the possibilities of investment that differences in wealth make very little corresponding differences in social position in Tusik. A man with money is not much better off than a man without it. Correspondingly, differences in wealth are not necessarily consistent with differences in social position. The elected chiefs, who serve for life, are almost the most consequential persons in the community. Yet one of them may work as a laborer for one of his subordinates with little or no loss of prestige. In Chan Kom, whether the difference be due to the greater practical advantages the expenditure of wealth brings or whether it be due to reflection of the townsman's view, it would be less acceptable for a village leader to be without resources and to work for another as an

ordinary laborer. And in Dzitas and in Merida the correspondence of social position with wealth is much more
prominent. These circumstances form a factor in the explanation of the classlessness of the village societies. The old social
classes in the city and in the town, as already set forth in much
detail, were based chiefly on genealogical connection with
originally distinct ethnic groups (although wealth was important in determining the social position of the individual in
relation to other members of his own class); the new social
classes are based on wealth, education, and occupation. In
Tusik there are no significant differences as to any of these
characters (except occupation which affects individuals, not
social strata), not even as to wealth. In Chan Kom, while
there are no classes, social differences based on wealth and
ability to assume leadership in dealing with the new ways coming from the towns are more important. In Tusik the "principal people" are the chiefs and the holders of the sacred offices;
in Chan Kom the people who have masonry houses on the
plaza and who carry on commerce and intercourse with Dzitas
and Merida are recognized as of greater social consequence
than the poor and backward who live chiefly off the plaza.

From what has been said it will already appear that the
people of Merida and Tusik, and certainly therefore also the
inhabitants of the intermediate communities, have in many
respects the same conceptions as to rights *in rem* and think alike
as to what constitutes property. Money, maize, tools, clothing,
jewels, and all sorts of personally useful or consumable
articles may be individually owned, and it is thought good to
have all these things. It is everywhere recognized in Yucatan,
as, of course, it is equally recognized far more widely, that an
individual has exclusive rights over certain property that he
himself creates or buys with his own money. But these rights
are less fully accorded to children, and especially to women, in
the peripheral communities. In Tusik a young man, even
though unmarried and living with his parents, keeps for his
own use money he receives for selling chicle or hogs or for fire-

wood he may occasionally sell to a visiting merchant. Even here, however, custom places a restriction upon his right, for it is expected that such earnings will go at least in part toward the expenses necessary in getting married and in setting up a household. The earnings which women bring about are more plainly accruals to familial estates. Although in the absence of her husband a woman may sell poultry, the proceeds go to the family treasury from which she may use (without the permission of the man) only small amounts of money to buy personal luxuries for herself. If an unmarried woman sells some garment she has sewed (as may rarely occur), she is expected to give the money to her father, under whose control she lives. In Chan Kom, on the other hand, it has become usual for a woman to keep the proceeds of sales of articles she manufactures. In Dzitas such individual transactions, independent of rights of the family or of male family heads, are commonplace, and in the town and in the city young boys often undertake little commercial ventures on their own account. In Tusik children do not sell on their own accounts.

A special form of individual property generally recognized is that making up the bride-gift. Though the nature of this property, its manner of creation, and the role it plays in the family organization all differ importantly in the various communities, as will later appear, yet everywhere there is the conception that, when a new family is created by marriage, the woman should be provided with certain articles of wearing apparel which remain hers and that the bridegroom or his family should provide these articles. In the villages, and among those wearing mestiza costume in town or city, the central article making up the bride-gift is one of the gold chains, already mentioned. In the villages the woman's right to this bride-gift is limited by one restriction: it constitutes a sort of pledge of her good marital behavior and reverts to her husband if she brings about a rupture of the marriage by going off with another man.[5] In Dzitas this limitation is not recognized, and in the city, where the bride-gift becomes a trousseau and is often selected with the participation of the woman, all notion of its role as a security for the woman's contribution to the success of the marriage is absent. But aside from this possibility, usually remote, that the woman may be guilty of such misconduct, in the village as well as in town and city, the gifts made the bride on the occasion of her marriage by the bridegroom and his family are completely hers and do not constitute a part of the familial estate. On her death the chain received at marriage goes to a daughter.

A consideration of the facts as to property as they appear comparatively in the materials from the four communities leads to the recognition of two matters of difference that appear worthy of presentation. One of these has to do with changing conceptions as to the permanence of familial estate. Aside from the bride-gift, the goods acquired for family use during the marriage, both articles made by the woman and food produced and articles made or purchased by the man, make up a family estate. In the view that prevails in the village this family estate should remain intact so long as either spouse is alive or so long as there are immature children. Therefore, in both Tusik and Chan Kom, the property of the family remains in the complete control of a surviving spouse even if all the children are grown. If the surviving spouse dies while one or more children are still immature, some selected male person, a brother or an uncle, takes over the property with the obligation to raise the children. Men make testamentary provision, leaving their "maize, horses, and children" to some kinsman. Chan Kom and Tusik are alike in this regard, but two details of difference have been noted. The inviolability of an estate is complete in Tusik to the degree that, even if a stepfather wastes the estate, the children, though grown, have no claim; the mother had the right to marry again and assume another partner to carry on the family responsibilities and participate in the enjoyment of the conjugal estate. In Chan Kom, on the other hand, cases were encountered where grown children made a claim before the authorities for a share in the estate under these conditions, and the partition of the estate was brought about. Further, in Tusik, Villa tells us that, when a widow dies without having remarried, the property is taken over by the oldest son living with her at the time of her death; he is expected to care for the other children if he is grown. But it is certainly true in Chan Kom[6] that, upon the death of a widow, all children share equally in the estate. In Dzitas the usages, whether responsive to formal law or not, have much less effect in preserving conjugal estates. There, if a man or a woman dies leaving grown children, the property is divided among the children and the surviving parent, the latter taking charge of the shares of immature children. Furthermore, cases were encountered in Dzitas where advantage was taken of the law, or of ignorance of the law, so that only legitimate children were allowed to inherit, making it possible for brothers and sisters to take the conjugal property of a sibling without assuming any of the responsibilities and obligations of trust which would be involved in the villages should a brother take over his deceased brother's estate and offspring. In the villages, where custom and not formal law governs, no distinction is, of course, made between marriages by law and without law. If a woman lives with a man and does his housework, for a substantial time, she is his wife, and she will have all the rights to his estate that she would have if married before the civil registry. In short, in the peripheral villages the customs with regard to family property emphasize the persistence of a family as an economic unit of wealth beyond the death of one or another partner and into the adult life of children, while as one goes to the town and the city there is greater disposition to recognize the rights of individuals to partition this unit and assume control over shares.[7] Merida was not studied with particular reference to the topic of this paragraph, and the materials available are not sufficient to make it possible to include practices characterizing the city in this comparative summary.

A more important difference among the communities lies in

the conceptions as to rights in land, and here the varying influence of Western European notions may be supposed to be
the principal influencing factor. Yet this conclusion may be
confronted with one puzzling fact: though the natives of the
Tusik group of settlements apparently recognize no individual
ownership of land, in the sense that land is permanently and
exclusively at the control of one individual and may by him
be sold, nevertheless apparently the buying and selling of land
was in earlier times common in east central Yucatan.[8] Is it
possible that individual rights over particular tracts of land
ceased to be recognized by those Maya who did not make
their peace with the government and who made new settlements in the southern forests and that they changed, or perhaps reverted, to a more collectivistic conception of rights over
land? Or is it possible that some of the natives of Quintana
Roo never took over or never developed notions of individual
landownership?

At any rate, the difference in this regard between present-
day Quintana Roo and Chan Kom is marked. In the former
region no land is the object of individual exclusive control.
The woods are free to anyone to make milpa (with the limitation that members of one settlement recognize a territory
within which they claim better rights than more distant neighbors), but after a used milpa has reverted to bush the first
milpero has no greater right there than any other. When the
Mexican government was seeking to force the X-Cacal settlements to accept ejidos, which are grants of land collectively
to a village, the natives resisted this and demanded and
secured a grant in the form of a single recognition of territorial
right in the whole cacicazgo. The ejido was not comprehen-
sively collectivist enough for these people. Neither are house
sites owned or sold in Tusik, nor are houses sold or rented. A
newcomer to a village may build his house on any unoccupied
spot, first communicating his wishes to the chief. Fruit trees,
though ownership in these is recognized independent of rights
in the land on which they grow, are not sold.[9] Yet a man's

house, or his fruit tree, is his as long as it exists, even if he goes to live in some other settlement.

In Chan Kom most milpas, ephemeral cultivations in the returning bush, are not owned any more than such are in Tusik. Yet the notion that real estate can be individually owned and bought and sold in not only common but is apparently of long standing. Several men own particular tracts of good land outside the ejidos to which they hold documents of title and which they may sell. Furthermore, with regard to the ejidos, the natives understand and depend upon the sanction of the Mexican government: they want collective ownership by formal transfer to the village and with a document of title. Certainly the native of Chan Kom is more disposed to buy and sell the fields and their products than are those of Quintana Roo. It is not uncommon to sell to another man a cleared field in the bush; in this case, of course, the buyer does not own the land; he has bought the fruits of the other man's labor and saved himself the trouble. Fruit trees are also bought and sold. Furthermore, the disposition to treat land as individually owned is expressed in the fact that during the period of observation people were coming to buy and sell house sites and houses. By older custom (and law also?) every settler in the settlement had a right to build his house on any unoccupied spot within the limits of the village (but, of course, not on the plaza or on a street); and his right to the house site lapsed when he left. By this older practice the house, then always a simple construction of poles and thatch, was built with the co-operative labor of the men of the settlement, and therefore the occupant lost his rights to the house upon leaving the settlement. But cases arose where a man sold part of his house site to another villager for cash, without objection from the village authorities, and, furthermore, men attempted, on leaving the village, to sell their house sites to outsiders. The latter attempts were not allowed, the village authorities holding that only a new settler could take an abandoned house site, and that, if he wished to pay for a better site than could be provided by lands not yet taken up, the proceeds would go to the village treasury, not to the retiring previous occupant. The village authorities also allowed a man who left the village to keep half the proceeds of the sale of an old-style house, the other half going to the village. The new masonry houses are coming to be regarded as entirely the property of the builder, to dispose of, at least to new settlers, as he likes.

In Dzitas the buying and selling of house lots, as well as of agricultural lands outside of the ejidos, is a commonplace. The custom of co-operative construction of houses as an obligation of the community to new residents has been abandoned. Many lands, both house sites and fields, are represented by documents of title, and it is not uncommon for an owner to deposit his documents with a creditor as security for a loan of money. This is, of course, not a mortgage; it may be that mortgages are made in Dzitas (as they are in Merida); the author did not meet with any.[10]

The differences just summarized as to the importance and development of commercial and pecuniary ways of life are accompanied by and interdependent with differences in the division of labor. When we speak of one society as compared with another as relatively "simple" or "complex," we are thinking often of differences as to the distribution of special functions among the population; and the development of civilization is perhaps most easily described, aside from technological changes, in terms of the multiplication and specialization of these functions and of changes in the character of the functions discharged. The differences as to division of labor that appear to the author when Tusik, Chan Kom, Dzitas, and Merida are compared seem to parallel changes which have occurred in the division of labor in the course of recent Western history. If use may be made of a form of expression strictly more appropriate to changes taking place over a period of time than to a comparison of four communities at a single time, the differences may be summarized as follows: (1) The division of labor becomes more complex in that individuals come to devote their time to particular functions and in that more functions are required for the maintenance of the life of the community. (2) The division of labor between the sexes becomes less rigidly defined. (3) Work becomes less commonly discharged by collective effort and more frequently performed as an individual enterprise. (4) The discharge of a special function, from being the exercise of a traditional prerogative involving prestige and esoteric knowledge as an aspect of an obligation to participate in the religious and moral life of the community, becomes the carrying-on of a practical activity in order chiefly to gain a livelihood.

It is not possible precisely to express the differing degrees to which there are recognized specialists in the four communities, but a rough computation including every locally named specialist (except holders of elected public office) indicates that in Tusik one family head in every eleven can make a claim to discharging a special function in his community, while the proportions in the cases of Chan Kom and Dzitas are about one in seven and one in four, respectively. In Tusik and its sister-settlements the few specialists include principally the holders of priestly office, a few musicians, a few midwives, and a family that sells baskets; in Chan Kom one can add storekeepers, a mason, a barber, and a baker. Dzitas provides a long list of specialists, some of which have been mentioned in an earlier chapter. In Merida almost every occupied male is discharging a special function; there is in the city no general basic economic activity comparable to agriculture in the villages. The comparison just made does not, indeed, fully express the differences that exist, because all the recognizable specialists in the villages (with a single important exception—the Nohoch Tata in X-Cacal) are also performing the basic operations of maintenance. Full-time specialists make their first appearance in Dzitas, where perhaps one-fourth of all the adult males might be so described. Even the men who discharge priestly functions in the Quintana Roo villages (always excepting the Nohoch Tata) carry on the same agriculture and hunting and do the simple construction of houses and other articles. In the villages practical knowledge is generally distributed among all of the sex to whom such knowledge is traditionally appropriate. This is even more true in Tusik than it is in Chan Kom, and it is true for old traditional activities as well as for newly acquired specialties. In Chan Kom there are a few women who are recognized as the prayer-reciters of the community; a man is the bone-setter of the community. In Tusik knowledge of these arts is more generally distributed among members of the appropriate sex, and no one can claim to be "the bone-setter" or "one of the" *rezadoras* of the community.

As is probably generally true, the acquisition of new functions by a community involves first the elaboration of the division of labor among men; women are much more conservative of functions traditionally theirs. After certain men of Chan Kom have become storekeepers and another a mason, all the women are still performing undifferentiated domestic work; and none of the specialists in Dzitas are women except one teacher, three midwives, an herb doctor, and a spiritualistic medium. It is, of course, in extensions of domestic functions, such as curing and nursing, that the women's professions begin. In the villages the healing functions (except those of midwifery) are closely associated with the priestly arts involving the yuntzilob, which are strictly confined to men; therefore, there are no women curers. But in Dzitas there are women herb doctors; and in Merida there are many more women healers by folk medicine and magic than there are men. The division of labor between the sexes whereby men do the farming and women the domestic work, and that whereby all participation in public affairs is the concern of men only, are traditional probably in both the Indian and the Spanish heritage, and have shown in Yucatan a high degree of resistance to change. The only woman known to have made milpa by her own labor in the villages studied was one who came down to the Dzitas–Chan Kom area from the city of Merida, and the extraordinary, almost monstrous, character of what she did will not soon be forgotten. In Tusik women do not attend public gatherings; they learn of the results later from the men. In Chan Kom, during the period of observation, it was thought well by the village leaders to have women present at gatherings at which edifying speeches were made, but when any really critical matter was to be discussed no woman was expected to be, or was, present. In Dzitas no one would seriously propose a woman for a public office, but teaching is open to women, and in the "cultural societies," where public theatrical performances are given, women play a part almost equal to that of men. In Merida the Revolution brought in new notions of feminism. During the early years of the new regime, the enthusiasm for innovation led a few women to assume public office and roles of leadership of some importance. But most of the people were shocked by the assumption of public office by women. After a time conservative opinion prevailed, and today the role of women in Merida is still insignificant. Although this experiment with militant feminism failed, in less sensational ways women's activities are expanding. Teaching is becoming primarily a woman's occupation; there is an increase of those employed as clerks, as stenographers, and even as executives; and one pioneer has established herself in medicine.

The statement made on a previous page that labor is more frequently expended by collective effort in the villages requires at once some limiting remarks. Readers of Landa are familiar with the passage (I, 164) in which he says that it was the custom among the Maya for a group of about twenty men to go about doing in turn the milpa work for each member of the group. It is also known that some years ago in Chan Kom houses were built by the co-operative labor of the community, and memory of such a practice, although longer extinct, is retained in Dzitas. (Apparently collective housebuilding has not been carried on in Merida within the memory of old inhabitants.) Yet Villa tells us that in the Tusik area the natives are little inclined to help one another with the work in the field, that when parties of workers do so assist one another it is a group of relatives that are involved, and that houses are built by the labor of the man who will live in it. In these respects, then, Tusik, Chan Kom, and Dzitas are substantially alike, and it further appears that Tusik, like the other communities, has abandoned old customs of mutual help in getting work done.

The differences that are to be pointed out with regard to collective labor have to do with festal preparations and the institutions of *fagina* and *guardia*. The annual festival in Tusik, as already mentioned in an earlier connection, requires that every adult and many children devote themselves for days to the fetching and preparation of firewood, water, festal food, and festal paraphernalia; and the important agricultural ceremonies, both Catholic and pagan, evoke the same collective effort. In Chan Kom itself the annual festival has been in recent years much simplified, but in other villages of the area it still involves the supreme effort of the community. The major ceremonies to the yuntzilob, in both Tusik and Chan Kom, also bring about common participation by all the adults of the community and the pooling of a large amount of labor. Of course, in the cases of these ceremonies and festivals the labor pooled is contributed in a sense of play, public responsibility, and worship of the gods. It is more than plain work. But all these occasions do unite the community in a single effort involving the exchange of services. In Dzitas these occasions are much rarer and probably never involve more than a minority of the population. The festival of the patron has been until recent years an important occasion in which many of the inhabitants contributed their property and their services; it is now apparently decaying as an institution. None of the other ceremonies for the saints, and no agricultural ritual, involves more than a very few of the inhabitants at any time. The work done in connection with festivity and worship in Dzitas is much more a matter of the individual or of small groups of individuals. This is as true in Merida, where even the neighborhood festal organizations are far from all inclusive.

Throughout Yucatan there is knowledge of that institution known as fagina by which public improvements and repairs are accomplished through the compulsory contributions of work by adult males at the discretion and order of the community leaders. The changes which this institution undergoes (again to adopt this manner of expression) as one passes from Quintana Roo through the other three communities in order convert the institution into something quite different: from a collective work drive to accomplish a common objective it becomes the payment by an individual of a tax. In the villages fagina is decreed, by the popularly elected chiefs in Tusik and X-Cacal, and by the popularly elected comisario and his assistants in Chan Kom, whenever public opinion, under the leadership of the community authorities, has decided that a road be opened or a public building be erected. No one receives remuneration for doing this work; it is a public duty. The institution not only gets public work done but it conduces to a solidarity of attitude toward social objectives, for, if a man fails to perform his fagina he is punished, and, if he remains unsympathetic to the enterprise and does not do his part, he may be forced to withdraw from the settlement and find a home in another. In Chan Kom a new settler may be tested by the imposition of a special task of fagina; if he does well and willingly what he is directed to do, he is recognized as a man who should be allowed to join the community. Fagina allows for the joint expenditure of energy in the accomplishment of new or occasional enterprises. In Dzitas the old people remember when there was much fagina, so that everyone had a sense of participation when the plaza was to be rebuilt or a road improved. But even then the wealthier people made a money contribution, instead of actually doing work, and looked on while their poorer neighbors toiled. Nowadays fagina is a trifling matter; those who do not pay a small tax are required to work only a few days each year on the roads. Therefore, only a very few of the adults actually work together at any time, and most never take part. Furthermore, the enterprise itself is to no important degree an expression of popular will, for the town authorities are the representatives of a self-perpetuating, politically minded minority controlled from Merida. And, still further, most of the public work is now done by prison labor, and many of the prisoners who do the work have been brought to Dzitas, as the seat of a judicial district. And in Merida the direct contribution of labor has almost entirely disappeared. With trifling exception—in the poorest sections of the city the residents are supposed to keep the street in front of their houses free from weeds—public works are maintained out of taxes. Hansen's oldest informants were able to recall a time when fagina was common; even then it was an obligation of the poor only. To the Meridano fagina is a rustic custom of the villages.

In the villages the institution of fagina must be considered in connection with that called guardia. By the latter custom every adult male who is not yet about forty-five years old (and who in Chan Kom has not been comisario) is required to give one or two weeks of service at the seat of the local government. The men who must perform guardia constitute the age group of adult but not yet old men. Their service maintains the regular operations of local government. In Dzitas and in Merida there is no such duty; the officers of the municipal government, elected or imposed on the community, maintain the functions of government themselves or employ labor out of the municipal treasury. But in the villages it is of first importance. In the X-Cacal group of villages guardia is of much more importance than fagina, and there is less fagina there than there is in Chan Kom, although two generations ago, when Chan Santa Cruz was still occupied by the Quintana Roo Maya, many public works were accomplished through this institution. Nowadays, on the other hand, guardia is the institution which more than any other maintains the cacicazgo as a political and military unit ready for action. Each of the five companies into which the subtribe is divided, and which have already been mentioned in chapter ii, must take its turn in furnishing a guard of adult males whose duty it is to remain in armed alertness, protecting the sacred precinct of the Most Holy Cross, the supreme religious symbol of the group. The members of this guard are military sentinels; they are also functionaries at a cult. They determine admission to the sacred precinct; they receive candles brought by worshipers; and they report the arrival of written messages from *La Santísima*. Other men of the group remain at hand and may serve as messengers or as officers to make arrests or preserve order. The entire guard is a military unit ready to resist invasion, always thought to be threatened, by Mexican authorities.

In Chan Kom the institution of guardia[11] is similar in form but serves simply the functions of carrying on the ordinary work of municipal government. Members of the guard carry messages, make arrests, and otherwise do the tasks required by the comisario. The guard is made up, furthermore, out of the population of a single local community (the village and its politically dependent hamlets) and represents that group only; in Quintana Roo it is a military-religious institution representing an entire subtribe. The situation with reference to the existence and role of institutions of compulsory collective service for the community in the four communities may therefore be summed up as follows. In Quintana Roo the paramount institution is one in which all the men of the subtribe contribute regularly and collectively at one and the same time to the preservation of the military-political organization of the group and to the performance of the major religious cult of the group. In Chan Kom compulsory collective toil is also of fundamental importance, but the institutions which maintain it are of more local consequence and are nonreligious and solely administrative and political. In Dzitas compulsory collective labor is weakly present, and in Merida it is not present at all. In Tusik only is the centrally important worship of the group intimately associated with and indeed inseparable from the political organization of the group. And we may say not only does the political organization become disassociated from the religious cult but also that, as one leaves the villages and goes toward the city, compulsory collective toil becomes secularized before it disappears.

The reader is asked to recall the situation earlier summarized as to the kind of professionals or specialized functionaries present in the four communities: in Tusik, the Nohoch Tata, the maestros cantores, the shaman-priests (h-mens), a midwife or two, a few musicians, and the family that sells baskets; in Chan Kom, the maestros cantores, the h-mens, midwives, and bone-setters, a marriage negotiator, and also baker, storekeeper, mason, and barber; in Dzitas, no priests, no h-mens, no maestros cantores (but women, not professionals, who act as reciters of prayer), and a great number of artisans, tradespeople, teachers, and specialized laborers of several kinds; in Merida, the number and proportion of specialized practical workers is still greater, and of religious professionals and other practitioners of traditional esoteric knowledge there are almost none. Apparently the remark made in the last paragraph with reference to the secularization of collective labor as one goes from Tusik to Merida can be given wider extension. The entire division of labor is relatively more sacred, less secular, as a more remote community is compared with any of the other communities that lies nearer the city. In Tusik the specialists that do exist, with insignificant exceptions, are of the sort that may be called "sacred professionals."[12] They perform specialized functions that involve esoteric knowledge; they tend to transfer their art to a disciple; their role is conceived as the performance of a social duty and responsibility; their chief recompense is prestige, not money; much of what they do is sacred in that it cannot be carelessly profaned or despised. These qualities are in great degree present in the functions of the Nohoch Tata, the maestros cantores, the secretaries, the h-mens, and the marriage negotiator of Chan Kom; to a lesser degree it is true of the midwives, bone-setters, and herbal curers. These sacred professionals diminish in relative number as one moves toward the city, and some kinds disappear entirely while many wholly secular specialties appear. Ritual offices[13] give way to enterprises and jobs, and the offices that do remain or that appear are secular, not sacred, offices.

It is in the Tusik communities, also, that the sacred professionals attain their greatest degree of sanctity. The Nohoch Tata is the supreme authority of the group. He has temporal as well as religious power. Alone of all men he does not make milpa; he is sustained by funds collected at the sanctuary. He maintains seclusive habits; he does not mingle with ordinary folk; and it is taboo to criticize him or even to touch him. The Chan Kom and Dzitas people do not often come in contact with a priest of the church, but, when they do, their attitude toward him is certainly less reverent than that shown toward the Nohoch Tata of X-Cacal; nor does any member of the Roman hierarchy in Yucatan have anything like the direct authority over parishioners that the Nohoch Tata exercises. The maestros cantores of Quintana Roo help maintain the cult under his direction, and their prestige and power are greater than in the case of functionaries of the same name in Chan Kom who, in turn, are more considerable personages than the equivalent rezadoras of Dzitas and Merida. In X-Cacal the maestros cantores help perform (simplified) masses in the temple, and they are also allowed to baptize and perform marriages. In Chan Kom a maestro cantor performs no sacraments, but he is respected as one called by God to lead in novenas and prayers for the dead. A rezadora, finally, in the town or the city, is just a woman who knows the prayers and is respected to some degree for this interest and ability.

In comparison with the mystical prestige in Quintana Roo accorded the Nohoch Tata, the maestros cantores, and the secretaries (chap. ii), the prestige of the h-mens of the X-Cacal cacicazgo appears small. The status of the h-men of Chan Kom (at least before the reform spirit had grown strong) seems to have been greater, relative to that of other functionaries in that community, than that which the h-men of the

Tusik region enjoys in his community. This may be due to the exalted role of the Nohoch Tata, and the greater sanctity of the cult which he, the secretaries, and the maestros cantores maintain, or it may be due, as has already been proposed in chapter iv, to the accidental character and knowledge of the men who happen to be h-mens in the X-Cacal cacicazgo. Villa tells us that the h-mens of the south have less specialized esoteric knowledge than do those of the Chan Kom region; it appears also (as has been pointed out in chap. iv) that some of the pagan ceremonies known in Chan Kom are unknown in the Tusik communities. The cult of the yuntzilob is so much dependent for its form, interpretation, and preservation upon the few h-mens that such an event as the War of the Castes could easily interrupt its transmission in complete form.

There is one circumstance, however, in which the h-men's importance to the community is more fully expressed in Quintana Roo than it is in Chan Kom. In Tusik and X-Cacal a ceremony is performed which is apparently unknown, or at the least is not practiced, in Chan Kom. The ceremony is performed every two years to cleanse the h-men of evil winds lodged in him by reason of his close association with the yuntzilob and to establish good relations between him and the supernaturals. The ceremony involves lustrative rites and the observance of a period of seclusion by the h-men. It is felt that it is essential to the well-being of the entire community that the h-men make this ceremony, and it is accordingly expected that every family in the community will contribute meat, meal, or seasonings to the offerings made by the h-men on this occasion to the yuntzilob and to the evil winds. To the degree expressed by this ceremony and the sense of group responsibility which it represents, the h-men is, even more strongly here, a sacred professional, an organ of the moral and religious life of the community. In this detail, as in others recounted in this chapter, special functions are, in the village, sacred and discharged by the community through a functionary with corresponding prestige. In the town and city they are general, secular, and discharged by an individual on his own account.

The differences among the four communities that have been discussed in this chapter are in large degree involved with differences as to commercialism. Tusik is certainly more commercial than many primitive societies. But, as compared with Dzitas or Merida, it is certainly far less commercial. This relatively insignificant commercialism consists not simply in the fact that there is less buying and selling. It consists also in a relative disinclination to deal with a friend and neighbor in such a way as to regard him as an opportunity for a practical advantage that can be expressed in terms of money. A person is one toward whom one acts through the medium of such human and sympathetic sentiments as one would one's self find pleasant or unpleasant. A customer is one whom one may use to obtain a commodity or a price. Whatever may be the circumstances under which the roles of person and customer may be combined, the situation in Tusik, like that in many primitive societies, suggests a disposition under certain circumstances to keep these roles separate. There is not much buying or selling among members of the settlement or the cacicazgo. When a native takes half a cent from a neighbor in exchange for an egg, and asks an outsider fifteen cents for the same, he is not so much, in either case, trying to consummate an exchange which will accrue to his advantage as he is in the one case expressing his good will and in the other his ill will or at least his lack of sympathy and confidence. The transaction is not genuinely commercial. One may suppose that the frequent situations in which one native agrees for a compensation to aid another in the work of the milpa are not completely commercial either; the compensation is a share of the crop; it is not money or a part of another sort of crop. The milpero shares his crop with one who helps him get that crop. The laborer works for another because it is maize that he lacks, and he works so that he may have maize to eat. The amount is fixed by tradition; therefore, one party to the arrangement is not put in the position of bargaining with another.

Related is the fact that the range of goods within which pecuniary valuation is possible, with either insider or outsider, is more restricted in such a community as Tusik than in a town or city. The native makes and consumes most of what he uses, and to this extent is unused to expressing the value of such articles to him or to another in terms of money. The chicle boom must have suddenly increased the number of goods so valued. Nevertheless, some very important goods— land, houses, and maize—are in Tusik outside, or almost outside, of the realm of valuation in money. Such goods are, of course, measured in terms of the effort required to produce them or to bring them into use. But as one does not buy or sell them, the relationship to them remains simply between the worker and the goods; the connections between the worker and his land or his house are the personal circumstances of his efforts; he does not have to think whether the goods would attract a buyer.

The attitude a man has in Tusik toward such a specialty as that of maestro cantor also has this noncommercial quality. This sort of specialty is not conceived as something that is to be sold at a practical advantage. It is a duty and a privilege, and its exercise is indorsed by feelings of obligation which are not practical but rather moral and religious. Even the discharge of work for the benefit of the entire group, in the institution called guardia, onerous as it is, is outside of money valuation. One cannot hire another to take one's place in this any more than one can hire a substitute godfather.

There is a sphere of relations, in short, within which bargaining and commercial valuation are out of the question, and another in which such are usual and proper. To some extent the former sphere coincides with the area of personal relations of the family, the settlement, and the cacicazgo, but there is also a degree of overlapping. Commercial dealings are not excluded from the in-group. Yet the reluctance to extend them

in this direction is to be observed. It appears that relationships defined as personal and confidential resist conversion into
commercial terms. After the abolition of peonage in Yucatan
it was not uncommon, nevertheless, for workers to refuse to
accept the employer-employee relationship but to expect a
continuance of the personal and human relationship of patronage, wherein the patron looked after his worker's needs while
the worker took care of other requirements of the patron. At
any rate the relatively noncommercial character of the Tusik
society appears if one places it in contrast with societies in the
highlands of Guatemala known to the writer. There, to give
a single example, the young daughter of the leader of the
religious brotherhood maintaining the cult of the Child Jesus,
and extending hospitality to all his neighbors on Christmas
Eve, decided to open a little store and sell sweets to her
father's guests and the Child's worshipers.

In this chapter the division of labor in the peripheral communities has been declared to be more sacred and less secular
than that characterizing the town and the city. The coinci-
dence in Yucatan of the more sacred with the less commercial,
and of the more secular with the more commercial, will be
mentioned again in this report. The relationship between the
development of commerce and the secularization of society
has been urged by more than one writer for Western European society.[14] Whether commercialization tends in Yucatan
to diminish the hold and sphere of religious and moral life, and
how it does it, if it does, are questions that cannot be answered
by these materials. One may, by the exercise of imagination,
suppose that, if one must think of one's land as something to
be made attractive to a possible purchaser, this may to some
extent interfere with that course of thinking about that land
which conceives it as a seat of deity and a privilege granted by
awesome supernaturals whom one must propitiate. But perhaps it is not difficult to maintain both attitudes. The native
seems to have established two compartments of thought with
regard to the maize itself. To the native of Tusik one's son

cannot go outside of the group without, practically speaking, being lost to one. A father in Dzitas entertains the possibility that a son may find work in the city or abroad and perhaps send money home, and so he may encourage the son to leave. Does this circumstance affect adversely the traditional attitudes maintaining between family members? It is not clear to the writer if and how it does. The secularization of life is to be reported in the town and in the city, but commercialization is only one of a number of possible influential factors. Another is the disorganization of the web of meanings which we call "culture," and still another is the direct example of secular habits of thought provided by the people of the more sophisticated communities.

CHAPTER VIII

FAMILY ORGANIZATION AND
DISORGANIZATION

IN THE course of the last chapter progressive differences among the four communities were reported which might be included under the general statement that in the peripheral communities, as compared with the less peripheral, the rights and activities of any individual tend more to involve the rights and activities of others. In the villages actions and attitudes take a more nearly joint or collective form; in the town and the city the same or corresponding institution gives greater opportunity for the independence of the individual. This general difference has been illustrated in the changing emphasis from specialized functions which are performed on behalf of the community to those discharged for the specialist's own benefit; in the development of individual rights in land and in conjugal estates; and in the diminution or disappearance of collective labor and of the exchange of services in connection with civic enterprises and religious worship. A consideration of the entire body of materials from the point of view suggested by this generalization results in the conclusion that increasing individualization is only incidentally to be recognized in changes in the division of labor and in property rights. The focus of these changes lies in the weakening of the familial organization. In the culturally well-organized villages social relations are in large degree those of kinship; and, when such an event as a marriage or a domestic ritual occurs, it is the families that are acting, so to speak, through individuals. In the town and in the city, on the other hand, the individual seems to be struggling to act in spite of the family groups. These statements are, of course, metaphorical exaggerations. They may stand as introductions to a chapter reporting differences in familial institutions in the communities studied.

Hansen's account of Merida emphasizes the breakdown of an old kinship organization in the recent history of that city. In chapter vi of this book brief reference was made to similar changes in Dzitas. Even in Chan Kom a difference between the more highly disciplined and self-consistent family system of two generations ago and the more recent situation is something of which older people are aware. In this feature of social life especially, changes have been rapid in recent years, and much more rapid in the city and in the town than in either of the villages. With regard to the subordination of the individual to the expectations and demands of his family group, the old situation even in Merida was perhaps more like the present situation in Tusik than it is like the present situation in Merida. If this statement were to be justified, it would probably be to the recent, and even today still partly persisting, situation in the aristocracy of the city that one would turn. The conservative propertied class, like the primitive Indian villager, depended for its organization on a tight family system. Both systems—that of the villager and that of the urban aristocrat—involved strong control by the old over the young and of women by men, marriages made for the interests of family groups, formalization of marriages, and the sanction of religion upon the family structure. In these respects Tusik preserves what the older upper-class Meridano is very conscious of being in process of losing.

This comparison is by the way. As usual in this volume, the comparison must be made between contemporary situations in the four communities, for there the materials are ample enough to allow it. A beginning will be made with the familial institutions in the Quintana Roo villages. These institutions cannot be assumed to be equivalent to, or even very similar to, the kinship institutions that prevailed among the Maya at the time of the Conquest. There is some evidence[1] that at that time the Yucatec Maya were organized in exogamous patrilineal groups. It has also been suggested, from a study of the kinship terms preserved in the Motul dictionary, that they observed bilateral cross-cousin marriage.[2] But of such institutions there is today no trace in Quintana Roo,[3] although exogamous patrilineal name-groups are still present among the Lacandones[4] and among the Tzeltal.[5] Although the differences as to kinship institutions which are reported below in many cases correspond to the differing degrees to which aboriginal elements are preserved in the periphery (e.g., the custom of service for the bride and temporary matrilocal residence and the importance of the hetzmek custom, both in Tusik), the differences are not invariably of that character. Thus the fact that it is only in the Quintana Roo villages that there exists a strong inhibition against marriage with a first or second cousin is probably to be attributed not to the survival of a pagan element but rather to the survival of a European Catholic element. Injunctions as to the Catholic impediments to marriage were included in Bishop Toral's diocesan instructions to the priests of Yucatan issued in 1565. This illustration repeats the general observation as to the survival of Catholic elements in Quintana Roo already made in chapter iv.

The principal differences among the family organizations characteristic of the four communities have to do not with their forms but with their relative stability and with the definition and importance of the rights and responsibilities recognized to exist among kindred. Throughout Yucatan the elementary (small parental) family is normal, and throughout Yucatan there are occasional extended domestic families which have social approval. In Tusik marriages are very enduring; there is no divorce, and either desertion or adultery is punished by the local authorities with flogging. A man and woman who have undertaken matrimony are expected to continue to live together, and sanctions, sacred and secular, enforce this expectation. A deserting husband is subject to reli-

gious, familial, and civil sanctions. Further, quarrels within
the family are uncommon. During Villa's residence he heard
of only one case in which a man struck his wife and of no case
in which a woman attempted violence against her husband,
and he further tells us that extra-marital sex relations are extremely rare (though cases occurred). When a young couple
are established in marriage, their adult life is assured; the relations they are to have to each other, to the kinsmen of each,
and to the sponsors of their marriage are fixed. Widowhood
does not release a woman from the control of her close male
relatives or from the tribal sanctions. Brief summaries of some
of Villa's cases from Quintana Roo may give a little substance
to what is barely stated in these lines: (1) a jealous husband,
suspicious of his wife, made her so uncomfortable that she
complained to her father (in whose house they were living).
The father warned the husband, who then left his wife. Later,
wishing to return to her, he was required to suffer a punishment of fifty lashes. The father suggested the punishment,
which was enforced by the chiefs of the man's company. (2)
A man who allowed his daughter to have sexual relations with
a married man was punished with fifty lashes, and the married
man with twenty-five. The girl, as the ward of her father, the
guiltiest party, was not punished. (3) A widow with children,
living with her brother, agreed at her brother's suggestion to
marry a certain man but thereafter, regretting of the agreement, left his home and returned to her mother. For this she
was punished with twenty-five lashes.

In Chan Kom the situation is similar, but the stability of
the elementary family is less, and the sanctions that conduce to
stability are less severe. Intrafamilial disputes there are rare,
although they are more frequent than in Tusik; desertion does
occur, and divorce is not entirely unknown.[6] In Chan Kom
a wife's adultery is still an offense against the husband, for
which he may punish the wife or bring about her punishment,
but it is not a reason for breaking up a marriage. And the
cases of desertion or of separation that did occur in Chan

Kom were all cases in which there were no small children of the couple. Yet in Chan Kom a man who tires of his wife may escape to a town; a girl who bears another man's child soon after marriage may run away similarly. These things are much more likely to occur in Chan Kom than in Tusik. In Dzitas separation, desertion, and divorce are common; marriages are brittle; many people have a number of consorts successively. The notion that a woman should endure everything from her husband without turning against him is preserved by the older people as an ideal, but in fact domestic disputes are notoriously common. There are even cases where a woman strikes her husband and then brings suit for divorce and secures a share of the family property. Opportunities for employment are open to women; there are women who prefer employment in Merida to being a wife in Dzitas, and say so. It is difficult in cases to tell when an elementary family comes into existence, because a man may sleep occasionally with a woman without public recognition until the association reaches such social acceptance that the woman comes to be called his "*esposa*"; yet he may have a legal wife in some other community and may be maintaining that home also. In Merida, too, desertion is frequent, and new elementary families are often set up without formality and at the expense of previously existing families. Legal divorce, though the rate is not so high as it was earlier in the Revolution, is probably resorted to more readily in the city than anywhere else.[7] The family quarrels that characterize many families in Dzitas are, from the evidence of Hansen's many cases, even more common in Merida. The triangle situation provides the principal occasion for the exercise of that black magic which, rare in the villages, flourishes in the city. The instability of the urban family finds one expression in the fact that wives of the masses are likely, at one time or another, to imagine themselves to be the victims of sorcery practiced by their rivals. This subject will be treated in more detail later in this volume.

It is in Tusik, and among some conservative people in vil-

lages in the Chan Kom region, that the extended domestic
family with patriarchal-matriarchal control is still to be found,
although there, as elsewhere, it is very much the exception. In
these households the father directs his married sons in the
making of a common milpa, while his wife maintains the
domestic funds and supervises the work of her daughters-in-
law and unmarried daughters. In Dzitas such households are
remembered and a few are spoken of as existing in neighboring communities, but the compound households that do exist
represent the sharing of a common roof by several related
married couples for reasons of economy. In these cases there is
no common treasury or milpa and little or no parental authority. Mothers ask sons who are living with them for maize and
hesitate to ask daughters-in-law to carry the maize to the mill
to be ground, lest the request be met with a refusal. Such compound families, both in Dzitas and in Merida, give rise to frequent disputes about money and about the control of children.
In the villages it is the father who tends to exert control over a
married son; in Merida, and also in Dzitas, it is more often his
mother, responsive to older tradition, who seeks to exert some
control over him and who expects respect and obedience from
his wife. Conflicts between a mother-in-law and a daughter-
in-law over the son and husband are common, both in compound families and in cases where separate households are set
up by the young couple. For example, a young man living in
a separate establishment with his wife is expected by his mother to make some contribution—perhaps the weekly supply of
sugar—to the household of his parents. The wife objects; the
young man either brings the sugar surreptitiously or arouses
the anger of his mother against his wife. Many households in
Dzitas have this character: they are neither wholly independent of the parental family nor are they interdependent with it
in ways that all its members understand and approve.

Villa reports from Quintana Roo cases in which sons do not
show the obedience to their fathers which is expected and are
not punished. Parental authority is not severe or tyrannical.

Nevertheless, the respect and obedience expected by a father of his son is most nearly realized in Quintana Roo. It is clear that dispute or open conflict between father and son which is not infrequent in Dzitas is very rare in Tusik. In Dzitas it is a matter of frequent lamentation by older persons that the young people do not respect their parents. It is remembered that children used to address their parents with the respectful form of speech, while now they are taught in the school to use the direct form. Some sons are attentive to their mothers, sending them food from time to time and responding to their requests, while others neglect their indigent mothers, residents of the same community, and allow them to go to more distant relatives or acquaintances for assistance. The discipline of young children is a source of evident worry in Dzitas, while in Merida, among the more sophisticated, expression is given to varying theories as to how children should be brought up, and among all classes corporal punishment is often unregularized and capricious.

The general principles of the family in Yucatan further provide that at the death of a father some other male member of the family shall assume responsibility and authority. This successor is normally the eldest son, if he be grown. In conformity with this expectation older brothers (as indicated in chap. v) are respected by younger brothers. An older brother may command; a younger, only request. The authority of the elder brother is greatest in Tusik and is also well recognized in Chan Kom. One looks up to one's zucuun and one comes to him for help or advice if members of the elder generation are not available. Dzitas again provides a variety of inconsistent instances. There is an occasional family in which a younger brother will rise when his zucuun enters or will throw away his cigarette; and older people will say that in mourning the period should be equally long for the death of an elder brother (but not for a younger) as in the case of the death of a father. Nevertheless, younger brothers more often than not regard their status as about equivalent to that of their zucuun, and there is little overt expression of the respect relationship. In Merida, too, control by an elder brother over a younger is often resented by the latter, and there is little respect unless the age difference is great. Hansen tells us that the terms approximately equivalent to zucuun and *idzin*, *hermano* and *hermanito*, appear to be going out of use, *hermano mayor* and *hermano menor* being used instead. As for the respect due an elder sister by a younger, its existence in Dzitas would not have been noted at all had the investigators not found it actually present in the villages.

The attitudes and practices which define the elementary family and its extension into a great family composed of related elementary families are, in summary, less well defined and less self-consistent as we go from Tusik to Merida. It is in the more peripheral communities that the activities of the individual are most subordinated to the functioning of the family as a unit. Something to the same effect may be said with regard to the great family. Here again the fundamental patterns of kinship are the same throughout the peninsula: kinship is recognized on both sides, as evidenced in the bilateral restrictions on marriage with kin and in the participation of relatives both on the father's side and on the mother's side in familial deliberations; on the other hand, the patrilinear side receives emphasis through the transmission of surnames through that line and as a result of the relatively greater authority of males. Nowhere is the great family a well-defined unit. Yet the definition is the clearest in the villages, and in Quintana Roo especially there are institutions, absent elsewhere, which maintain a certain cohesion in the patrilineal groups. One of these is the custom whereby a man ordinarily sets up his household, when he marries, in a house near that of his father. So brothers seek to maintain intimate contact with one another, and so it comes about that a settlement is made up of clusters of adjacent houses containing elementary families of which the males are related by blood. Along with this custom goes that whereby every newly married man secures a

cross to stand for him and his elementary family, and by which
these crosses are often kept in an oratory sheltering the crosses
of several brothers or other men related in the male line.
Moreover, certain crosses, originally representatives of elementary families, come to take on special prestige and sacred
quality and to stand for the entire patrilineal group. There
are five such great-family crosses, each with its oratory, in
Tusik. In these cases the annual festival of that cross is a matter for the lineage group: brothers, fathers, and uncles may
participate in the festival.

In Chan Kom it is remembered when crosses and santos
were kept in separate oratories, but nowadays santos are kept
in the house or left in the village church. There is no custom of
obtaining a cross for each household, and the obligation to maintain the cult of the santo one owns does not extend with any
clearness outside of the elementary family that owns it. That
is to say, if a man owns a santo, one of his sons will inherit
it and take over the duty, his alone, to recognize the day of
that saint in the calendar. Patrilocal residence is the rule also
in Chan Kom, but exceptions do occur of residence near the
wife's father; and there are many instances of young men setting up their households at some distance from their father's
house. In Chan Kom there are many elementary families that
do not form parts of well-recognized great families, but, on the
other hand, there are a few great families, patrilineally connected, that show considerable solidarity. Two of these in particular manifested rivalry throughout the period of the observations in spite of the fact that they had intermarried. Several disputes occurred between these two groups, at one time
amounting to a factional division of the community.[8] The introduction of Protestantism was facilitated by the fact that one
of these two family groups found in conversion to the new cult
an opportunity for leadership and status denied its members by
the dominance of the other great family in local affairs. In
Dzitas great-family household clusters are less common, there
is no religious cult depending upon lineages, and in fact great

families have little strength or definition of outline. Here, as in Merida, the great family is recognizable chiefly in the use of terms (nephew, uncle, cousin, etc.), by the tendency to choose friends and godparents from its members, in the preference given such kin in asking or in granting aid, and in the disposition for relatives to come together at such crises as death and at social occasions. The patronymic group, or the group of male relatives with their wives and children, hardly exists, except as pride in the family name among members of the upper class. These differences as to the great family may be summarized by briefly contrasting the two extreme situations. In Merida the fact that one is related to someone else, outside of the elementary family, affects the behavior of individuals with regard to each other, but the great family does not conventionally act as a defined and recognizable group. In Quintana Roo one may recognize the existence and the functioning of such a group in the settlement of adjacent houses of related men and their wives and in the cult of the lineage cross which certain of these groups maintain.

The included diagrams summarize the kinship terminologies in use in three of the four communities. Hansen's materials do not include confirmation by genealogical method of terms in Merida, but it is very probable that the terms used there are closely similar to or identical with those used in Dzitas. These, as will be indicated below, are practically the equivalent, term for term, of terms used in Maya discourse. A comparison of the three systems confirms certain general conclusions reached as to differences in kinship behavior in the communities in that certain of the differences in terms are consistent with the reported differences in behavior. But other features of the terminologies do not seem to express corresponding conventional behavior and so raise other questions. The matter is complicated by the fact that each of the societies is changing, and the terms may in part represent kinship institutions that have disappeared. An examination of the diagrams representing the three communities will show that the Chan

Kom system resembles that of Dzitas more closely than it does that of Tusik. Then, as the Chan Kom people separated from those of Quintana Roo less than a hundred years ago, the changes represented in the difference between the Chan Kom system and that of Tusik must have taken place within that time.

The only data on early Yucatec kinship terms known to the writer is the analysis of the terms listed in the Beltran and Motul dictionaries published by Eggan.[9] These terms are apparently those in use toward the end of the sixteenth century. This system is very different from that now current in Quintana Roo. This is not the place to make a comparison in detail. The old system included a tendency to link alternate generations through the use of the same or similar terms; this tendency is entirely unrepresented now. The old terms for affinal relatives were numerous and made fine distinctions; these are almost wholly gone. The terminological distinction made among the grandparents of the same sex have also given way to a simple pair of terms consistent with Spanish categories in regard to these relatives. Although Villa's materials from Quintana Roo are not full enough to declare completely on the point, it is also apparently true that the present system is without most or all of those terminological correspondences between certain consanguineous and certain affinal relatives which Eggan found to suggest the existence of bilateral cross-cousin marriage. Like the Spanish terms, those of the ancient Maya in most cases indicated the sex of the relative; of course, that tendency is present in the Tusik terms. The old Maya terms also indicated the sex of the speaker in many terms used for the descending generations; the Tusik terms do not indicate it except in that a woman calls her sister's child by the same term she uses for her own child, while a man has a different term for his sister's child. The present system is like the old in the emphasis on seniority among the speaker's siblings and in the extension of these terms to certain cousins (although the extension is now somewhat different) and to relatives-in-law.

TUSIK—CONSANGUINEOUS RELATIVES

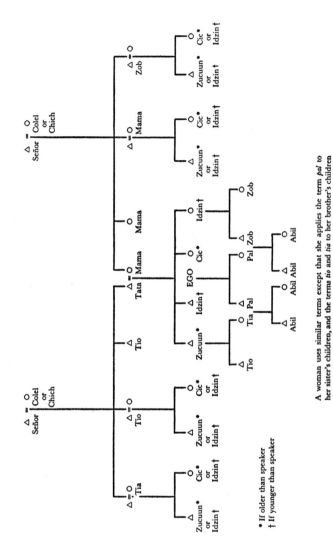

* If older than speaker
† If younger than speaker

A woman uses similar terms except that she applies the term *pal* to her sister's children, and the terms *tio* and *tia* to her brother's children

198

TUSIK—AFFINAL RELATIVES

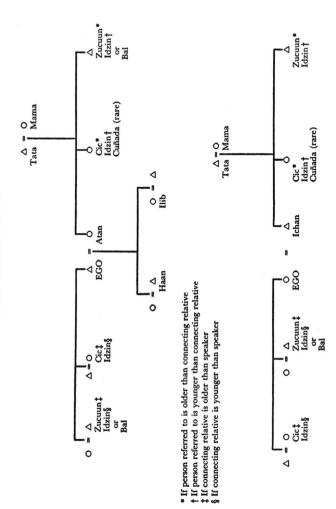

* If person referred to is older than connecting relative
† If person referred to is younger than connecting relative
‡ If connecting relative is older than speaker
§ If connecting relative is younger than speaker

199

CHAN KOM—CONSANGUINEOUS RELATIVES

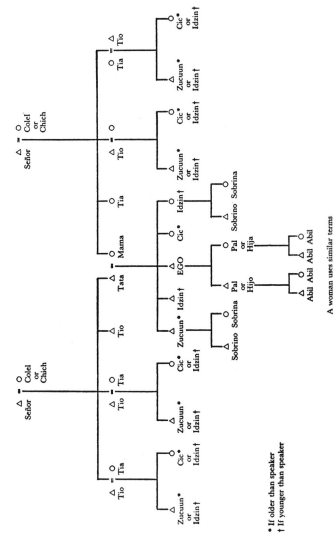

* If older than speaker
† If younger than speaker

A woman uses similar terms

CHAN KOM—AFFINAL RELATIVES

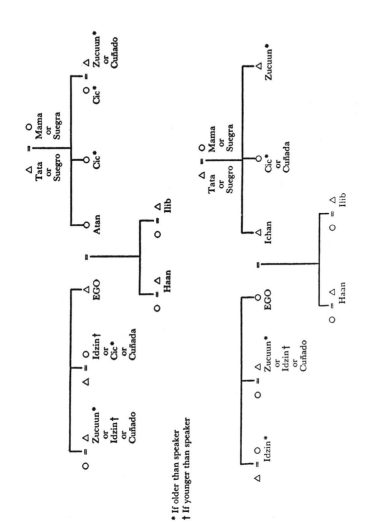

* If older than speaker
† If younger than speaker

201

DZITAS—CONSANGUINEOUS RELATIVES

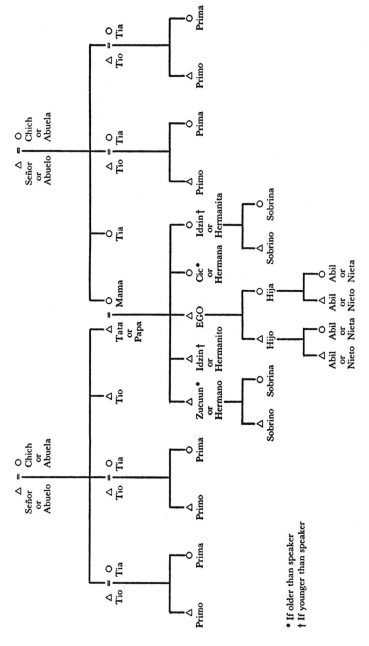

* If older than speaker
† If younger than speaker

A woman uses similar terms

DZITAS—AFFINAL RELATIVES

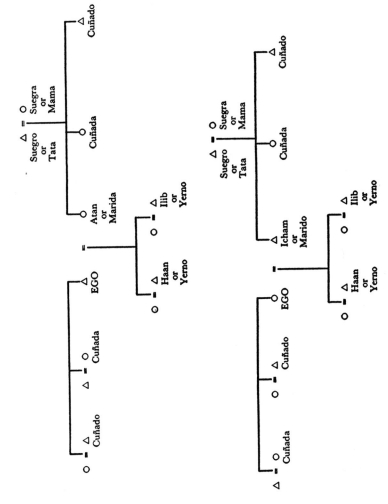

The sixteenth-century system was "classificatory" in that a father's brother was called "little father" (as also the mother's sister's husband) and in that the mother's sister (and also a man's father's brother's wife) was called "little mother," while there were special terms for mother's brother and for father's sister. A man called his brother's son by the same term he called his own son but used a special term for his sister's son. A woman called her sister's child by the same term as she called her own children but addressed her brother's children by a different term. The present terminology in Tusik includes the use of the "mother" term for mother's sister, while the father's sister is called by another term. Also, a woman calls her sister's child by the same term as she calls her own child (but not by the same term which anciently she used). On the other hand, a father's brother is now terminologically distinguished from the father, and a man does not call his brother's offspring by the same terms which he uses for his own children.

In view of the relative emphasis upon the father-line, already indicated, it might be argued that the equivalence of siblings of the same sex would be a matter of greater importance among brothers than among sisters and that therefore we might expect the reverse of what in Tusik is the case and anticipate a terminological identification of father and father's brother rather than of mother and mother's sister. On the other hand, it might be argued that the importance of age distinctions is greater among males than among females, that making such a distinction would restrict any tendency to identify terminologically the father and the father's brother, and that therefore what we find in Tusik is just what we might expect. Speculation on the point does not seem fruitful. It seems safer to admit that no clear reason appears, from what is known of Tusik society, why it should be more necessary, or natural, or functional to distinguish the mother from the mother's sister than to distinguish the father from the father's brother.

There are also, in the Tusik list, certain reciprocal terms

which apparently do not conform to any special relations of reciprocity between the relatives so terminologically identified. A single term denotes both a man's sister's child and a mother's brother. One's brother's children and the siblings of one's father are also grouped together: the Spanish words *tio* and *tia* are used for all these relatives, the masculine form applying to male relatives of the group and the feminine form to both the nieces and the aunts. Nothing has been reported for Quintana Roo that would single out these pairs of relatives as of special complementary significance. Nor does it readily appear that these usages are survivals from early times. In the list published by Eggan different terms occur for a man's sister's child and a mother's brother, and, although it is true that according to that list a man called his brother's children by the same term that he called his own children, there are no terms used both for avuncular and for niece or nephew relationships. Neither the little we know of antecedent usages nor the fuller knowledge we have of current kinship attitudes provides an explanation for these reciprocal terms.

Other features of the Tusik system are consistent with conventional behavior already reported. In conformity with the social emphasis upon seniority, especially among persons of one's own generation, brothers and sisters are distinguished as to whether they are older or younger than the speaker. Furthermore, in accordance with the disposition to regard other collateral relatives of the same generation as more distant siblings, the terms are applied to first cousins, to spouse's siblings, and to siblings' spouses.[10] There are other features of the terminological usages which do not appear from the diagrams but which are also expressive of the prevailing attitudes. The terms for mother and father are almost regularly applied to the parents-in-law. The Quintana Roo native usually marries by the institution called "son-in-law service" (*haan-cab*): a man lives temporarily under his father-in-law's roof, owing him much of the obedience of a son. After a fixed period the couple move to the house of the man's father or to a house near it; the wife is expected to show respect and obedience to her mother-in-law.[11] If Eggan's interpretation of the older terms is correct, in the sixteenth century a man called his parents-in-law by the same term (*han* and *ix han*) which he applied to his mother's brother, because he looked to his mother's brother to provide him with a wife in the person of one of his daughters. But later, it may be suggested, with the disappearance of the custom of cross-cousin marriage, and the persistence of the custom of temporary matrilocal residence with the obligation to work for one's father-in-law in exchange for one's wife[12]—now no longer one's cousin because the priests forbade it—the father and mother terms came to be applied to the parents-in-law. A woman was already calling her husband's father "great father."[13]

The hierarchy of age and authority outside of the elementary family and the parent-in-law relationships is also, in Quintana Roo, frequently expressed by appropriate terms. The word for "father" is applied by extension to other persons toward whom the speaker bears special sonlike relationships: to the chiefs of his own company (but not to the chiefs of other companies) and to the male sponsor of his marriage. The priestly leader of the entire community is to everyone the "Great Father" (Nohoch Tata). The fact that almost any old person is respected is expressed in the use of honorific parental terms for such persons: *tatich* and *mamich*.

The terms of the Tusik system, it will be noted, are linguistically Maya with three or four exceptions (*mama, tio, tia, cuñada*).[14] The Chan Kom list of terms includes additional Spanish terms: *hijo, sobrino, suegro,* cuñado, while the term *zob* is not used, and the term *lak*, much used in Tusik for any sibling, is apparently falling into disuse in Chan Kom. The Chan Kom terminology differs from that of Tusik in respects which can be interpreted in part as modifications bringing the system into closer conformity with the European terms and corresponding categories and in part as changes consistent with differences in the social organization of the two societies. With reference to the former, there is to be noted the fact that the classificatory use of the term for mother and that for child as applied to a woman's sister's daughter do not occur in Chan Kom. None of the Chan Kom terms merge lineal and collateral relatives. The reciprocal use of terms for the uncle-aunt-niece-nephew relationships are also absent in Chan Kom, and in their place are the two pairs of Spanish terms, tio and tia, sobrino and sobrina, used as in Europe.

The terminological differences to be noted in Chan Kom that have evident consistency with differences in social organization express a diminution of the tendency to extend terms with primary significance for members of the elementary family to more remote relatives or to persons not related to the speaker at all. The differences, therefore, amount to a shrinkage of the group of persons who are treated in terms of rights and obligations appropriate to kinship relationships or to an expression of a reduction in the strength or importance of these rights and obligations in the cases of more remote individuals. The terms *primo* and *prima* are coming into use, the term "zucuun" tends to be used for older male first cousins only where the difference in age is considerable; a man who does not feel any particular respect for a cousin who is an approximate age mate will call him by his first name or explain that he is a cousin. The use of the corresponding term for older sister is even more rarely used for female cousins. The Spanish terms for parent-in-law are available to the son- or daughter-in-law who does not want to express a filial attitude toward his or her parent-in-law; and these terms are not infrequently used in place of *tata* and mama. The marriage sponsor is called "padrino," the relationship is considerably less important than it is in Tusik, and to call this ceremonial kinsman "father" would seem inappropriate. Finally, there are in Chan Kom no chiefs or priests to be called "father," and the general terms of respect for older persons, although they would no doubt be recognized in Chan Kom, probably sound quite old fashioned there. In Chan Kom the use of kinship terms tends to be limited to persons who are really kin, and to the closest of these.

What remains in Chan Kom of the extended use of kinship terms is the use of older-brother terms for distinctly older male cousins, of the sibling terms for brothers- and sisters-in-law, and of the parent terms for parents-in-law when sympathy and affection are felt. In Dzitas, at least among the Maya-speaking native vecino people of Dzitas, these features (with the exception of the last which is, of course, common in Europe and North America) are gone. A zucuun is one's own elder brother. The Spanish terms for brother- and sister-in-law are used in Maya discourse. There remains a system of terms which may be translated into equivalent Spanish terms. This translation is, of course, frequently made, for both languages are spoken in Dzitas. The system is one which does not carry the feelings of kinship much beyond cousins and grandparents, and in which the closer relatives are terminologically distinguished from those more remote. This comparison of kinship terminologies may therefore be concluded with the formulation of a general observation that, just as the importance of attitudes and behavior toward more distant relatives or toward persons who are not relatives declines as one goes from Tusik to Chan Kom to Dzitas, so, in a considerable degree, do the terms used change so that kinship terms are not applied to these more distant persons, or so that terms indicating greater relative distance are applied to them.

These differences cannot be dismissed by saying that all that is involved is the change from a Maya system of terms to a European system. The latter will also vary according to the state of the social organization. The European system, in the form in which it appears in Dzitas, does not have application to very distant relatives; and, in using it, people are uncertain as to its limits or confused as to what term should be applied to more distant kinsmen. This reflects the fact that family connections are not strong in Dzitas and that one is not sure whether to treat a more remote relative as a kinsmen, or how to treat him. The terms are used or misused much as they are in North American cities. By what term shall I address my father's first cousin? The word "cousin" is available as a sort of catch-all for all distant connections; but, if the man is much older than I and exhibits a fatherly interest in me, I may well call him "uncle," if I call him by any kinship term at all. The European terminology is, however, adjustable to a society in which distant relationships are recognized and in which the outlines of the kinship group are well defined. Among the Spanish-speaking peasants (*Ladinos*) of the western highlands of Guatemala, as the writer can report from his own knowledge, the terminological system is entirely European, very extensive, and definite in its expression. The word for cousin is applied to a parent's sibling's child (distinguished as primo hermano), to a grandparent's sibling's child's child, and to children of these on down. The uncle and aunt terms are applied to siblings of parents, to siblings of grandparents, and on up. They are also applied to first cousins of parents, but no further—not to children of grandparents' first cousins. By extension ("*político*"), these terms may be applied to spouses of the parents' siblings and very rarely to spouses of other "uncles" and "aunts." "Sobrino" and "sobrina" are applied to children of siblings, and to their children on down, and to children of parents' siblings' children and their children on down; these terms are not extended to spouses. Even young persons in these societies can give one genealogies with accompanying terms, all without uncertainty and with complete inner consistency. In Dzitas this cannot be done because the family system itself is less systematic.

Before summarizing the foregoing discussion, the reader may be reminded of the procedure adopted in the comparison of the kinship institutions of the several communities, as a specific illustration of the general method employed in the investigations on which this book is based. The differences here reported were discovered, first, because questions were asked of the facts suitable to the discovery of this kind of differences and, second, because plenty of case materials were secured indicating how events work themselves out characteristically in the several communities. The questions asked were of the following sort: To what extent does the society exist in institutions and relationships of kinship? How standardized is behavior with reference to kinship and the family? To what extent does the behavior of the individual conventionally depend upon and involve certain kindred? The questions which guided this inquiry were asked, by implication at least, when Henry Maine wrote of the supposed historic change whereby society from being a system of families had become an aggregation of individuals. As one examines, in the several communities, instances of the arranging of marriages, of the selecting of godparents, and of disputes involving families, one receives at least partial answers to these questions and finds, also, further questions arising.

One would with difficulty, if at all, arrive at the determination of the differences reported here if one attended merely to the forms of familial institutions. If one asked if certain institutions, listed in advance, were or were not present, one would secure answers that would certainly obscure the differences here discussed. Does the culture of Tusik include elementary families? It does, and so does that of Merida. Are there bilateral kinship, transmission of the surname through the father, respect for elder brothers, separate terms for older and younger brothers? The answer might well be affirmative to questions as to all these elements in all the communities. On the other hand, elements which might be reported as absent in Merida and present in Tusik, or vice versa, would, after all, not reveal the differences essential to the inquiry as it is here defined: son-in-law service, lineage crosses, reciprocal terms, divorce. One wants to know the way in which each custom enters into the total life of the community. What must be known about the respect for elder brothers, for example, is just how serious is the attitude, under what sorts of situations is it manifest, and with what sanctions of ritual or religion is it provided. An in-

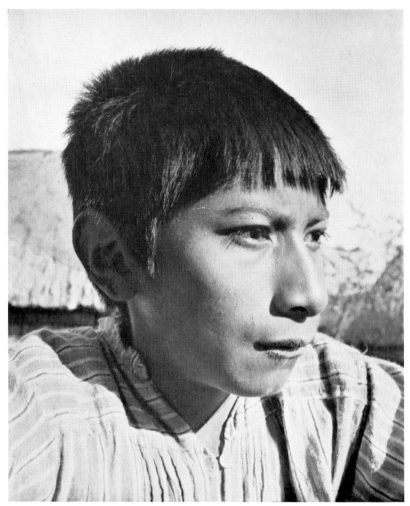

Photograph by Frances Rhoads Morley

stitution recognizable as formally the same in two societies may, in its total role in the life of each society, be quite a different institution. Of course, the differences as to elder-brother respect in Merida and in Tusik might be resolved into a large number of more restricted elements of culture—is it customary to deliver an order to a younger brother but not an elder; if a girl is to be married will her elder brother, in the absence of her father, give or withhold approval to her marriage? etc.— but these more special questions can hardly be formulated until, by acquaintance with the societies through case materials and direct observation, one already knows so much about them that the questions with which one began are already answered. A culture trait is what you make it.

In returning to the comparison of kinship institutions, the writer may summarize the conclusions already advanced. As one goes from Tusik toward Merida there is to be noted a reduction in the stability of the elementary family; a decline in the manifestation of patriarchal or matriarchal authority; a disappearance of institutions expressing cohesion in the great family; a reduction in the strength and importance of respect relationships, especially for elder brothers and for elder people generally; an increasing vagueness of the conventional outlines of appropriate behavior toward relatives; and a shrinkage in the applicability of kinship terms primarily denoting members of the elementary family toward more distant relatives or toward persons not relatives. Attention may now be turned toward the customs with regard to marriage.

Mention has already been made of the fact that in Tusik there is strong reluctance to marry a first or second cousin. Indeed, such marriages are not allowed, in spite of the small number of persons with whom marriage is possible. One may not marry the daughter of one's parent's compadre. It is also forbidden to marry a deceased spouse's sibling. (The existence of explanatory myths for this custom has been noted.) And, further, a widower may not marry a girl who has not before been married. These restrictions on marriage, based chiefly on real or ceremonial kinship, are most strict in the Quintana Roo villages. In Chan Kom the restriction on marriage with a deceased spouse's sibling is gone. Marriages with a first cousin are still much disapproved, but there are socially approved marriages with relatives of the degree of distance of second cousins. Although the relationship is regarded as making the marriage to some degree unsuitable, yet there is much support for these marriages even among the more religious and morally demanding in the community. In Chan Kom we did not encounter any rule or restriction against marriage of a widower with a girl never before married. In Dzitas there is little or no reluctance, among most of the population, to marry even first cousins, and there are several such unions, as well as unions with a deceased wife's sister. Cases are reported there from other towns of established unions between uncle and niece. Neither in Tusik nor in Chan Kom did we encounter instances of sexual relationships between persons yet more closely related, although, of course, surreptitious intercourse may occur. In Dzitas a number of instances of casual incestuous intercourse were matters of common gossip, and a brother and a sister had for several years been living together as man and wife, with children. The reluctance to have sexual intercourse with a godchild or with the daughter of one's godparent is very strong. We cannot say that it is stronger than in the case of relationships by blood; but no instance of an established household composed of such persons came to our attention. The situation in Merida is similar to that observed in Dzitas. Established unions between first cousins are not uncommon, and even between uncle and niece, while cases of closer connection, defined by all as incestuous, are reported. A myth collected in Merida includes the assertion that incest between compadres is even more terrible than that between father and daughter, which in turn is said to be more terrible than that between mother and son. Breach of the taboo with respect to compadres is certainly the commonest of the three; the myth is probably to be interpreted as putting the pressure of moral control where it is most needed.

In the villages marriage is an arrangement made by parents for the adult security of their children and for the establishment of relationships between the two bodies of kindred of which the parties to the marriage are representatives. In the town and in the city there is still a disposition by parents to make marriage have this character, but in fact it there tends to be an arrangement entered into at the initiative of two young people as a result of the fact that they have been attracted to each other. The differences among the four communities that amount to this contrast have in this instance also a progressive character. In Tusik the fact that the normal form of marriage involves temporary residence with the wife's parents and labor by the boy for his parents-in-law, followed by usual residence near the boy's family, emphasizes the subordination of the new elementary family to the older families and also serves to unite the two bodies of kindred that are linked by the marriage. The arrangements for the marriage are there accomplished by the parents and other relatives of the young people. The girl is wholly passive, and the boy does not put in an appearance to express his wishes until, ordinarily, the third of four meetings occurs. After he has been accepted, the boy is expected to bring firewood to his future parents-in-law; before the wedding he sends over food to be served at the wedding; and on the trip to X-Cacal, where the marriage is performed, he carries the baggage. The negotiations for the marriage involve participation by the relatives of both young people in a series of nocturnal meetings. One principal subject for negotiations is the period of service which the young man is to give to his new relative-in-law. Another is the composition of the bride's gift to be made by the boy, with the help of his father. This gift (muhul), including both clothing and jewelry for the girl and rum, food, and cigarettes to be consumed at the wedding, is formally delivered and formally accepted by the parents in the presence of relatives on both sides.

In Chan Kom service by the boy for his father-in-law is reduced to occasional and ill-defined gifts, and the requirement

of residence for a period with the girl's parents is practically
extinct. Many of the older generation, however, have married
by haan-cab. Nevertheless, in Chan Kom the usual marriage
is one arranged by the parents for the benefit of their children,
and during the period of the observations it was more common
than not for the parents of the boy to propose to him the name
of a girl whom they wished to make his wife. The nocturnal
petition for the girl by the boy's relatives takes place in Chan
Kom much as in Tusik. The negotiations are similar, except
that in Chan Kom no period of haan-cab is, of course, included
in the discussions. The muhul is, however, similarly subject
to negotiation, and there also its formal acceptance signalizes
an unbreakable contract between the families—although cases
of breach are not unknown. Nevertheless, in Chan Kom there
is a disposition among the more town-wise young men for
them to take the initiative in suggesting to their parents the
young lady whom they favor. What are the circumstances
which tend to admit romantic love as a social convention? In
either Tusik and Chan Kom one may live for weeks without
seeing two young unmarried people otherwise alone and in
conversation together and without seeing any endearment pass
between husband and wife. The conventions are strongly
against such behavior. Yet passionate and exclusive attachments between couples do occur, and, if one is unobserved,
one may once in a while note repeated caresses and love-mak-
ing between a recently married couple. It is in Dzitas that one
first begins to hear "falling in love" spoken of as something
happening frequently around one.

In Chan Kom one much respected man of mature years is
known as the casamentero of the community and acts as the
negotiator of all marriages which take place. In Tusik there
is no such single functionary, although some respected elder
person, preferably a chief or a maestro cantor, acts as the intermediary between the parties. The absence of a special
functionary in Tusik and the presence of such in Chan Kom
may be due to the accident that in the latter community there

is someone especially fitted by inclination and temperament to fill the position. Or, possibly, the Tusik people may be disinclined to recognize such a functionary because the early missionaries, in teaching that young persons should not be married simply because older persons wished them to, included marriage negotiators in their condemnation.[15]

In Dzitas only the older, more conservative, and more rustic inhabitants remember what was meant by "haan-cab," although most people can mention cases known to them in the villages where boys were expected to do work for their fathers-in-law. The older generation recall their own marriages as arranged by parents; older persons will speak almost with pride of the fact that they knew almost nothing of their brides before marriage. At the present time the situation is very different: practically all marriages follow an understanding by young people. Love matches, as has been remarked, are common and socially accepted. Parental pressure is still strong, but among the cases of marriage by decision of the young people is one in which, after two young people belonging to two of the "better" families had become engaged with the support of both families, the young man broke his engagement, married a girl of no family, and nevertheless settled down in a house near the girl and family he jilted. There is much courting, and not infrequently recognized unions, with or without marriage, are set up following intercourse. As in the villages, it is regarded as proper for the parents of the boy to make formal calls upon the girl's parents to ask for the hand of the girl and to make arrangements for the marriage, and it is still regarded as improper for the boy to be present at the first visit. But the number of visits is more often than not reduced to two; they are not made very late at night; and commonly the young man will come into the discussion as soon as indication of a favorable reply is received. As occasional marriages occur between a boy in Dzitas and a girl in such a village as Chan Kom, conflicts between the more sophisticated and the more conservative expectations do take place. The parents of a Dzitas boy, for example, will conform to what is expected of them in a village where their son has formed an attachment and, feeling a little foolish, call at the girl's household late at night, bringing bread and chocolate. The callers are disposed to raise the matter at issue at once; the hosts regard this as indelicate and proceed to a postponement that is purely formal.

The gift to the bride is in Dzitas part of the normal marriage, but the word "muhul" is going out of use; indeed, a number of the people asked about the matter could not properly identify it. It is not the subject of formal negotiation between familial groups. It is a traditional gift made to the bride by her future husband. The garments and jewelry of which it consists are still conventionally fixed. But there is no formal delivery; it is merely sent over to the bride not long before the wedding. Among the more sophisticated, as is true also in Merida, the girl participates in the selection of the articles which compose the bride-gift. In Merida, as Hansen's account fully shows, marriages are today increasingly romantic and individualistic. In the lower class as well as the upper there is little in a marriage which could be called the linkage of two familial groups. Practically all marriages arise out of mutual understanding between two young people. The street, the market, the school, and the motion-picture theater provide abundant opportunities for meeting and courting. There remains the conception that a visit is to be paid to the girl's father to express the petition, but the asking is done directly by the boy. After he has been accepted, there may or may not be a meeting between the two pairs of parents; no gifts are made to the girl's parents. And what is still more to the point, Hansen's investigations indicate that not less than one-fourth of all the recent lower-class marriages in Merida are substantial elopements, taking place without any previous participation of the older generation whatsoever. In most of these cases the couple go off to begin living together with the expectation that thereafter the girl's father will permit or more probably insist upon a formal union.

It is only in the Quintana Roo villages that the ceremonial celebration of marriage invariably has the character of a sacrament. The other communities provide instances of progressively decreasing form and sacred quality in the matrimonial rituals. The marriage ceremony in Tusik is required in all cases, even in cases of remarriage (except that in the latter cases haan-cab and the muhul may be omitted); in Chan Kom, in Dzitas, and in the lower class of Merida, a remarriage is commonly without ritual recognition. The Quintana Roo couple go to X-Cacal, and at the entrance to the temple which houses the Most Sacred Cross they kneel upon a *zarape* and here recite seven times the six basic prayers called "the doctrine." It is the obligation of the marriage sponsor to see that boy and girl can recite these prayers correctly, and failure in their recitation may cause the Nohoch Tata to refuse to marry the couple. The Nohoch Tata performs a mass and then declares the couple united in marriage.[16]

In Chan Kom and in Dzitas the law is observed requiring declaration of intention to marry eighteen days before marriage takes place and making civil marriage a prerequisite to marriage by the clergy. The requirement of civil marriage and the difficulty and expense of church marriages are themselves factors tending to reduce the sacredness of marriage rituals. In Chan Kom almost all first marriages are attended by the civil formalities: the bridal party—consisting of the couple, both pairs of parents, the sponsors of the marriage, and, in some cases, additional witnesses—makes two trips to the town to appear before the civil registrar (more recently such an office was established in Chan Kom, making these trips unnecessary). The older people still value the church marriage, but there are now few priests in Yucatan; church marriage is expensive, and, in fact, it is decreasingly valued. In Dzitas the attitudes and practices with regard to forms of marriage ceremony are similar, but a considerably larger proportion of unions occur without any ceremony at all. In Merida, too, the church ceremony is declining in frequence and significance, and in both upper and lower classes, a wedding tends to be a party, an occasion for gaiety, rather than a religious observance.

There is to be recognized a third aspect of the marriage rituals, a ceremony neither of the church nor of the state but rather of the families that are involved. The ritual is, in fact, a sort of sealing of connubial connection between the boy's parents and the girl's, as well as a solemnization, independent of the church, of the new relations between the spouses. It is perhaps remarkable that Villa's materials from Quintana Roo give no evidence of such a ritual there or any indication that the ritual was ever practiced there. He says that the ceremony at X-Cacal is concluded when the Nohoch Tata has given the couple advice as to their future conduct and that then the members of the wedding party return to their respective homes but that "on some occasions the ceremony is followed by a feast given in the bride's house."

A feast, often at the bride's house (like other outlays in connection with the wedding at the expense of the boy and his family), is a feature of weddings in all the communities. The point here in view is that—with the possible exception of Quintana Roo, as already stated—there takes place at this feast some ritual in which is signalized the breaking of old connections and the formation of the new. In the old-style weddings of Merida, even among the upper class, there was a formal leave-taking of the bride by her parents, accompanied by the giving of a formal blessing. Nowadays this leave-taking is private and informal, even among the lower class. In Dzitas some families cling to the custom whereby the couple kneel before their parents (of both) and receive their formal blessing in the presence of the guests, but here, too, the custom is passing.

In Chan Kom this little formal blessing is still common. Moreover, in the old-style conservative wedding, now remembered rather than fully observed, there is (or was) an elaborately ritualized familial procedure. This has been described in the Chan Kom report.[17] The bridal party proceeds from the church in fixed order, representing the sequence of respect and authority in the family. The bride kneels at the door of the house where the feast is to be and salutes her parents-in-law and her parents in fixed order, and the groom does likewise. The sponsors of the marriage (properly two, man and wife) salute formally the four parents. There is ritual drinking and smoking by the older persons involved. The male sponsor of the marriage delivers a formal speech to the four parents in which he hands over to them the young people who during the period of the marriage have been in his charge. Rum and cigarettes are distributed again, and then a turkey dinner is formally presented by the bridegroom's father to the bride's father; thereafter another similar preparation of festal food is presented by the bridegroom's father to the sponsor of the marriage in token of gratitude for the responsibility the latter has assumed. After the feast, at the request of the bride's parents, the male sponsor of the marriage formally charges the bridegroom and the bride with their new duties and responsibilities. The sponsors escort the bride to her parents' home (if the feast takes place elsewhere), where these older people formally take leave of their daughter. All these salutations and leave-takings involve many gestures of respect and mutual confidence, and the speeches are delivered in traditional phrases. This solemn and elaborately detailed ceremonial expression of the changes in familial organization which a marriage brings about existed in these villages further to define and to sanction the structure of society. But in Dzitas, and still more truly in Merida, this ceremonial is represented by only trifling elements.

In parts of Indian Latin America of which the writer has knowledge the institutions which depend upon the ritual of baptism are of first importance in shaping the organization of society. This fact is due in part no doubt to the emphasis placed upon the sacrament by the missionaries—baptism was greatly stressed in the instructions given his diocese by Bishop Toral of Yucatan. In other parts, one feels from some knowledge of American Indian societies, the acceptance of baptism and fictitious co-parenthood was favored by the existence of conceptions as to the appropriateness of ceremonial kinship in connection with sponsorship of individuals passing from one social condition or age to another. In some Indian societies anciently converted to Catholicism the godparental institution has been developed greatly to bring about a long series of god-parental and co-parental relationships through a correspond-ing series of events in the life of the individual.[18] Among the Maya of Yucatan this tendency to repeat the pattern of bap-tism or to assimilate it with pre-existing pagan rites of transit has been represented by the adjustment of the Christian rite to the pagan ritual known as hetzmek.[19] Here again we encoun-ter an illustration of the fact that pagan and Christian ele-ments are most closely integrated in Quintana Roo, for there and there only are the sponsors of the baptism and of hetzmek one and the same persons. The persons selected by the par-ents to share with them responsibility for the moral and practi-cal welfare of the child are bound to the child and to their compadres by a double ritual. A married couple are selected; one of the two acts in connection with the baptism, the other in connection with the little ritual wherein the sponsor holds the child and successively places in its hand objects symbolizing the future skills and capacities which it is the objective of the ritual to assure.

The baptismal and hetzmek customs of the Tusik area[20] fur-ther differ from those of communities nearer the city in that they tend more emphatically to express the linkage of two adult couples and in that the relationships established are more seriously binding and morally consequential. Baptism is invariable: no parent would forego the trip to the shrine vil-lage of X-Cacal necessary to secure baptism; and the impor-tance of baptism to the child is expressed in the belief that an unbaptized child becomes a certain mysterious nocturnal bird that flies above living children, seeking to kill a child so that it may pass to heaven in its place. To assure the baptism of their child, and to provide themselves with compadres, it is the rule in Tusik to make the request of the couple selected soon after the prospective parents know that a child is to be born to them. The persons selected as sponsors are always persons whose relationship to the petitioners is already such that respect is properly felt toward them. If either pair of prospective grandparents are alive, these are properly the first choice; otherwise chiefs and maestros cantores are preferred. From the moment when the couple besought express their willingness to act—and refusals are extremely rare—they become compadres of their petitioners, and the obligation of respect and expression of gratitude prevails. The child learns to hold his godparents in equal respect with his parents; he calls the former by the same kinship terms as he does the latter; in the event of the death of both parents the godparents will as a matter of course bring up the child. Furthermore, the same godparents function for all children born of that couple; it is thought a sin to change godparents.

In Chan Kom the hetzmek sponsors are nearly always different persons from those chosen to act as godparents. They are thought of as occupying a secondary position of responsibility; nevertheless, there are cases where the hetzmek godparents bring up their godchild. Both pairs of sponsors are selected because their age and character make it appropriate for the child's parents to respect them. The importance of baptism was in this village also unshaken until the arrival of Protestant missionaries; and the corresponding myths have great effect. But in Chan Kom it is usual to wait until the birth of the child to ask the godparents to act (although there are occasional conservative persons even in Merida who think it improper so to delay). A child shows his respect for his godparents in manner of speech and in occasional service, but he does not use the parent terms in addressing them. With the small differences noted, the institution of godparenthood has about the same importance and solemnity in Chan Kom as in Tusik.

In Dzitas there are several circumstances which contribute toward a reduction in the importance of the institution. The Protestants throw doubt upon the ritual of baptism by the priest. The story about the nocturnal birds is only half-believed. The selection of compadres is not a matter considered at length and far in advance; the choice may be made not long before the baptism occurs. As there are great differences in social status and wealth among the members of the community, there is a temptation to select compadres for the practical advantages which may accrue. A young married woman, for example, said to her male cousin who had just asked the well-to-do Syrian merchant to take his child to baptism: "You are pretty smart to pick a rich compadre. As for me, I wouldn't dare, because I am poor." It results that there are cases where a man makes his compadre a man who is much younger than himself, in violation of the general patterns of respect for elders. It is common for indios to ask vecinos to act as godparents; a well-to-do and respected vecino will therefore come to have a great many godchildren; toward these, and toward all their parents, he can hardly maintain the sentiments of respect and affection which should be properly maintained. Indeed, in Dzitas the word "compadre" tends to become a general word of intimacy, used even though the relationship is not properly maintained. In Merida the discrepancy is even greater between what older people think should be done about baptism and what is actually done, and the relationships established are more casual and secular. Although people say that children should be baptized within a month of birth, the rite is often deferred a year or more. The selection of godparents is often guided by considerations of wealth or influence, and upper-class godparents are desired, although such persons may be reluctant to act. A case is, however, reported of a Meridano with over a thousand godchildren. The incompatibility between such a situation and the theory of sacred, special, personal relationship is obvious. In Merida "compadre" is often used for persons not united by ritual, and it is sometimes used ironically for one who is overly friendly or who claims favors to which he has no right.

The relative reduction of importance of the hetzmek ritual and of the relationships it brings about, already noted in Chan Kom, is still greater in the town and the city. In Dzitas the rite is performed for the large majority of children, but its performance tends to be casual, and the godparents of the hetzmek are not regarded as occupying anything like the important place which do those of the baptism. "One soon forgets them." An orphaned child would hardly look to these persons —or more commonly to a single person—for support. In Merida the ritual is more often omitted than performed (and is not performed by the upper class), although people know about it. It is regarded as a little magical safeguard for the child. That it creates adult relationships is hardly recognized; no real respect relationships are formed.

Corresponding with the decline in the importance of the institution of baptism as a means toward the forging of new links of social relationship, the rituals which attend the selection of co-parents and which express the parents' gratitude for the obligation incurred undergo a progressive simplification and secularization. The ritual of baptism, important though it is in bringing about the safety of the child's soul, is a single brief ritual, performed in all the communities, in X-Cacal by the Nohoch Tata or the maestro cantor and in other communities by a priest of the church. In the remoter communities it is the rituals which signalize the relationships between the co-parents that are the most elaborate and numerous. In Quintana Roo, where hetzmek is but an aspect of the baptismal rituals,[21] the relationship which these two crisis rites jointly create between two adult couples is solemnized by four successive ceremonies, each recognizing a stage in the formation of the relationship, in addition to the baptism and hetzmek rituals themselves. The request made by the parents that a known and respected couple will act as godparents takes place at a nocturnal visit in which the petitioners, after conversing on other matters to establish a friendly atmosphere, then make the request in formal and traditional language. A short time after the request has been made there takes place the *tzicil*, a ceremony in which the parents express the respect which they have for their child's godparents. This involves the formal presentation of certain traditional cooked food and three white candles. If the godparents respond fully, they then prepare a table on which are placed seven clay dishes containing the food they have just been given and a vessel of water and rue leaves. The child's father kneels beside the table and sanctifies the act by praying the six usual prayers. The articles are then carried to the oratory of the godparents, are there offered to the familial cross, and, only after this, are eaten by both couples. The third ritual occurs when the parents send word to their compadres of the birth of the child. The father brings two live hens and a measure of maize; the godparents return the visit, bringing certain clothing for the infant. It is now the obligation of the godparents to go to X-Cacal to find out the child's name by consulting the secretaries. After the godparents have acted as sponsors for two or three children of the same marriage, a fourth ceremony, called *poc-kab* ("handwashing"), is held in the little oratory of the godparents. A banquet of traditional foods is prepared in vessels and with decorations appropriate to this occasion only. The prepared food is offered to the cross through the mediation of a maestro cantor. In the central feature of the ritual the parents kneel and wash the hands of their godparents, first by one spouse before the banquet, and then after the banquet by the other. The godparents must return a gift of money, and the parents complete the exchange by sending to their co-parents' home a bowl of cooked food that has been placed beside the table but not consumed. In all these rituals, be it emphasized, the child plays little or no part; it is the union of the two adult couples that is solemnized.

In Chan Kom the request made by the parents that the other couple act as godparents is similarly attended with formal entrance to the house of the godparents-elect; by bowing and kissing of their hands; by the delivery of the petition in formal terms through an intermediary; and by the presentation of traditional food and drink which are then and there consumed in token of the inviolable agreement reached.[22] It is similarly thought proper in Chan Kom to hold a ceremony about a year after the birth of the child in which the parents show their gratitude toward their compadres. But, as the request is not made until after the birth of the child, there is no notification ceremony, and the tzicil and poc-kab ceremonies have become fused into a single ritual which bears either name. The parents kneel before their co-parents and ceremonially wash their hands. If the ceremony is fully performed, a cooked turkey is formally presented, and the intermediary functionary delivers a charge to the four adults that they love and respect one another.[23] In Dzitas it is the custom to give something to the elective godparents when the request is made, but the gift is a turkey only in the case of very conservative and pious persons or in the case of a villager coming to ask a Dzitas native to act. The petition is delivered by the father himself, without the use of formal language, and there are no ritual speeches or ritual drinking of rum. There are indeed many cases in which no present is made at all when the request to serve is expressed. Nevertheless, one would not, even in Dzitas, send the message containing the request through someone else; one must come one's self on so important a matter. After the baptism there is usually a small familial feast, or serving of light refreshments, in the home of the child at the expense of the parents, the godparent or godparents (for in Dzitas it is not essential that there be two) receiving chief attention. Yet there are cases where the godparent is wealthier than his compadres and himself provides the little festival in opposition to the direction in which respect should properly lie. The Dzitas people are aware that in the more rural settlements it is customary for the parents at some later time to wash their co-parents' hands and to offer them a turkey dinner, but this

custom does not exist in Dzitas. In Merida the situation is
similar: the request to act is made late; it may even be deferred until the child is sick. The request is informal, and generally the mother asks a woman friend to act, whereas even
in Dzitas it is thought too important a matter to leave to
women, and more commonly the father comes to make the request. No gifts are brought when the request is made, and it
is common for the parents to make no gifts at all. After the
baptism there is a little party, which is no more than that; and
the godfather may contribute to its cost. The formal respect
rituals are entirely absent in Merida.

The manner in which the baptismal name is determined
varies among the four communities in a way which further
illustrates the progressive differences as to individualization
and secularization. In the villages it is taken for granted that
the name the child will bear will be that of one of the saints
appropriate to the day on which the child is born. "They have
not yet looked in the almanac" is a way of saying that the
name has not yet been determined. There is thus small choice
in the matter, and everyone has in the calendar a day appropriate to him, anniversary of his birth, just as each saint is to
be specially recognized on its name day. In Quintana Roo,
where no one can read but the two secretaries, and the almanacs are in their custody, the finding-out of the name is the occasion of a trip to X-Cacal and the making of a request of one
of these two respected functionaries for the name of the child.[24]
But in Chan Kom a number of people have almanacs, and
any literate person may look the name up for himself. In
Dzitas it is common for children to be given the name of a saint
appropriate to the day of birth, and if another name is given
people will sometimes say that it is unlucky "to change the
name." Nevertheless, children are not infrequently given the
name of a saint other than that appropriate to the birthday;
a child may be named after a relative. A few people give
names which are not saints' names at all (in the baptism the
priest will add a saint's name); these instances are not well

regarded by the older people. In Merida the tradition that a child should be named after one of the saints of the day of its birth is known to exist, at least by the people of the lower class, but only a small conservative minority follow the practice with any consistency. Of 114 consecutive baptisms in one of the principal churches of Merida in 1930, only eleven children were named after a saint of the day of the birth. Even the members of the lower class follow more commonly the upper-class custom of long standing of naming the child after a relative, or to bestow any saint's name which the parents fancy. Hansen's materials indicate that there are fashions in saint's names, as in more secular names. The names now chosen in Merida for children often have no relation to Catholic practice. The names bestowed by the more modern include those of movie stars and in one case that of the chief prophet of communism, Karl Marx.

The materials summarized in this chapter represent both the greater individualization and the greater secular character of the town and city as compared with the villages and of each community as compared with that southeast of it. In the less peripheral communities the acts of the individual are relatively independent of the acts and rights of others. The individual is relatively more free to break up the elementary family of which he is a part; his actions do not so much concern more remote relatives; there is less expectancy that he will show respect toward or receive it from certain relatives; he has more to say about selecting his own wife, or she, her own husband; he may more nearly ignore his parents-in-law; and to progressively greater degree is he free to treat his godparents or his compadres as he would other persons. But the word "free" misleads; it suggests that in Tusik the native feels himself unfree. This is probably not the case. In the isolated village, where only one manner of life presents itself, there is no great sense of constraint. Customs, being self-consistent, carry to the individual a recommendation of the rightness of the way of conduct toward which all tradition conduces. It is in

Dzitas, probably, or on the margins of the developing middle class in Merida, that the sense of unfreedom is greatest. There one set of ways direct the individual in one direction, while another denies the rightness of this course and points to another. When one is of two minds, or when the customs are at variance with another, then one cannot feel fully free to act. The sense of freedom is lost just at the point where liberty is gained.

In the familial organization of the remoter villages the sacred and moral quality of the conduct expected of kinsmen is expressed and supported in ritual. As the ritual declines, so do the institutions expressed in the ritual become more secular. Or perhaps it is that, as the institutions become more secular, so do the rituals decline. The marriage ceremony, from being a sacred rite performed by the supreme native pontiff at the seat of the supreme sacred symbol of the group, becomes a party, or a formality required by the state. The obligations and rights of adults brought into relationship through a marriage, or through baptism, become less real and less solemn; correspondingly, the ceremonies which express these relationships lessen and disappear. A society, with a culture, exists in the moral and conventional relationships which obtain among its members and in part by reason of the solemn and collective gestures wherein the people reaffirm these relationships.

CHAPTER IX

THE DECLINE OF THE GODS

I

REFERENCE has just been made to the sacred and moral quality of conduct in the villages. The presentation of the native's view of life attempted in the fifth chapter should suggest the existence of this quality. The organized conventional understandings that compose the culture of the villages have more than the force of mere habit or convenience or practical efficacy. To a large extent notions as to behavior are suffused with a moral value and are expressed in symbols that have sanctity. The point has been further illustrated in the comparison of kinship institutions made in the immediately preceding chapter. It is most true in the more remote communities that the behavior expected of kinsmen rests under the warrant of ritual and religion. To state the matter in the form of an absolute contrast—and, of course, the contrast is not absolute—in Merida one behaves toward an older male cousin as personal predilections and convenience suggest, but in the villages one behaves toward an older male cousin in accordance with that pattern of respect for elders and kinsmen compliance with which people believe to be essential to virtue. In city and in village a child is taught that to be impudent to his godparent is a sin; but it is only in the remoter villages that the uncontrovertible gravity of the relationship is announced to the individual again and again in the rituals of "paying respects" and of "hand-washing." So it is with other aspects of the culture. The plan for conduct to which the conservative native responds is a sacred plan, well documented with ritual and belief.

The decline and disappearance of the pagan gods and ceremonies as one goes from Tusik to Merida may be regarded most obviously as the supplanting of indigenous culture by European, but it may also be recognized as an aspect of the relatively more secular character of life in the town and city. In the villages the gods of the forest, the cornfields, and the hives are close at hand, plainly defined and distinguished, and are worshiped in fixed ritual. The chaacs are closely identified with the rain; when the rain clouds gather, the native may announce that "the chaacs are riding the sky." The balams that guard the milpa and the village are heard in the whistlings and rustlings of the forest by night. The kuilob-kaaxob, spirits of the wood, are probably more vaguely conceived than are the other two principal classes of deities associated with aspects of nature; but any mature native will distinguish them from the other yuntzilob, and at the time of felling the trees for new milpa it is these beings that receive propitiation. The cosmogonic notions sketched in the fifth chapter provide for the native of the village a sort of topography of the unseen world. The unseen side of nature, the "beings of wind" that are felt in animals and trees and in the godlike spirit copies of the animals they protect—deer and cattle, peccary and turkey—are frequently recognized and are always to be treated with circumspection. The Yucatecan Maya does not have an intensely religious personal life; he does not have characteristically mystical, let alone ecstatic, experiences. Yet his life is religious in the sense that there are unseen beings close about him to whom he must constantly appeal. He may sometimes circumvent them by the use of "secrets," those magical charms which gain man's end directly without mediation of supernatural wills. But he is frequently in awe of these beings, and their propitiation, while it is in large part prudence, is in a large degree piety. In the villages one would not scoff; uncertain and uncanny results, it is felt, would follow.

In Dzitas those who scoff are not lacking. The differences in beliefs as to the pagan gods are wide. Some hold the chaacs to be the powerful rain-gods recognized in the villages.

Others are skeptical, saying that "other people say" that they are gods of the rain but that they must be, like all things, "of *Dios*." Others are disbelievers. "Of course, it is only the wind. It is the wind that brings the rain; it whirls the water up from the sea and rushes it across the sky and pours it on the land. . . . . In books it explains that the lightning is electricity." The situation for conflict among these various attitudes is presented in the occasions of agricultural ceremony, when a group of milperos cultivating adjacent lands participate, according to the prevailing sentiment, in a joint ceremony. Then various shades of belief are present. "When I go to the u-hanli-col,[1] of course, I have to say 'Yes' and 'All right,' and I don't argue with them. Because many of them believe what the h-men tells them. They are my friends—I bring the rum and the other things they need. Sometimes they say that the lightning will strike me. But the lightning won't strike until one's hour has arrived." Another man said: "When I am with the others, poor creatures, my mouth is one way and my heart is another. They say the offering is for the *kunku* (great rain-god), but they eat it all themselves! It is not true. The *zaz-tuns* (divining crystals) of the h-mens are just bottle tops."

On the whole, the pagan religion has in Dzitas much less influence over the agriculturalist's life. The difference lies partly in the disappearance of conceptions as to the super-natural world and partly in the lessening of the awful or sacred qualities of such beings as are still recognized. This has been briefly stated in chapter vi. The townsman does not know as much as the villager about the gods of the rain and of the bush, and such beings as he does know about are to him not so tall or so terrible. They become blurred, while they shrink from gods to goblins.

No one in Dzitas among those who discussed the matter with the writer could give the meanings of the figurative expressions used in the prayers of the shaman-priest.[2] The "door-way in the clouds" (*holhuntazmuyal*), through which the chaacs are supposed to emerge, could not be identified. Few people can identify the four directional rain-gods with colors or with the proper directions, although it is generally felt that there are four or five of these gods. Nor can people give the names of the special chaacs. The balams are confused with the kuilob-kaaxob, and the bee-gods and specialized guardians of the cattle and the deer are not recognized at all by these same natives of Dzitas, or they are barely known.

Especially are the balams, chaacs, and kuilob-kaaxob confused with the alux. The alux,[3] goblin-like little beings, are properly the animated form of the ancient idols and effigies, mischievous little terrestrial creatures rather than gods controlling nature. To the agriculturalists of Dzitas the confusion of the alux with the yuntzilob is such that it is the former rather than the latter which are foremost in their minds when they feel fearful at night in their milpas or when they set out the calabash dishes filled with cornmeal and water. The materials abundantly support this statement. "The balams watch over everybody. The alux guard the milpa." "The alux say, 'If you don't pay me, I don't work.' And that's fair, isn't it?" "The aluxes are like little children. They stay in the milpas where the bush is high and protect the milpas so no one can rob them. That is why, when new ears are ripe, you must perform loh [ceremony of lustration and appeasement]." "We do not make offerings to the balams, but to the alux." The association of the yuntzilob with the evil winds (chap. xi)[4] is in Dzitas more often than not converted into an association of the alux with these winds. "If you pass a place where an alux has just been, often the alux has left a wind there, and it gets into you, and you suffer an attack. That is why there are *yerbateros* (h-mens); so they may drive out the winds. They do it with their Maya prayers. But we do not know how." From being the dwelling-places of the gods, the milpas become the lurking-places of mischievous fairies.

A corresponding change occurs in Yucatan on the side of ritual. The agricultural ceremonies are performed in Dzitas, but with less fulness, regularity, completeness, and consistency.

Only the most conservative put out any offering at the time of burning the milpa or at sowing. When the ears are ripe, most milperos leave first fruits in the milpa, "for the balam" or "for the alux," but there is no group ceremony of *pibil-nal*[5] under the leadership of a h-men. In the villages the cha-chaac is a ceremony performed by all the men of the village collectively on occasions of threatening drought. In Dzitas the ceremony is frequently performed, but by small groups of milperos cultivating certain lands particularly endangered. Some agriculturalists have never participated in a cha-chaac. In Chan Kom u-hanli-col is a ceremony to be regularly performed by each agriculturalist to maintain good relations with the yuntzilob. In Dzitas it tends to be regarded as a ceremony necessary to certain lands if they are to produce a good crop.

This is the essential difference in emphasis. In Chan Kom the agricultural rituals are to a marked extent acts of piety. In Dzitas they tend to be acts of safeguard. In Chan Kom and in Tusik the relation of the ceremony is not only to the land; it is also to the person of the native. If he is sick, the milpero calls the h-men, who probably tells him that his illness comes from his failure to make the proper rituals to the gods. He must atone for the wrong he has done by making a more expensive ceremony to the yuntzilob. In Dzitas, on the other hand, the h-men is rarely called in for illness. But if the land does not yield a good crop, and no simple explanation appears, the milpero may ask the h-men to perform a ceremony, "to fix up the land," so to speak. "Two years ago Filomeno Dzul made u-hanli-col at his milpa at Popola. That was because his milpa was not growing properly, and the animals were eating the corn. . . . . You don't have to make it always, but only on lands that are accustomed to it. Some are, and there you have to make it or the corn doesn't grow or is eaten by animals. Especially where there are alux you have to make it." "There is a place not far from here where there is a stone like a horse. It is a horse of the chaac. The man who had the milpa there one year felled the bush and let the trees fall on it; then he burned the bush. After that no one was ever able to get a crop on that land. Now for six or seven years they have been making u-hanli-col on that land, and at last it is beginning to yield a harvest again." The personal security of the milpero is here not involved; there is little thought of danger to his body, let alone his soul.

The loh ceremony, which is lustrative of the evil winds rather than a prayer to the yuntzilob,[6] is not infrequently performed in Dzitas. A man will have it done as another elsewhere would put fertilizer in his field or would spray a crop with insecticide. It is simply a prudent precaution. The postmaster at Dzitas, a sophisticated mestizo vecino, had the ceremony performed in his cattle pen. His uncle, also a vecino but himself a simple agriculturalist, urged him to. The postmaster's account of what took place is characteristic of the attitude of the more sophisticated townsman:

It was very nice. All night long and all day that fellow [the h-men] sat at the door of the corral and didn't sleep. He kept praying in Maya. I couldn't understand anything he said. He asked me to answer several times, but I didn't know what to answer. It was all in Maya, but said backward. He didn't put up any table in the corral. He did put a table in the house— I think there were four dishes of zaca on it. In the four winds [i.e., corners] of the corral he planted crosses of wood, and he put lime leaves with each. It was just praying and rum. . . . . The bad wind gets into the ground and you have to get rid of it.

Thus the contrast between the field rituals of the villages and those of Dzitas is expressed in the contrast suggested by the terms "religion" and "magic." Certainly the performance of the rituals of the milpa in the villages has a "magical" component in its motivation to the extent that they are performed as a technique to assure a good crop. On the other hand, much if not all of the moral and religious meaning of the rituals that is present in the villages is lacking in Dzitas. The loss of religion in these rituals is probably due to a number of interacting factors. There can be no doubt that the example of urban nonbelievers and the effects of education in which natural phenomena are rationally explained play a considerable part. Some of the skeptics in Dzitas offer as disproof of the rain-gods rational explanations of astronomical and meteorological phenomena. The prestige of the city man and hence of his ideas favors a growing disbelief. The fact that some neighbors do not perform the ceremonies and yet are successful agriculturalists at least raises questions as to the importance of the ceremonies.

> My cousin Fernando has a milpa. And he never puts out zaca; even at harvest he doesn't. He says it is foolishness. But he doesn't get any harvest. Last year he planted forty *mecates*, and he got only ten cargas. He doesn't believe in it. But he has been making milpa only two years. Goodness knows what will come of it. None of the storekeepers make milpa except Bernardo, and he just began. He says he never made milpa before, and he is beginning here. And his milpa burned beautifully this year. It is strange.

The emphasis, it may be noted, is upon efficacy rather than moral or religious virtue. The doubter does not ask, "Is it wrong?" He asks, "Does it work?"

> This year my uncle Pepe did not put out zaca when he made his milpa. He always did before. I don't know why he didn't this year. I did, and my milpa burned well. But he didn't, and his burned well too. I guess maybe it isn't necessary to put it out at the burning. But what *is* necessary is to put out zaca at the sowing and at the harvest.

It does not appear that the group of Evangelical Protestants constitute an important center of skepticism with regard to the pagan gods and ceremonies. As a whole, the Protestants pay relatively little attention to the yuntzilob, yet many of these men make offerings and some take part in the group ceremonies with other agriculturalists. The evangelical missionaries direct their proselytism against the Catholic faith rather than against paganism.

In looking over the materials from Dzitas, the writer forms the impression that indirect factors are as important as the direct influence and example of nonbelievers in bringing about a decline in the pagan religion. It seems to him that the simplification and obsolescence of the ceremonies is not only a result of the loss of faith but is also a cause of it. People cease to believe partly because they cease to understand and cease to participate in those once dramatic gestures of the group by which the nature of the gods is proclaimed. They do not perform the rituals or do not perform them with such understanding for the principal reason that in Dzitas the shaman-priest is not a member of the local community. In such villages as Chan Kom there is likely to be at least one h-men, a relative and a close neighbor, who talks in the evenings with his fellows about the yuntzilob and about the significance of the ceremonies he performs. When the ceremonies are carried on, a group of men who truly represent the local community take part. They are all agriculturalists and all are equally concerned with matters of the milpa. But in Dzitas there is no h-men, nor has there been for many years. The h-men is a fellow with uncanny powers brought in from a more rustic settlement to do something which ought to be done lest harm come to the harvest. The Dzitas people are unaccustomed to his liturgical language, and few of them understand it. "The h-men prays in Maya, but we don't understand it. That's because he talks the true Maya, and the Maya we talk isn't the real Maya." The postmaster, in the instance cited above, felt a little foolish when he could not make the responses the h-men required of him as owner of the land being purified. "It was all in Maya, but said backward." Even the cardinal numbers above five, expressed in Maya in the prayers, are not understood by many participants whose usual Maya makes use of Spanish words for these quantities. For certain of the ceremonies that in the villages are performed with the leadership of the h-men, as that in which new ears of corn are offered to the yuntzilob, the townsman substitutes the mere leaving of new ears in his milpa—for whom? The many-times repeated invocations of the h-men are not there to remind him.

This is also one of the reasons why the alux tend to become the principal objects of propitiation. The yuntzilob are everywhere—Tusik, Chan Kom, or Dzitas—approached chiefly through the shaman-priests. The h-mens know the words to use and the acts to perform. But the alux, while they are included in a few of the rituals maintained by the h-men,[7] are not his specialty. Anyone can hear them, occasionally see them, and often seek to propitiate them. One deals directly with the alux. But the tall gods become less accessible when their mediators are not present.

A related circumstance contributing to the weakening of the religious faith in the yuntzilob lies in the fact that in the town the ceremonies, if held at all, are less likely to occur at moments of genuine crisis. This needs little explanation in the case of the principal rain ceremony (cha-chaac). Every instance of the performance of this ceremony reported in Chan Kom and in Tusik corresponded with the culmination of a season of drought and involved the participation of every man in the village. The sense of common cause among the villagers is, naturally, much more intense in the village than in the larger and more heterogeneous town. In Dzitas the cha-chaac, as already stated, is a ceremony brought about by a small group of milperos. Many of their neighbors are disinterested or ignorant of what is going on. The ceremony, therefore, is a relatively minor episode in the town, while in Chan Kom and Tusik the entire community—and the women, too, for they are busy preparing part of the offerings—devotes itself simultaneously to the appeal to the pagan gods. A similar observation may be made about the lesser ceremonies which are effected at the instance of a single milpero. In Dzitas, where the h-men is not ordinarily called in to treat a sickness, the explanation for the sickness in the failure of the patient to perform a ceremony is rarely given; therefore, the lesser ceremonies are not so often made coincident with the anxiety of sickness. In Chan Kom a man performs the ceremony because he is prudently and piously regular or, alternatively, because he believes that his relations with the gods are unsatisfactory, and thus he is experiencing some personal distress. Since in Dzitas the regular offerings are usually without the benefit of the illuminating and explanatory formalisms which relate them to the moral life of the individual, they are less often than in the villages made on occasions of personal emergency. They are acts directed more immediately to the practical end: a successful crop. They tend to become part of the technology—of the nonrational technology—in another word, of the magic, of the agriculturalist. To a less extent do they provide expression for that critical state of mind conducive to prayer. So a man in Dzitas will merely say, for example, that "when you are taking out the honey, it is a dangerous (*delicado*) time when winds might strike you"—without making any ceremony and without very definite conceptions as to deities. Or he will set out the corn gruel at time of planting without prayers, just to be sure that the crop will turn out all right.

When we turn from the villages and the town to Merida, it may almost be said that we leave the pagan gods behind. They are associated in the minds of residents of the capital with the backcountry, the bush, and milpa agriculture. Only a few of the semirural inhabitants of the periphery of the city who cultivate maize with some regularity ever have occasion to be actively concerned with pagan ceremonies. A fair number of other persons have seen one or more of these ceremonies on the invitation of friends or relatives who live in the country. But they understand little of what goes on, and they can be characterized better as sight-seers than as participants. The great majority of people know only what they have learned through listening to accounts of rituals to bring rain, of fields delivered to the care of supernatural guardians, and of the ill fortune that befalls those who offend the guardians by attempts at theft.[8]

Among the peripheral Merida agriculturalists one hears reports of many of the ceremonies described for Chan Kom. But it is difficult to get any details or to find out how general the observances are. Such practices are secret. An individual does not confide even to his neighbor, unless he feels certain that the neighbor is friendly and sympathetic, for fear of being ridiculed or denounced before the city authorities. For important ceremonies a h-men is brought in from a village. There is, however, in at least one suburb a man who sometimes officiates in milpa ceremonies. But he devotes most of his time to curing sickness and working black magic. He is usually, and properly, called a curer rather than a h-men. His functions are more those of a practitioner in folk medicine and a sorcerer than those of a shaman-priest.

Knowledge of the pagan gods is more vague and confused than in Dzitas. Most people connect the chaacs with the rain in some way, but ordinary rains do not seem to be thought of seriously as the work of the chaacs. Other beings of bush and field are rarely differentiated at all. They are commonly referred to collectively as *dueños del monte* or *dueños del cerro*, or simply as *vientos*. The use of this last term reveals a disposition to identify them with the "winds" that operate in disease and black magic. Caves and artificial mounds are dangerous because disease-producing vientos are likely to reside within them. These places are suggested as the special habitations of the dueños as well. But the confusion is not complete. There are many who insist that the dueños are less malevolent than are other kinds of winds; that they do no harm, beyond a little mischief, unless they are provoked. Nevertheless, nobody seems quite sure, and "winds" of any sort are to be treated with caution.

The association of the pagan deities with black magic was made explicit by the suburban curer mentioned above. He says that he calls on the balams for aid in curing sickness and that in one instance he employed the help of nine balams to bring about the death of a milpa thief who had insulted him. The same man defined the alux as figures of clay *or wax* which are found *or put* in the fields to protect the crops. The identification of the alux with a well-established technique of sorcery would have been complete in this case, except for the fact that the curer went on to explain that some alux inhabit the bush permanently without having been placed there.

The general attitudes and beliefs of urban residents regarding the pagan cult vary widely. A part of the small number of

agriculturalists who live in the city believe sufficiently to induce them to keep up some of the agricultural rituals. Their
attitudes in doing this are probably similar to those described
for Dzitas. Large numbers of the less sophisticated members
of the lower clsss, though they have had no direct experience
with the pagan cult, are credulous nevertheless. Many of them
vouch for the efficacy of rain ceremonies and show respect for
guardians of the milpa, even after they have begun to question
some of their other folk beliefs. Their position seems to be that
the Indians, especially those in faraway places, are closer to the
ancient people and preserve better their secrets and magical
powers—secrets and powers that have been lost in the life of
the city. The more sophisticated tend to look upon pagan
practices as unfortunate superstitions of rustics. It is they who
favor education and repressive state action to put a stop to
such folly. Then, there are a few who interpret the cult as interesting local folklore and who collect and publish stories on
the customs of the Indians.

From the foregoing it is evident that, with the exception of
an insignificant number of milpa cultivators, the inhabitants
of Merida do not consider the pagan cult a part of their own
existence, no matter what beliefs they hold concerning its reality or efficacy. It is separated from the city in space and is
identified with a kind of people and a way of life that are regarded as inferior. When people of Merida think of the cult
at all, they look outward or backward toward the hinterland—
and downward.

II

In this chapter it is being said that religion plays a relatively
larger part in the peripheral societies than in the town and in
the city. What is sacred in the villages tends to appear as more
secular in Dzitas and Merida. The reader has already been
told (chap. iv) that many elements of Catholic belief and
ritual exist in Quintana Roo which are not now present in the
other communities. What is now in addition to be said is that
the elements of Catholicism common to all the communities

are relatively more sacred in the peripheral communities than in the others. The symbols of divinity and the rituals that attend these symbols are more highly sacred in Tusik than in Dzitas or in Merida. The secularization of life that is to be noted in the progressive comparison that is now familiar to the reader is not confined to the pagan gods and ceremonies but extends also to the cult introduced from Europe. This might not have been said had the comparison been made a hundred years ago, or even seventy-five years ago, but the influence of an anticlerical government and the effects of recent mobility and other changes in the towns and the city have altered the Catholic practices and conceptions of the people. Today the most religiously minded communities, taking them as wholes, exist farthest from the episcopal authority.

The objective symbols of sanctity in Yucatan are chiefly crosses and images of saints. The yuntzilob are, since the Conquest, without effigy representation. In the Quintana Roo communities there are very few effigies of saints, but wooden crosses receive the greatest attention and worship. This is probably due in part to the fact that the Quintana Roo people are largely cut off from the wood-carvers of religious images, but the extreme emphasis upon the worship of the cross in the outlying region may be a result of emphasis placed on that symbol of the early missionaries and may have roots in an ancient worship of some analogous pagan symbol. In the Chan Kom area villages and families have wooden santos where the Quintana Roo people have crosses. Both groups of people also recognize in their prayers, and in certain beliefs, particularly named saints appropriate to certain activities or human needs.[9] If one looks at the way in which these two conceptions—effigy and named saint—enter into the activities of the people, it appears that the conceptions, while related, are distinct. The saints appealed to in special connections—St. Mark in connection with agriculture and St. Isidore in connection with hunting deer—receive appeals without the necessity of the presence of any effigy, and even independent of an effigy of St. Mark or

St. Isidore that may exist in some village. They are beings of special interests or functions existing in heaven or in the woods. But the patron saint, whatever his name, is the symbol of the group of which it is patron, village or family as it may be, and of all the needs that that group may experience. He exists in the village or family shrine in the form of an effigy which in itself has power and sanctity. You cannot honor the patron without the presence of the effigy. One might distinguish the saints from the santos. If the matter be looked at in this way, then it appears that both in Quintana Roo and in the Chan Kom area there are both saints and santos but that in Quintana Roo the santos are crosses, not images of saints.

What is to be recorded in connection with the subject of this chapter is the loss of sanctity, especially of the santos. At least it may be declared that it is the crosses of Quintana Roo that are attended with the greatest veneration and awe. The Most Holy Cross, kept in X-Cacal for the respect and worship of the entire cacicazgo, is so sacred that few of its votaries are allowed to see it. Kept in a special precinct behind a screen, it is constantly protected by an armed guard. A worshiper may not himself place a candle before it; the candle is handed to the priest to place on the altar. Its power is expressed directly: if it is displeased with a votary, the cross indicates the fact by causing the flame of the candle to go out. It expresses its particular wishes by writing letters, and in former times it spoke with a human voice. No effigy in any other of the communities has this degree of awful power. Some of the same sanctity attends the other crosses of the Quintana Roo people. The village and family crosses are too sacred to be taken out of their chapels and carried about in procession; instead, equivalent substitute crosses are provided for the purpose. In Chan Kom, while the patron santo is venerated as greatly miraculous, it is maintained in a little oratory accessible to anyone, without guard. While in Quintana Roo it is thought wrong to keep crosses in the houses where people carry on everyday affairs, in Chan Kom many santos and crosses are kept there, although it is remembered that years ago all effigies were kept in special oratories. Nor do the santos of the Chan Kom area rule their people by any such direct method and explicit instructions as characterize the Most Holy Cross of X-Cacal. Except in the Quintana Roo villages, the sacred effigies are kept in ordinary dwellings and moved about as it seems convenient. If a man wishes to make a novena for a certain santo, he may in Chan Kom or in Dzitas or in Merida borrow it from a neighbor. It even occurs that a santo not properly suited to the occasion may be used "as if it were" the right santo: in Dzitas a small Virgin is borrowed from an individual and used as *La Concepción*, the original La Concepción having been destroyed during the Revolution.

Throughout Yucatan the santos retain much sacred quality. But it is the few widely recognized santos of especial potency that receive the attentions of the faithful. Most notable are the Three Kings, patrons of the town of Tizimín. The annual fiesta in their honor is attended by thousands of people, coming from as far away as Campeche. Many stories are told of the miracles these effigies perform. A miracle, as often as not, is the expression of supernatural power in the form of punishment of the unbelieving or the impious. A man, for instance, treats the fiesta lightly and is visited with sickness or blindness or other trouble. By some it is thought difficult even to gaze steadily upon these images because of the awful power they exert. Copies of the Three Kings are on hundreds of household altars in various communities throughout Yucatan, and on January 6 many people who are not at the fiesta in Tizimín dedicate celebrations to them at home. Somewhat similar prestige formerly attached to La Concepción of Izamal, but of late its reputation has declined sharply with the decay of its fiesta. Indeed there is in Merida something akin to fashion in the concern with santos. A few years ago San Nicolas was popular. Today he is almost forgotten; an image of the *Virgen de Perpetuo Socorro* has emerged from relative obscurity and may almost be said to be "the rage." In addition to these santos, associated with specific communities and certain particularly efficacious images, there are a few outstanding santos whose popularity is manifest chiefly by the fact that their effigies are to be found in an unusual number of homes and receive an unusual number of individual and family devotions. The main examples of this class are the *Niño Dios*, San Antonio, and the *Niño de Atocha*.

While a genuine religious feeling attaches everywhere to all santos and especially to certain of them, at the same time the general trend of change as one goes from the remoter villages toward the city is one of secularization. The unbelievers, from none at all in Tusik, become in Merida perhaps more numerous than the believers. In Tusik everyone attends to the great and supernatural authority of the Most Holy Cross. In Chan Kom the power of the patron has already been challenged by the coming of Protestantism. In Dzitas, while stories of the power of the patron, Santa Inez, abound, there are many people who from one year to the next never burn a candle before her. In Merida many of the inhabitants of the city, or of one of the barrios of the city, do not even know which santo is the patron of their local community. The prestige of the santos is in the city corrupted not only by competing cults (Protestantism, spiritualism, theosophy, and naturism) but also and more importantly by the anti-Catholicism associated with the political liberalism of recent times. The city includes the few very Catholic conservatives who follow all the ways of the church and identify themselves with her interests, the great number of partial or nominal Catholics, and a large minority of frankly dissident or disbelieving cultists or other individuals. The lower class in Merida, in Hansen's words, "seems to be drifting toward a situation of no important or effective religion."

Of the special aspects of the general trend there is to be recorded in particular the progressive individualization of the santos. By this is meant the change wherein the santo, from being the universal and necessary religious symbol of all members of the group, becomes a private and adventitious symbol of divine power. The number of santos known to any one per-

son increases as their average sanctity declines; and as their
number increases their attachments to particular people become more variable. In Quintana Roo there is a hierarchy of
crosses closely corresponding to the organization of society.
At the top there is the Most Holy Cross, representing the entire subtribe, then the village crosses, then the familial crosses,
and finally the crosses each representing an adult man and his
wife and children. Thus everyone knows from childhood just
what symbols of sacred power are of consequence for him, and
the order of their relative consequence. One is born to one's
gods; one does not elect them. Furthermore, everyone who belongs to one's lineage, or one's village, or one's tribe, attends
to the same symbols of divinity. There is no choice. The santos reflect the structure of society, not the predilections of the
individual. In Chan Kom, as in Quintana Roo, the santos on
the whole express the collective attitudes of the people rather
than individual preference. It is to the patron, to the Niño
Dios, or to the Holy Cross that people make their prayers. All
the villagers address themselves to the same santos, and these
are all santos felt to belong to the local community. But, as
there is no tribal organization in the Chan Kom area, there is
no tribal god corresponding to the Most Holy Cross at
X-Cacal. There is, to be sure, a vague feeling that the cross—
not any particular cross—appertains to the mazehua, and that
the Day of the Holy Cross (May 3) is a sort of ethnic festival.
But there is no defined group more comprehensive than the
village that might be marked by its own symbol of divinity.

On the other hand, in Chan Kom certain tendencies toward
the individualization of society are reflected in some small
changes taking place in the religious symbols. It will be recalled that in Quintana Roo there are familial crosses. Every
family has the same kind of religious symbol which is a simula-
crum of the village and tribal symbols. Furthermore, every
family has such a symbol, and still further all the familial
crosses are brought together at the occasion of the important
village ceremonies so that no individual or family is unrepre-

sented in the chief collective rituals. In Chan Kom, on the other hand, the familial symbols are not so regularly and systematically distributed according to the division of the community into family groups. Some families have santos and some do not, while there is no custom, as there is in Quintana Roo, that upon marriage every man secure his own cross and house it in some suitable oratory. The few private or familial santos that do exist in Chan Kom are effigies of different saints, involving different days of recognition. There is, in Chan Kom, some room for individual choice. If you want a santo, you may buy one from an image-seller.

In Dzitas, and still more in Merida, the inclinations of the individual have still greater opportunity, and the relative predominance of the community patron is still further reduced. One man may have half-a-dozen santos on his domestic altar and observe the name day of each of them by novena or by simple burning of candles, while his neighbor may have no santos at all. Still more important, in the towns and the city it is common for an individual to make an attachment to a santo that is particular to him and that does not involve his family or his community. A woman may go to the fiesta at Tizimín, become convinced of the miraculousness of the santos there, and bring back a picture of them. She may then privately ask the aid of these beings without causing other members of her family to take part in the supplication. In both Dzitas and Merida, men, or more usually women, make vows to saints other than the patrons of the community, especially to the Niño of Atocha or to the Three Kings of Tizimín. While in Chan Kom seven or eight households have santos which are not regarded as patrons of the community, in Dzitas and in Merida the community patrons if not actually unknown are very unimportant in the galaxy of santos, and the elements which chiefly determine the santo to which the individual in town or city directs his prayer are the widespread fame of miraculous images in communities other than Dzitas or Merida and the separate attachments formed by chance and preference between the individual and such images. The high degree of instability in the relation between a person and the santo to which he is devoted reflects the mobility and disorganization of life in the city.

The essential facts are these: in the peripheral village the symbols of European form and apparently European origin have a sanctity recognized by all members of the group to which each symbol pertains and are worshiped in a series of ceremonies which are carried on either by small families, by lineages, by the village, or by the subtribe. These ceremonies involve all members of the group concerned, and all share common religious attitudes. In the city the degree of sanctity attached to these symbols varies between wide extremes as one individual is compared with another; and the ceremonies which involve them tend to be more individual and less collective and more secular and less sacred. The foregoing paragraphs have summarized the facts about the santos so far as they contribute to this general conclusion. The generalization may also be approached through a review of the rituals of Catholic form.

Throughout Yucatan prayers are recited in the presence of santos or of equivalent crosses as forms of appeal or as expressions of gratitude or of propitiation. The prayers are in part learned through oral tradition and in part (Quintana Roo excepted) are read from books. The principal prayers recited are the Our Father, the Hail Mary, the Creed, the General Confession, the Salve, and the Act of Contrition. Especially in Quintana Roo these six prayers are referred to as "the doctrine" (*payalchi*). Except in Quintana Roo, where it is usual to recite these six prayers successively, there is knowledge of the combination of certain of these prayers in fixed symmetrical groups (rosaries). In the more sophisticated communities these prayers, known to most people, are combined with various anthems and litanies which are less generally known. It is recognized that on the more important occasions these prayers are to be led by persons (maestros cantores or rezadoras) specially qualified by their knowledge of the less widely known elements of liturgy. The recitation occurs before altars including the effigy of the santo and is followed by the distribution and consumption of food and drink; this consumption is itself in some part a religious act, although it may be largely secular. It is generally understood that these prayers are to be recited on the days appropriate to the saints honored in the Christian calendar but that they may also be held on occasions which are suggested by the interests or needs of the persons who bring about their recital.

Such is a formal statement of the formal resemblances among the Catholic rituals in the four communities studied. The interesting points of difference appear from a consideration of the varying functions of the Christian cult in the various communities. In Quintana Roo the Catholic cult is most elaborate and is expressed in the most specialized ceremonies. Both the community and the individual (or small family) are provided with rituals for both calendrical and occasional celebration. On the vespers of the days appropriate to the "great saints," the entire village holds a ceremony called "oxdias." The ceremony includes the recitation of the usual prayers under the leadership of a maestro cantor, with all laymen of the community participating. Every family must make a contribution of food, and to each person of prestige in turn falls the duty and privilege of preparing the special ritual breads (oxdias, hostias) from which the ceremony takes its name, and of which everyone partakes. A series of six oxdias is held when the village is threatened by drought (and is followed by the pagan ceremony called "okot-batam").[10] The oxdias, therefore, expresses the worship of the entire community, either on those days fixed in the calendar which tradition has sanctified or on those occasions when the community is collectively in greatest need. The celebrations of calendrical festivals are without exception community matters.

Oxdias and okot-batam, being community matters, are held in the village temple. The rituals of Catholic form which serve the individual and his family are held in the familial chapel. Two kinds of ceremonies are distinguished. *Edzcunah gracia* is performed whenever it is thought appropriate to maintain good relations with the crosses. The occasion may be the sickness of a child, concern over the crops, or the corresponding situations when a benefit has been received or thanks are to be given. This ceremony is also held—but in such cases in the chapel of the individual and before the substitute crosses—to assure harmonious relations with the spirits of the deceased relatives, especially the parents, of the individual. The edzcunah gracia requires no participation from outside the family. The votary and his wife prepare ritual foods; he himself places them on the altar or the table specially prepared; he himself kneels and prays "the doctrine" three times. After the offerings have been left for a time on the altar, they are eaten by the votary and his family. The other private ceremony, *chen rezar*, or *rezo*, is performed only when the shaman-priest has declared that an illness has resulted from the anger of the souls of the dead relatives of the sufferer. The ritual asks pardon of the offended souls and of God as a means to the restoration of health. This ceremony takes place in the familial chapel and requires the help of the maestro cantor, and it differs from the edzcunah gracia also in that the food offered on the altar is afterward in part distributed among members of the man's great family and among his neighbors.

There should be added to this list of Catholic rituals in Quintana Roo the prayers recited on the Day of All Souls and on the Day of All Saints (*hanal pixan*) and the annual or biennial festival of the patron saint. The latter, as it occurs in different communities in Yucatan, will form the subject of a succeeding chapter. What is here to be emphasized is that in the exercise of the Catholic cult in Quintana Roo there is, on the one hand, a worship in which the entire community is engaged, and, on the other hand, private or small-family worship which occurs when a feeling of unease suggests it. The oxdias, held in the village church, requires the chiefs and h-mens of the settlement, as well as the maestros cantores, to perform special roles. Leadership, as in all public and ritual matters, is in the hands of the men, but both men and women kneel and pray and partake of the food of communion. The oxdias may be calendrically determined or it may follow from a general need, but in any case it is a common simultaneous expression of piety by the whole community. The individual, on his part, holds private ceremonies when there is a special reason to pray. The edzcunah gracia and the chen rezar (rezo) are also genuine expressions of piety, and their occurrences coincide with states of mind appropriate to prayer.

In Chan Kom it is usual to employ the word "novena" for any ritual recitation of Catholic prayers, whether on one afternoon or evening or on nine successive evenings. (As the prayers recited always include a rosary, the ceremony is sometimes called a *rosario*.) Only the prayers for the souls of the dead are distinguished as "rezos." The terminological distinction made among novenas is that between "name-day novenas" and "open-the-mouth novenas."[11] The former are those held on the calendrical day appropriate to the santo honored and so correspond in function to the calendrical oxdias of Quintana Roo. But, as there are a few individuals in Chan Kom who have special santos, there are a few novenas, held on the responsibility of individuals, that are calendrically determined. Yet the most important name-day novenas are those held for the santos recognized by the entire community: San Diego, God, and the Holy Cross. These are usually full novenas of nine nights (distinguished as *novenarios*), while (with rare and recent exceptions) a man who has a private santo recognizes its name day with only a single night of prayer.

It is the *novenas de promesa* that are most common in Chan Kom. They are held whenever a man wishes to express thankfulness for a blessing received or to pray for a benefit sought. Thus they correspond to the edzcunah gracia of Quintana Roo. It may once more be emphasized that the object of supplication or the recipient of gratitude, though not a familial cross as in Quintana Roo, is in Chan Kom always one of the local santos, or is God, or is the Holy Cross—beings to whom all members of the community similarly appeal. "Outside" santos are not involved. It may also be pointed out that the novena functions in Chan Kom, as does its corresponding ritual in Tusik, chiefly as an expression of a genuine and occasional impulse of recognition of divinity. Although the novena is in large part social entertainment for the participants, the people who give the novena do so because they thank the santo or appeal to the santo. The calendrical novena is an obligation that goes with ownership of a particular effigy. The owner knows he has to recognize the santo on the appropriate day and feels that misfortune might follow if he failed to do so. But the day is fixed by the round of days; it is not one selected according to the immediate religious impulses of the worshiper.

The Chan Kom novena initiated by an individual is more of a neighborhood function than is the edzcunah gracia of Tusik. (It will be noted that in this respect an institution is more individualistic in Tusik than in Chan Kom.) It is the custom for persons outside the family to attend. A man's closest kinsmen will know that they are welcome, and they are likely to attend. Members of the family may speak of their plan to hold a novena and invite others to come. The people who attend are themselves performers of the ritual, for many of the prayers are known to all, and everyone joins in some of the responses. At the same time it is customary (as it is not in the case of the edzcunah gracia) to get one of the local maestros cantores to lead in the recitation and chanting of prayers and anthems; the occasion is, therefore, dignified by the presence of one of the men looked up to in the community for their religious knowledge. Men and women join equally in these village novenas; husband and wife are jointly votaries and hosts; and men friends attend as freely as do women.

The rezo of Chan Kom is similar in function to ceremonies

of the same name in Quintana Roo. Rezos are held at certain intervals after the death of a member of the family or when one is sick by reason of the anger of the soul of such a close kinsman to whom not all the expected ceremonies have been made. In the latter sort of situation the rezo, like the edzcunah gracia and the novena de promesa, is a religious ritual occasioned by immediate needs. In Dzitas the prayers for the dead are held only in commemoration of the death on days fixed by the date of the death. The h-men is not there to tell a sick person that it is the souls of his kinsmen who are bringing the sickness upon him as a punishment for his failure to perform the rituals. So the occasional rezo, an expression of propitiation and of wish to be well, does not occur in Dzitas or in Merida; at least, no word of such a rezo was heard by the field investigators.

But there are more important respects in which the relatively more secular character of the Catholic ceremonies in Dzitas is evidenced. With the exception of the annual festival of the patron, the ceremonies held in the church on behalf of the entire town are far less inclusive of the people of the community than are the corresponding ceremonies in the villages. A small minority of the population attend masses on those exceptional occasions when the priest is there to perform them. When the priest is not there, a simple rosary is held; very few people attend. When the priest is not present on the important saints' days novenas are held in the church. This may occur on the day of the Three Kings, on that of the Virgin of Guadalupe, and on Christmas Eve; the last is a full novenario. But it is a few families of the town that take the lead in these novenas, and a great many people take no part whatsoever. A large part of the population is indifferent.

The situation with regard to individual, or familial, novenas is the reverse of that in Chan Kom in that the large majority of novenas held are name-day novenas, while novenas de promesa are relatively uncommon. (Some of the name-day novenas are referred to as "novenas de promesa" because it is remembered that an ancestor who had the image vowed to make the novena annually. But in cases known to the writer the reason why the vow was made has been forgotten; they are in substance like any other calendrical novena.) Because some people have many santos, and have different santos from their neighbors, there results a calendar of special obligations to perform novenas: it is known that so-and-so has a santo of San Isidro and therefore makes a one-night, or perhaps a nine-night, novena on his name day, while another man has a San Pedro and makes a novena at a different time. When these private santos are celebrated with full novenarios, relatives and friends are asked to take nights, providing the hospitality and food for that evening. Although the situation was different a generation ago, nowadays men take little part in novenas, either those of the church or those held in private houses. Occasionally in a list of *devotos* a man's name will appear, but the man himself will rarely take active part; the night is listed in his name merely as an acknowledgment of his authority in domestic matters. Men will remain outside the house until the praying is over and then enter to enjoy the refreshments. Furthermore, the reciters of the liturgies appropriate to particular saints are, in the town, women, not men. The maestro cantor of the village has the prestige of his sex and also of a permanent and appreciated office in the community. But a rezadora is just a woman who knows the prayers. Thus a number of circumstances contribute to reducing the religious importance of the Dzitas novena: the atmosphere of indifference toward or even disbelief in all saints and santos; the fact that the occasion of a novena is a date in a calendar of little importance to persons not having the corresponding santo; the absence of a prayerful motive in most novenas; the fact that the santos honored are in most cases not the important symbols recognized by everyone but more special beings; and the deprofessionalization of the functions of the prayer-leader. After this citation of easily verifiable points of difference, the writer may be permitted to record also the impressions of the field workers who have participated in these Dzitas novenas that they are not characterized by any strong religious sentiment and that they do not evidence any strong neighborhood solidarity. This is in distinct contrast, of course, to behavior in the villages.

Although the statement may not hold for the more rustic indios milperos of Dzitas, it is otherwise true that agricultural interests do not there play any important part in the motivation of the novenas de promesa. The cases of novenas de promesa that the writers have from Dzitas are few at best, and among them is none with a motivation that arose from concern for the harvest. In the village the novena is certainly much more closely integrated into the predominant concern of the people—agricultural success; in the town, if the novena is not wholly secular and social, its motives are various and conform less to a pattern. Some cases from Dzitas followed vows made to a saint as conditional upon recovery from illness. One occurred because a mother wanted to ask a saint to reveal to her who had got her half-witted daughter with child. There is a certain magical or divinatory flavor to many novenas, clearer in the town than in the villages. "Some think it is good to have novenas for the sick. Some think it is bad and that then they die more quickly. It is the same way with confessing when one is sick. Some people think it makes them feel better, but others say, 'No, as soon as I confess I will die.'"

Merida presents one important general difference from the other communities with regard to Catholic ceremonies. The fact that it is the seat of ecclesiastical authority means that the ordained functionaries of the church play a more important role there than elsewhere. This is especially true since the advent of anti-Catholic legislation. Priests are permitted to conduct regular services in only nine churches in the state of Yucatan; four of these churches are in Merida. It follows that it is chiefly in the city that an individual has the opportunity of attending ceremonies carried on by the official clergy. At the same time he can direct his devotions to the santos on his household altar and offer prayers for his dead relatives in his own home, as do the people of Dzitas and Chan Kom.[12]

These two kinds of religious activity are distinct in many ways. It is common, especially among the lower class, to think of the formal church organization as belonging to the clergy. The rituals the priests provide tend to be accepted as a matter of course. They have always been available and presumably they always will be, unless the government interferes. The ordinary individual needs to make no contribution or to feel any responsibility. The organization seems to function independent of him. A person's household santos, on the other hand, are his santos, and the novenas he offers them are his novenas. He knows that only his continued interest and effort will keep the ceremonies going. Also, it may be noted, that, when an individual attends mass, he is among strangers with whom his contacts are casual and secondary. In a novena he is surrounded by his friends and relatives. Another difference is that participation in official Catholic activities is urged upon people by the established ecclesiastical leaders, using every device at their command. Although the priests must have implanted the cult of the household santos in Yucatan in the first place, at present they give it no encouragement. The sole authority that now supports it is the authority of tradition. Tradition, however, is documented with a large number of stories that point out how the santos punish people who fail to honor them with the appropriate celebrations. It is significant that no corresponding myths were encountered depicting the rewards and pains that come from faithfulness to or neglect of the official church, except for a few which illustrate the necessity of baptism. A further distinction derives from the circumstance that novenas held at home to which one invites one's relatives and friends are primarily a lower-class institution. It is not uncommon for pious lower-class persons to express their religious devotion by diligent attention to the images on the family altar, while they are rather lax in going to mass and in carrying out their other obligations as members of the church. In contrast, pious upper-class people tend to participate fully in the program of formal Catholicism and to limit their religious behavior at home to simple acts of worship performed individually and privately.

It is even possible to observe some signs of antagonism between these two aspects of Catholicism. Persons who are deeply attached to their santos think of themselves as being good religious people, though they may be quite negligent with reference to mass, confession, etc. It is not that they really question the formal cult. They look up to the clergy and accept the things the clergy does as entirely right and proper. Their attitude appears to be that they want the church available to be used as and when they wish but that the santos are nearer and the ceremonies addressed to them are more meaningful. When a priest exhorts them to greater faithfulness to the formal institution, they listen politely and respectfully. They agree and make promises, which they often fail to keep. But if they are urged too much, they are likely to feel annoyance instead of contrition. In the conversations of lower-class people who consider themselves to be good Catholics, one hears certain priests criticized for their zeal in trying to induce their parishioners to discharge all their duties to the church. Other priests who are more tolerant of partial participation are commented upon approvingly. Among the clergy and among devout upper-class Catholics there is a disposition to disparage the traditional cult of the household santos. Novenas are described as profane celebrations of little or no religious value. More often than not, according to these critics, the prayers are a mere excuse for a party. The only real religion, they hold, is that offered by the church, supplemented by private devotions of pure prayer. It is their view that worship should be a specialized activity, unmixed with entertainment. They would certainly deny the right of an individual to call himself a good Catholic who did not fulfil all or most of his obligations to the formal organization. Aside from strictly religious considerations, novenas tend to be looked down upon because they are associated with the lower class. Everybody knows that the church derives its most loyal support from the old upper class. The prestige of this class is identified with its characteristic mode of religious behavior in some degree, thus raising the rating of the formal Catholic cult and setting it off in contrast to the cult of the household santos.

We can return now to a consideration of novenas in Merida as compared to the other communities. But, first, it may be well to record that, as in Dzitas, prayers for the dead (called "rosarios" in the city rather than "rezos") are held at fixed intervals determined by the date of the death of the person they commemorate. Much that has been said of novenas in Dzitas applies equally well to Merida. There is the same diversity of santos from household to household. Novenas de promesa are rare and, when given, are likely to be simple affairs involving only the immediate family. For full novenarios friends and relatives are invited to take nights. The arrangements are almost entirely in the hands of women, and the women alone do the praying, led by a rezadora. Other similarities with Dzitas could be cited, but we are more concerned with differences which reveal the greater secularization of these rituals in the city.

It is necessary to glance at the past of a generation or two ago to see one evidence of secularization that was more apparent then than now. At that time novenas played an important role in the lower class as means through which families could express their social status. As one family vied with another, the nonreligious features of novenas became very elaborate. On the final night the guests sometimes numbered more than a hundred. The house and lot would be decorated. There would be a jarana, provided with the best orchestra that could be afforded. Instead of the simple refreshments in vogue today, for the "better" novenas these would consist of chicken and turkey or perhaps barbecued pig. It was customary for the owner of the santo to entertain the *nocheros* (leaders of the eight previous nights of prayer and festivity) of the first eight nights and their families throughout the last day in order to repay them for their contributions earlier and to have their assistance in preparing for the final night. Certain families acquired fame for the splendor of their novenas. Since these were distributed throughout the year, they might be described as constituting the "events" of lower-class "society." With all this elaboration of the more secular aspects of the celebration, the part concerned directly with the santo remained relatively modest. The altar was highly adorned, and the leader of the prayers was often accompanied by one or two chanters and by a person playing a portable organ, but that was all. Although the foregoing refers chiefly to a few outstanding novenas, they represented the pattern that many people formerly sought to emulate, and they exhibited characteristics that have little in common with the domestic religious practices of Chan Kom and Tusik.

The novenas one finds in Merida today are generally much simpler than they used to be. There are other sources of entertainment and more effective ways to gain prestige. The guests do not often exceed thirty or forty, and the usual refreshments are sweetened rice water or commercially produced soft drinks, with some small edible delicacy. If there is a dance, a phonograph or a radio frequently suffices for music. Sometimes the affair is shortened to one night, which is definitely felt to be an inferior substitute for a full novenario. The more elaborate pattern of the past does have enough validity, however, to induce some people to cease giving novenas entirely in preference to making a show so modest that it might give rise to adverse comment among the neighbors. Reflecting the nature of social relations in the city, novenas are purely invitational. To attend without being specifically asked would be construed as "crashing the party." The guests come from anywhere in the city the host happens to have friends. Consequently, novenas have little of the character of neighborhood gatherings. Modern dancing has completely replaced the jarana. This means more than a mere change of style. The jarana had a certain amount of religious connotation due to its long association with religious festivities. In fact, it persisted in connection with novenas after it had ceased to be popular entertainment indulged in for its own sake. Modern dancing, on the other hand, is entirely secular. A few conservative old people even suggest that it is an offense to the santo for dancers to embrace in its presence as they do today. A further sign of secularization is the almost universal practice of requesting the male guests to contribute to the cost of the orchestra, if there is one. This is a direct violation of the traditional conception of the function of the social enjoyment that went with a novena. The santo was thought to be pleased by the festivity as well as by the prayer. Both were offered to honor the santo, and both were part of the obligation of a person who undertook to give a novena. By collecting from his guests, the owner of a santo is escaping some of his duties. Moreover, it was the traditional idea that anyone who contributed in any way became to a degree a devoto, a participant in honoring the santo. Investigation disclosed that the men who help pay for the music for a modern dance are not considered devotos in any sense. Everybody with whom the matter was discussed agreed that they are merely paying for the privilege of dancing. Ordinarily this practice of charging the guests serves only to make a novena a better party and to reduce the expenses borne by the host. But one case of outright commercialization was encountered. The novena in question had been given annually for a long time and was always an elaborate affair. Over the years it acquired a reputation for gaiety that made it very popular. During the period of study full advantage was being taken of the opportunities it presented. To increase the attendance, four or five hundred printed invitations were distributed throughout the city. There were several dances in addition to the one on the last night. All of them were organized by the owner of the santo, not by the nocheros. The nocheros provided only the prayers, in which few people participated, since most of them came just for the dances. At other novenas it is usual to collect from the guests informally during the course of the evening while the dancing is going on. In this instance, admission was paid at the door. Even the refreshments were sold, and, to increase the revenue, hard liquor was included. All in all the novena returned a net profit. It may be observed that in this case the arrangements were not left to the women of the family; the male head himself was in active charge. What had happened can be summarized by saying that the santo had become the excuse for a celebration, the owner of the santo an entrepreneur, and the novena a business enterprise.

In addition to the apparent secularization of such novenas as are still maintained in Merida, the fact is to be reported that novenas are becoming less common there at a rate which suggests that the whole institution may be dying out. There are two partial exceptions to this picture of decline. They are the novenas offered to the Infant Jesus and to the Three Kings at Christmas time. Although they, too, show some signs of weakening, they have suffered far less than have other novenas. The reason for their continued popularity is that they are established features of the general holiday celebration; that is, they are the customary Christmas parties. Their association with this important holiday provides them with a kind of support no other novena has. Even people who are quite indifferent to the santos and to religion generally still feel that it is appropriate for Christmas parties to have a slight religious flavor, a result which can be achieved by following the traditional practice of organizing them as novenas to the Infant Jesus or to the Three Kings. Owing to the special factors operating in these two cases, they should be considered exceptions and omitted from a discussion of the decline of novenas. Leaving them out of account, then, we may begin by observing that, outside of the lower class, novenas are already practically extinct. Within the lower class one finds family after family reporting that it used to give them but does not now. Often a statement is added to the effect that the last novena was held four, five, or perhaps eight, ten, or fifteen years ago. An estimate of how far this trend has gone would be little better than a guess. But it seems perfectly safe to say that not more than one family in five still gives novenas to which outsiders are invited; and one in ten would probably be nearer the truth. Moreover, an observer gets the impression that the majority of novenas are kept up by the older generation and that they are rare in families founded within the last two decades. After people stop giving novenas, they may retain their interest in the household santos and express it by burning candles and reciting prayers individually or in company with other members of the domestic group. Or they may pay almost no attention to the images on the family altar either because they have become unconcerned with religion in any form or because they are content with the religious experience provided by formal Catholicism or some alternative cult.

The factors undermining novenas in the city are many and varied. The most obvious is the antireligious propaganda maintained by the government, which is stronger here than elsewhere in the state. Although it is often discounted because of its political source, it does show, nevertheless, that some people can attack the santos openly with no apparent evil consequences to themselves. Moreover, every individual has friends and relatives, persons he knows intimately, who ignore the santos more or less and yet enjoy health and prosperity. Faced with a growing number of such cases, all but the most faithful question the efficacy and necessity of novenas. The old stories that point out how forgetting the santos brings misfortune are not told so frequently or so widely as they used to be. People do not have time to listen; they are too busy "going places" and "doing things." When the stories are recounted, it is usually an older person who tells them; and age today has no great authority or prestige. They are either frankly disbelieved or are rationalized into ineffectiveness by those who are somewhat credulous. It is said, for instance, that, if a person lacks money for a novena he is accustomed to give or if he diminishes his attentions to the santo little by little instead of all at once, the santo will understand and not take offense. Probably the abandonment of a novena in itself contributes to a further loss of interest and faith. As long as it is kept up, even though it be quite secularized, the very effort it requires tends to reaffirm whatever concern its sponsor still feels. At the same time it serves as a kind of public announcement that he feels something. One suspects that many of the families who have substituted simple acts of devotion performed in private for the traditional celebrations in honor of the santos may be on the way toward a more complete neglect of them. The simplicity and privacy of these rituals may make them less capable of sustaining the individual's interest, particularly in a world where numerous and varied stimuli press upon him and compete for his time and attention. Finally, it will be recalled that participation in formal Catholicism is proclaimed as a form of religious expression superior to that provided by domestic ceremonies; superior because it is pure religion, uncontaminated by profane elements as are the traditional rituals addressed to the household images. In a similar way, though less directly and explicitly, new kinds of purely secular diversion strike at the entertainment features of novenas. Without being told, most people judge novena parties to be second rate as compared to the movies and the dances of social clubs. Their sole function is to divert, and they are deliberately designed to be glamorous and exciting.

III

The subject of this chapter has been the secularization of Yucatecan life. More specially it has dealt with the decline in religious faith and the reduction in sanctity of the acts and images in which faith is manifest. But the facts do not allow one to deal with this general trend apart from others that have been urged upon the reader in earlier chapters. Apart from the aspect of secularization, the differences in such an institu-

Photograph by Frances Rhoads Morley

tion as the santos, as these are revealed by a comparison of the several communities, contribute to the documentation of other propositions set forth in this volume. The cult of the santos presents materials on individualization; it demonstrates the fact that the individual is in the villages less free to act independently of his family or settlement. It presents material on the disorganization of culture, for it shows that the interdependence and consistency of customs and belief are most marked in the peripheral communities. In Tusik and Chan Kom the yuntzilob express matters of universal and paramount concern: the rain, the bush, and the milpa. In Dzitas the yuntzilob still stand for these things, so far as they stand for anything, but these are not the paramount concern of those townsmen who are not thinking about crops but rather about their stores or their jobs. In Quintana Roo the crosses are not only objects of sanctity but they are also objectifications of the hierarchy of groups which make up the social organization. The santo of the city man expresses, in many cases, chiefly his own personal and private experiences in fixing upon that santo as helpful to him. Both yuntzilob and santo, in Dzitas, are less well integrated into a system of interdependent ideas. The separation of the novena from agriculture and the fact that in the towns the yuntzilob are less regarded as the causers of disease by way of punishment for moral wrong are instances of the way in which the network of meanings breaks apart, here and there. Connections that existed in the village, so that one realm of thought and practice offered justification for another, disappear in town and city. May it be that secularization is in part a result, simply, of this loosening of the web of meanings? Where the cross one prays to is the cross addressed by everyone in one's family, or one's village, or one's tribe—where, in other words, the symbols to which one points one's prayers remind one by their very arrangement and manner of treatment of the form of the society in which one lives, and where there are many other institutions about one that declare the rightness of that form of society, may it be that the political and social institutions thereby contribute to the sanctification of the religious symbols, and vice versa? And perhaps when the connections with social organization *are* gone, the santos become less sacred, just because those connections are gone. In the villages a man thinks of the yuntzilob when he plants his corn, or harvests it, and also when he has become sick and the h-men has told him that the yuntzilob have punished him with sickness. The townsman may or may not still be a farmer, and so concern himself with the yuntzilob, and it is not customary to attach to sickness a meaning involving the yuntzilob. There is at least one less source of support and justification for the divinity of the yuntzilob. It seems to the writer not unlikely that, even if there were no schools and no urban skeptics, religion, both pagan and Catholic, would decline with the appearance of specialized occupations or with the moving-away of the h-men because those are circumstances that disorganize the culture. It seems probable that the loss of tribal independence by the X-Cacal Maya will, even without other contributing causes, bring about a decline in religious faith among that people. There will be no subtribe for the Most Holy Cross to stand for.

Returning to the subject, the decline of the gods, and reviewing what has been said in this chapter, the writer notes the instances in which the summary of differences has amounted to saying that what is religious in the peripheral communities becomes merely magical in the town or the city. The awful beings of the sky and the bush, the yuntzilob, are displaced by little goblins, the alux. The ceremonies from the yuntzilob, from being "acts of piety," become "acts of safeguard." From praying in the milpa, one hires a man to say some spells that "cure" the land. The edzcunah gracia of Tusik is a form of prayer. The corresponding novena de promesa in Chan Kom is more prayer than party. In Dzitas it is more party than prayer; and indeed, in so far as it is not secular entertainment, it is something that is done because it would be unlucky not to do it. People raise the question as to whether or not it is lucky to perform this or that novena or to leave it unperformed. Even the santo, religious symbol that it does remain for the true Catholic and the religiously minded individual in the town or the city, becomes for many a mere charm. One wears the image in the town, or puts it on the autobus one drives in the city, along with other luck symbols.

It appears that, under the circumstances that prevail in Yucatan, magic, while it is present everywhere along with true piety and worship, is a sort of intermediate station on the road to complete secularization. When an object is sacred to a man, he will not tolerate a critical or rational exposure of its nature. For him it is protected by an uncertain, emotionally rooted aura. It has qualities that move him and that may not be explained away; he will resent it if you try. If, moreover, it is a religious object, it embodies, and often personalizes, qualities that are ultimate moral goods. These he seeks in the object, relating it to his own person in prayer, propitiation, and appeal. The yuntzilob cease to be gods; they leave religion; yet the woods remain uncanny. The old acts that once attested the yuntzilob are not to be given up entirely. One's neighbor perhaps disbelieves in the yuntzilob; so one doubts— but is is better to be on the safe side. Not to do anything at sowing is to feel uncomfortable. One is not entirely matter-of-fact when dealing with the bush and the uncertain rain. There is so much luck about the results. Maybe to do the act will help to bring a good crop. So the ritual is done, now not as worship but as a spell or charm. The santo, too, takes on this magical quality. It is not a chair or a hat; it has qualities which are not rationally to be dealt with. You may not have much faith in it as a supernatural person, but it might be unlucky not to perform a novena on the name day. The concern is no longer with the propitiation of a being that cares for one if one remains virtuous. The attention has shifted to the luck of the field or to uncertain mishaps that might occur if one did nothing. The object cannot be entirely explained away; it still has power. If the right words are said, it can be made to work.

Catholic and pagan elements in the religion exhibit this disposition to become more emphatically magical (once more speaking of the comparison in terms of a trend or change), while they are separating from each other and moving apart. In the villages there is, to the native, no paganism to be distinguished from Catholicism. Only an outsider, with knowledge of history, would make such a distinction. Indeed, in Tusik it would not represent the native's point of view to speak of religion as something distinct from the rest of life. There are the proper ways to do things; and included are prayers and offerings, just as are included work and behavior toward chiefs and kinsmen. To say that one is a Catholic, if it is said at all, is about the same as saying one is a proper human being of one's own world of affairs. In Chan Kom and villages like it, where there are Protestants, there are, for the first time, so to speak, Catholics. And being a Catholic rather than an *Evangélico* does not set either in contrast to paganism. Paganism, in the villages, is not recognized as a cult in opposition to anything else. Evangélicos do not believe in the saints, while Catholics do; but everybody makes the rain ceremony. It is in the towns that paganism begins to separate out, as it were. It is seen as a cult of value to the agriculturalists in the community or to some of them. It is in some disrepute. At least the leaders of the community, the men who have prestige, tend to be detached from it or to treat lightly such connection as they have with it. The cult of the yuntzilob becomes a useful magic—a little humorous, a trifle embarrassing. Beyond that, in the city particularly, it becomes a superstition. It is something somebody else mistakenly believes. And finally, if detached from all moral judgment, the ideas as to pagan deities become only folklore, quaint stories and beliefs which can be enjoyed by adults or told to children. Then secularization is quite complete; all the uncanny power has been drawn; the gods have become figures in fairy tales.

Paganism simply fades away. It leaves almost no institutions in the life of the city. It is connected with all the rustic and backward elements of life which a spreading, dominant urban viewpoint depreciates. It is frowned upon by the state and condemned by the established churches. Its leaders, the h-mens, are suspect to city authority. So it retreats to the forests or shrinks to almost nothing.

Catholicism, of course, remains. The Christian elements in the religion of Yucatan have been supported for centuries by a vigorous organization and by the approval of the élite. They have long been identified with the sociologically superior. Yet the trend of secularization affects them, and piety declines. At the same time Catholicism appears as a distinguishable body of thought and practice. In Chan Kom there are, as there are not in Tusik, Catholics who are in opposition to Evangélicos. In Dzitas the opposition is more marked: the Protestants are more set apart; they maintain their own chapel; they are looked on by Catholics, who now feel themselves as something different, with distaste or fear. And in Merida the Catholics are fully recognizable as a special interest group in rivalry with other interest groups.

It is in the city that there is to be recognized a separation within Catholicism itself. On the one hand, there is the cult of the santos; on the other, is the formal church. The cult of the santos is a kind of folk Catholicism. It is local, is without formal organization, is sanctioned by a body of folklore, and is carried on by ordinary persons with the assistance of a few individuals from among their neighbors who possess some knowledge of prayers not shared by everyone. It flourishes in a situation where a need is felt for supernatural aid in the course of daily existence and where the common experiences of all members of the community reaffirm the efficacy of such aid and the rightness of seeking it. In the city, as the crises people face grow more diversified and as secular attitudes come to characterize larger and larger areas of behavior, concern with the supernatural becomes less constant and less urgent. The cult of the santos, therefore, tends to disappear, since it is dependent on the active interest of common people. The decline is hastened by antireligious propaganda, by disparagement from the church and from the élite, and by the multiplication of things to do, places to go, and ways to spend time and money that characterizes the city.

At the same time the church, with its followers of orthodox faithful, exists as a semisecular institution in competition with other groups and institutions for the attention and support of the people. It is part of an international organization. It has specialized, full-time leaders. It survives in the urban environment, defending itself against competitors, self-consciously proclaiming vigorously and insistently the value of its program, and modifying its program as necessary to give it greater appeal. In doing this, it is transformed into an interest group which functions to provide certain people with a ready means of religious expression that tends to become a specialized segment of their lives.

All this will be fully presented, in terms of the recent history of Merida, in Hansen's book under preparation. Here the point is more briefly made in terms of the comparison between village and city. In the remote villages, where conceptions we may regard as Catholic are generally held by everybody, there is no Catholicism as something set apart from or opposed to something else. In the city, where Catholicism takes on some of the characteristics of a political party, many people are relatively indifferent to the conceptions supported by the church.

The principal differences among the four communities with regard to religion, including both pagan and Christian elements, may now be briefly summarized. In Tusik there is a single body of beliefs and practices, in which everyone participates; religion is not distinguished from the rest of life; and, of course, therefore, there is no distinction between Catholicism and paganism or between Catholicism and anything else. In Chan Kom the integration of pagan and Christian elements is less nearly complete than in Tusik; religion is still an important concern of everyone and is still integrated with the rest of life. Catholics here appear, because there are some Protestants. In

Dzitas religious activity is less well integrated with the rest of life; religion is recognized as a distinguishable interest or activity; paganism occupies the attention of only part of the population and is in disrepute among the "better" people; and Catholics and Protestants are well-defined groups. In Merida paganism is practically gone; it is associated with the back country and is viewed as superstition or as quaint folklore. A division appears in Catholicism. The traditional cult of the santos, carried on by the common people, decays. The Catholic church remains, competing with Protestantism and other cults and struggling to maintain itself against antireligion and indifference. Even for those who continue faithful, religion has lost much of its connection with the rest of life and is to a considerable degree a separate and specialized division of behavior. One is a member of a church rather than a participant in a society and a culture.

CHAPTER X

HOLY DAY TO HOLIDAY

A S IN many other parts of Latin America, a principal recurrent event in the life of each local community of Yucatan is the annual celebration of the santo which is its patron. There is probably no village, town, or barrio in which this occasion is allowed to pass entirely without cere-monial recognition, and in many of them it gives rise to the supreme collective effort of the people. The activities which make up these fiestas are much the same in all communities of Yucatan. They form a regional style, a special type, within the more general outlines of Middle American, or of Catholic American, folk festivals of patron saints.[1] Behind the festal forms one may look to the motives which the forms express. Varied and complicated as the motives are—they no doubt in-clude piety, local and personal pride, desire for relaxation and play, sociability, commercial interests, and a fear of misfortune which might follow if an obligation regarded as traditional should be neglected—they may be broadly investigated in terms of that pair of categories which have been used in the preceding pages: the sacred and the secular. Whatever else the festival is, it is both worship and play. The presence of these two elements is recognized in the program of the festivals and in such accounts of them as appear in the news-papers: those features which are *religiosas* are set off against those which are *profanas*. Every festival includes both sacred and secular elements. But the sacred elements are much less important in some festivals than in others, and, moreover, the same formal activity may be found in one community to rest under sacred sanctions while in others that same activity is wholly secular. In general, as one may suppose, the more

270

urban the festival, the more secular; and, so far as a small amount of materials indicate, the recent historic trend has been one of secularization. It also seems plain that the secularization of the festival is closely connected with the appearance of circumstances making it possible for people to regard the occasion as an opportunity to make money. Extreme cases may be found in the peninsula: a festival which is an integral and necessary part of the system of religious observances upon which the life of the community is felt to depend as compared with a festival promoted in order to enrich the promoters. In these two instances, which are to be described below, many of the same conventionalized activities are present, so that, considered simply as forms of overt behavior, both cases conform to the Yucatan festal style.

Considered as worship, the name-day festival is an annual homage offered to the santo by the people to whom the santo gives special protection. The people make the expected offerings, and the santo gives them health and good fortune. A sort of perpetual vow, which must be annually renewed, exists between santo and community. Failure to perform the festival in the traditional manner is regarded as a breach of the obligation. If for such a special reason as a year of relative poverty the people find themselves unable to perform the festival as usual, it is felt that the obligation is added to the commitment to perform the festival at the next anniversary. In such a case some prayers will be offered, perhaps a mass will be paid for (a sort of token payment), and the individuals in that year responsible for the festival will "explain" the situation to the santo.

The central and almost invariable element of the worship offered the santo is a series of nine nights of prayer. In most cases this is a ninefold recitation of a novena, prayers and hymns composed by ecclesiastics and published as particularly appropriate to the saint honored. In cases where the worshipers do not know or do not have the text of a novena, the recitation of nine rosaries may be substituted. Formerly, in the larger communities, nine masses were held; but in recent years it has been exceptional for a community to secure the services of a priest. It is the custom to distribute the primary responsibility for the conduct of these evenings of worship among nine individuals or nine groups of individuals. In this manner the leadership of the period of prayer passes from one to another. It is felt that the care or custody of the santo passes from one to another also. It is customary to mark the termination of one twenty-four-hour period of responsibility and the beginning of another with a procession in which the transfer from one group to the next is formalized. Each individual or group has a number of duties to perform which are incidental to the prayers, but which also constitute offerings to the santo: the preparation and placing of candles; the decoration of the church. The novenario is begun so that the last night of prayer falls on the evening before the name day of the santo. It is the core of the festival, considered as worship. The other activities, playful as most of them are, at the same time are regarded as contributing to the glory of the santo. This is true in so far as a feeling of piety animates those who participate. The novenario, or the nine masses, constitute the principal and the essential offering of the community, as a collectivity, to the santo.

The traditions of the festival are such as to allow also for the making of offerings to the santo by individuals as individuals. The obligation of the community is perpetual and is annually renewed. But the sense of obligation of a particular individual toward the santo, or his feeling of need of help from the santo, will vary with his fortunes. A man may make a vow to the santo in praying for recovery from sickness. Or, after an unusually abundant harvest, he may wish to give thanks to the santo. The organization of the festival provides several ways in which he may do this. He may assume one of the principal places in the group managing the festival as a whole. He—or in urbanized communities more commonly she—may "take a night" of the novenario, or take membership in one of the groups among whom the novenario is distributed. And there are many ways in which one may assume lesser commitments which also, in their smaller degree, are offerings to the santo. One may simply burn a candle before the image. If one cannot come one's self, one can always send a candle by another person. If one attends a festival not of one's own community but in a distant town or village where the santo is known for special miraculousness, then the trip to the festival takes on the character of a pilgrimage, and the very exertion of going there becomes itself an offering. Or one may provide rockets to be set off or contribute one's labor to help in the preparation of festal foods or equipment. As will appear more fully below, in some communities and in some cases one may participate in the traditional folk dance (jarana), which invariably attends the fiesta, in fulfilment of a vow and as an offering to the saint, or one may participate in the bullfight, which is also a common part of the festival, or contribute a bull to the sport, in the same spirit of offering and even of discharge of a sacred commitment made to the santo.

Of course, the people who do these things are not in every case or entirely in any case moved by religious sentiments. Even the man who steps forward to assume the principal leadership of the festival in a community in which pious motives prevail is likely to be influenced by considerations apart from his personal and private relations with divinity. One element is certainly the prestige which attaches to the assumption of leadership in the chief collective act of the community. A man must also be responsive to the expectations of his neighbors; they will expect a man with the necessary resources and the appropriate character to make the largest offering, to assume a principal share of the collective burden. And also there is the widespread desire to bring about a festivity which is anticipated as an opportunity for fun and excitement.

Considered as secular entertainment, the center of the festival is the jarana. A jarana may be held to render festive any occasion, periodic or occasional; it is certainly present in every fiesta of a patron saint. The jarana is the Yucatecan form of those Latin-American folk dances descended from the *iota* and its cousins of Spain. It involves a certain style of musical accompaniment with heavily marked rhythm usually expressed by brasses and drums, a form of dancing which is based on a characteristic step and in which couples dance opposite one another without embracing, the use of a wooden platform to accentuate the beat of the dance steps, the erection of a leafy bower (*enramada*) to shelter the dancers, and a number of strongly marked conventions of the dance floor. The rhythm of the jarana music converts a lonely settlement in the bush into a center of excitement and charm. The opening of a jarana invites young men and women to the opportunities of self-display, of association with and judging of one another, and of play and self-expression in traditional and glamorous forms. While young men and young unmarried women are prominent in the jarana, older people also take part. A jarana usually begins soon after nightfall and lasts until dawn. In the towns and the city dancing occurs at these festivals also in the form of more modern European dances (*bailes*). These involve different music, costume, and manners. They are much less closely connected with the traditional festival and are entirely secular.

Of second importance in the secular aspects of the festivities is the bullfight (*corrida*). A fiesta without a jarana is hardly possible, but in small and poor communities there may be no corrida, because suitable bulls are lacking. The corrida varies from a rustic teasing of bulls, that are too valuable to be killed, by the young men of the village, to corridas in which bulls are slain by professional bullfighters imported for the purpose. The corrida also has its traditional concomitants, its characteristic style. Elements which are practically universal are the construction of a bull ring of poles and vines (*kaxche*) and the provision of a band to play at the ring during the sport. A somewhat less common custom is that whereby the lassos and other paraphernalia of the bullfight are paraded around the bull ring before the corrida. This is spoken of as "consecrating the bull ring." (A parade around the plaza, whether by members of one of the prayer groups, by dancers, or by bullfighters, is called "crowning the plaza." Done after a jarana just before dawn, it is called a *nona;* it is customary in many communities for the then presiding chief of the fiesta to serve free refreshments to all after a nona.) The corrida and the jarana are interrelated in that the jarana is on such occasions as these usually spoken of as a *vaquería,* and the young men, both bullfighters and dancers, are called *vaqueros,* and the girls, *vaqueras.* According to tradition, the last dance of each vaquería is one called *El Torito,* in which the girl simulates the part of the bull, her partner that of the bullfighter. In the more remote communities there is a further custom wherein, early in the festival, a ceiba tree is felled in the bush and ceremoniously erected to music in the bull ring.

The entertainments of the festival are provided chiefly by the vaquería, by the corrida, and by the opportunity to consume festal food and drink. The drink is commonly rum, although in a few of the communities where an ancient tradition is still adhered to balche (bark beer sweetened with honey) is served at certain times. The festal foodstuffs are based upon three staples: maize, hogs, and fowl. The maize is in many cases mixed with lard and baked into cakes of special form and flavor; it is also prepared in the form of atoles and of ordinary tortillas. The pork is boiled, or put into tamales, or made into cracklings. In the more rustic villages the pig's head is cooked and decorated in a special manner; so prepared it becomes a symbol of the perpetual obligation to perform the festival, and ceremonial delivery is made of it from the retiring chief votaries to those who take over the responsibility for the coming year. Though hens will do if turkeys are not available, turkey meat is (except in Quintana Roo) as important a part of the festal food as is pork. Throughout Yucatan it is characteristically prepared for festivals in one of two ways: *escabeche,* a dish in which turkey is cooked in spices and served, cut up, with a sauce of onions, garlic, peppers, and spices, or *relleno*, turkey stuffed with meat and seasonings and boiled whole. Either turkey or hen is cooked into broth (*kol*); thickened with corn meal, the broth becomes another festal dish known as *hek*. The preparation of these foodstuffs consumes a large amount of labor and time in the days before the festival: firewood must be cut and brought to the village or town; maize must be ground, hogs slaughtered, and the lard rendered; and many other raw materials, including honey, fowl, sugar, and many kinds of seasonings, must be assembled and cooked. The community is host to guests from many other communities, and in the villages that adhere to an old tradition food is given, not sold, to visitors. Especially is food and drink to be supplied to the musicians (who are usually hired from some larger community) and to distinguished visitors. The primary responsibility for discharging this hospitality rests on the men who occupy the leading posts in the festal organization, but the organization of the festival is such as to distribute the responsibility and the cost among others of the community.

For in every community there is a festal organization: a number of permanent offices to which attach the obligations and the honors incident to leadership in the celebration of the fiesta, and traditional devices by which one group of incumbents leaves these offices and their successors enter them. It is not expected that the same man will continue to assume the burden in the following year; the trust must be handed over from one man to another. The structure of the festival is preserved in latency during the year between anniversaries of the patron, and the institution includes features whereby it is called into activity in time to accomplish the festival. A further invariable feature of the festal organization is to be found in usages whereby the labor and the cost of making the festival, while assumed in the first place by one or a few leaders, are distributed among many other members, or even all members, of the community.

In communities where the sense of pious obligation to the patron is strong, the division of labor is incident to a division of responsibility, to a division of the relation between the community and its supernatural guardian. Accordingly the transfer from one group of leaders to the next, and also the subdivision of responsibility from the principal holders to the lesser, is ritualized. These transfers are expressed in traditional gestures; they have a binding effect. The vow by which the community is perpetually bound to its supernatural guardian, and which must be annually renewed, is discharged by a changing series of particular individuals or groups of individuals. In the conservative villages the central organization of the festival is spoken of as *cuch*, "burden," and there are rituals by which the holy load is shifted from one set of shoulders to the next. Always there must be someone, or some group of people, who have the sacred obligation upon them; they are the ones who will next year take the leadership in making the festival. The rituals take the form of an actual handing-over of certain of the festal foods from one man to another and from some men to others. Where the sense of sacred obligation is strong, this act is the culminating moment of the festival; then the sanctified custodianship passes. Where the pious obligation is not paramount, these rituals are absent. "At the fiesta of so-and-so there is no cuch," people say. "It is just an undertaking."

In the following comparison of festivals of the patron saint in Yucatan the writer passes beyond the limitation of his data to those provided by the four communities especially studied and considers material on the festival in communities other than Tusik, Chan Kom, Dzitas, and Merida. Recent emphases on secular progress in Chan Kom have caused observance of the festival there to lapse. So fiestas in neighboring communities enter into the discussion. Merida is not suitable because patron fiestas are extremely attenuated there, and to get a full impression of the fiesta in that city one would have to go back twenty years or more to a period in which the materials would refer to a less urban period than the present. So two still flourishing festivals which Meridanos frequently attend are considered in this chapter. Fiestas can be studied with a somewhat less intimate knowledge of the entire community than can be some other institutions discussed in this book.

The Quintana Roo festivals contain all the elements already mentioned as characterizing the pattern universal for Yucatan. Nine nights of prayer are offered to the patron. The obligation to make the chief offerings (those occurring on the days immediately following the novenario) is distributed among five groups of persons who, taken together, represent the entire group over which the cross or saint is patron. The principal obligation rests upon pious volunteers, while lesser shares of this responsibility are assumed by others. The chief element of entertainment is the vaquería (jarana), which is attended with most of the ancillary features that have been mentioned above. In spite of the fact that the Quintana Roo people are without cattle, their patronal festivals include corridas: a man, half-concealed within a frame of vines, wood, and sacking built to resemble a bull, prances about the ring while toreadors equipped with deerskins used as capes bait him and seek to lasso him. The corrida takes place in a bull ring (kaxche) specially constructed for the occasion; the corrida is preceded by a procession around the plaza; in advance of the corrida a ceiba tree is set up within the ring. The festal foods and drink are rum, pork prepared as relleno and in the form of another seasoned dish known as *tzahbil keken*, crackles, and atole. The culminating feature of the festival is the delivery of certain ritual foods and objects from the incumbent group of organizers to their successors.

Within the limits of the usual pattern the patronal festival, as performed in Quintana Roo, has many local features. Some of these are certainly survivals of elements which were at one time more generally present in Yucatan. In many of the rustic communities of Yucatan it is felt that new ceremonial equipment should be used each time that the festival is performed, but the idea is much more plainly defined in Quintana Roo than elsewhere. Villa tells us[2] that there, whenever a cross is honored with an annual or biennial festival, it is customary to destroy the old altar and make a new one; to provide a new cloth for the altar; and, if money is available, to supply new clay dishes for the offerings. That this was ancient Maya custom is well known.[3] The planting of the ceiba tree, which is omitted in most of the present-day festivals of Yucatan and which is merely a piece of traditional sport where it is still performed, is in Quintana Roo carried on in a manner which still makes plain its connection with religion and agriculture. The tree, as it is borne along to the bull ring, is accompanied by musicians playing religious hymns. It is surmounted by a boy who simulates a *coati* (*pisote; chic*). He performs antics for the amusement of the crowd. Once the tree is planted, he throws squash seeds to the winds as a sign that the tree has flowered and ties yams and gourds to the branches to symbolize the bearing of fruit. To the ancient Maya the ceiba was a sacred tree and a symbol of fertility.[4]

Even more conspicuous in the festival in Quintana Roo are certain survivals which are plainly of Christian origin; indeed, the general impression made on the observer is that the festival is a Christian rite. The ceremony includes both low masses and high masses on the chief days of the festival. The fiesta is inaugurated with a mass of great importance, held at dawn on the first day, called the *alborada misa*. (In such a town as Tizimín, in Yucatan, where nowadays no masses are held at the festival, the word "alborada" is retained for the secular jarana with which the festival begins.) The crosses are paraded in processions involving certain stations, the singing of hymns, and praying by the people while kneeling out of doors. Penance and purification are expressed by the ritual of *kat zipil* ("ask pardon") in which the devout move to the altar on their knees. Furthermore, some of the older folk customs which bear no certain correspondence to either Christian or pagan customs are preserved in X-Cacal. The solemn delivery of the ritual objects embodying the vow is made according to an old traditional form that will be described below. A ceremonial making of atole by selected vaqueras (*puc keyem;* "dissolve atole") is practiced, and there are other old customs later to be mentioned.

On the other hand, some festal customs of indubitable antiquity that are known from some of the communities of Yucatan are not present in Quintana Roo. The two customs of *dza akab* and *hadz pach,* later to be described in connection with the festivals of the Chan Kom region, are not known in X-Cacal, although Villa obtained evidence that the former custom, involving a night of vigil by the vaqueros and vaqueras and their going about receiving food and drink at the houses of organizers of the festival, was practiced two generations ago. The appearance of masked individuals who announce the festival and frighten little boys, the dance of a man dressed as a woman, the management of the jarana by a *cacique,* a sort of festal dictator, the ceremonial strangling of turkeys to be made into festal soup, and the use of balche are all elements of the patron fiesta which are not practiced in Quintana Roo and are apparently not known there but which have survived in the far more sophisticated community of Dzitas, or in some other town or village known to the writer in Yucatan. The fiesta in Quintana Roo is undeniably archaic in many features; but, on the other hand, it is far from a complete record of the corresponding festivals of Colonial times.

Two statements can be made about the Quintana Roo festivals which are of interest in relation to the matters taken up in this volume. The organization of the festival is very closely integrated with the political and social organization of the group, and the emphases of the ritual are strongly upon its sacred aspects. The Quintana Roo festival is not only an elaborate expression of the collective vow of the people with regard to their patron; it is also a manifestation of their prevailing social structure. The men who take the lead in the festival are in part the men who exercise civil authority throughout the year. The festival throws into activity the hierarchy of subtribal leaders. The Nohoch Tata is the supreme personage at the festival, while the chiefs of the companies that compose the subtribe maintain supervision of their companies and take important places in the processions, in the conduct of the ceremonies, and in the feasting. Thus these officers have ceremonial as well as secular civil functions. More striking is the fact that in Quintana Roo the selection of the votaries who assume the burden of the festival is done in such a manner as to depend upon the subtribal structure. Though each village maintains its own annual fiesta of the cross which is patron to that village, these village festivals are of much less importance than are those maintained by the subtribe as a whole. The village crosses are regarded as owned by some particular residents of the villages, and the corresponding festivals are maintained by the owners as their private responsibilities; there are no volunteering burden-bearers; and, although other members of the community may contribute to the cost of the festival, the contributions are modest and unsystematized. In Tusik, for example, the family that has inherited the cross regarded as the village patron asks no help from others in maintaining the festival; the fiesta is regarded as for the benefit of the village, but the one family undertakes it and acts as host to the other villagers. The festivals of the cacicazgo, on the other hand, are the supreme religious acts performed by the people of that group. There are two of these subtribal festivals: one in honor of the Virgin of the Conception, which is held on December 8 or soon thereafter, and another held on or about May 3 in honor of the Holy Cross. These are the same two festivals which were held by these natives generations ago when their political and religious center was Santa Cruz del Bravo. It is now customary to hold these festivals alternately, one each year. The responsibility of the fiesta is divided among the five companies that compose the cacicazgo. Each company must supply four chief organizers (although if one company has met with unusual hardship it may be excused in that year from making its contribution). The festival is held at X-Cacal, the present shrine village. The people assemble there and camp in the *cuarteles*,[5] each company occupying one cuartel. Each company has the responsibility of preparing festal foods and of delivering them solemnly to the santo. The festival, therefore, consists of the usual series of nine nights of prayers (here rosaries); but within this series, on each of the five last days that constitute the important part of the fiesta, there is a repeated cluster of acts in which the companies by turns take leadership. Hogs are slaughtered, maize is ground, festal foods are cooked, and these are arranged on a special table; a procession takes place in which the offerings are carried to the temple; the foods are formally delivered to the santo; two masses are performed; the foods are distributed to the people and eaten; and a vaquería is held. The foods are distributed to the people of the cacicazgo according to companies; that is, each company which is host for that day sends a proper share of the food to the cuarteles of the other companies by turns, the host company being served last. Furthermore, the distribution in each cuartel is done in such a way that the chiefs are served first, according to rank.

The requirement that each company provide four leading organizers is found only in Quintana Roo; only there are the Maya organized in companies. But within each company the choice of those men who will act as organizers is brought about, as elsewhere, according to the wishes of the volunteers and according to the expectations of the other people of the group. The leaders for the fiesta to be held two years thereafter are determined at meetings held on the two last days of the festival. This meeting is held in the church at X-Cacal. It is led by the principal chiefs. The promises made, both by the men who will assume the twenty posts of chief organizers and by those who promise to act as helpers to the leaders, are recorded by the only literate men of the cacicazgo—the secretaries. This is one of the duties attached to the office of secretary.[6]

The Quintana Roo festival, entertaining as it is to its participants, is emphatically a religious enterprise. As compared with the corresponding occasion in the less isolated communities studied, it includes proportionately greater manifestations of religious sentiment. Religious exercises are more numerous, their performance is attended with more solemnity, the participation in them is more general, and the expression of pious offering to deity is more fully and plainly made. Where festivals in other villages and towns include characteristically a novena, or a series of nine recitations of rosaries—or, where a priest is available, may include nine masses—the X-Cacal people, remote and primitive as they are, celebrate nine rosaries, five low masses, and five high masses. Many of them are attended by only a few individuals, but the most important—as, for example, the first mass which begins the festival—are attended by most of the people. These masses are held by the Nohoch Tata, that religious leader whose person is sacred. The maestros cantores and certain persons selected to function as would acolytes have important parts, as do the chiefs of the companies. Both men and women take part in the religious exercises. At several times during the ceremony the images are carried in procession around the plaza to music regarded as religious. Men and women kneel in the open air, as they also do inside the church, to pray. The reader will recall the sanctity which attends the secluded altar in the sanctuary which is the focus of religious attention during these rites. Except for those holding religious offices, approach to the altar is much restricted: one may come up to it only at certain times and with the consent of the Nohoch Tata; no one may come to the altar except with a candle to be placed on it as an offering; shoes may not be worn in the sanctuary. Kneeling, praying, crossing one's self, the burning of candles offered by individuals, money contributions by the faithful for the masses, and a pervasive atmosphere of devotion and appeal to divinity, all evidence the sacredness of the festival.

A striking feature of the X-Cacal ceremony is the solemnity

and elaboration with which the festal foods are arranged and
offered to the divinity honored by the festival. Elsewhere,
while the principal festal foods may be regarded as prepared in
honor of the santo, the sentiment is much more casually entertained and is practically without formal expression. But in
X-Cacal the offering is a principal part of the complex of repeated acts with which each of the five groups of chief votaries
worships the saint or cross on the five principal days of the
fiesta. It is apparent that the arrangement of these festal foods
is accomplished in the same spirit and with much the same
form as attends the arrangement of offerings made, in quite
other ceremonies, to the yuntzilob. This is true, although in the
case of this ceremony to Christian divinities the offerings are
very different, and the matter is not in charge of the h-men. A
special functionary is appointed: some man of religious temperament who in this office is known as *kub-mesa* ("table-
deliverer"). He directs the four votaries of the day how to prepare the offering. The principal festal foods are represented:
relleno, tzahbil keken, tortillas, crackers, and chocolate.
These are arranged in piles or bundles each of which must
contain certain numbers of component parts: three, five,
seven, ten, and thirteen. The napkins and vessels in which the
offerings are placed should be new. Certain numbers of black
wax candles are added. All these articles are arranged in a
symmetrical order on a special table set up in the cuartel of
the company responsible for the offerings of that day. The
votaries formally deliver the whole to the kub-mesa, stating
that it is the table which they have promised to the santo.
They then bring from the temple the most sacred symbols of
deity which are allowed to leave the sanctuary. One is a small
cross, which stands for the Most Holy Cross, the patron of the
cacicazgo. The other is the Holy Seat,[7] a small chair decorated with basil. Two black wax candles are set upon this
chair; no one is allowed to sit in it. These objects are brought
in a solemn procession with music to the cuartel, while the
votaries, their wives, the kub-mesa, and the chief of the com-

pany involved kneel and pray. The symbols of divinity have now been produced; they are present during the performance of the acts which dedicate the offerings to them. When the votaries come out from the cuartel, the kub-mesa distributes the offerings among them, giving each something to carry. The procession, bearing the offerings, the cross, and the Holy Seat, enters the temple where the articles are placed on the altar. A high mass is held, after which the offerings are removed from the altar and distributed to the people in the order that has already been described. This solemn dedication of the festal foods is repeated for each of the four other companies.

Other rituals, also of strong religious import, are present in the X-Cacal ceremony and absent in the other representatives of the annual festival or else are present in other communities in a more secular form. The making of a certain beverage of maize with a sweetmeat of squash seeds and chaya leaves (puc keyem) is a mere traditional and entertaining custom as met with in Dzitas and in villages of the Chan Kom area. In X-Cacal the act is attended with "an air of great seriousness and importance."[8] The atole is placed on the altar, and the people pray before it is eaten. During the festivities not a few individuals, as matters of personal devotion and lustration, practice the kat zipil penance. On the afternoon of the day on which the fifth and last offering is made to the santo there is performed a terminal rite known as "the church offering" (u tzicil iglesia). The kub-mesa prepares a table with festal foods to be eaten by the chiefs while they are secluded from the common people. Before they partake, all the chiefs go to the temple and perform kat zipil to cleanse themselves of sin. The table is set in the temple, and there the chiefs alone eat of the food, in something of the spirit of communion, while armed guards stand at the door.

The rite just mentioned immediately precedes the ceremony known as "dance of the head" (okoztah pol), by which the vow is renewed and the responsibility is intrusted to other hands. The principal symbol is a roasted pig's head, decorated in a certain manner. (On more than one occasion Villa saw maize and honey cakes, similarly decorated, used in place of a pig's head.) The head is given a "crown" of vines. Five sticks, four in a square, and one in the center of the square, are set up on it. The central stick transfixes an *arepa*, a cake of maize and honey. Two little dolls, one dressed as a man, the other as a woman, are set upon this cake. To the sticks are tied corn-husk cigarettes, cruciform arepas, and strips of colored paper. These decorated sticks are sometimes called *ramilletes*. Within the pig's mouth are placed two arepas. The whole is set in a wooden tray. The meaning of these symbols has been almost entirely lost.

The handing-over of the head with ramilletes is attended with much religious significance. The head is first placed upon the altar by the offering chiefs, the secretaries, and the maestros cantores. A rosary is then recited. Eleven persons selected in advance from the participants in the fiesta stand in a row in the cuartel and face the door opposite the temple in such a way so that they look toward the altar. They then sing a song in praise of the Holy Cross. The eleven persons leave their seats and, after making the sign of the cross, begin to dance around a table placed in the center of the corredor. Nine circuits are made in a clockwise direction and nine in a reverse direction. The principal chiefs keep count of the movements around the table by moving cigarettes from one pile to another. On each revolution the dancers cross themselves and repeat the song. The dancing procession is led by the chief of the company involved. He bears the head and is followed by a man who shakes a rattle and acts as though calling a hog. The dance ended, the head is again placed on the altar.

It is surprising that in view of the obvious emphasis in X-Cacal upon the fiesta as the performance of a vow to the santo, the obligation is not called "cuch," and the votaries are not called "burden-bearers" but *diputados*—a word, of much more secular connotations, used for the organizers of the festival in the commercialized towns. Nevertheless, the sanctity of the festival in X-Cacal is apparent. In the more isolated and rustic settlements of the Chan Kom area the festival is expressed in the organization and ritual called "cuch." During the period when these field studies were made, cuch was observed in X-Kopteil and X-Kalakdzonot. There was also cuch, if not in these same years then in years not long before, in Calotmul, Uayma, Dzitnup, and, probably, Tixcacal. In the neighborhood of Tizimín it is similarly the backward communities off the railroad, such as Kikil, Lohche, and Suhcopo, that maintain cuch. These are all rural communities where the older folk tradition is still strong in many aspects of life. That Chan Kom has not had a cuch for many years is to be explained chiefly by the unusual emphasis given in that community to "progress." The interests and energies of the people of Chan Kom have gone to the building of roads and the erection of schools.

The festivals of this area, as compared with those of central Quintana Roo, have fewer religious exercises. There is only a novena and no masses. The solemn dedication of the festal foods upon special altars is lacking. There is no Holy Seat, no kneeling penance, no public processions, no kneeling and praying out of doors. Nevertheless, the conception of discharge of a sacred obligation is central. A brief description of the festival in one of these villages, X-Kalakdzonot, has been published.[9] The leadership of the festival is in the hands of one man, the "burden-bearer" (cargador). He and his wife have principal charge of all arrangements. Their house is the center of activities. Here hospitality is offered to all comers; here the enramada for the dancing is erected; here the musicians are received and fed. He leads in making arrangements to bring musicians, in inviting the people of other settlements to come and dance, in building the bull ring and arranging for the corrida, in buying rockets, and in collecting and preparing the festal foods. But in all these activities he has the assistance of men who, subordinate to him, have assumed shares of the responsibility. In many of these villages the subordinates are called *nakulob;* commonly there are three of them. The cargador is the head of the festival and assumes the largest share in the cost. The nakulob assume lesser and equal shares. The cargador and the nakulob who are to assume the burden in the following year are determined upon at a meeting which takes place at a calendrically fixed date well in advance of the festival this year. The outgoing cargador, who will be in charge of the immediately coming fiesta, will make a speech, or some other man will make it, inviting someone to volunteer to take the cuch as cargador. If no one offers to take it, someone may suggest a name, and the matter may be put to an informal vote. In a similar way the nakulob are decided upon. Thus at the time of every festival the burden-bearers for two festivals are known. The next incumbents stand ready to take over the charge which the outgoing cargador and nakulob are about to lay down.

The chief symbols of the cuch are the decorated pig's head and the ritual objects called ramilletes. In X-Kalakdzonot these are separate from the head and have a somewhat different form from those of Quintana Roo. A ramillete is a pole from the top of which are suspended five hoops. Pole and hoops are wound with colored paper. To them are attached certain traditional objects: paper streamers, cigarettes, dolls made of cloth, and loaves of wheat bread made in the form of eagles. In some communities the cigarettes must be corn-husk cigarettes, and they are fastened in a peculiar manner to objects called *x-muuch.* To make a x-muuch, an entire corn husk is dyed with aniline dye and soaked so as to soften it. Then the outer leaves are split but left attached to the whole, and each is crimped by being folded back and forth. To the end of each of these strips of corn husk is tied a cigarette. The manner of decorating the pig's head has been described. The delivery of these objects takes place on the day following the last jarana. The outgoing cargador, with his nakulob, calls upon the incoming cargador, offers him rum, and invites him to come to his house, the center of the festivities. In preparation for his coming a table has been set in the house of the outgoing car-gador. On it is placed the pig's head, tortillas, rum, a few cigarettes, chocolate, and a small wooden cross. Holding the ramillete, the outgoing cargador addresses his successor and utters a traditional short speech, expressing the handing-over, in the name of the Trinity, of the cuch. The other accepts the ramillete and solemnly declares his promise to make the fes-tival in the following year. The event is witnessed by every-one; the promise is so important that men will say that death might be expected to follow its breach. The new nakulob, at the direction of the new cargador, now take up from the table the objects upon it and, with them, perform a slow dance around the table to traditional music. When they have danced with the objects, all, excepting the pig's head, are divided into parts equal in number to the number of nakulob. By accept-ing these shares, the nakulob express their vows to give the as-sistance to the cargador which tradition expects of them. Be-sides other assistance, each nakulob must return next year to the cargador for use in the festival a double amount of the ob-jects that they take.

The cuch ritual expresses the fact that in these villages the festival is performed in discharge of a vow. The principal ac-tivities take place at the house of the cargador and under his direction. In this way the sacred office of the cargador is made prominent. The jarana which is felt to be in honor of the santo, takes place under the enramada, and, that the santo may be present, the image is moved to that structure. Even the corrida is in some part a sacred undertaking. To express honor or gratitude toward the santo, a man may contribute a bull to the corrida or, in the same spirit, may vow to take part in the dangerous sport of bullbaiting. Generally, however, it is expected that all young and able-bodied men of the village will take part in the corrida, just as all the girls will dance in the jarana. As vaqueros and vaqueras they expose themselves, in the performance and enjoyment of the festival, to an espe-cial danger: the exposure to evil winds which the festal activities entail. The bulls, as fierce animals belonging to a super-natural guardian (X-Juan-Thul), are carriers of these evil winds. The bullbaiters must be prepared, must be strength-ened, for the corrida. So in the remoter villages it is custom-ary before the corrida and before the last jarana for the h-mens to make offering to the balamob and to X-Juan-Thul to keep the vaqueros and vaqueras safe from the evil winds. The va-queros spend the night in vigil (dza akab, "give the night") away from their wives and under the care of a h-men. The ropes with which the bulls are to be bound are purified with balche by the h-men and are kept from contamination; they may not be brought into an ordinary house after purification The vaqueros visit the cargador, and each of the nakulob in. turn, keeping awake by drinking and playing. Always they keep their lassos with them. After the corrida, there takes place a last short jarana which is thought to finish off the fes-tival. At its conclusion the vaqueras are brought to the h-mens, who cleanse them of the evil winds to which dancing and close association with men have exposed them. The h-mens strike them with twisted handkerchiefs; this act gives its name to the ritual (hadz pach, "strike the back"). The h-mens also strike them with branches of *zipche* and blow rum upon them. So are they purified and made safe.

The materials we have collected include no example of the full performance of these two ceremonies in very recent years. It is probable that they are still performed in some of the re-moter villages. They were certainly a characteristic part of the festival of the patron in villages of the Chan Kon area a gen-eration ago. They further expressed the nonsecular character of the festal activities and indeed integrated the festival, an offering to a Catholic saint, with the cult of the yuntzilob. In-formants who witnessed the fiesta in Tekom (east of Chan Kom) in recent years say that there hadz pach is still prac-ticed, but without the services of a h-men. Only the vaqueros are purified, and by the vaqueros: each vaquero in turn holds onto a rope and allows a vaquera whom he selects to hit him with his neckerchief. "This they do to get rid of the winds that have been around the animals they have been fighting. Then the people say: 'Now you are not a vaquero any more. The fiesta is over.'" It is not known by the writer whether dza akab is still practiced in Tekom. In Dzitas younger informants knew nothing about either custom, but some of the old people recalled a purificatory rite, which was apparently hadz pach, that was once practiced there. One old woman said that when she was young in Dzitas, during the last dance of the last jarana, the dancers hung leather whips from their wrists so that in dancing they struck one another "to get off the evil winds." It is plain that at one time the association of the jarana and the corrida with the yuntzilob and with the evil winds was well recognized.

At least up to 1939 (with the exception of 1933), Dzitas observed its festival with a cuch organization and ritual like that characteristic of the villages, and in this respect Dzitas is very exceptional among the railroad towns. Dza akab and hadz pach are lacking in the Dzitas festival, as has just been said, but many of the older folk customs are preserved there. The cuch organization is large and detailed, in proportion to the size of the community. The word "cuch" is used for the organization and for the chief organizers as well as for the obligation or perpetual vow. In the former sense a cuch in Dzitas consists of three cargadores: one "great cuch" and two "small cuch," each of whom has three assistants (noox). The festal organization is perpetuated in three annual calendrical ritual feasts. The festival of Santa Inez, the patron, is celebrated on the Sunday nearest January 21. Apparently it is usual in Dzitas for each cargador to find his own successor or to be approached by some man who wishes to take his place. These private understandings are reached between the time of the festival and Holy Week. No cargador may succeed himself, but in the second year the same man may again be cargador. On Holy Saturday a meeting is held in the public building (cuartel). This meeting is called chuc-hel ("seek out a successor").

Each of the three cargadores who are to make the festival in the following January—who are, in other words, the present bearers of the vow—goes to the house of his successor and escorts him to the place of meeting. On this occasion, or before it, each new cargador has asked three men to be his noox. So, if all arrangements are complete, the meeting consists of twenty-four men. The current cuch are the hosts; they offer cigarettes and balche or rum to their successors and in so doing bind their successors to their obligation. In the evening it is usual to hold a jarana, the costs of which are paid by the current cargadores.

Chuc-hel brings into being the next cuch. *Kah ik* ("notification") assures the readiness of the new cuch to take over the pious burden at the termination of the coming festival. This second meeting takes place on Christmas Eve. Again balche is distributed, again a jarana is held, and again the cargadores of the current year bring their successors to the place of meeting, with their noox, and, by giving them drink and cigarettes, recall their promises. If through death or other causes substitutions have to be made, they are arranged on this occasion.

Now the present cargadores are assured of the readiness of their successors. Soon after Christmas they and their noox, and the three assistants customarily found by each noox, begin to assemble the money and food and other materials necessary. Each cargador and each noox is expected to furnish a large hog (in some years two), a turkey, one or more hens, certain amounts of maize and honey, cacao cooked with ground purple maize and flavored with anise and pepper, and (for the ramilletes) six cloth dolls and six x-muuch. The costs of the rockets, of the musicians, and of the masses, if there are any, are borne by the cargadores and the noox equally except that the chief cargador makes the largest contribution. But already these costs have in part been distributed to others. Each helper of a noox may contribute a small amount of money besides his services. On the occasion of both the chuc-hel and of the kah ik, it is customary for the cargadores to send boys about the town offering balche to the people. Everyone who accepts balche is expected to give a few cents toward the cost of the festival.

On the Wednesday just preceding the fiesta, the preparation of the festal foods begins at the houses of the cargadores and of the noox. The wives of these men have found other women to help them. Each helper of a noox brings a load of firewood, one measure of maize, a bottle of honey, and two chickens. On this day the maize is boiled, the hogs are slaughtered, and the lard is rendered. During the night the maize is ground for the cakes called "arepas."

On the following day the arepas are taken to the baker to be baked, and chicken broth (kol) is made. When the arepas are done, some are eaten at once by the cargadores and some are given to their helpers. If anyone comes to a house where these activities are in progress, it is customary to offer such persons arepas, and they are expected to contribute a few cents to the cost of the fiesta.

The rest of the festival is similar to what has been described for X-Kalakdzonot, except, of course, that the festival is larger and more elaborate, as the community is larger and richer. There are (at least) two jaranas—one held on Saturday night, the other on Sunday. There is usually a corrida. The delivery of the cuch takes place on Sunday afternoon. The cargadores do not themselves dance with the ritual objects but select six men to do it for them. There is one pig's head and one ramillete for each of the three cargadores, hence six men are used in the dance. The ramilletes and the pigs' heads are prepared as in the villages. The delivery is made with solemnity and is expressed in short traditional utterances. Each new cargador receives from his predecessor one of the pigs' heads, one of the ramilletes, seventy small arepas, twelve large arepas, one bottle of rum with a flower stuck in the neck, one measure of cracklings, and four gourd vessels of that thickened turkey broth called "hek." Each new cargador begins at once the organization of the group of assistants who will help him to make the festival in the following years by dividing what he has just received equally among his three noox. The noox in their turn invite others present to promise to be their helpers, and distribute among the people small fragments of their share. Each person who accepts a share obligates himself to bring wood, honey, and maize next year on the Wednesday preceding the festival and must help in the preparations at that time. Ordinarily each helper receives four arepas and some hek. People may take dolls, or x-muuch, or breads from the ramillete; by doing so, each promises to bring two of the same next year. The organization for the next fiesta is now begun. Soon after this festival the cargadores and their noox, bearers of the vow, must find successors who will take the festival when it is performed two years from now. With the meeting of the new cargadores and their successors on Holy Saturday the cycle of meetings is repeated.

Besides the all-important cuch, the Dzitas festival preserves a number of customs which suggest meanings of the festival now lost. At the end of the first jarana it is customary to strangle the turkeys used for the hek while dancing with them. Each cargador finds a man to do this, giving him half a bottle of rum and some cigarettes. At the dance of the ramilletes and the pigs' heads there also dances a man dressed as a woman, wearing a wig of henequen fiber and carrying a calabash rattle. This person, known as *La Encamisada*, is arranged for by the cargadores. During the dance balche is sprinkled over the dancers and anyone who is near them. On the day of the fiesta two men known as chic ("fool," also "coati")[10] appear as buffoons. One is dressed in rags, with a headdress of feathers; the other, as a woman. Just before the jarana they go about blowing on conch shells and announcing the festival. As they go about, small boys try to avoid them, for, if they catch a small boy, they rub a little gunpowder and fat on his anus. At the jarana it is sometimes arranged to have two pretty vaqueras sell dishes of a special atole; this custom (already mentioned in connection with X-Cacal) is called puc keyem ("dissolve atole").

And still another custom is that whereby, to get funds for the festival of next year, the cacique (as is called a sort of master of ceremonies appointed to lead the jarana) "sells" a vaquera to a man present: she sits beside him for a little while or dances with him, and the cacique collects money.[11]

With the exception of the "dance of the turkeys" (*cutz-cal-tzo*), which has been reported to us from no other community but Dzitas, the customs just mentioned are present, or have recently been present, in other communities of the area—more commonly in villages, of course, than in towns like Dzitas. The people of Dzitas take pride in the traditional character of their festival. Although the form of some of the customs mentioned suggests that they, like the ceiba-planting ceremony in X-Cacal, once had significance in connection with agriculture or religion, nothing said about them by the people of Dzitas would suggest that they have any such meanings today. As performed in recent years these customs are enjoyed because they are traditional and because they are amusing. They contribute to the excitement and to the fun, and that is all that there is to them. They are not like the cuch, for the cuch is the expression of serious commitment that rests under strong religious sanctions.

That the Dzitas fiesta had two generations ago a much more religious character than it now has is indicated by information given by the oldest natives of Dzitas. In the middle of the nineteenth century the festival of Santa Inez, with cuch, was celebrated only by indios. The vecinos celebrated the festival of the Virgin of the Conception, and without cuch. The cuch of that time was organized much as it is now, and the ritual objects and foods were very similar (informants say, however, that the ramilletes of that time were not adorned with paper but with shells and baskets of wax and that money was hung upon them). But the cuch was more closely related to the church and probably to the prayers for good crops. At that time the twelve cargadores were locked up in the church during the night preceding the jarana. When they came out, they came out dancing with dishes of kol. They passed under an enramada in which the santo was placed, and, after paying their respects to the santo, they offered the kol to everyone. There was a parade of the santos; the wooden cylindrical drum (*tunkul*) was beaten at the door of the church; people who came out of the church were given a taste of seasoned corn gruel (*pinole*) from a wooden paddle; it was customary to set young maize plants on each side of the path along which the procession passed. In later years the activities were moved to the house of the chief cargador and still later to the secular public building (*juzgado*), where they are now held.

The central idea of the vow was given wider expression in those times. The cargadores themselves danced with the ritual objects. At the beginning of the first jarana, after they had come out from their period of seclusion in the church, the cargadores were required to dance first with their wives. Many of those who took part in the jaranas did so in compliance with a vow. The woman who assumed the principal responsibility for the cooking of the foods did so as a vow or offering; in later days the wife of the head cargador came to assume the duty. Arepas and balche were then not sold but offered free to all comers, as "the guests of the santo." Nowadays people take the offering of balche lightly, some throwing it out; but then it was regarded as a sacred offering to be treated with respect. These fragments of information as to the old-time fiesta probably include errors and no doubt omit much, but they surely point to a stronger religious meaning of the festival. It may be added that it is only in recent years that, imitating the customs of Merida, the more Catholic women of Dzitas have organized gremios to take charge of the novenas, to decorate the church, and to give new jaranas, independent of those of the cargadores. In earlier years all these activities were subsumed under the responsibility of the man making cuch; thus there was then a single organization, led by men, for the festival.

As compared with the festival in Tusik, that of Dzitas is the more secular. Although it remains a collective effort of a large part of the community and is still based on the worship of the santo and the serious and pious undertakings of the leading votaries, the reference to the divine and moral world is less explicit than is the case in Quintana Roo. As compared with the festivals in most Yucatecan towns, that of Dzitas is unusually complete with details of traditional ritual and entertainment. It is probable that the festival in Dzitas has not suffered a great diminution. It remains the important regular collective action of the people. But its great function seems now to be to emphasize the structure of the community and to express the pride and solidarity of the town: the intensely religious sentiments which support and complete this function in the case of the festival of Quintana Roo are less present in Dzitas.

At any rate, the Dzitas festival is not primarily a commercial undertaking. Many vendors of foods and drinks take advantage of the presence of the crowd to make a little money, but these commercial opportunities are unorganized. On the whole, the Dzitas festival, in so far as it is not prayer, is a party; it is not a business venture. The case of the fiesta of Tizimín is interesting because it adds this third aspect: it *is* a commercial undertaking. It happened, for reasons which are unknown to the writer, that the Three Kings of Tizimín became for Yucatan as a whole the most miraculous santos in the peninsula. As stated in an earlier chapter, for many townspeople and for many people of Merida these are the santos to whom one prays in time of trouble rather than the patrons of their own communities. The fiesta, therefore, attracts a large number of people from all over the peninsula. Especially since the railroad reached Tizimín at the turn of the century, Tizimín has become a Yucatecan Mecca. The fiesta retains most of the traditional forms. It includes jaranas and corridas. The novenario is divided into the usual nine parts, and the handing-over of the responsibility for the worship of the santos from one group to the next is attended with the usual processions and fireworks. The jaranas have special traditional names. At the conclusion of the first jarana the ceiba tree is brought, with music, to the bull ring and planted there. Those who take part in this ceremony immediately at its conclusion go to the house of the chief organizer of the fiesta and are given rum. The ceremony of "crowning the plaza" by the vaqueros and vaqueras is observed after the second jarana and again after the corrida. The early-morning procession around the plaza after the last jarana (la nona) is likewise observed. People make arepas, and cook turkey meat in the festal dishes. Sometimes they observe the custom, mentioned above, called puc keyem. Ramilletes are made and paraded around the plaza together with the paraphernalia of the bullfight.

Nevertheless, in Tizimín the festival is not organized around the pious vows of men religiously obligated to the santo. There is no cuch in Tizimín, and no dance of the pigs' heads and the ramilletes. There is no ceremonious handing-over from incumbents to successors. Ramilletes are made, but apparently only by some of the organizers, and they are not handed over to a successor but are at once distributed to any who will take part, with the expectation that each recipient will make a contribution in the following year. The fiesta is in general charge of a commission appointed by the officers of the town government. The posts are profitable, and they go to political favorites. The commission must hire the musicians for the three vaquerías and for the corridas. To secure funds, the commission holds an auction at Christmas. The various concessions to be involved in the fiesta are auctioned off: the corridas, the vaquerías, the merry-go-round, and forty or fifty "locations" (*puestos*) in the market place at which the buyers are entitled to sell food or drink or operate gambling games. Each concessionaire comes to make money. The net profits which accrue to the commission are supposed to be turned over to the municipal treasury to pay for public improvements, but it is widely said that a part remains in the pockets of the commissioners. Certainly the primary purpose of these men, who control the organization of the festival, is to make money. Under their general supervision two other organizations maintain, respectively, the fiesta *sagrada* and the fiesta *secular*. The former, the nine novenas, is in charge of nine gremios. These are composed of both men and women. Only a minority of their membership comes from Tizimín. By participating in these gremios, pious and socially inclined people from elsewhere in Yucatan may offer worship to the santos. Because there are three santos, a term of membership consists of three years. Those who belong contribute to the cost of the novena, help in the work, and take part in the procession. So many are the participants that some gremios are divided into sections, and the labor is divided among the sections. In some cases all the members of a section come from the same town or from Merida. The fiesta secular is in charge of eight *diputaciones*, each headed by a diputado. The corridas and vaquerías are maintained for nine days and nights; the events of the last day and night are arranged directly by the commission. A pious man may assume one of the posts of diputado as a matter of vow. The writer does not know how often this is the case. He is informed that some diputados operate their enterprises as if they were concessions and make money by commercial dealings with the hogs and other materials which they collect. The accounts given as to the operations behind the corridas leave little doubt but that the organization of the Tizimín fiesta gives a place for both profit and piety. A man who offers a bull to the fiesta has a choice: he may offer it "to the death" or he may restrict his offering so that the bull may be only baited (*lidiado*). Apparently in many instances of the first class the owner sells the bull to a butcher on the hoof and after the corrida recovers all but the difference between this price and the value of the bull alive. Or one may rent a bull from a cattle dealer and offer it, technically de promesa, but restricted to lidiado, in the fiesta; so that all one has offered is the cost of rental. Cases are reported of men going into such an enterprise on shares.

The fiesta of Tizimín is, therefore, a business enterprise so arranged as to make it possible for the genuinely pious also to take part. The concessions at Tizimín bring higher prices, probably, than any others in the peninsula. On the other hand, more people kneel in genuine prayer before the santos than can be found in other fiestas, and many who dance in the jarana do so because they have vowed to *Los Reyes* to come take part in their festival. The fiesta of Tizimín has a modern and secular administration. But also it retains a great number of elements of the old folk festival. This combination of features is probably due to the fact that the Tizimín fiesta began to be famous and also commercialized at a time when the folk culture was still strong in the eastern part of the peninsula. The especial sanctity of the santos of Tizimín attracted many outsiders. When the railroad made communications easy, the opportunities for financial gain shifted the central organization from votaries of the santos to promoters and politicians. The pious sought to maintain the old customs because related to a sacred tradition, while the profit-seekers saw in the preservation of old customs something to attract the public. So piety and profit have got along together in Tizimín.

What happens to the festival of the patron saint under modern conditions in an area where the folk tradition is less strong and where the santo celebrated enjoys no unusual prestige appears from consideration of the fiesta of Chicxulub. This is a village on the coast north of Merida and not far from the port of Progreso. In this area the settlements are small and poor. The area was early affected by European influences. The folk culture has greatly declined here as compared with culture in the eastern part of the peninsula. Nevertheless, most of the coastal villages maintained the festival of the patron saint, although in most instances, probably, without cuch. The festival of Chicxulub was until recently a very minor affair. But in the 1930's the coastal strip east of Progreso experienced a boom. This occurred because it became fashionable for people with money to spend some weeks during the hottest part of the summer on the seacoast. The automobile road to Progreso was opened in 1928. The summer colony grew, and people of the middle class also came to enjoy a vacation on the seashore. From Progreso the *temporadistas* spread to other settlements on the coast. They began to attend those local festivals which happen to fall in the summer season. The increasing size of the crowds attracted vendors from Merida and elsewhere. The municipal governments of these settlements began to develop the festival as so to realize on the commercial possibilities. Competition grew keen. In 1934 it is said that over ten thousand people visited Chicxulub on a single day of the festival. The fiesta of Seyé happened to fall on the same date and was that year a complete failure. In order to compete with Chicxulub, Chelem changed the date of its festival from the date proper to it according to the calendar of saints to a day falling before the fiesta of Chicxulub. But by this time Chicxulub had become the fashionable place to go, and the attempt of Chelem failed.

The fiesta of Chicxulub still centers around a novenario, corridas, and dances. It is still possible for a pious person to make offerings to the santo (here a Virgin) and even to contribute a bull to the bullfight in the spirit of a vow. But the religious aspect of the fiesta has been reduced to almost nothing. The novenario is in the hands of women, chiefly from the community. They do little more than decorate the church and arrange for the rosaries. They receive no assistance from the municipal authorities who are busy promoting the secular festival. Occasionally some of the summer residents help decorate the altar "just for fun." The secular festival has become the chief enterprise and the biggest business of the village. The date is now fixed for that Sunday in August when the moon is at its best. At this time the summer season is at it height. The authorities spend money in building an ample bull ring and a large platform for dancing and in hiring musicians and professional bullfighters. But there is a large income from paid admissions. The jarana has been reduced to a very small affair; few of the people who come to Chicxulub wish to dance the jarana. Most of the visitors are young people from Merida. They have no thought for the Virgin and every thought for having a good time. They attend in large numbers the modern dances (bailes). Admission to these is free to women; men pay a peso—a large charge for Yucatan. The dances are policed, and there is a problem of dealing with vice and disorder. Admission to the corrida costs fifty cents or a peso for a seat. Although the paid bullfighters furnish most of the entertainment, amateurs are allowed to enter the ring to discharge promesas by riding or baiting the bulls. Except in the customs whereby the few local women, almost unnoticed, maintain their organization for arranging rosaries for the Virgin, there is nothing in the festival to suggest the perpetuation of a sacred charge. There is no sacred charge. There is instead commercialized entertainment. In 1934, when these coastal villages were experiencing a boom, there was a movement to call the principal festivals of the patron saints "fairs" instead of "festivals of saints." It was proposed that each community name its festival after some conspicuous local product —the cedar, the *jícama*, etc. The village of Komchen did in fact hold a "Maize Fair" consisting of "dances, bullfights, and other pleasures." Some journalists in Merida praised the movement and tried to find in the alleged fact that the ancient Mayas had a "beautiful succession of agricultural festivals" a justification for the change. So when secularization has destroyed the old meanings do reason and rationalization invent new ones.

CHAPTER XI

MEDICINE AND MAGIC

THE generalized description of the festival of the patron saint that occurs in the first pages of the immediately preceding chapter will remind the reader that, notwithstanding the local differences that are emphasized throughout this book, there is a Yucatecan culture. Like every other relatively isolated community, Yucatan as a whole has customs and institutions which characterize it and distinguish it from every other such community. It is, of course, among the common people that these regionally peculiar customs most plainly appear. The educated classes of the city carry on ways of life which tend to be international. Golf, automobiles, and scientific medicine do not characterize Yucatan so as to distinguish it from other countries. The local culture is to be found in the ways of life of the uneducated and of the rustic.

So in Yucatan a culture, characteristic of the peninsula, exists in the traditional behavior of the common people, including the remote tribesman, the isolated Maya peasant, and the masses of the town and the city. To distinguish it from the ways of the well educated, which are not, in the same sense, Yucatecan, and not, in the same full sense, culture, we may call it the folk culture of Yucatan. That this culture undergoes disorganization in the urban environment and is less completely present there should appear from a reading of foregoing pages. In chapter iv, in connection with questions as to the extent and nature of Indian as compared with Spanish influence upon the ways of life of the peninsula, mention was made of many of the principal customs, tools, and institutions which are generally known and accepted throughout Yucatan, at least among the common people. In describing Yucatecan life as a

303

whole one might ignore the elements of conventional behavior which are found only in the city, most of which have been relatively recently introduced there. One might also neglect those vestiges of early customs that survive in certain of the villages, such as the pagan agricultural rites and conceptions, or the New Fire ceremony, or the custom of public penance. One would have left, nevertheless, enough to describe Yucatecan culture and to distinguish it from other cultures.

The "common Yucatecan" knows the local techniques of maize-growing. He is familiar with the apsidal thatched house of poles and thatch and with a great many elements of domestic equipment and practice, including most of the objects described in the chapters on the material culture of Chan Kom and of Tusik.[1] He sleeps in a hammock, eats tortillas and beans, drinks coffee or chocolate, and wears the folk costume that has often been described. He is familiar with citrus fruits, the metal handmill, metal knives, axes and hoes, kerosene lamps, candles, firearms, and cattle- and bee-keeping. He uses the European calendar, observes Sunday, and celebrates certain saint's days with play, abstention from labor, and often ritual practices. The festival pattern described in the last chapter, in its essential features, is known to him. He can recite some of the principal Catholic prayers; he understands something about novenas and rosaries, octaves, masses, heaven and hell, punishment after death, God, Christ, the saints, baptism, hetzmek, the balams as uncanny supernatural beings of the wood, the x-tabai, and the alux. He regards himself as related to his kinsmen in both the line of his father and that of his mother; he thinks it natural that a man should make his home, after marriage, near his father's home, although settlement with the mother or apart from both is also proper to him. He is used to the institution of godparenthood, and he thinks it improper to marry one's godparent, or godchild, or the child of one's godparent.

In no aspect of living is the existence of a widespread Yucatecan folk culture more evident, in spite of local differ-

ences, than in the beliefs and practices with regard to disease
and its treatment. The materials collected from the four communities are in the most nearly complete agreement (excepting
those relating to methods of farming and housebuilding) where
they deal with the popular conceptions as to health, sickness,
and the treatment of sickness. In speculating on the probable
historic causes for the wide spread of these conceptions, one
observes that they are not the sort of thing which the Spanish
missionaries and administrators would have forced upon the
natives. Indeed it is clear that they are not entirely Spanish in
origin; Indian contributions are apparent. Notions as to sickness and health must have been spread among the people of
Yucatan without important coercion. They must have spread
because they were interesting and because their application
was believed to be effective. In so far as the conceptions are the
same in the four communities, they constitute a sort of primitive pseudo-science and corresponding healing art: they are
the technology of the folk to provide health, as building the
thatched house meets the need for shelter, and maize agriculture and the folk cookery provide food. The differences among
the four communities in connection with the customs relating
to sickness become significant, however, when one considers
the ways in which these ideas of folk physiology and the art of
healing are connected with religion or with aspects of social
organization or disorganization.

Of fundamental importance in the folk conceptions as to disease is the concept of evil winds.[2] These are in part associated
with actual movements of air, in part regarded as malevolent
supernatural beings, and in part considered as groups of symptoms making up diseases. The concept exists both in generalized form, "wind," and as many separately distinguished and
often semipersonified "winds." They are connected with
wells, caves, and water generally. The wind that blows in the
evening when a yellow light shines against the background of a
dark sky is a particularly dangerous wind; so also are whirling
winds. Persons going into the bush are in special danger from

these winds; so also are those who become heated from exercise, or who are tired, or who become sexually excited. The winds are thought of as somehow entering the body of the affected person, and treatment consists in removing them, either by entreating them or by compelling them to go, as supernatural beings, or by removing them through lustrative actions, as if they were infecting substances. Specialists, curers or shaman-priests, are required in all serious ailments resulting from attack or possession by evil winds. Certain plants are especially appropriate to cure or to prevent the maladies caused by evil winds: the zipche plant is used to sweep away the winds; the seeds of the oxol are worn as a preventive.

The foregoing summary is far from a complete statement of the conceptions and practices which are general in Yucatan among the uneducated with respect to the one subject of the disease-bearing winds, but it will serve to indicate that the common understandings throughout the area studied extend to points of considerable detail. A similar group of generally held beliefs and practices center around the idea of the evil eye.[3] Certain persons are born with the power to cause sickness by merely looking at one; they may be recognized by the presence of some sort of a mark in their own eye or of a mark near the nose. Some animals have the power. Children are the usual victims of those with evil eye, and an ailment known as "green diarrhea" is the common result. Treatment is either with certain herbs, of which rue is most important, or by "homeopathic" application to the child of something associated with the one who, usually unwittingly, caused the sickness by exercise of his unfortunate power.

Many other elements of thought and practice go to make up the Yucatecan folkways with respect to sickness and its treatment. The conception of the division of most foods and many herbal remedies into two categories, "hot" and "cold,"[4] is held by the citizen of Merida and the remote tribal Indian. Everyone can at once mention foods which are more or less "hot" or "cold," and the lists of such foods collected in the four communities are very similar in detail. A person who is heated should not eat of "cold" things. "Cold" things are debilitating or otherwise dangerous, and persons much weakened or chilled should take of "hot" foods or remedies. A person in fever may be helped by taking "cold" remedies. So good health is in considerable part a matter of maintaining proper equilibrium between these opposite extremes. It is thought (at least in the villages and the town) that some people are by nature "cold" while others are "hot"; the marriage of persons representing the same extreme is likely to result in the sickness of one or the other.[5] Persons with "cold hands" will be unsuccessful in certain activities such as cooking or raising certain kinds of domestic animals. A well-known sickness associated with a condition of "cold" and usually affecting women is known as *pasmo*.

A supernatural nocturnal bird, blue in color, brings illness to children when it flies above them as they sleep. A person with a wound should not go near a corpse; the sickness or evil associated with the corpse may enter the wound. Smallpox, whooping-cough, and measles are carried by a trio of supernatural beings in miniature human form; when these diseases are prevalent, the beings should be propitiated with offerings. Useful in the treatment of certain ailments are bathing, massage, bleeding, and cupping. The professional curers use flint points or rattlesnake fangs to make the incisions for bleeding. They know methods of divination or prognosis: looking into a crystal or casting grains of corn. Tuesday and Friday are days of particular danger from evil winds; they are also days especially suited to the treatment of diseases in which the banishment or propitiation of the winds is a consideration. Many of the ritual acts performed in connection with medical treatment should be ninefold. The wood of the tree known as *tancazche* is a specific and amulet against many maladies. Although there are great local differences as to the amount of imputed witchcraft, some ideas on the subject are probably universal in the area: that certain persons can turn themselves into animals and in this form go about at night doing evil and indecent acts; that extraordinary skill is the result of a pact made with the devil; that certain persons can bring sickness and death upon others by magic worked on the victim from a distance.

The list of widespread elements could be considerably extended. Nevertheless, taken as a whole, the ideas and beliefs as to sickness and its treatment are conspicuously different as they appear in the villages in comparison with the corresponding ideas as they enter into the lives of the city dweller. As in some other features of customary life which have been here compared, the tribal and peasant villages are much alike, and the situation in Dzitas lies somewhere between that characterizing the villages, on the one hand, and that of Merida, on the other.

In the villages the ideas as to disease are closely interdependent with moral and religious conceptions; in the city they are much less so. In the villages the ideas as to sickness and its treatment form a relatively simple and stable body of interrelated parts. In the city the conceptions are more numerous and are less consistently and less stably related to one another. These two general propositions may be expanded in a single discussion.

In the villages a principal cause of disease is believed to lie in the failure of the sick man to make one of the ritual offerings expected of the pious man. The ritual offerings, in turn, are in the villages inseparable aspects of the agricultural activities. In chapter v it has already been indicated that prudence, piety, and physical welfare are thus closely interrelated. "The man whose soul is at peace can expect to be in good health." To make milpa, and to make the offerings that go with making milpa, is to safeguard one's self against one of the chief dangers to health and life: the punishment of the gods. In Tusik, and in Chan Kom (excepting the opportunity given the natives there to visit a clinic established for several years at Chichen Itza), the only special knowledge to which the sick man may turn, should his ailment get beyond the bounds of domestic ministration, is that of the h-men, a functionary who both leads the natives in the rituals addressed to the pagan deities and also diagnoses and treats their ailments. In many cases the h-men declares the cause of the malady to lie in the failure of the sick man (or of the sick person's husband or father) to make the expected offering. The winds, the universal bringers of diseases, are everywhere in Yucatan regarded as acting of their own volition or as entering the body of the sufferer by mere accident. But in the villages it is also common to regard the winds as coming because sent by the deities of the fields or of the hives. "Is it the dinner-of-the-milpa or a wind that comes?" runs the divinatory formula of the h-men; that is, is it because this man did not make the ceremony that the gods punish him, or is it simply chance encounter with a wind? In many cases the former explanation is given, and the sickness is considered to follow a lapse from piety.

A further connection with religion and morals is made in the villages by the meaning given to the ceremonies (Catholic in form) performed for the souls of dead kindred. Not a few of the cases of sickness observed in Chan Kom[6] were believed to be occasioned by the failure of the afflicted person to have recited the prayers for the dead. "The soul of her mother is troubling her because she has not prayed for her for a long time." It is the h-men, leader in pagan ritual though he is, who makes these diagnoses; the Catholic prayer that must be made to bring about the patient's recovery is later conducted by the maestro cantor. The point is that the concentration of all power of professional diagnosis and treatment into the hands of a single functionary, the h-men—and that functionary the leader in the important agricultural and lustrative rituals—allows for a consistency of conceptions as to sickness and for their integration into the religion of the people, which the notably different situation in this regard in the town and city does not allow. The materials from Quintana Roo[7] also show the importance of this belief that inattention to the souls of the dead is a cause of illness. None of the cases of sickness

reported in Dzitas involved this cause of sickness, nor did
Hansen ever hear the idea expressed in Merida. The point of
the healing cult of spiritualism that is so important in Merida
is the communicating with the dead to get their advice on
treatment; it is not a propitiation of dead ancestors. In the
villages the souls of the dead are nearer and more dangerous
to men than they are thought to be in the town and in the city.
The Day of the Dead in the villages is a day when the spirits
return and stand close at hand to watch the conduct of their
living kindred. It is feared that on these days a dead soul might
invade the body of a child.[8] The rituals performed after a
death in Chan Kom have for their purpose, in considerable
part, the safe separation of the soul from the earth and the
speeding of it to heaven, where it will not trouble the living.
So, in the villages, the man who is stricken with illness at once
thinks, "Have I done my duty.to the yuntzilob? Have I made
my prayers for my dead father and mother?"

The knowledge and practice of the h-men holds religious
and medical conceptions together in something that approxi-
mates a system of ideas. The laymen differ greatly among
themselves, of course, as to the degree of interest they take in
the special knowledge. It is safe to say, however, that in the
thinking of the ordinary villager there are not a few lines of
connection between disease and religion which are lacking in
the view of the ordinary townsman. The city man, in talking
of the evil winds, does not associate them with the coming and
going of the balams and chaacs and kuilob-kaaxob in the bush
and in the cornfield. The villager, as he goes about these
places, thinks of the unseen presence of his deities and fears to
meet them or to pass near them, because the winds accompany
them: the supernatural is dangerous as well as good. He is
reminded of this idea every time he attends an agricultural
ceremony, for the h-men's ritual acts express the dangerous-
ness of an occasion to which the yuntzilob are bidden and include conspicuous cleansings and sweepings-away of the winds
that have attended the dangerous moments. The dual divi-

sion into cold and hot extends, in the villages, into the plants used to adorn the altar prepared for the yuntzilob; there is a tacit parallel, already noted in chapter v, between fever, the sickness of man, and drought, the fever of the milpa. In Quintana Roo the celebration of the New Fire ceremony in Holy Week brings to the foreground certain men in the community who have "hot hands"; they kindle the sacred fire and so relate the cold-hot dichotomy to the religious life. In the town and city the conception is quite secular.

A parenthetical statement, repeating what was more briefly said in chapter ix, suggests itself to prevent an apparent misrepresentation. It is not the intention to convey the impression that the Maya of the villages are an unusually religious people. They do not so impress the writer. In Chan Kom the h-men is appreciated, but with a strong skeptical qualification. In Quintana Roo the authority and respect granted the h-men are much below that given to the more secular officers (but the Nohoch Tata receives the greatest respect of all specialists). The attitude of the villager in both communities, when he participates in a ceremony, is as much one of prudence as of religious devotion. Nevertheless, in terms of degree, the relatively greater role played by religious conceptions in the village life is hard to deny. In many cases of sickness in the village the afflicted person thinks of his gods or the spirits of his dead, and much treatment takes the form of a prayer and propitiation. Conversely, there are symbols, such as the evil wind or the "cold" plant or the "hot" person, that suggest both matters of health and matters of the gods. These statements cannot be made of the ideas of the "average" city man.

In Quintana Roo the folk conceptions of disease and the leadership of the h-men in these matters have no rival for the faith of the people. A single body of customs exists, interrelated with other aspects of the culture. In Chan Kom this is less true because the inhabitants include persons who lived in the city and because communication with the teacher, with the Americans at Chichen, and with visitors and travelers brings about the communication of new and conflicting ideas. The course of treatment in Chan Kom does not always run smooth. The materials presented in the "Diary" of events in that village in 1930–31 show the effects of competing notions as to treatment of disease. Don Fano, a simple and pious man who lived all his life in the village, accedes only briefly to the recommendation of the teacher that he take medicines provided by the Americans; almost at once he sends for a h-men and makes a ceremony to the bee-gods in expression of a pattern of ideas he well understands, and then makes a novena to God and the saints.[9] Don Nas, who spent some years in Merida and is Spanish-speaking and literate, passes through gyrations of suspicion, opinion, hope, and experiment, in trying a series of ideas and applications, from the exorcising of evil winds to hypodermic injections. The behavior of Don Nas presents in Chan Kom a single case of a sort that is common in Dzitas and still commoner in Merida.

The extended published account of the treatment of disease in Dzitas shows a situation there which differs greatly from that prevailing in the village. The difference may be stated in three propositions of related fact: (1) the folk medicine is exposed to great competition from other, recently invading, ideas and practices; (2) the folk medicine is associated with what is depreciated, while the rival ideas, though less well understood, are connected with superior social position; and (3) the folk medicine is almost completely without the support of religious connection and sanction.

The inhabitant of Dzitas may consult the local curer (Aurelia, a woman), or he may consult a city-trained doctor who occasionally comes to Dzitas, or he may visit other doctors in towns near by. He may ask the advice of a Mexican practitioner of spiritualistic healing—a matter occult and of doubtful merit to the ordinary inhabitant of Dzitas. He may go out into the country and ask the aid of a h-men in some small village or hacienda settlement, in which case he has recourse to someone who is little known to him personally and whose conduct of religious ceremonies he does not well know or much understand. Or he may pay a good fee to the ambulant practitioner, Don Petronilo, who impresses his patients with long words and long hair and knowledge gained from books. Many single cases of treatment in Dzitas in fact involve several of these conflicting sources of authority and help.

So the individual is presented with a number of alternative and often inconsistent lines of conduct, no one of which is closely integrated with the other institutions and conceptions by which his life is ruled. A man may find his neighbor or his kinsman expressing lack of confidence and even contempt for the course he chooses to follow. In serious cases of illness a native may follow first one course and then another; it is not rare for a patient to consult within a short time Dr. A. of Espita, Aurelia, and Petronilo. Each source of medical authority receives support from one or another consideration, but each of those is a little reason by itself, incomplete or even adventitious.[10]

The only one of these practitioners who offers patients a body of practices which are at all well understood and which connect with the local tradition and the lore of the ordinary person in Dzitas is Aurelia, the curer. She makes the most of the evil winds, of hot and cold, and of the herbal medicine. She agrees with the common man that Tuesday and Friday are the best days on which to take certain cures; she trusts the preventive worth of tancazche; she understands the lustrative value of rum. She burns a candle before a cross when she heals; and she knows about bleeding and massage. The common people may be induced to trust her just because she carries on conceptions which they were brought up to trust; she knows much more about those matters and can better control the powers involved. But it does not clearly work out in this way, for in Dzitas superior status is accorded the modern and the urban. "To consult a city doctor is to add to one's prestige; it is beneath the dignity of the upper class in Dzitas, and for most men, to consult Aurelia."[11] The traveling healer and the city-trained doctor are symbols of the privileged class and of the greater power and social position of the city, and even the most ignorant people of Dzitas apply to those experts for aid if opportunity and money are available. But the medical knowledge of these specialists is, on the whole, mystery to the uneducated inhabitants of Dzitas. Two motives chiefly impel such a person to consult one of these "outside" practitioners. The first is the hope or conviction that the famous man can effect a cure. The second is provided by the fact that in doing so one identifies one's self with the socially superior. The exercise of these motives tends not to preserve the old folk culture but rather to destroy it, for in making this choice one turns one's back on the whole organized body of traditional conceptions and ideas which are still transmitted within the home and the neighborhood and which—back in the villages— were enmeshed with the agriculture and the religion.

The secularization of the folk medicine results in great measure from the fact of transfer of the functions of healing from a man who is priest as well as shaman to a woman who is only a healer and practitioner of beneficent magic. The point is that, according to fundamental conceptions of the Yucatecan folk, the worship of the yuntzilob must be carried on by men and not by women. In all the important agricultural and apicultural ceremonies, as described for Chan Kom,[12] it is men who congregate, keeping themselves apart from women, and assist the h-men, who must, a priori, so to speak, be a man. Even the festal cookery is in the hands of men, although all secular cookery is done by women. The important ceremonies involve sexual continence. When, during the rain ceremony, the women participate by preparing the fowl broth, they do so at a distance, and the materials are delivered to them and called for by a man or a boy. So it is that in the villages the h-men is both leader of religious ritual and healer, and, as has been said, the healing and the praying are closely interdependent.

It would be important to discover, by investigation of the matter in a number of villages and towns, especially in the area marginal to strong urban influence, how it is that the healing functions—divination, exorcistic ceremony, and the rest— come to be carried on by women. The writer does not have

Photograph by Frances Rhoads Morley

enough facts to answer the question. Aurelia, the curer of Dzitas, said she learned her specialty from a woman curer like herself; other inhabitants of Dzitas said that she had lived for some years with a h-men of the villages and that she had picked up from association with him enough of his knowledge for her to set up in practice. It may be pointed out that the general tradition of the folk emphasizes the woman's part in the practice and transmission of herbal lore (quite apart from the agricultural rituals). As in many societies, so in Yucatan, homely healing is particularly appropriate to women. It may next be said that no h-men had lived in Dzitas for many years. A woman could practice the healing art without competition from a man. Reference may again be made to the fact that, as there is no h-men in Dzitas, the people there do not well understand the occasional rituals carried on in milpas of the neighborhood by shaman-priests brought from outlying settlements. These are all statements to show only that the practice of the healing art, by a woman, without connection with the pagan religion, might, consistent with circumstances, be carried on in the towns. One would have to study the careers of many Aurelias to find out by what characteristic course of events the transfer to a woman comes about. To these suggestions Hansen adds others to the effect that the assumption of professional curing by women may be an aspect of the breakdown of family life which sets many women free of family ties and obliges them to support themselves. He also points out that interest in sickness is greater in town and city than in the villages. With reference to factors which perhaps dispose men to abandon the field of folk medicine to women, he suggests that, with the secularization of medicine, its practice becomes socially less significant and argues that in such a society as this, where the dominance of men over women is stressed, there is a tendency for men to abandon an activity that declines in importance. The change from male h-men to female herbalist is paralleled by the change from male reciter of Catholic prayers to that of female chanter—a substitution which occurs as one goes from the villages to the city. Further-more, with the opening of more secular occupations to men, curing, now secularized, is compared practically to its disad-vantage, and men take up more rewarding means of livelihood. This suggestion gets some support from the fact that some men in Merida have been known to take up curing during periods of business depression when other jobs were difficult to find. Of course, it may be supposed that, once the occupation comes to be associated with women, it is less attractive to men.

However this question may be answered, the fact here to be stressed is that Aurelia's practice is largely secular. True, her practice calls "for faith as a necessary element in treatment, and emphasizes the supernatural power centered in her divin-ing crystal."[13] But this is a vague and greatly diluted super-naturalism compared with the implications attending the prac-tice of the h-men in the villages. Aurelia does not use any of the prayers recited by the shaman-priests in their ceremonies; probably she does not know them. She does not carry on any acts of worship. She appeals to no deities. Her recital of short Catholic prayers, like her use of candles, tancazche, and rum, involves merely the utilization of supernormal power inherent in these articles, substances, and formulas. Aurelia is, in gen-eral, a medical technician and, more especially, a magician, a practitioner of white magic.

The disintegration of medical conceptions and practices which is to a small degree observable in Chan Kom as ex-pressed in the conduct of such a man as Don Nas, and which becomes really significant in Dzitas, is carried to a greater degree in Merida. The conflict between the older folk medi-cine sanctioned by tradition and the new modern art of heal-ing which carries the prestige is in the city intensified by the fact that in the city the government attacks folk and popular healing with propaganda and with police. The folk medicine, therefore, takes on a certain character of secrecy. Further-more, in the city there is a still greater number and variety of competing practitioners and kinds of practice. Hansen has collected many well-reported cases of sickness[14] that occurred among the lower working class of the city—people born and bred in the urban environment. Most of these, where the sickness is at all prolonged, involve consultation with two, three, or many different specialists and consideration of a great number and variety of elements of belief. In Dzitas there was to be noted the existence of a few conceptions not recorded from the villages. Not a few cases of "attacks" occur; this is a vaguely defined ailment, identified with almost any sudden seizure and often associated with quarrels or other emotional disturbance. There is in Dzitas a single and little patronized "spiritualist," a representative of a cult there little known. In Merida "attacks" are common, and spiritualism flourishes. This cult involves a new set of practitioners, rivals of others, and a long list of new elements: "magnetic fluid"; summoning of the spirits of dead doctors; the administration by beings of invisible injections and the performance of invisible operations; the use of flowers, water, and candles in a combination new in aggregate though not in the elements that compose it; and possession by the spirits of the dead. The practice of black magic, a subject that is to receive treatment later in this chapter, brings with it in Merida another list of elements, some of which can be traced to West Indian influence orally transmitted and some of which have been derived from the reading of manuals on the magical art which circulate in Merida. Included are the use of powder made from corpses; the sending of a sharp object to wound the victim; the use of toads, frogs, and bats in witchcraft; divination with playing cards; divination through spirit possession.

The disintegration of the folk medicine in Merida is apparent not merely in the fact that there is a wider range and larger number of elements of treatment among which the sick person has to choose, and in the detachment of medicine from agriculture and religion, but also in the instability of the new combinations which are formed in the conditions which prevail in the city. On this, Hansen says:

Instead of being organized into stable configurations, each trait tends to move as a unit and is capable of entering into a large number of combinations. Such combinations are mutable and impermanent. Unlike the more fixed patterns characteristic of less mobile societies, the constituents are not bound together by reciprocal, definitive relations. Frequently they seem to be associated as a result of fortuitous circumstances rather than because of any necessary connections. The meaning of a given trait changes as it moves from one context to another. One derives the impression that magic is a mere agglomeration of confused and oftentimes conflicting elements. It lacks form and integration. Any new idea may be taken up readily. The agglomeration contains so many inconsistencies that one more makes little difference.[15]

This summary is based on three years of study of Merida and specifically on a large number of cases reported in great detail. In view of the regrettable fact that Hansen's materials have not been published, one case, somewhat more extensive and elaborate than many, and yet not unrepresentative of the whole collection of elements involved in the diagnoses and treatments, appears below:

One afternoon Bicha went into her yard to look after her chickens. She had taken only a few steps when she felt a sharp pain in her right leg. It was so severe that she could hardly stand and could not walk at all. Her husband had to help her back into the house. From the first a wind was suspected, but it was hoped that it was only rheumatism. She had long been troubled with this, but mostly in her left leg rather than in her right. Massages and occasional bloodletting had proved sufficient to enable her to get around.

The first remedy consisted in rubbing the affected leg with alcohol into which some sprigs of rue had been broken. Rue is rather effective against winds and is a potent all-round medicine. Nearly everyone keeps a few plants. But in this case the treatment did no good. She became worse. Her leg swelled from the knee down and the veins stood out.

In the evening her husband went to find a medium whose services had been sought in another illness some six years before. The medium expressed the opinion that the ailment was due to a wind and gave "passes" several times, which she shouldn't have done, theoretically, since a wind was involved. Her ministrations brought no relief, however.

Late that night, after the medium had gone, an old man who happened to be staying with Bicha came in. He had some reputation as a masseur and mender of bones and made a very modest living at the trade. He gave Bicha two massages during the night. She felt somewhat better after each one. The partial success of this procedure induced the patient and her husband to seek the services of a more accomplished specialist of this sort. The next day, therefore, "Dr." Ignacio Lopez was called in. He applied hot packs and massaged the ailing part thoroughly. It brought real but only temporary relief. The treatment was repeated twice during the next few days.

When the massages gave no indication of bringing about a definite cure, Bicha became more and more convinced that her ailment was due to a wind, not to rheumatism, and that what was needed was a specialist in winds. The fact that the "doctor" charged two pesos for each massage had an influence in bringing about this decision. So the following Tuesday the sufferer was taken to see Crescencia, a well-known yerbatera (curer). She told the patient's fortune with cards and then announced, "What attacked you was more than a mere wind, it was an evil wind. It is a miracle that you are still alive. If it had struck your heart instead of your leg, *ay Dios!* But do not worry. I shall cure you." Thereupon she performed the simplest and most common of the traditional ceremonies for exorcising evil winds. (It contained many nontraditional elements, however.) Then she gave instructions for fumigating Bicha's house the following Friday in order to drive out any evil winds which might be hanging around. She also recommended the use of three kinds of perfume. Bicha was to have some of each kind on her body at all times as a protection against the winds.

Two other visits were made to Crescencia on succeeding Tuesdays. They were increasingly expensive. After the second one Crescencia told the patient, "Since you are a friend of mine I shall speak to you frankly. Your illness is caused by evil spirits that are in your house. What you need is a spiritualist medium. This will not cost you so much." As a matter of fact, Crescencia knew that Bicha had little money and could not long continue with the treatments. Had it not been for this, the yerbatera would probably not have been so frank.

Crescencia recommended a medium who was a friend and disciple of hers. This medium was in charge of the case for nine weeks. During this period the explanation of the difficulty changed little. It was rather confused, but the idea seemed to be that an evil wind had lodged in Bicha's leg and that three evil spirits were haunting the house. The object of the cure was to get the wind out of the patient so that she would become well and the spirits out of the house so that she would stay well. Why the spirits and the wind were there does not seem to have been considered. Only once was another interpretation advanced. In the first seance a spirit which presented itself in the medium said the ailment was due to a spell wrought by the mistress of Bicha's husband. The spirit further stated that the mistress was a native of Campeche. The husband was furious. He had a mistress, but she was not from Campeche. Furthermore, he told her that if she ever sought to injure his wife through black magic he would kill her. The spirit dropped the accusation and in a later seance explained that the evil wind had been encountered by accident.

An elaborate exorcistic ceremony at the end of the nine weeks was to have made everything all right. Bicha did feel somewhat better afterward and she continued to improve slowly. Her husband, on the other hand, developed a toothache and began to get thin. About two months later he became very ill. Two explanations for the new trouble presented themselves. The final ceremony had not gone off as it should have done. Through the medium a spirit had explained to Bicha's husband how certain offerings were to be prepared and dedicated. He carried out the instructions and delivered the things to the spirits and the winds at the appointed hour. Shortly afterward the medium was supposed to have arrived to hold a seance. Due to unavoidable obstacles, she came ten hours late. Meanwhile the spirits and winds which had been called to partake of the offerings became angry at the delay and took their spite out on the one who had called them. This interpretation seemed adequate until he became seriously ill so long afterward. To explain this more acute crisis his mistress was suspected of witchcraft.

They went to see a yerbatero, a practitioner who had not been consulted before. But they confined themselves to describing only the physiological symptoms of the sickness and said nothing of the ceremony or of their suspicions of black magic. The motive for this was to avoid, if possible, a diagnosis involving evil winds or sorcery, the treatment of which is expensive. They wanted the yerbatero to recommend herb medicines first. If the patient recovered, they would save some money. If he did not, then they could tell the rest of the story and take the consequences.

He recovered, that is, his acute sickness passed. There followed a period of three months of comparative calm. But they were uneasy, discontented. Life was bearable, but things were not as they should be. Bicha was much better but not really well. Her husband continued to be thin and had no appetite. He had been out of work for a long time and for all he hunted he could not find a job. For two years the fruit trees in the lot had produced almost nothing and the chickens were always dying. The house seemed haunted somehow. Bicha, who had never liked to leave the place except when necessary, found that she could be content only when visiting friends and neighbors.

One day they heard of a very good yerbatera who did not make excessive charges for her services. They decided to see her and have their fortunes told. It was a momentous visit. They learned the answer to all their questions, the explanation of all their difficulties. This worker, Carmita, was a thoroughgoing diagnostician. They were the victims of three cases of black magic. The fruit trees did not produce and the chickens died because of a spell which had been worked by one Julia Poot. She was a comadre of Bicha and had lived with her for several months two years before. Trouble developed between them and Bicha asked her to leave. She did so, but not until she had buried in the lot her own soiled petticoat, that of Bicha, and a live rooster. She died a month or two later, but her spirit remained to guard the things she had buried. As long as they were there, Bicha and her husband could not prosper. It was a purely economic curse and did not affect the health of anyone.

The second spell was due to a former neighbor, Juana. She was always borrowing things, including money. One day when Bicha needed money, she tried to collect. There was a quarrel. A few days later Juana found a toad in her teakettle. Immediately she became very ill. She accused Bicha of attempting to kill by sorcery and swore vengeance. It was she who sent the evil wind which lodged in Bicha's leg. Shortly afterward she died and her spirit went to haunt Bicha's house and see to it that she did not get well.

The mistress of Bicha's husband was found to be working to cause him to leave his wife and live with her. Her object was only to win his love. The sorcery had no effect on Bicha and his sickness was due to evil winds he had caught in the ceremony which had gone wrong.

There was one additional source of trouble. The yerbatera and the medium who had attempted to cure Bicha's leg had been worse than incompetent. Everything they did was wrong. They did not really want to cure her. The worst error they made was to bury a bundle—composed of three kinds of herbs, two kinds of flowers and a large candle—into which the evil that had caused the ailment had supposedly been transferred by means of the final ceremony. The fact that it was buried meant that at the end of two years Bicha would die.

Carmita, the new-found specialist, set about making everything right. The evil winds which were bothering Bicha's husband were removed by means of exorcistic ceremonies. Within two or three months he had regained his lost weight. Carmita not only drove the spirit of Juana out of the house but returned the spell she had wrought before her death. Since Juana was dead, it fell on her sister; this was all right since she had helped produce it. Thereafter Bicha was able to recover completely. The rooster and the two petticoats were taken out of the lot and delivered to the winds in the bush at midnight. At the same time the spirit of Julia was sent away. This was accomplished by convincing her she was dead and commanding her to depart. Since then the fruit trees have been producing, Bicha has less trouble with her chickens, and her husband has a part-time job. The bundle which had been buried was disposed of in a manner similar to that used in getting rid of the petticoats and rooster.

Only the question of the mistress remains. Bicha's husband, now that life is running smoothly, does not think the mistress is working magic. His wife and Carmita are of a different opinion. According to them the mistress is spending all the wages she earns as a servant to defend herself and to keep up the spell. She has two yerbateros and three spiritualists working for her. For this reason Carmita has been able to accomplish nothing against her. But Carmita is on the alert. She is waiting for the time when the mistress becomes careless and ceases to employ her defenders. Then she will settle this matter as she has the others.[16]

In these cases from the city evil winds often appear confused with the "magnetic fluid" which the spiritualists claim to control. If a comparison is made between cases of spiritualism that conform most closely to the more sophisticated and literate wing of this cult, on the one hand, and cases in which rural h-mens treat for evil winds, on the other, it becomes clear that in historical origins the conceptions are quite different. They became blurred in the thinking of the urban lower class. One of Hansen's informants said that evil wind and fluid were the same and that the only difference lay in the word used: a spiritualist would call it "magnetic fluid," other people would call it an evil wind. In many of Hansen's cases a practicing medium diagnoses the illness as due to evil winds. In some of these cases the treatment follows the procedure historically appropriate to evil winds, and in others it conforms with the much newer teachings of the spiritualists.

In one of Hansen's cases the cure lasted nine weeks, and a seance was held in the house of the patient on every Tuesday and Friday. On each occasion the house was purified with incense. Besides the procedure usually carried on by spiritualists in which "passes" are given, the spirits of two dead doctors presented themselves and operated invisibly. The medium then became possessed, not by the spirits of urban doctors, as is the usual pattern—so far as there is any—but by the spirits of two h-mens and, so inspired, performed a confused variation of the exorcistic ceremony which, in the tradition of the folk medicine, serves to remove evil winds from a sufferer. The offerings included corn gruel, fowl, and rum, which belong in the context of the agricultural-therapeutic rituals of the village h-men; flowers, water, and candles, which are common to spiritualistic ceremony; and herbs such as curers like Aurelia of Dzitas use in dealing with the evil winds. To all this was added an offering of chocolate and sweet bread which, in theory or old tradition, are used only in the Catholic ceremonies for repose of, or in commemoration of, the souls of the dead. On this occasion, when the assembled articles were proffered to the winds, a spiritualistic prayer was used, and offerings to the spirits of the h-mens were accompanied by Catholic prayers. The patient was instructed to take elaborate baths, one of which, to be repeated daily for nine days, was to contain three kinds of flowers, nine leaves of each of eleven kinds of herbs, and two kinds of perfume. For the last nine days before the final ceremony the patient slept surrounded by nine small crosses made of two certain herbs and salt—protections against the evil winds.

Nothing approaching this multiplication of elements and confusion of traditions appears in any of the cases from the village, and it is only remotely approached in the materials from Dzitas. In cases such as this the reasons, the sanctions from tradition which give an ideational and specifically symbolic justification for what is done, have all but disappeared, and the procedure is felt to have magical power chiefly because it is colorful, impressive, highly formal, and elaborate. Hansen comments on this and similar cases by saying that "one observes a disposition to increase the effectiveness of a procedure merely by multiplying its constituent elements" and continues:

In this treatment elements were brought together which had probably never been in association before. The medium in charge gave the impression that she was selecting items from her experience which presented themselves at the moment. It is doubtful if she ever recalled them in exactly the same order twice. It is not uncommon for treatments to be recommended in one seance and revised in the next.[17]

The comparison of therapeutic custom in the four communities has now reached a situation, present in the city, where the practices may be called magic and not religion. In the city medicine is a technique of control unconnected with religion and piety. Religious behavior is in a separate sphere of activity from the therapeutics represented in such cases as that of the ninefold seance or that of the much-plagued Bicha. Hansen says of the observances of Christian religion as he saw them in the working classes of Merida that

the ideal of piety is methodical worship without thought of material reward or punishment. In so far as this ideal is attained religion becomes a separate department of behavior existing in terms of itself. The proof of piety is the performance of certain rituals and the holding of certain attitudes; not economic success and bodily health.[18]

In Merida appeal to the supernatural in connection with sickness is not wholly lacking, but it plays a much smaller part. Many lower-class people burn a candle and say a prayer when there is sickness in the house before or at the same time when they turn to curers, just as upper-class people appeal to the Virgin and call a physician. There are also cases in which the sickness of persons regarded as very wicked is attributed to their wickedness. But the treatment carried on by the popular curer in the city is on the whole a treatment carried on without reference to religion. Urban popular medicine is secular; it is magical rather than religious. Generally speaking, sickness is due to an invasion by winds or bad magnetic fluid or germs, or it has been done to one by the magical and malignant action of an enemy. In any case the gods have not caused it, and appeal to them plays a relatively small part in the attempt to cure it. The pious and the wicked are both susceptible to misfortune, and the principal remedy for disease is not prayer but direct dealing with the cause through appropriate techniques.

Hansen's materials show the secular nature of the popular medical practitioners of Merida and the heightened competition that prevails among them. It is an intensification of the situation that prevails in Dzitas, where Aurelia the curer competes with Petronilo the ambulant healer and both compete with the city-trained doctor. The activities of the urban curers are independent of the gods. Hansen has reviewed his materials with care to see what exceptions they offer to this statement. The apparent exceptions are very few. He found that one yerbatera (curer) had the habit of burning a candle to her favorite saint after each consultation. But the candle was furnished by the patient as a part of the fee, and it was made clear that the idea behind the act was to increase the curer's efficiency. It also served to show that her magic was "white," not diabolic. The same woman recommended that an object which had been used to carry a spell be presented to the Virgin. "Let the Virgin do justice," she said. Investigation showed that the yerbatera thought that the execution of her advice would result in a cure: the Virgin, offended by the nature of such a gift, would punish the sender of the spell, and the patient would recover. This is a more complicated form of the same technique in which the images of saints are stood on their heads or locked up until compelled to do what is wanted. Hansen has such cases. None of them represent acts of piety, and they are not like the prayers to the yuntzilob in the villages. The urban workers in magic have no priestly functions.

The city magicians and curers carry on their special functions as a means of livelihood. It is true that some of the h-mens of the villages receive enough in fees for their services so that they do not have to practice agriculture. But most do practice agriculture, and all that came into the direct knowledge of the writer discharged their roles as servants of the community. The urban curer is not a traditional leader of a community; his duties do not constitute a prerogative. Hansen's materials are full of attempts by one curer to discredit another. The educated physician is not spared. The popular healers point out that the educated doctors do not know how to cure diseases arising from supernatural causes—that their training gives them no power over evil wind or malignant fluid. In not a few cases the last specialist who treated the case is declared by his successor to be the causer of the sickness. These yerbateros charge as much as they think they can get.

Witchcraft is probably the most feared as well as the most frequent cause of illness; and for combatting sorcery huge fees are collected. The rivalry and the commercialism of the curers are illustrated in the case of Bicha. The generally commercial trend of the healing art in the city is tested by the case of the spiritualists. In the "pure" form of the cult, that is, as it appears in the talk, acts, and writings of its more educated exponents, it is a semireligious cult in which the mediums, through their unusual natural gifts, make available to participants in a congregation or assembly the benefits to be gained from consultation with the spirits of departed physicians. In this strict view the medium should offer his services free, as a voluntary dedication to humanity. But the practitioners of the cult among the uneducated masses have less sense of responsibility to this ideal. Practicing a healing art, and finding themselves giving services without substantial reward, some of the spiritualist curers accept fees. One yerbatera, realizing the demand for both kinds of service, took in a spiritualist as a sort of junior partner. The yerbatera then offered both kinds of treatment in her establishment—and she took the fees.

The rest of this chapter will be devoted to a discussion of witchcraft or black magic as it appears in the four communities studied. Consideration of the subject makes apparent important differences among the communities with respect to interpersonal conflict and suggests relationships between the amount of sorcery and its role in the society, on the one hand, and the disintegration of culture and personal insecurity, on the other.

As one reviews the four communities from Quintana Roo to Merida, the frequence of imputed witchcraft progressively increases. It is hardly possible to prove this statement by any quantitative index of sorcery, but the accounts of the matter prepared by the men who did the field work in the four communities hardly leave the generalization open to dispute. Of Tusik, Villa writes: "Cases of witchcraft are very rare; it can hardly be said to exist at all." During the months of his residence in Quintana Roo only a single case came to his attention, and this was one in which the people merely suspected witchcraft and did not become convinced that it had occurred. In all the cases of sickness which he followed, witchcraft played no part.[19] In Chan Kom "although black magic is generally recognized, and although death from sorcery is a not uncommon allegation, witchcraft is not one of the leading causes of sickness and death."[20] The information secured about witchcraft in Chan Kom was chiefly information given by natives in general terms and did not relate to cases of sickness occurring in the village during the period of study. The common causes of sickness in Chan Kom are the accidental invasion of the sick person by evil winds or the punishment of god or spirit. In the ordinary course of events, within the village, sorcery plays little or no part in the explanation of ailments and misfortunes. Yet sorcery is feared, and it remains in the background as a possible explanation and one to which credence will be given, in the last resort, or if personal conflict strongly suggests it. The case of Don Eus, given in his autobiography,[21] illustrates the place of sorcery in the history of a protracted disease. It is only after three months of sickness that he accepts the diagnosis of witchcraft made by the h-men, and the ground is laid for this explanation by the quarrel the sick man has had with people in another village. It is notable that in every case of witchcraft of which the investigators heard in Chan Kom, the accusation was made against someone who was not a resident of the village. Of course, the same statement can be made of Tusik (where the cases reported were of witchcraft alleged to have taken place some time in the past). The only act of sorcery that was imputed to have occurred in the Chan Kom area during the period of investigation was the appearance of a *uay-chup*, a witch in animal form, in one of the neighboring settlements; as a result of this, some inhabitants fled the place.

The significant fact is that in the villages sickness does not easily lead to or become an expression of hatred or fear of human beings. In the villages one does not often carry on one's quarrels by doing black magic to one's enemy. In Tusik one practically never does, and in Chan Kom, rarely. And, when it does happen in Chan Kom, it is not one's immediate neighbor or kinsman who is suspected. It is someone outside, some person with uncanny characteristics, or a h-men, or a man whose resentment has been aroused by the sick person. On the whole, the course of sickness in Chan Kom goes on without involving quarrels. It is not that there are no quarrels. The reader of the "Diary"[22] will meet with many disputes— about property, about women, about political rivalry. But participants in these quarrels do not fight with sorcery, and sickness is not commonly linked with them.

The course of sickness in Chan Kom may be compared with its course in the town and in the city by reviewing briefly the principal cases mentioned in the "Diary." March 26, 1930: A child has the whooping-cough; the h-men says it will die; it is God's will; it does die. May 9: Some children have whooping-cough; the mothers put out offerings to propitiate the supernatural beings supposed to bring the disease. June 17: The h-men gives herbal treatment in a case of dysentery. July 6 ff.: Don Fano, long sick, goes to Chichen Itza for medicines, and, when these do not bring relief, he summons the h-men. The h-men declares that Don Fano is being punished by the bee-gods, and the appropriate ceremony is held. July 18: A man moves his residence, because, finding his horse unaccountably dead, he concludes that evil winds are about. August 5: A girl has fever; the h-men says three winds have possessed her; he performs an exorcistic ceremony. August 11: A child with an intestinal infection is given no treatment. August 20: The death of an infant is ascribed to the effect of the supernatural bird that causes such deaths. October 10: The h-men performs a ceremony to exorcise evil winds from a sick man. November 14: Another infant dies; no explanation is reported. December 12: An epidemic of colds is somewhat speculatively ascribed by laymen to a recent shower of meteors. March 18, 1931: Another infant dies; the explanation as to the bird is given. March 23: A young girl has a sore on her side; the h-men is called; he performs a ceremony to exorcise the evil winds. April 29: Natives refuse to buy an electric machine offered by a traveling merchant to cure diseases. May 15: A woman has a cold; she goes to Chicken Itza for medicines. July 8: A man is sick; the h-men is called; he says the sickness was sent by the pagan gods because of the man's failure to make a ceremony; the ceremony is held. July 10: A boy is sick; the h-men says the sickness is caused by the spirit of his grandfather because the boy's father did not make the proper prayers. July 11: A girl, Ursena, is sick; a similar diagnosis is made. The prayers are held. July 21: A boy dies of dysentery; no treatment is reported. August 10: Ursena is still sick; the h-men says she has evil winds in her and prescribes a bath with rue. September 5 and October 14: The case of the uay-chup, mentioned above. No sickness is involved. September 27: A man is sick; the h-men performs kex to drive out the evil winds.

This summary omits only the worries of the one man, Don Nas, who came from the city, and his vacillating programs of treatment.

In general, then, in the villages, cases of sickness receive simple treatment. In the large majority of cases the remedy, recognized as appropriate by everybody, is soon applied; or the appropriate explanation is given for disease or for death. People know what to do, and it is done. Much of what is done by the layman takes the form of herbal or other traditional remedies. In nearly all serious cases the h-men is called; his advice is trusted; there is little to rival him or to cast doubt on his effectiveness. Although sickness gives rise to thoughts of sorcery in some serious cases, it does not commonly do so, and it is probably present only in the background of fearful thinking of the people. Sicknesses do not, often, therefore, involve or express disputes or enmities. On the whole, it has seemed to these investigators that sickness does not give rise, in the villages, to extraordinary uncertainty. Ordinarily a native of the village expects that the treatment will cure his child, or he expects that the child will die. In either case he seems to an outsider indifferent or apathetic. Visitors say that the native is "callous" or "fatalistic."

The impression made by the townspeople and the city residents is in marked contrast:

> The amount of worrying over sickness appears greater even than would be expected. People talk much about sickness, complain greatly about their own ailments, and take serious or desperate views of the illnesses of their relatives. A young man will take to his hammock for an ailment that seems minor to such observers as we.

The publication on sickness in Dzitas[23] reports fifteen cases of witchcraft, many of which were recent or current cases. Of the cases treated by Aurelia, the curer, and reported in the same publication, half involve quarrels or enmities and witchcraft. It is said in summary:

> It is probably safe to say that at least one adult out of ten in Dzitas has been talked about as either a promoter or a victim of witchcraft. No instance was reported of a self-confessed witch. Sorcery is alleged of one's enemies, and it is most easily believed of any practitioner of ritual art. Almost everyone believes that the shaman-priests of the villages, uncanny people, practice sorcery.

In Dzitas the course of the treatment of sickness runs much less smoothly than in Chan Kom; there is much greater disposition to vary the treatment or to go from one source of possible aid to another; and sorcery is a frequently imputed cause. In the town, as compared with the village, sickness is not connected with religion. But, again as compared with the village, it *is* connected with interpersonal conflict. A suggested explanation of this situation has been stated as follows:

> The anxiety over sickness, we suggest, is one expression of the personal insecurity in Dzitas which in turn is related to the heterogeneity of the population and the incompletely organized and partly secularized culture. It seems to us that the weakness of familial and community organization and the incompleteness of a cultural organization are specially manifest, in the

realm of sickness, in the frequent suspicion of witchcraft, and in the importance of quarreling, with resulting "attacks" as a supposed cause of sickness.[24]

The contrast between the village and the city is suggested by the case of Bicha, given in detail earlier in this chapter. This is one of many cases collected by Hansen in which there is a long course of shifting choice of cause and of curer, a recurrent sense of insecurity, and especially an association of the ailment with unsatisfactory personal relations and therefore with witchcraft. Bicha and her husband pass from administration of a domestic remedy to appeal to an old man who happens by. He gives simple treatment, and Bicha and her husband then seek out an expert in a folk art of healing. When the ailment remains, they seek another specialist who can look beyond ordinary to supernatural causes: Crecencia confirms their apprehensions that evil spirits are involved. The afflicted Bicha comes under the care of a spiritualist; a period of unsuccessful treatment culminates in an exorcistic ceremony. By this time the idea is firmly in Bicha's mind that witchcraft is being done against her. The ceremony fails; Bicha is still sick; she seeks new help from another yerbatero, and then her case is firmly taken in hand by Carmita, a curer, reputed to have great power over diabolical influence. The cumulative anxiety of Bicha and her husband is now centered in the fear of witchcraft; in Carmita's drastic handling of this peril, with the aid of countermagic, they get a feeling of at least temporary security.

Hansen reports that suspicion of sorcery is extremely common in the city. In many of his cases it is the first cause considered. A woman goes into her yard one evening, hears a whizzing sound, feels a pain, and almost faints. After a week she dies. The family without hesitation attributes her death to witchcraft sent by her daughter-in-law with whom she has had a quarrel. A man steps into his yard to pick oranges, and a bird falls dead near him. The man tells his wife and at once arranges for a yerbatero to come and exorcise his yard. The following statement by one of Hansen's informants is a more extreme statement of the beliefs as to witchcraft than is typical, but nothing approaching it appears in the material from the villages or even from Dzitas.

> Everything that happens today is a *maldad* (the most common term for injury done by magical means). Some persons say there used to be more than there are now, but it is not true. People make maldades on the slightest pretext. A family wanted to borrow a setting hen from the neighbors. The hen had just finished hatching one hatch of eggs and the neighbors wanted it to begin laying again. So they refused to lend it. The family that wanted to borrow it became angry and made maldades. Another family sent to the neighbors to buy eggs. The neighbors had three, and they were saving them until they had enough to set a hen and so would not sell them. Offended at the refusal, the family made maldades. Think of it, making maldades over three eggs! And I know many more cases just as bad.

In reviewing the situation as to witchcraft it is necessary to make it clear that the belief in witchcraft is present in all four communities. The Quintana Roo people are not skeptics on the subject; indeed, of all the peoples here concerned they take the idea of witchcraft most seriously. But witchcraft rarely occurs there. In the few cases where it was reported as having occurred in the past, it was said that the sorcerers had been punished with death. In one such case it was said that the evildoers were publicly shot when the people were gathered for a festival. Where, in Yucatan, witchcraft is the rarest, it is most greatly abhorred. In Quintana Roo witchcraft is not practiced, but it is a great theoretical sin. In Dzitas and in Merida it is believed that it is much practiced, and nothing much is done about it except by the injured or endangered person, who combats it with countermagic.

The explanations of this situation are probably double in character: one may give an explanation in terms of differences in historical events and one may give an explanation in terms of the consistency between one element of the society or culture and some other element. In the former case—to speak now in terms of the immediate problem—one "explains" the greater amount of witchcraft in Merida by telling about something that happened in Merida or that did not happen there. In the latter case one "explains" the greater amount of witchcraft in Merida by pointing to a condition there which might be supposed to provide a favorable situation for witchcraft. The condition is the disorganization of culture in the city with the consequent personal insecurity. Truth can be claimed for the latter explanation as it can be claimed for the former; and there is no inconsistency between the two explanations.

One might suppose that a more "primitive" community would show more sorcery than a more "civilized" one. This is not the case in Yucatan. We do not know to what extent the ancient Maya recognized and practiced sorcery. We do know that Spaniards of the time of the Conquest believed in black magic, and we know that the missionaries identified much of the pagan practices with the black art, that they taught that witchcraft was a great sin, and that in the Colonial period severe punishment was meted out to practitioners of black magic. The abhorrence of sorcery in Tusik, and the rarity of the offense, may be regarded as a survival from early Colonial times. We may suppose that the most isolated natives of the peninsula most rarely make accusation of sorcery because they carry on in traditional form that teaching which said it was a great evil, just as they carry on traditional Catholic rituals which have largely disappeared nearer the city. This explanation is not quite satisfactory, either to explain the situation in Quintana Roo or to explain that in Merida. If the people of Quintana Roo know of sorcery, and believe it a great sin, as appears to be the fact, one might yet expect them to accuse someone of sorcery if they were strongly tempted to accuse someone of anything. A part of the explanation may lie, then, not in the possible greater adherence to earlier teaching but in something in the contemporary life which does not provide frequent occasions when witchcraft would be an appropriate thought or remedy. At this point we have left the explanation in terms of the teachings of the early missionaries.

The specific historical explanation suggested does not tell us why there is, in the belief of the common people, much witchcraft in the town and city. This may still be in part explained, however, in terms of historical event, by pointing out that there is evidence for the diffusion of many conceptions as to witchcraft into the city from outside of Yucatan. Not a few Cubans live in Merida, and some elements of the magical art may have come from the West Indies. Books of medieval magic are on sale in Merida, and the number of people who have read these or looked into them cannot be insignificant. So the means to learn more ways to do black magic have been made available. One may argue that there is more magic in Merida because the city dwellers have had more opportunity to learn about it. The force of this argument is greatly diminished, however, when it is remarked that the Meridano has had greater opportunity to learn scientific and rational habits of thought which are unfavorable to magic and that he has had greater opportunity to forget the kinds of magic which the old tradition, from Colonial times and before, preserves better in the more remote communities.

The fact is—to repeat it for emphasis—that in all the four communities the common people believe in black magic. In the village the belief is least challenged and that is where cases of witchcraft are thought rarely to occur. In the town and city, where some people are skeptical of the reality of witchcraft, there is a great deal of it. These facts suggest that an explanation in terms of past events and of differences in diffusion and in preservation through tradition is not a complete explanation.

It may therefore be proposed that in Yucatan—and the proposition is not meant to extend beyond Yucatan—magic, and especially black magic, is an expression of the insecurity of the individual in the unstable social milieu of the city. Life has greater uncertainties in the city than in the village. The forces of economic competition affect people in different ways and therefore tend to isolate the individual from his family and his local group. The lack of an integrated culture and the breakdown of the familial and religious controls, which have been stressed in earlier chapters, make it difficult to predict the behavior of others. The social world in which an individual moves is large and complex, and the roles of individuals within it are often unclear and are unstable. It is to be remembered that none of those cases of black magic which were encountered in the villages involved its practice by one resident of a village against another of the same village. The solidarity of the local and the familial group is great. But in the city one's neighbor may be one's enemy and not rarely is. No case was collected in any of the communities, not even in Merida, of witchcraft between close consanguineous kin; the blood tie is strong even in the city.

But a large majority of all the cases of witchcraft collected in both Dzitas and in Merida involved ill feeling or worse between a woman and persons connected with her through marriage. A woman is bewitched by her husband's sisters, or her mother-in-law, or her husband's aunt. But, most commonly, the injured person is a wife, and the supposed doer of sorcery is another woman, a rival for her husband's affections and support. This conclusion was independently reached by the writer and by Hansen from analysis of the two collections of cases. It seems a fair suggestion to connect the fact of the great role of sorcery in the triangle situation with the much greater insecurity of the married woman in the city as compared with her position in the villages. In the village, as has been stated,[25] almost every adult marries, and marriage is an arrangement for the economic and social security of the individual, supported by important familial and religious sanctions. In the city more women are unmarried, men are freer to make secondary unions, brief or more lasting, and, what is more important, their doing so endangers the economic security of the wife. Practically the only career open to the urban woman of the masses is serving a man as wife or mistress; yet the looseness of marriage ties puts in perennial danger her hold upon this career. This is probably not the only factor in explaining the great number of urban witchcraft cases in which two women, rivals for a man, are involved. Hansen[26] has pointed to the predominance of women over men in the city.[27] But it is probably one of the important factors. In case after case, a woman, struck suddenly with an ailment, thinks of her husband's known or suspected infidelity and of the enmity that the other woman may be expressing in sorcery. Some of Hansen's cases show this fear to the point where one is tempted to speak of a neurosis. One woman had for years eaten nothing not prepared with her own hands because of fear of her husband's mistress. Another saw magical spells in simple incidents such as the flight of a bird through her house or the appearance of a night-flying insect in her hammock. When this woman rose in the morning, she looked fearfully at her doorstep to see if some evil thing might be found there. Less extreme cases of the sort appear in the collection from Dzitas.[28] None were reported from Chan Kom or from Tusik. The woman, and especially the married woman who has little support from her kinsmen and cannot control her husband, is the most insecure of the many insecure in the mobile and disorganized life of lower-class Merida.

There is a greater amount of black magic in Merida than in the villages (proportionate, of course, to the number of occasions which might give rise to it) in spite of the fact that it is in Merida that science and rational thought exert the greatest influence. The attention that has been given in this chapter to the beliefs and customs of the lower class should not obscure the fact that in the capital there is a large number of doctors with modern training (158 of the 206 who in Yucatan are licensed by the federal government). Members of the upper and middle class rely largely on the medical profession and look down on the people who employ curers and mediums. This strong attitude of the socially dominant groups exerts an influence, of course, upon the thinking of the masses. More generally, the expansion of education tends to discredit the folk medicine and to dispose the common people to a more rational and scientifically tested medicine. The situation that has been described is a situation in which lower-class people, who have a recent background in folk culture, find themselves living in an increasingly mobile community. They continue to depend on many of the traditional methods of dealing with sickness; they adopt uncritically new techniques brought in from outside; and they expand the use of magic to meet the multiple uncertainties of the city. While the disorganization of city life finds one expression in the frequency with which black magic is considered as an explanation for sickness, at the same time the expanding influence of modern urban ways, including scientific medicine, tends not only to displace the folk medicine but to increase skepticism with regard to magic.

CHAPTER XII

THE FOLK CULTURE AND CIVILIZATION

SOME novelty attaches to the method employed in this study: the approximately simultaneous investigation of a series of contemporary communities differing chiefly with respect to the degree to which each has been affected by communication with a single important center of modifying influence.[1] In this chapter there will be presented the author's conclusions as to the results of this method as applied in Yucatan.

The most general conclusion is that the same relative order —an order corresponding to their relative positions on the map: city, town, peasant village, and tribal village—serves to range the four communities studied so as to represent the progressively increasing or decreasing extent to which several general social or cultural characters are present. In a preliminary paper[2] it was asserted that the peasant village as compared with the tribal village, the town as compared with the peasant village, or the city as compared with the town is less isolated; is more heterogeneous; is characterized by a more complex division of labor; has a more completely developed money economy; has professional specialists who are more secular and less sacred; has kinship and godparental institutions that are less well organized and less effective in social control; is correspondingly more dependent on impersonally acting institutions of control; is less religious, with respect both to beliefs and practices of Catholic origin as well as to those of Indian origin: exhibits less tendency to regard sickness as resulting from a breach of moral or merely customary rule; allows a greater freedom of action and choice to the individual;

and—a conclusion then more tentatively advanced—shows a greater emphasis upon black magic as an ascribed cause of sickness. In the present volume these conclusions are particularized by the reference to facts as to certain customs and institutions as they appear in the four communities. They are also further generalized in that most of the cultural characters as to which differences are found are grouped under three headings. The changes in culture that in Yucatan appear to "go along with" lessening isolation and homogeneity are seen to be chiefly three: disorganization of the culture, secularization, and individualization.

The contribution made by the present application of this method to research on the history of Yucatan is small. It is true that the investigation has revealed the persistence in a more peripheral community of certain elements of custom which documentary evidence or the oral testimony of old people shows to have been once characteristic of a less peripheral community. Examples are: the persistence of the vecino-indio distinction with emphasis on the status significance of Indian surnames in Dzitas after its disappearance in Merida; the various native customs and institutions listed in chapter iv and marked with an asterisk to show that there is evidence that, although now absent in Chan Kom, they were once present there as they still are in Tusik; the important and conspicuous features of Catholic ritual still present in Tusik of which many are attested to have existed in former years in less remote communities; the persistence of compulsory collective labor for the public benefit (fagina) in the villages with evidence of its earlier existence in Dzitas and even in Merida; the use of separate oratories for domestic santos, which is a practice in Tusik but only a memory in Chan Kom; the decline and substantial disappearance in the city of the custom, usual in the villages, of choosing the child's baptismal name from among those of saints appropriate to the day of its birth. To the degree to which the investigators obtained information as to earlier custom in the communities they studied, there appears a certain rough overlapping of the courses of history of each, so that, if their accounts are superimposed on one another at the points where the past condition of one community coincides with the present condition of the next most isolated community, there results a single historical account, although a very rough one, of culture change in Yucatan. Even where confirmation is lacking as to the earlier presence in a less peripheral community of elements of culture now present in a more peripheral community, the different forms of custom and institution may be arranged in an order consistent with the spatial order of the communities so as to suggest a possible actual historical sequence. This was done in chapter iii with reference to differences as to the conventional definition given to status and ethnic groups. This could be done more systematically with reference to many other aspects of Yucatecan life. It could be done with reference to differences in familial organization and ritual and with regard to many elements of religious and festal practice. It would be assumed that, because the more remote communities have had less contact with the one important center of influence, what is to be found in the more remote communities represents on the whole an earlier condition of the same general custom or institution than what is found in less remote communities. As with the definitions of ethnic and status groups, so these differences could be connected so as to suggest how each might have given rise to the next. There would result, as in the case of the general conclusion reached in chapter iii, a sort of generalized hypothetical account of the history of the culture of what might be called an "ideal type" of Yucatecan community, or of Yucatecan society taken as a whole. In a similar way it might be validly asserted that a comparative description of communities encountered as one goes from Paris southward through Marseilles, Algiers, the Sahara, and then the Sudan would provide the vague outlines of the culture history of western Europe. Such a method of reaching an approximate and generalized culture history probably comes somewhat nearer the facts as they might be determined by true historical research in such a region as Yucatan where the culture history is already known to have been very simple: a single Indian culture came in contact with Spanish colonial society four hundred years ago and remained largely undisturbed by other influences or local movements until the introduction of more modern ways through a single port and a single city. Nevertheless, that the more archaic feature is always preserved in the most peripheral community is not always true, and instances have been given in this volume where it was found not to be true. In Yucatan as elsewhere each community has its own special course of culture history. The method is certainly a crude way to derive even the most tentative historical conclusions.

The most that may be claimed is that the work of the professional historian in working out the history of culture in Yucatan through study of artifact and document may be to some degree supplemented by the student of the contemporary cultures—provided that student does as much local history as he can. There is doubt that the documents and the artifacts will ever yield decisive information on such problems as changes in the kinship system, on forms of courtship and marriage, or on the steps by which some of the saints were incorporated into the pagan pantheon while the pantheon in other respects also was changing its character. The opinion may be ventured that, if we are interested in the history of such changes as these in Yucatan, we are well advised to pursue historical inquiry through study of present-day communities. The outlines of historic trends of change in such institutions as were mentioned above might be expected to appear more clearly if carefully prepared histories of local cultures were written (by asking old people what they remember, and by comparing results with what informants report as more recent and with what is observed to be characteristic today), and if the results in one community were compared with the corresponding results in communities progressively less affected by recent influences. But in none of the four communities studied in the present connection was any systematic effort made to recover the older conditions of the local society by asking informants. Hansen's study of Merida, as yet in the course of composition, comes closest to being an exception. On the whole the investigation of the course of historic change in any one community by consultation of either document or informant has been casual and unsystematic. On the whole the results here achieved follow a comparison of present conditions in one community with present conditions in the others. Attested historical changes in any one community supplement in a secondary fashion the results of the comparison of contemporary situations.[3]

In the preliminary paper there was shown a disposition,[4] here further developed, to seek through this method of comparison of differently affected communities some general knowledge as to the nature of society and of its changes. It has been discovered that the less isolated and more heterogeneous societies of the series of four in Yucatan are the ones which are more characterized by disorganization of culture, by secularization, and by individualization. These conclusions are generalizations on many particular facts. The assertions are "on the whole" true. To reach these conclusions it is not necessary to report the history of any one of the communities: they may be compared as if all existed at the same moment of time. At the same time, when questions come to be raised as to whether changes in any of the characters are related to or conditioned by changes in any of the others, and as to how they are interrelated, such knowledge as the writer has about particular events in the history of the communities is very welcome and he wishes he had more. The simple comparison of contemporary communities is not a method to be recommended to those wishing to do historical research in Yucatan, in view of the availability of documents and in view of the opportunity to determine the recent history of any community studied by consulting old informants as to earlier conditions. It is, however, a satisfactory way somewhat to clarify certain problems as to the nature of isolated-homogeneous society as compared with mobile-heterogeneous society.

In the preliminary paper it was suggested that the characters of the more isolated communities might be grouped to constitute a "type" in opposition to the "type" formed by assembling the opposite characters of the less isolated communities. The characters there asserted to identify the first "type" are: isolation; cultural homogeneity; organization of the conventional understandings into a "single web of interrelated meanings"; adjustment to the local environment; predominately personal character of the relationships; relative importance of familial institutions; relative importance of sacred sanctions as compared with secular; development of ritual expression of belief and attitude; tendency for much of the behavior of the individual to involve his familial or local group. These conceptions (which obviously derive much, as has been earlier remarked, from Maine, Durkheim, and Tönnies) were offered in that paper to point a direction in which studies of changes in primitive or peasant societies under influence from modern civilization or cities might be systematically and comparatively pursued. The line of thought suggested by the discovery or creation of these "types" leads to some hypotheses: (1) The primitive and peasant societies (which will be found to be, as compared with other societies,[5] isolated and homogeneous local communities) have in general characters of the first type. (2) When such societies undergo contact and communication with urbanized society (or at least with modern Western urbanized society), they tend to change in the direction of the opposite of these characters. (3) There is some natural or interdependent relation among some or all of these characters in that change with regard to certain of them tends to bring about or carry with it change with respect to others of them. The present study, an examination of four particular communities in Yucatan, does not, of course, establish the truth of any one of these possible hypotheses. It may be claimed that it moves a little distance toward their more precise formulation and toward the development of ways of bringing particular facts to bear upon them.

The problems suggested in that earlier paper are too comprehensive in scope and too vague in definition to be suitable guides for research. Nine or ten characters, each simply denoted by a phrase or two, are thrown together and called a "type." It is not clear how we are to determine how any particular society partakes more or less of any of these characters. It is not made clear how we are to determine which of these characters is naturally associated with any other. It is necessary to ask many more special questions, and relate them to particular fact, to define more precise lines of inquiry. The facts given in this report lend themselves to this effort.

The problem is seen as one of the relation among variables. No one of these is the sole cause of the others, but it is assumed, subject to proof, that, as certain of these vary, so do others. For the purposes of this investigation the isolation and homogeneity of the community are taken together as an independent variable. Organization or disorganization of culture, secularization, and individualization are regarded as dependent variables. The choice of isolation and homogeneity as independent variables implies the hypothesis that loss of isolation and increasing heterogeneity are causes of disorganization, secularization, and individualization. Even if this should be established, it would not follow that these are the only causes of these effects or that these are the only covariant or causal relationships to be discovered in the same data. There may be, for example, covariant or causal interrelations between disorganization and secularization or between disorganization and individualization.[6]

If these questions are to become guides to empirical research, the terms must be sufficiently general to make it possible to compare what is done in one field, as Yucatan, with what is done in another. But they must be sufficiently precise to enable the investigators, while operating within the definitions given him by the broad concept, to ask more special questions of particular fact and get answers which can be recognized as evidential for the more general question implied by the term. One must know how to find out whether the particular fact reported within a particular setting of time and place represents the presence or absence of some quality generalized in the concept.

As is, or ought usually to be, the case, the present investigation has involved some interaction between the guiding general term, on the one hand, and the particular facts, on the other, with resulting redefinition of the general terms and propositions. The use of the term "primitive," for the purposes of this study, as referring to the "enduring isolation" and the "homogeneity" of a society, arose from the attempt to specify just what sort of facts could be compared in the various communities in order to determine their relative primitiveness. The relative lack of emphasis placed on size of the community, development of the technology, degree of literacy, relative importance of sacred as compared with secular sanctions, or complexity of the division of labor does not mean that these characters might not be found to be variables interdependent with one or more of the others already mentioned or with each other. It means merely that the four communities were found to be readily comparable with reference to their degree of isolation and homogeneity and that it is assumed that simple, easily verifiable facts, such as those given in the second chapter, are available to justify placing them in the order given with reference to these qualities. Also implied is the assumption that other communities, similarly situated in other parts of the world, might be similarly ranged according to the same guiding conceptions and so make possible a comparative study of the problems sketched in this report.

The conception of organization of culture with its reciprocal, disorganization, has undergone change and development in the course of the study.[7] The original question remains: To what extent may each of these four communities be described in terms of an organized body of conventional understandings?

In the preliminary paper one character of the supposed type of society was asserted to be the fact that "the ways of life form a single web of interrelated meanings." As one leaves the village and goes toward the town, one encounters, it was stated, a situation in which "the ways of life are less closely interrelated; group-habits exist more in terms each of itself, and do not to the same degree evoke a body of closely associated and definitive acts and meanings."[8] As the matter is now considered, this contrasting characterization of cultural organization and disorganization appears valid but inadequate in that it covers what appears now to be a number of different though related characters no one of which has been adequately defined. Four of these may be recognized: (1) the unity of the culture of the society, that is, the extent to which it may be described as a single culture and to which it must be seen as a series of related subcultures, some subordinate to others; (2) the extent and nature of alternative lines of thought and action, conventionally made available to the individual; (3) the extent to which there exist relationships of interdependency between the various elements of culture; and (4) the extent of relationships of conflict and inconsistency between various elements of the culture.

The first of these has to do with the extent to which the society may be described in terms of a single—only one—organized body of conventional understandings. If the conventionalized activities of all the kinds of people making up the society—men, women, specialists, and nonspecialists—express meanings which have a relation one to another and which can be described as a whole, and if that whole represents the understandings of all these people, then to that extent there is but a single culture. This situation is never realized in fact. There is in the case of each society "an aggregate of subcultures,"[9] characteristic of local groups, classes, occupational groups, or other subdivisions of the entire society. The existence of subcultures in Dzitas, especially as characterizing indios in contrast to vecinos, in the society in which the present

older generation was raised, has been mentioned in chapter
iii, and the introduction of Protestantism into Chan Kom, as
described in chapter vi, may be recognized to have resulted in
a new subculture—that of the Protestant converts. But no
systematic comparison of the four communities with respect
to the relative number and importance of subcultures as compared with a possible general or "over-all" culture has been
attempted. The writer supposes that in the more isolated
homogeneous communities it is more nearly possible than in
those less isolated and homogeneous to describe the society in
terms of a single organized body of conventional understandings. The conclusion is indeed in part already reached by
defining the former class of societies as homogeneous, for, if
we say that the society is composed of the same kind of people
doing the same kind of thing, we have probably also said that
the behavior of these people has the same conventional character for all of them.

The second character comprised in the observation that as
one goes from village to city in Yucatan it is less possible to describe the ways of life as a single web of interrelated meanings
lies in the increasing number of what Linton has recognized
under the name of "Alternatives." In Linton's book "Alternatives" is allowed to stand for what on closer analysis appear to
be two different phenomena of culture: (1) elements "which
are shared by certain individuals but which are not common to
all members of the society or even to all the members of any
one of the socially recognized categories"[10] and (2) elements
known to every normal adult or to all the members of a socially
recognized group but among which the individual may "exercise choice."[11] The former (which, following a suggestion
from Dr. Sol Tax, who pointed out to the writer this distinction, one might call "Variants") are elements known only to
certain individuals of the society; each member of the society,
so far as the Variants are concerned, has one way, conventionally shared with certain other individuals who do not together constitute any socially recognized group, to meet a cer-

tain situation; other members have other ways. Alternatives in the more restricted sense (as, for example, in the choice open to us to go by train or by bus) are two or more ways open to everyone in the society or socially recognized group to meet a certain kind of situation; they are, in fact, a kind of Universal. The increase of Variants and Alternatives as one goes from village to city has not been systematically investigated in the present work, but the fact of the increase is suggested many places in the manuscript; it is especially noted in the chapter on "Medicine and Magic," where material is presented to show that in the town and city there is a much wider range and a larger number of elements of diagnosis and of treatment from among which the native has to choose, and it is shown that therefore the lines of conduct followed by neighboring individuals are in the city more variable, inconsistent, and unstable. It appears to the writer that the relative importance of alternative lines of conventionally recognized action may be inquired into in the manner suggested by the comparison of treatment of disease in Chan Kom as compared with Merida: the collection of equivalent cases to which the same crisis, as observed first in the one community and then the other, gave rise. If, as in the case of the materials from Chan Kom, each individual tends to follow the same line of thought and action as does his neighbors, and tends to follow the same line in each recurrent instance of the same class of situation, while, as in the materials with regard to sickness from Merida, each individual experiments and vacillates among a variety of lines of conduct so that the courses of action in the second group of cases are not parallel but inconsistent and various, then in the latter community there are, in respect to this class of situation, more Variants and more Alternatives. Denoting the primitive (and peasant) cultures as "folk cultures," Linton recognizes that the difference between the folk cultures and modern civilizations is "primarily a matter of the proportion which the core of Universals and Specialties bears to the fluid zone of Alternatives."[12] We may understand Linton to mean by "core of Universals" those elements of culture which are general for all the members of the society and which do not consist of conventional competing ways of acting in the same situation; we may understand him to mean "core of Universals which are not (in the restricted sense) Alternatives." Then the "core of Universals" is about the same as "the extent to which the entire society can be described in terms of a single organized body of conventional understandings." It is the breakdown or reduction of this core which is noted by the present writer in comparing the villages of Yucatan with the city and town, and that is declared by Linton to characterize modern civilization as compared with the folk societies:

Folk cultures are borne by small, closely-integrated social units or by aggrégates of such units which have already worked out satisfactory mutual adjustments. In such cultures, new items are not appearing with any great frequency and the society has plenty of time to test them and to assimilate them to its pre-existing pattern. In such cultures the core constitutes almost the whole.

In modern civilization on the other hand, the small, closely integrated social units are being broken down, giving place to masses of individuals who are much more loosely interrelated than the members of the former local groups and classes. . . . . In modern civilizations, therefore, the core of culture is being progressively reduced. Our own civilization, as it presents itself to the individual, is mainly an assortment of Alternatives between which he may or frequently must choose. We are rapidly approaching the point where there will no longer be enough items on which all members of the society agree to provide the culture with form and pattern.[13]

Following this line of thought we are made to see that the investigation in Yucatan has been, *in parvo*, a study of certain aspects of the historic process of civilization itself.

By way of digression it may be said that the two characters so far mentioned bear different relationships to the general problem of culture change and culture disorganization. The number of subcultures may increase in a society that develops a complex division of labor or may be increased by the inclusion of people with a different tradition or cult, but the presence of a large number of subcultures is not an indication of a rapid rate of social change. Any culture, "sub" or otherwise, requires some isolation for its development. The materials with regard to the fusion of Catholic and pagan elements in Tusik, and the facts as to the adjustment of Protestantism to other elements of culture in Chan Kom, help to show how understandings become common, and develop interrelations among themselves, when a people are left alone to communicate freely with one another and not too much with outsiders. It does not seem appropriate to speak of an increase in the number of subcultures as an aspect of the disorganization of a culture. Indeed it is the conversion of both the universal elements of culture and those which are special to subcultures into Alternatives which is a feature of modern civilization and of Dzitas and Merida as contrasted with Chan Kom and Tusik.

A correlative proposition is that we may expect to find a relatively large number of Alternatives associated with a relatively low degree of interdependence of the elements of the culture and of consistency among them. A review of the materials from Yucatan does not yield a demonstration of this relationship in their case. Such a relationship is plausible. Where there are many alternative lines of conduct and thought open to the individual, the situation is favorable, one may argue, for the presence of inconsistencies between what he does on one occasion and what he does on another, and it is probably less likely that such lines of thought and action as he does follow will be found to be extensively and in many places interdependent.

The discussion may now be allowed to return to consideration of the characteristics of cultural organization. The last two characters of the four enumerated on a previous page of this chapter may be set forth in the form of questions. The first question is: "To what extent does any element of culture have interdependent connotations with others?" The answer to this question is to be found in the act of reducing the culture to written description. If the elements of a culture require, for its full exposition, exposition of other elements, this aspect of culture organization exists. In describing the agricultural activities of the people of the villages one cannot deal fully with the subject without also dealing with sickness and its cure, and vice versa; but in reporting the bee cult there is no need to take account of the beliefs and practices with reference to death. There is an interconnection in the first case, and none in the second. But in Merida little or no account of agriculture need be taken in dealing with sickness and so, where there is an interconnection in the villages, there is none in the city.

Finally, the investigator of cultural disorganization[14] may ask, "To what extent are there conventionally recognized lines of thought and action within the same culture which are inconsistent with one another in that they call for a choice whereby one must be abandoned in favor of another?" He may find conventionally recognized actions or attitudes which at least apparently contradict one another, as in the case of the belief that men who marry their deceased wive's sister go to hell, and the practice of contracting such marriages. The mere fact of apparent contradiction is itself probably an indication of imperfect operation of the tendency, here again asserted or assumed to exist, of cultures to develop consistency of parts. If the belief is a genuine belief and not a mere saying, and if the practice is general, then there must be, in the individuals who both believe and yet so marry, a sense of conflict. It is in the evidences for conflict and distress in such individuals that the existence of such deeper inconsistencies must be sought.

The study of these materials has thus led to an understanding that the matter of the organization of those elements of conventional understanding that make up the culture of a society may be studied in terms of more special questions each of which directs the investigator to the examination of corresponding particular sorts of facts: (1) the number and identity of cultures, some of which may be subordinated to others, going to make up the total conventional life of the society; (2) the extent and nature of alternative lines of thought or action conventionally made available to the individual; (3) the extent to which the elements of culture are connotatively interdependent; (4) the presence and nature of conventionally recognized elements which are inconsistent apparently as asserted or even in that one calls for a course of behavior which makes impossible the other.[15]

In order that societies may be more precisely compared as to the degree to which they are sacred or secular, a clearer understanding of the meaning of these terms is required than has been expressed in the preceding pages. The conclusion has been reached that the city and town exhibit greater secularization than do the villages. The principal facts offered in support of this conclusion are (in the order in which they have been presented): the separation of maize from the context of religion and its treatment simply as a means of getting food or money; the increase in the number of specialists who carry on their activities for a practical livelihood relative to those that carry on traditional activities which are regarded as prerogatives and even moral duties to the community; the change in the character of the institution of guardia whereby from being an obligation, religiously supported, to protect a shrine and a god it becomes a mere job in the town hall; the (almost complete) disappearance of family worship; the decline in the sacramental character of baptism and marriage; the conversion of the pagan cult from what is truly religious worship to mere magic or even superstition; the decline in the veneration accorded the santos; the change in the novena in which from being a traditional form expressive of appeal to deity it becomes a party for the fun of the participants; the alteration in the festival of the patron saint in which it loses its predominant character as worship and becomes play and an opportunity to profit; the separation of ideas as to the cause and cure of sickness from conceptions as to moral or religious obligation.

What definition of "sacred" will embrace all of the first members of the pairs of facts implied in the foregoing summary and direct the investigator to particular data relevant to a comparative study of secularization? Durkheim's formulation of the antithesis is that of an absolute differentiation of two realms of human thought: the sacred is to be recognized in distinction from the profane (secular) by the very fact that one may not be brought in contact with the other; we are to look, apparently, for those rites of transition, purification, and interdiction which will mark for us the boundary between the two realms.[16] But the materials from Yucatan have not yielded to the present writer any confirmation of the possibility of distinguishing the sacred from the secular by attention to such ritually guarded portals. Rather it seems that objects and sanctions may be more or less sacred. The secularization of maize, or of the festival of the patron, or of the loh ceremony,[17] is a gradual change, not a leap from one realm of thought to another. And in each of the four communities studied it seems to make sense to say that certain things are more sacred than other things. Indeed, the people themselves will approximately say it: "Maize is more to be respected than beans."

The statement just quoted recalls the customs, to which at least the older people in the villages adhere, not to step on maize kernels or crack them idly between the teeth or in other ways treat them with disrespect. The reluctance to do so is supported by the connection maize has with the gods and with other conceptions regarding the virtuous life. It is not good to treat any food wastefully or rudely, and especially not maize. The reluctance is not merely a matter of practical convenience; it is just believed, and there is a feeling of distress which cannot be fully accounted for in terms of practical advantage or disadvantage that attaches to a violation of the injunction. It may be suggested, therefore, that an object is sacred to the extent that there is reluctance, emotionally supported, to call the thing rationally or practically into question. Secular objects are treated in a practical or even critical manner without reluctance. What makes it appropriate to say that maize is sacred as it grows in the fields in Chan Kom and secular when it gets to market is that in the fields reasons of practical advantage are not enough to make a man decide whether or not to step on the kernels or even to plant or not to plant: he just feels uncomfortable, his words and actions lead us to believe, if the corn is stepped on or if, though able-bodied and free to do so, he does not make milpa. But the actions with regard to maize in the market are readily adapted to considerations of expediency: show the man how to get a better price, and he will follow the suggestion.[18]

Of course, it is in the area where the gods are that lie most of the objects and actions which give rise to strong reluctance if rational or practical criticism of them is entertained. So in the materials here presented it is decline of the gods or the separation of one element of custom or another from religious thought and sanction that make up the largest part of the evidence for secularization. The great cross at X-Cacal we conclude to be more sacred than many of the crosses encountered in Yucatan because of the evidences in customary action of the awe in which it is held: the screen which stands before it, the armed guards, the requirements to take off shoes and make offerings, the belief that it talks and that it gives signals of its displeasure, etc. But moral conceptions are sacred too, as the word is here defined. So also are those elements of the nonrational which are impure rather than pure, and which Durkheim recognizes as one of the poles of the sacred,[19] to be included within the definition. The decline in the sacred in Yucatan includes also —although the matter has not been discussed in these pages— the diminution or disappearance of belief in the danger of menstrual flow and of corpses.

The recognition of some such definition for the sacred as has just been suggested should help to bring about a more effective comparison of societies, and of the succeeding phases of change in an element of culture, with respect to secularization. It is a good thing not to have our attention too attentively drawn to matters of formal religion in connection with the sacred. In our own society, for example, some of the most sacred elements, in this sense, are probably some outside of the usually recognized religion. The definition gives some promise of guiding investigation; it should be possible to devise more special interrogations to ask of more special facts.[20]

The third general conclusion that has been reached with respect to the differences among the four communities in Yucatan is that the least isolated and the most heterogeneous of these are the most individualized (or individualistic). The principal facts which support this conclusion are the following (again expressing the progressive differences among the four communities as if a single historic change were involved): the relative decrease in importance of specialized functions which are performed on behalf of the community and the relative increase of specialties discharged for the individual's own benefit; the development of individual rights in land and in family estates; the diminution or disappearance of collective labor and of the exchange of services in connection with civic enterprises and religious worship; the decreasing concern of the family or of the local community in the making and the maintaining of marriages; the becoming less common of the extended domestic family; the lessening of emphasis and of conventional definition of the respect relationships among kin; the decline in family worship and the disappearance of religious symbols expressive of the great family; decrease in the tendency to extend kinship terms with primary significance for members of the elementary family to more remote relatives or to persons unrelated genealogically; the increasing vagueness of the conventional outlines of appropriate behavior toward relatives; the change in the nature of the marriage and baptismal rites so as less to express the linkage of the families and more to concern the immediately involved individuals only; the decline in relative importance of the santo patron of the local community; the suggested relation of the increase in sorcery to the separation of individuals, especially of women, from the security of familial groups.

We may understand a society to be individualistic to the extent that the socially approved behavior of any of its members does not involve family, clan, neighborhood, village, or other primary group. The villages in Yucatan, as compared with the town and the city, are relatively more "collectivistic" or "nonindividualized" in that such important and recurrent situations as labor, ownership, selection of spouse, entering upon the married state, and religious worship are more controlled by and have greater consequences for the family and the local community. In the villages it is relatively easy to say "the family did this" or "the community did that"; in Merida it is not so easy.

It may be pointed out that a comparison of two societies as to their relative individualistic character, on the one hand, and to their collectivistic character, on the other, does not necessarily involve a consideration of the degree to which either is undergoing change. It is the impression of the writer that the society of the rural Ladinos of the midwest highlands of Guatemala is a little-changing society which is much more individualistic than is the society of Tusik: families have a much smaller share in the arrangement and maintenance of marriages, and individuals are free to make occupational choices and enter into business enterprises at their own sole responsibility, to cite only two respects in which the statement just made could be shown to be true. In the Guatemalan case the social norms allow for much independent action by the individual; in the case of the Yucatecan villages less such allowance is contained within the conventions. The rural Ladino society of Guatemala and the society of Tusik are alike in that in both the existing social rules are followed by most people; the difference between them is in the character of the rules. In the one case the rules give the individual much independent liberty of action; in the other case they give less. In considering the matter in such a more changing society as that of Dzitas, we encounter situations in which norms of the latter sort are giving way to norms of the former sort. The older people lament the fact that young people do not obey familial controls. There is, in Dzitas, what Thomas and Znaniecki call "social disorganization: decrease of the influence of existing social rules of behavior upon individual members of the group."[21] But if the ways of the younger people should become the customs of the succeeding generations without further change there would result a society without social disorganization but more individualistic than that which had existed before. In the materials from Yucatan it is not possible to recognize such an outcome; both social disorganization and the development of more individualistic norms are apparently occurring together in the town and in the city. The modes of conduct shift toward the more individualistic pole of the collectivistic-individualistic scale, but there is a decrease in the degree to which the courses of conduct of the members of the society tend to conform to whatever mode there is.

The foregoing discussion of the three major conclusions of this volume should make it possible by review of the materials on which this study is based or by collection of new materials to verify the general conclusion that in Yucatan the long-isolated, homogenous society is the sacred, collectivistic society characterized by well-organized culture, as compared with the less isolated, more heterogeneous society. If this is established, questions of greater significance arise. One question, created by the attempt to universalize the conclusion, may be stated: "Are all long-isolated, homogenous societies sacred, collectivistic, and characterized by well-organized cultures?" The question invites examination of the primitive societies and their comparison with reference to the three qualities here stressed, a comparison to be made with each other and then with at least that less isolated, heterogeneous society that we know best— our own. A reading knowledge of some of the primitive societies suggests that in general the answer to the question is likely to be in the affirmative and that there is indeed a natural association between long isolation and homogeneity, on the one hand, and sacredness, collectivism, and the organization of culture, on the other. In various ways this has been declared in the antithetical concepts offered by Maine, Durkheim, and

Tönnies, already referred to (Preface). But it may well turn out that the correspondence is limited by special circumstances, that the association among some of the various characters is more necessarily close than among others, and that besides the long-isolated society with its attendant characters, on the one hand, and the less-isolated, heterogeneous society with its characters, on the other, we may recognize subtypes, or types in which various kinds of compromises or combinations of character are found. A recent paper by Dr. Sol Tax[22] points out that, while certain Guatemalan nonliterate societies of which he has some knowledge are characterized by local cultures (presumably well organized), are homogeneous, and are isolated at least in the sense that the contacts with persons outside the local community are not intimate, nevertheless family organization is low, and on the whole the conventions allow for much individualistic behavior, and the secular character of the social life is great (he also points out the impersonal nature of many institutions and controls in these communities, a matter not much discussed in the present pages with reference to Yucatan). These Guatemalan societies are, as has been remarked above in connection with the rural Ladinos, in relative equilibrium, that is, social disorganization is relatively small. Tax concludes that a primitive (long-isolated, homogeneous) society can be "mobile, with relationships impersonal, with formal institutions dictating the acts of the individuals, and with familial organization weak, with life secularized, and with individuals acting more from economic or other personal advantage than from any deep conviction or thought of the social good."[23] His conclusion requires much more analysis of particular facts in Guatemala to enable us to regard the results of the comparison as established, but the avowedly tentative conclusion may be rephrased: There are long-isolated, nonliterate, homogeneous, culturally well-organized local communities in relative equilibrium which are characterized by predominance of secular and impersonal behavior and sanctions and by individualism with relative unimportance of kinship institutions.

It is hardly possible long to pursue the task of classifying societies in such terms as these without developing an interest in problems of becoming. Reverting to the conclusion reached with reference to the four communities in Yucatan, one asks, once that the general conclusions as to the differences among them are at all accepted, "What has brought about these differences?" One possible answer would be that the four communities differ in the respects mentioned according to their degree of isolation from the single important center of influence, which center has been transmitting to the various communities, first the ways of the Spaniard, and later the ways of the modern city, in proportion to the degree of isolation of the communities from that center. It might be argued that the differences between Tusik and Chan Kom, and between Chan Kom and Dzitas, are merely the different degrees to which Spanish and modern elements of culture have diffused, as the anthropologist says, to these communities. It might be said that there is no natural interrelation among the various changes that have apparently occurred in the four communities, that each is independent of the other and, to give a single example to illustrate the whole possible line of argument, that Dzitas has both a less well-organized culture and a more secular society as compared with an earlier condition in that community simply because its people have borrowed from the city a set of customs which happen to have less organization, and at about the same time, following example from the same source, have learned to take religion less seriously. It might be contended that all that has been accomplished in this study is to summarize the events of diffusion into the hinterland of Yucatan and that the results that have here been expressed in general form depend upon the accident that the societies that exerted influence over the peripheral communities were characterized by less well-organized culture, by secularism, and by individualism. Such a line of argument, if consistently followed, would involve the contention that the extension of these three kinds of social behavior or qualities of society into the peripheries of the modern Euro-American area has no more significance for the understanding of the general nature of society and its changes than has the spread of trousers or the gasoline tin.

If this should be the only conclusion to which the study leads, it might, nevertheless, have a value in providing a general guide for the comparative study of the extension of modern Euro-American ways into other societies. It is certainly to be recognized that the present study does not establish that any isolated, homogeneous society, or that of the hinterland of Yucatan in particular, would have become less well organized culturally, more secular, and more individualistic if it had become less isolated and more heterogeneous through contact with some other kind of society—a society, let us say, that was also sacred and collectivistic and well organized culturally. Recent history does not readily provide us with opportunities to study such a situation. It is probable that different readers will find different values in the materials herein presented with reference to possible contribution to the understanding of general problems of social change. It seems to the writer that the materials indicate that there is some interrelation of the characters which constitute the progressive differences noted. It seems to him impossible to report the situation in Yucatan simply in terms of different degrees of diffusion of elements of culture. Account has also to be taken of the consistency of the total social situation with the new element of culture that is presented by example. If it appears that in Merida as compared with Dzitas there is less bargaining and more disposition to announce a fixed price for goods offered for sale, it is significant to point out that merchants in the city imitate foreign standards. It is also significant to point out that, where the stores are large, the employees are more impersonal, and the saving of time is important, the fixed price instead of the protracted haggle is more adaptive, more "natural." Perhaps the merchants of Merida, once having developed their business in other respects to its present point, would have begun to announce fixed prices even if they had not heard of the custom. We cannot say as to this. But we can say that the borrowing, if it was a borrowing, was made easier by the fact of the other changes. There is no necessity for a clear choice between an explanation in terms of borrowing, on the one hand, and in terms of necessary interrelation of changes, on the other. Contact and communication initiate changes which go on partly under the guidance example provided by the source of the communications and partly of the adaptive necessities of the social situation as it comes to be.

It would be difficult to support an assertion that the lesser organization of culture in the town and the city is due simply to the fact that the people of the city have learned how to have less organization in their conventional life. The comparison of the four communities indicates that the greater disorganization comes about as a cumulative result of many particular changes, some of which are not on the level of communication at all. What is borrowed are particular tools, modes of conduct, and ideas; these in turn do things to the lives of the borrowers so that the total result is a kind and degree of disorganization. The appearance of opportunities to make a livelihood in ways other than agriculture causes some men in the community to give up agriculture. Having given up agriculture, they do not participate in agricultural rituals. In this way they cease to share in the attendant understandings as to, for example, the relations between agricultural ritual and disease. But meanwhile the pressure of city opinion has made it difficult for the shaman-priest to practice his calling in the town community. So he moves away, and the people of the town are without his immediate and frequent example and instruction. At the same time new ways of treating illness, without reference to agricultural piety and ritual conformity, are introduced from the city. So far as these are followed the individual is in this way also led aside from the interrelated patterns of thought and action which characterized the older way of life. The connections between sickness and ritual practices are broken down. In many such interacting and cumulative ways as this the phenomenon that has here been called the disorganization of culture has come about in Yucatan. It is also to be emphasized that the complementary process of reorganization of culture is certainly not brought about by learning to have organized customs and institutions in direct imitation; rather it is brought about by living in isolated intimacy for a long time. This is attested most convincingly by the fact that it is in the isolated communities that elements of Catholic origin are most closely integrated with elements of the pagan religion. Organization and disorganization of culture are not directly learned. They are aspects of society which "go with," respectively, isolation and outside communication and heterogeneity.

Similar questions can be raised about secularization and individualization. Do the people of Dzitas (for example) come to take a more secular view of life and to recognize the rights of the individual to act on his own independent account because they are presented with the example of citizens of Merida, whom they perhaps admire, and who are skeptical and behave in a more individualistic manner? Can there be effective education and propaganda to inculcate a generally secular view? Perhaps there can be. Or perhaps, until the experience of an individual is such as to impair his conception of the sacredness of an act or an object, his observation of skepticism in others will have little effect on him. Whether or not secularization and individualization may be directly and generally learned or inculcated is not established by the materials from Yucatan. The materials do suggest that these results may come about more indirectly. The specialized activities in Dzitas are on the whole more secular than those of Tusik partly because new arts unconnected with religion have been introduced to Dzitas and partly because old arts have lost those connections for a variety of reasons. It was probably the advent of a more general literacy that made the secretary, as a sacred specialist, unnecessary. If we attempt to explain the fact that guardia is a sacred duty in Quintana Roo and a secular chore in Chan Kom, we cannot say much that is con-vincing as to the effect of an example of a secular government upon the people of Chan Kom as an influence that may have caused them to take a less religious view of guardia. It is more probable that, when the ancestors of the Chan Kom people ceased to guard a shrine containing a talking cross, or some equivalent symbol of great religious power, they continued to carry on guardia, but now without the religious connection. Or it may be that guardia, once more secular among the Quintana Roo people, became more sacred when, after the War of the Castes, they became organized tribally in defense of their isolated land from the whites.

The impossibility of describing all the differences among the four communities solely in terms of different degrees of diffu-sion from the city appears from an attempt to offer such an ex-planation for the facts with reference to black magic. It may be argued that black magic is regarded with less horror in the city than in Quintana Roo because the people of the city, even the lower class, are more exposed to examples of rational and skeptical thinking and especially to disbelief in magic. But the fact that in the city black magic is more frequently believed to have occurred than it is in Quintana Roo cannot be accounted for in such terms. The explanation offered in the preceding chapter in terms of the breakdown of the family and other primary group controls, with attendant personal insecurity, will seem to many readers more acceptable. Nor can it be plausibly argued that there are more family quarrels in Dzitas than in Quintana Roo because the people of Dzitas have di-rectly imitated the example of Merida in this respect.

It appears to the writer that interrelation between the dis-organization of culture and secularization is rather strongly suggested by the Yucatan materials. One of the principal im-plications of chapter ix is that people cease to believe because they cease to understand, and they cease to understand be-cause they cease to do the things that express the understand-ings. The community is so large that not all the men can participate in a single rain ceremony. Or new arts have been introduced which give some men employment other than in agriculture; as a result some of the men, having no milpa, have no occasion to participate in the ceremonies. Or the shaman-priest moves away from the local community. For any or all of these reasons, and for others, fewer of the people find themselves participating in the rituals and hearing or reciting the prayers. As they do not do these things, they cease to understand them. There remains merely the feeling that, if the rites are not performed, misfortune will follow. The disorganization of culture has also involved secularization, for the content of belief, myth, and ritual which expressed and supported the emotionally colored attitude—the sacredness of the agricultural activities—has been lost. The materials are no more than suggestive at this point, but they seem to the writer sufficient to point out the likely possibility that, whatever might have been the effect of direct example upon the religious cults of the villages, the mere increasing heterogeneity and complication of the division of labor would have brought about some secularization. It is notable that the secularization proceeds, as one compares the four communities, with regard to both the Christian and the pagan cults and in not very different degrees.

Pursuit of these questions fails for the lack of sufficient historical data on the course of change in each of the communities. The comparison of the four communities as they were found to be at the time of investigation suggests general hypotheses for the study of cultural disorganization, secularization, and individualization, now considered as processes, not simply as characters of unchanging societies. While such investigations are awaited, further guidance in the formulation of these hypotheses may be derived from a widening of the comparison. Once more the reader's attention is called to the much more briefly reported societies in the highlands of Guatemala. The question may be asked how these Guatemalan societies came to be (if they are) secular and individualistic, while being culturally well organized and homogeneous. Again the question cannot be answered without greater knowledge of history than we now have.

Some speculations as to alternative possibilities may be offered as a guide to historical research. In the first place, it is a probable assumption that at some time in their early history the Indian societies of Guatemala were more sacred and collectivistic than they now appear to be. This assumption is an application of the generalization already offered, subject to examination, that most primitive societies tend to have these characteristics. One possibility is that the Guatemalan societies became more secular and individualistic due to contact with the Spanish society following the Conquest. If this were true, the situation there would be similar to that in Yucatan, with the differences that, though becoming secular and individualistic, the Guatemalan societies retained their local, nonliterate, homogeneous, and culturally well-organized characteristics and reached an equilibrium retaining these characters. However, another and different assumption might be made: that the Guatemalan societies, even before the Conquest, were relatively secular and individualistic. To this assumption we are directed by the fact that the secular and individualistic character of these societies appears to be dependent on aspects of those societies which we have reason to suppose existed before the Conquest: the complex and important system of trade with some use of money and the form of political organization whereby an élite secures the participation of all members of the group in ceremonial and practical activities of the state by the exercise of impersonal controls. By this second assumption the Spanish invasion, by increasing the division of labor, extending the use of money, the system of markets, and further enlarging the impersonal state, merely carried further a secularization and individualization that had already begun.

Both the secular quality of contemporary Guatemalan life and its individualistic character are bound up both with the important commerce and with the highly developed political institutions. Almost everybody buys and sells, and everyone goes to market. Haggling for goods in terms of one outstanding measure of value—money—is carried on by man, woman, and child. So doing, anyone, even a young unmarried girl, will act independently to secure a practical advantage. Success in such dealings is readily measured in monetary terms. It is understood by the people how the possession of money increases freedom and personal mobility, and its acquisition is freely employed to secure these results. Where most goods are measurable in terms of money, and where much time and attention are devoted to practical, competitive bargaining by means of a mundane and universal measure of value and of achievement, it is easy to add the conclusion that intense personal religious life and a nonrational sanctification of social objects are not likely to occur.

Another striking feature of the societies of at least the midwestern highland part of Guatemala is the large part played by impersonal political and juridical institutions in social control. Public opinion and family organization do not have the greatly dominant roles in controlling the individual that they have in many simple societies. Much use is made of the courthouse machinery; many quarrels lead quickly to complaints before the local authorities; in the case of hamlets these courts are not even in the local settlement but in a village or town some distance away; in these formal actions and litigations brother may be pitted against brother, and father against son-in-law or even son.[24] As the ultimate sources of power that support these courts are in the city of Guatemala and in the national government, the individual who so easily resorts to them throws himself upon a very impersonal authority indeed. A related fact is the almost automatic character of public office in many of these Guatemalan communities. Participation in a hierarchy of office is a duty required of boys and men; the individual submits himself to the system, it might be said, passing through a graded series of public duties until he emerges, an old man, free of the necessity. It is not hard to see a connection between these exterior and impersonal systems of controls and the individualistic and secular behavior which appears to characterize this part of Guatemala.

These considerations suggest some possible causes, independent of the breakdown of cultural organization, for secularization and individualization: trade and a money economy and the development of a formal, hierarchical government with authority exercised by remote control. A consideration of some other societies, notably some in West Africa, might tend to reinforce these hypotheses or it might tend to contravene them. But, with reference to the Yucatecan and Guatemalan materials alone, the suggestions appear to have force, especially with regard to the influence of money and markets. The most isolated communities of Quintana Roo are like those of Guatemala in that they are primitive societies in equilibrium. They are unlike them in that they are more sacred and less individualistic. It has been seen that especially in Quintana Roo the market plays a small place in the life of the people and that money valuation of goods is much less general than in Guatemala. It has also been shown that in Quintana Roo as compared with Guatemala practically all social control is exerted by institutions arising from within the local community. The suggestion that a money economy is an agent of secularization is an old one in connection with the history of our own society. The line of thought suggested in this and the preceding paragraph indicates that it is important to determine the history, in both Guatemala and Yucatan, of the regional division of labor, of the system of trade and the use of money, and of the institutions of government, particularly of the civil-ceremonial government of Indian communities of the highlands of Guatemala. It is important to determine to what extent these institutions existed in pre-Columbian times and what was the effect of the Conquest and of later events upon them.

The indicated hypothesis is that the secular and individualistic character of highland Guatemala life is a result, in part, of the great regional division of labor and of trade. These features were in turn dependent, we may suppose, on the topographic and geographic diversity. Yucatan does not have this diversity. Yet apparently before the Conquest, Yucatan participated in the trade[25] and was perhaps characterized by greater regional division of productive labor than it now is. Cacao and cotton were grown; the coast people exported salt. Perhaps Quintana Roo was before the Conquest more commercial than it is now because a form of society based on regional division of labor, trade, and even money, and characterized by impersonal, hierarchical government, developed in the highlands where the habitat made such development possible, and was then extended to the Yucatan peninsula. And perhaps when the Maya state broke up before the Conquest, and when after that event contact with Guatemala largely ceased, such villages of Maya as remained relatively remote from the later modern civilization of the white man reverted from a secular, individualistic condition to a more sacred, less individualistic condition.[26] In such case the Maya of Quintana Roo have taken elements from two civilizations—one Christian, the other pagan—and have gone back to the more usual sort of primitive society. The Indians of the Guatemalan highlands, on the other hand, according to this view, retain the characters of the mixed society—a secular, individualistic, primitive society—which they began to develop before the Conquest out of the social and technical conventions which their habitat favored.

The contribution of speculation-as-to-facts to the line of thought has now become large, and the argument has probably gone beyond the point where it is of value to science. The principal tentative generalizations to which we are led by the Yucatan materials, combined with some knowledge of the Guatemalan societies and of other societies less particularly denoted here, may be summarized. A consideration of Yucatan, set against a background of general impressions as to the primitive societies on the whole, and with limitation suggested by Guatemala, indicates that in the absence of a money economy, isolated, homogeneous societies tend to have well-organized cultures and to be sacred and collectivistic. A comparison of what Tax reports for Guatemala with the materials from Yucatan leads to the conclusion that there is no single necessary cause for secularization and individualization. The Yucatan materials, in spite of the possible objection that the differences are simply learned or diffused directly, induce the writer to propose that increase of contacts, bringing about heterogeneity and disorganization of culture, constitutes one sufficient cause of secularization and individualization. And the case of Guatemala, fortified by certain interpretations of the history of our society, suggests that the development of important commerce and a money economy may be another such sufficient cause.

NOTES

"CK" refers to *Chan Kom: A Maya Village*, by Robert Redfield and Alfonso Villa; "QR" refers to *The Maya of East Central Quintano Roo*, by Villa; "DDZ" refers to *Disease and Its Treatment in Dzitas, Yucatan*, by Margaret Park Redfield.

CHAPTER I

1. QR, chap. iv.
2. QR, chap. iv.
3. The principal other differences between communities known by the author to exist in Yucatan and disregarded in the formulation of this project include: (1) the difference between a community of hacienda employees and a community of independent farmers, such as Chan Kom (this difference would be of importance in any study planned with immediate reference to the practical social and economic problems of Yucatan); (2) the difference between typical agricultural communities, such as those dealt with in this volume, and the (relatively few) coastal settlements which depend in large part upon fishing; (3) the difference between the "standard" Yucatecan culture which concerns the reader of these pages and the somewhat different, marginal culture of Campeche. The Campeche culture is the one notable regional culture in the peninsula (British Honduras might be added as another). The communities that have been chosen, however, lie along the northwest-southeast line of diminishing communications, and therefore Campeche is not involved.

4. It has been suggested (Benedict, *American Anthropologist*, 39:342) that it would have been wise to select for first study a village long established and conservative rather than one made up of relatively recent colonists because the older culture would presumably be better preserved in such a village than it is in Chan Kom. Should one seek such a village within the region controlled by the government of Yucatan, one might look to some village at the extreme eastern part of the state, as Chemax or Nabalam, or perhaps to one of the communities that lie beyond the southeastern range of hills, such as Santa Elena, southwest of Ticul. Aside from the practical convenience of studying Chan Kom rather than some other peasant village, justification for the choice lies in two circumstances. In the first place, as the Quintana Roo village also included in this study has been practically cut off from modernizing influences for a century, many of the older elements of culture might be expected to occur there, with at least the degree of probability that they might be found in Chemax or in Santa Elena, and so receive recognition in the completed project. In the second place, the very fact that Chan Kom is an extreme deviate in the degree to which the ideas and

actions of its people have been organized and directed toward modernization makes sharper the contrast it is desired to make between it and Tusik, where extreme conservatism prevails. The objective of this study is not the recovery of early Maya culture but the description, in terms as general as are warranted by the facts, of the differences among four communities differently situated with respect to isolation. Chan Kom is determined to overcome its isolation; Tusik is determined to preserve it. Nevertheless, it must be recognized that the circumstance that Chan Kom is a community of colonists introduces into the comparison of the four communities a factor which cannot be identified with differences in the degree of accessibility to ideas and examples from the city, namely, the circumstance that a community made up chiefly of young persons who choose to leave their ancestral villages to make new homes in a territory not well known to them may be, or by the experience become, more radical than is "on the average" true in an old village. The writer recognizes that the unusual interest in "progress" that prevailed in Chan Kom during the period of study makes Chan Kom atypical for the region in which it lies. The reader will note in the following pages how the writer in part redresses this atypicality by making the comparison between Tusik and Chan Kom, or between Dzitas and Chan Kom, in terms of what was characteristic in Chan Kom just before the great period of progress, or with what Villa and the writer learned about other communities in the Chan Kom area. The comparison of patron festivals is made with villages near Chan Kom, because Chan Kom was not at the time maintaining its festival; the account of marriage rituals represent the older custom in Chan Kom; the role of the *h-men* in Chan Kom is dealt with as it existed toward the end of the period of study before the last h-men left Chan Kom.

5. Radcliffe-Brown, 1939, p. 20.

6. The behavior of some human aggregations is homogeneous by reason of similar separate individual responses to the same situation (see Blumer, *Publications of the American Sociological Society*, 29:115–27). The four societies studied, especially those remote from the city, are homogeneous in that behavior is standardized by tradition, i.e., is cultural.

7. The reader may raise a question as to whether or not some of the differences stated to exist among the four communities are not related simply to another factor: the size of the community. It is true that Tusik is less than half the size of Chan Kom and that Chan Kom is smaller than Dzitas, and Dzitas smaller than Merida. Yet X-Cacal, another Quintana Roo community near Tusik which is twice as large as Tusik and four-fifths as large as Chan Kom, and which might as well have been used for the study as Tusik, exhibits the same features which are present in Tusik. Furthermore, the author has sufficient familiarity with villages near Chan Kom and almost as large as the town of Dzitas (Tekom, east of Chan Kom, with a population of over eight hundred, is one of these) to assert that, if one of these had been studied instead of Chan Kom, the results of the comparison would not have been much affected. It may be supposed that the size of a community puts limits upon the possibilities as to which certain characters of social life may be present, but it appears to the writer that two communi-

ties differing considerably in size may exhibit similar degree of development of the characters hereinafter emphasized in carrying through the comparison based on the materials from Yucatan.

CHAPTER II

1. These descriptions are of conditions in 1934.

2. This description of Merida was prepared by Asael T. Hansen. The account represents Merida at the time the study was made. In recent years changes have occurred, especially in the economic life and in the position of the wealthy, chiefly as a result of agrarian reforms.

3. All figures are from the 1930 census. The population of Merida given here includes 1,645 people living in three areas on the periphery of the city which the census lists separately. All three are integral parts of the city.

4. Based on a list of the members of the Co-operative of Sisal Producers given in Rafael Mendiburu M. and Pedro Góngora R. de la Gala, 1934, pp. 188–97.

5. Except for the Customs Office and the Immigration Office, which are located in Progreso.

6. The information is from the Federal Health Office in Merida. Only doctors that that office recognizes are included.

7. Information furnished by A. T. Hansen.

8. There is no official source of information regarding the number of migrants from the towns and villages of the hinterland residing in Merida. Studies of three small areas, widely separated from one another in the city—one in a middle-class section and the other two in lower-class districts—showed that, of 197 persons fifteen years of age and over, 52, or 26 per cent, were born in the hinterland.

9. Census of 1930. Information on place, i.e., state and nation, of birth is given in the census only for the state as a whole. It is assumed here that the full range is represented in Merida, an assumption which seems fairly safe.

10. The city of Merida accounts for 87.7 per cent of the population of the *municipio*.

11. The figures refer to the municipio.

12. The 1930 census gives no figures on English apart from other foreign languages. According to the 1921 census, there were in the state 886 persons whose native language was not English who spoke the language. The number has certainly increased since then, and, as they are concentrated in Merida, the figure of a thousand seems reasonable.

13. The figure for the city itself would be about 76 per cent.

14. This refers only to copies distributed in Merida. The figures are for a sample month in 1936.

15. This is the subject of a paper by Hansen, 1934a, pp. 124–42.

16. This assumes a rather generous estimate of the population of Merida seventy-five years ago. The earliest official figure is 36,634 for 1895.

17. There were approximately 2,800 in the state in 1933. The figure for Merida is an estimate based on this.

18. Population figures for Dzitas (pueblo and municipio):

Source	Dzitas Alone	Entire Municipio
Federal census, 1895.............	737	....
Federal census, 1921.............	1,398	2,703
Shattuck's census, 1929..........	1,177	....
Municipal census, 1930..........	....	2,426
Federal census, 1930............	1,338	2,411

According to the 1930 municipal census and to Shattuck's census, females slightly outnumber males. The federal censuses of 1921 and 1930 indicate the reverse.

19. DDZ, pp. 55–57.

20. A map of Dzitas is to be found in Shattuck, 1933, p. 106.

21. Roys, 1939.

22. Hansen has classified municipios of the state of Yucatan into three groups: (1) two "urban" municipios of Merida and Progreso; (2) twelve "town" municipios each of which includes a town with a population over 2,000 which constitutes 75 per cent or more of the total population of the municipio; and (3) thirty-two "rural" municipios, twenty-three of which contain no town with a population over 1,000 and nine of which contain a town with a population between 1,000 and 1,500 which constitutes less than 60 per cent of the total population of the municipio.

With reference to this classification the municipio of Dzitas falls—barely—into the rural group. The town itself contains 1,200 people, constituting 55 per cent of the population of the municipio. The municipio is one of those of the rural group whose characteristics most closely approach those of the town type. The figures in the following table express these characters as they occur in the entire municipio of Dzitas and may be compared with the corresponding figures for classes of municipios as they will be given by Hansen.

Foreigners per 10,000	Single Persons per 100	Divorced Persons per 10,000	Non-Spanish-speaking Persons per 100	Maya-speaking Persons per 100	Literate Persons per 100	Non-Catholics per 10,000
21	20	43	35	78	42	348

23. CK, pp. 1–16. 25. CK, p. 97, n. 7.

24. CK, pp. 42–47, 51–60. 26. CK, pp. 6–11.

27. On the details of political organization in Yucatan at this period see Redfield, "Notes on the Political Organization of Yucatan," pp. 77–83, in Shattuck, 1933.

28. CK, pp. 27–30, 102–6.

29. CK, pp. 11, 15–17.

30. CK, pp. 68–77.

31. CK, pp. 100–101.

32. CK, pp. 31–42.

33. CK, pp. 18–30.

34. CK, p. 13.

35. QR, chap. vii.

36. QR, chap. vii.

37. QR, chap. vii.

38. QR, chap. v.

39. QR, chap. ix.

40. QR, chap. viii.

CHAPTER III

1. The materials of this chapter have been presented, with different emphasis, by the author in Redfield, *Cooperation in Research*, 1938, pp. 511–32. As the reader will discover, many other factors besides race enter into the definition of socially recognized groups in Yucatan. For purposes of a title the word "race" is convenient to refer to the original distinction between Spanish whites and Maya Indians upon which most of the ethnic and class differences are based.

2. The general statement made in this paragraph, to be quite true, would require qualifications and additions. It ignores, among other factors in the situation in Yucatan, the role played by social classes previously existing in the Spanish and Maya societies in determining, by force of tradition, the social classes which developed in the later Yucatecan society.

3. This word is Nahua in origin. In Mexico it was used, apparently before the Conquest, to refer to a member of the commoner class, as distinguished from a noble. So it had originally a significance with regard to status. It was in use in Yucatan before the Conquest, or soon after.

4. *Mazehualob* and *dzulob* are the two principal ethnic groups recognized by the Quintana Roo natives, but other lesser groups are ignored in this discussion because the central argument does not require dealing with them. The negroes, known through contacts with British Honduras, are known simply as "black men" (*box uinicob*). They are not depreciated; they are thought to be different from but akin to the mazehualob. The Chinese, called *chinos*, are depreciated; children of Chinese and Maya women are insulted by reference to their Chinese origin.

5. With respect to *dzul* see n. 21 below.

6. The change from folk to city costume (*mestizo* to *vestido*) is generally made first by the man rather than the woman, for the reason (among others) that he may make the change gradually, adding a garment of the city at a time, whereas for her no such easy transition is possible; she must, practically speaking, put on the city costume all at once.

7. The facts given briefly in the text are further summarized in the accompanying table.

This census does not take into account further complications introduced by the circumstance that in not a few mestizo households a son or daughter has adopted city attire, or that some sons of milperos, still living with parents, have risen in the occupational scale. It is based on the parental generation in each household. As in nearly every case a married son sets up a separate household, the simplification does not seriously affect the distribution of the features in the population, but, on the other hand, the classification as presented does not call attention to the frontier of culture and status change between the generations.

		No. of Households
GROUP	I. Maya-speaking mestizo *milperos*, woodcutters, etc.	136
GROUP	II. "Transitional"	
	A. Maya-speaking mestizos who have specialized occupations (carpenters, barbers, and trackworkers)........................	10
	B. Maya-speaking, *de vestido*	
	1. Milperos...................... 4	
	2. Specialized occupations........... 8	
	Total of "B".....................	12
	C. Spanish-speaking; women mestiza	
	1. Milperos...................... 5	
	2. Specialized occupations (from porter to mason and horse dealer)........ 11	
	Total of "C".....................	16
	Total, Group II.....................	38
GROUP III. Spanish-speaking, de vestido, specialized occupations.......................................		39
Data lacking...		12
Total..		225

8. The Korean tinsmith is, of course, an exception.

9. In Colonial times certain civil rights were denied to Indians. The word "vecino," as implying full civil rights, was naturally applied to people not Indians. In many Colonial documents *indios* are contrasted with *vecinos*. (The matter is not entirely clear, however, because in at least two documents persons undoubtedly Indians are referred to as vecinos.) Vecino, as a more or less legal or technical term, included in Merida two groups socially distinguished: whites and mixed-bloods wearing the same garb as did the Indians. In Dzitas the supreme class was apparently unrepresented. The mixed-bloods with Spanish names were the only ones enjoying full civil rights. Perhaps that is why in such a place as Dzitas the word persisted in general use to denote the upper of the two classes present.

10. The municipal government of Dzitas is now chiefly in the hands of indios. A man such as is described in the text sat one afternoon in the plaza at Dzitas watching the activities in the municipal building, amused, he said afterward to a friend, also a vecino, to see "what a mess those Indians are making of the job of government."

11. Doña N.'s two grandmothers and her mother's father all bore Maya surnames and were therefore indios. Her father and his father had a Spanish surname. Her neighbors, knowing all this, say that Doña N., in spite of her own surname, is india. Doña N. lives the life of the poor and ignorant milpero; in

spite of her Spanish surname, she cannot quite claim to be as good as one with four vecino grandparents. But, she says, "anyway, I am half-vecina. I am *mulata*. I always go where the vecinas are." The difference in status between india and vecina is much on her mind.

Doña P., an impoverished mestiza whose family has lost its solidarity and gives her little support, clings to the fact that she is vecina and resents the un-respectful demeanor of the indios toward her. She is so poor that she begs; she wears the *huipil;* her daughter-in-law, a mestiza of no family, is not respectful to her; and she lives in a miserable house far from the plaza, among indios. And all this, she feels, is wrong, for were not all four of her grandparents vecinos?

12. Don P. and his family live in great poverty, but his ancestry and his wife's are entirely vecino, and he counts among his kinsmen a priest and a well-to-do Meridano. Don P. and one of his three sons are milperos. The old man and his sons wear the mestizo costume, but all the women of the family are de vestido. With Don P. and his wife live two daughters and one son, the spouses of these, and their children. The daughters have vecino husbands who are not milperos. These husbands treat their wives badly, and one, indeed, has left his wife. Into this household some years ago an india came as a servant. The son, Francisco, began to sleep with her, and now she lives as his wife and the children have been legitimized, although no marriage ceremony has been performed. If this daughter-in-law had been a vecina of equal status to that of her husband, her husband's kinsmen would refer to her as Francisco's *esposa*—it is not usual to deny the term to women living as wives, even though the union is informal. (They speak of one of the daughters' husbands as her "esposo," although he has an earlier wife living to whom he was properly married.) When the other grand-children wish to tease Francisco's children, they call them by their mother's Indian surname. When Francisco "takes a night" at a novena, his mother, and not his india consort, arranges it for him, and the wife's name is not given as one of those participating in the novena.

Doña C. and her husband are vecinos, and she is de vestido. Doña C. holds her head very high, in spite of her reduced circumstances. She lived for a time in Merida, one son is in school there, and she was among those women active in the first *gremios* (religious sisterhoods) organized in Dzitas in imitation of Merida. But the other two sons have disappointed her by marrying indias. These daughters-in-law have better character reputations than have the sons. Doña C. speaks of them, however, with disparagement. "I do not have to be at home. My sons' wives are mestizas. They can do the housework." One of these india daughters-in-law was not even from Dzitas; she lived before her marriage in a village. Doña C. and her husband had then to go to this village, bearing presents of food, and at night, in order that the village courting customs should be observed. This she did because her son urged her, explaining that it would be expected by his future parents-in-law. But Doña C. felt foolish carrying it out, and she is quite willing you should know that she felt so.

13. The cross-stitch embroidery designs of that period were geometrical. The realistic patterns now common were introduced later.

14. Of the thirty-six marriages recorded in the books of the civil registry

for the three years 1867–69, only 8 per cent were between a person with Indian surname and a person with Spanish surname, whereas in two four-year periods ending, in the one case, in 1900 and, in the other, in 1932, the corresponding figures are, respectively, 18 per cent and 16 per cent. Records of church marriages were not seen; presumably in marriages solemnized by the church the difference would be greater.

15. It is said that in those days the Maya language was spoken generally in all homes, indio and vecino. In 1760 an official traveler "heard not a word of Spanish in all the pueblos visited from Carmen to Campeche and from the latter to Merida" (*Discurso sobre la constitución de las provincias de Yucatán y Campeche* ["Documentos para la historia de Yucatán," Vol. III (Mérida, 1938)], p. 78).

16. How did it come about that the surname became the important index of social position? Historical research should give an answer to this question. Meanwhile it may be supposed that in the cases of the first children born of white fathers and Indian mothers, if the father recognized the child as his (through marriage with the mother or otherwise), it took the father's surname and was accorded a superior occupational and social position. If the child was the product of a more casual union and went unrecognized by the father, it was brought up among the mother's people and bore the Indian name. So a Spanish surname came to attest membership in the superior mixed-blood group. In Dzitas the even more superior white group disappeared, through absorption with the mixed-bloods (vecinos) or withdrawal to the city. As amalgamation and assimilation progressed, the vecinos, especially those with respect to other indicia sinking lower in the social scale, clung to the pride of name and race.

17. The situation as it exists today can be made manifest by relating the indio-vecino distinction to the culture classification summarized in the table in n. 7. Of the Maya-speaking, mestizo milperos (Group I), 75 per cent have Maya surnames (i.e., are indios), and several of the others may be persons whose surnames were changed to Spanish forms just before or during the Revolution. Of the 39 Spanish-speaking family heads who habitually wear the city costume and carry on specialized occupations, not one is an indio. On the other hand, not all the vecinos fall in this superior group (Group III), nor are all the indios humble milperos. Half of 108 households where the man is a vecino use the Maya language habitually; 39 (36 per cent) gain their livelihood as simple milperos; in 48 (44 per cent) the wives wear the folk dress. All the households of indio men are Maya-speaking, with perhaps two or three exceptions. All are mestizo in the sense that the men do not wear shoes or dark trousers; in many the men have assumed some of the garments of the vestido group—they wear, for example, colored shirts and have given up the apron. In three indio households the grown sons have adopted city dress, in five the woman is *catrina*, and in a dozen or more the grown daughters wear city attire. The fourteen indios who have specialized occupations include two masons, two trackworkers, one barber, two carters, two tailors, one wall-builder, one baker, one brakeman, and two porters. About half of these also work their own milpas.

18. Nowadays most of the posts in the municipal government are filled by indios, but a few, notably that of secretary, are usually occupied by vecinos. At

the time of the Revolution a few of the vecinos took the side of the indios; but most vecinos were identified with the opposite faction.

19. "Now there are four or five indios who even wear shoes. And they used to be servants at the *finca* of San Juan. . . . ." "The indios nowadays are very stuck-up (*orgullosos*). Some are good, but others are ill-bred (*malcriados*). Isidra and José Capul, our neighbors, don't behave well toward us. They used to bow, and now they go by with their hats on. The indios began to be proud at the time of Felipe Carrillo. He spoiled them. Now many of them are rich; they have all sorts of things in their houses, while we are poor. . . . . You see, there is an india who has been to visit the ruins [at Chichen], and I have never been there. . . . ." "When Don Francisco Canton was fighting his battles, he came to Dzitas and asked them why they kept the indios apart; he changed some of their names to Spanish names. This broke down the feeling of respect that the indios had for the vecinos, and they began buying silk huipils."

20. In the case of men it is possible, by assuming some of the garments of the modern Western world and discarding corresponding folk garments, to assume a costume equivocal with regard to these two generally mutually exclusive categories.

21. The Tizimín *Chronicle* declares that in Katun 8 Ahua "Mayapan was depopulated by foreigners (dzulob) from the mountains," evidently referring to the Xiu. On pp. 83–84 of Roys's translation of the Chumayel we read of "dzulob" who seem to be the Itza. Another reference to foreigners (dzulob) occurs on p. 142 of Roys's translation of the Chumayel. In the Chontal *relación* of Paxbolon it is said that the Acalan rulers had a war with the "dzulob," apparently in the Usumacintla Valley. From other references it appears that these dzulob were Nahua-speaking (information supplied by R. L. Roys). For "dzul" the Motul dictionary gives "estrangero de otro reino."

CHAPTER IV

1. Redfield, *American Anthropologist*, 1934, pp. 57–59.

2. Parsons, 1937.

3. Where Merida is involved in the comparison, reference is to the middle and lower classes, unless there is special reference to the contrary. The heterogeneity of Merida is so great that few elements of convention characterize every inhabitant. It is obvious that it is the lower classes that most closely resemble the townspeople and the village folk.

4. Wauchope, 1938, pp. 16 ff.

5. CK, pp. 364–66, for citations of authority as to the aboriginal origins of elements mentioned in these two paragraphs.

6. On the aboriginal origin of *hetzmek* see CK, p. 374.

7. For evidence that the *x-tabai* is an Indian concept see Parsons, 1937, p. 230.

8. On the supernatural connotations of the ceiba to the ancient Maya see Redfield, *Maya Research*, 3:231–43.

9. ". . . . y que se lavan las manos y la boca despues de comer" (Landa, chap. xxv, Book I).

10. QR, chap. xiii; CK, pp. 164–68.

11. Parsons, 1937, pp. 214–15; Carr, Master's thesis, University of Chicago, 1937.

12. As stated in chap. viii, it is in the villages that one finds most commonly a grouping of married sons living close together or even in the same household with the father; in some of these instances the father exercises patriarchal authority. There is reason to suppose that this form of family was common among the Maya before the Conquest. In a census of Cozumel taken in 1570 each house contained, besides the head and his wife, from one to seven other married couples (Roys, Scholes, and Adams, 1940, p. 14). These authors quote a letter written in 1548 by Fray Lorenzo de Bienvenida to the Crown Prince: ". . . . In this land there is hardly a house which contains only a single householder. On the contrary, every house has two, three, four, six and some still more; and among them there is one paterfamilias, who is the head of the house."

13. QR, chap. xiv.

14. Except in Quintana Roo, where the dead are buried uncoffined.

15. On the question of Spanish and Indian contributions to Latin-American notions of witchcraft see Parsons, 1937, p. 493; also Parsons, *Man*, 27:106–12, 125–28.

16. CK, pp. 93–94.

17. QR, chap. iv.

18. CK, pp. 127–47; QR, chap. xi.

19. It should be added that, of course, primitive elements of custom do not survive only on the periphery of any changing society. There are always special local circumstances which may cause the retention of old elements in certain communities. The coati impersonation and the erecting of the ceiba tree are elements of festal practice which Chan Kom has given up. They are retained in not a few Yucatecan communities more sophisticated than is Chan Kom, partly because local pride helps to maintain old customs. The mock calling of the pig, as part of the dance with the pig's head, is still practiced in other villages in Yucatan where the coati impersonator is unknown. In Cacalchen it is not unusual to select the godparents before the birth of the child, and even in Merida there are a few old people who refuse to act as godparents if not asked before the birth of the child. This community is archaic in this respect, and that community in another.

20. CK, pp. 144–46.

21. CK, pp. 173–75.

22. CK, pp. 142.

23. The customs of *dza akab* and *hadz pach* (CK, pp. 158–59) might be added to this list in a qualified sense. The customs appear to be native in origin rather than Spanish. They are not observed in Chan Kom today, but they were observed in festivals attended by the Chan Kom people a generation ago. They are fresher in the memory of the Chan Kom people than they are in the memories of the Tusik people. Again it is probably the special decline in the h-men, his numbers and authority, that accounts for the fact cited.

24. Perhaps similar reasons account for the absence of a special marriage

negotiator (*casamentero*) at Tusik, whereas there is such a functionary at Chan Kom.

25. In other matters of custom Tusik presents a certain abraded, or simplified, appearance, resulting, apparently, from poverty and the harder conditions of life in Quintana Roo. It is there understood that the domestic utensils and tablecloths should be renewed on All Souls' Day. But, because of poverty, this is not done in Tusik, although it is done in Chan Kom. Similarly, at the annual fiesta in Quintana Roo a mock pig's head was decorated instead of a real one; and, as the people have no bulls to use in a bullfight, a man takes the part of the bull in a mock bullfight that attends the fiesta.

26. CK, pp. 117–18.

27. Pacheco Cruz (1934, p. 58) reports proverbs.

28. CK, p. 370.

29. About sixty years ago members of the lower class in Merida (and no doubt in the towns also) observed daily recitation of prayers. But these were domestic, not recited in church.

30. Parsons calls attention to the fact that, among the Rio Grande Pueblos, Santo Domingo is the most conservative of both pagan and Christian elements.

31. QR, chap. xii.

32. The ancient Aztec (and presumably the Maya) had a ceremony at the end of every 18,980 days in which new fire was kindled by priests with a fire drill, the householders first putting out their domestic fires, which were then relighted from the new fire (see Juan de Torquemada, 1723, pp. 292–95).

CHAPTER V

1. Linton, 1936, pp. 273–74.

CHAPTER VI

1. CK, p. 192.
2. CK, pp. 198–204.
3. CK, pp. 116–17, 144–46.
4. CK, p. 119.
5. QR, chap. ix.
6. QR, chap. x.
7. QR, chap. xii.
8. CK, p. 125.
9. CK, p. 137.
10. CK, pp. 146–47.
11. CK, p. 176.
12. CK, pp. 158–59.
13. Sumner, 1907, p. 5.
14. CK, pp. 164–68; QR, chap. xiii.
15. CK, p. 227.
16. CK, chap. xiii.

CHAPTER VII

1. When this chapter came to be written, it was discovered that there were lacking many facts required for a thorough comparison of the economic life of the communities studied. Notable deficiencies exist with reference to details of sale, loan, and hire in Dzitas. The author has also failed to find out to what extent practices in the town and city express national or state law.

2. Blom, 1932, pp. 533–50.

3. The unimportant and casual exchange of locally produced goods includes maize, minor foods, brown sugar, hammocks, and baskets. The amount is very small; relative to the trade with the town and the city it is insignificant.

4. QR, chap. vii.

5. CK, p. 62.   6. CK, p. 63.

7. The right and custom of testamentary disposition appear to be as generally recognized in Tusik and in Chan Kom as in the town and in the city. The early missionaries urged the Indians to make lists of their possessions so at death they might go to their wives and children (Bishop Toral's instructions). As the people of Tusik cannot write, these testamentary dispositions are orally given; and such provisions are regarded as sacred and usually upheld without question. In Dzitas written wills are more common, and it is there less uncommon to refer to constituted formal authority for the carrying-out of their provisions. In Tusik disputes about inheritance are extremely rare. Probably this is in part due to the greater degree of family organization there; partly it is due to the poverty of the Quintana Roo people.

8. Roys's study of early land documents in Yucatan indicates to him the existence of individually owned and inherited tracts of land in the Chan Kom region a few years after the Conquest. A document of 1561 suggests such ownership, and in another, probably only a few years later, dealing with the same property, the owner refers to the land as "the forest of my ancestors." Roys inclines to the view that just before the Conquest in this part of Yucatan most land was held by a landholding organization similar to the Aztec *calpolli*, that other land was then held by individuals, and that after the Conquest the calpolli ownership became converted into ownership by towns, both of farmlands and of town lots (personal communication to the author from R. L. Roys). The conceptions of land held in Quintana Roo appear to be copies neither of the calpolli ownership of very early times nor of the later town ownership. While the absence of notions of individual ownership of land in Quintana Roo may be hard to account for in view of the fact that individual landownership was apparently well known in ancient southeastern Yucatan, on the other hand, the fact that the entire subtribe, or group of villages, rather than a single village, claims rights over agricultural lands and bush may go back to old traditions. Roys (in personal correspondence) cites early seventeenth-century documents in which it is clearly shown that Cuncunul, Tekom, and Tixcacalcupul (in the Chan Kom area) had joint control over their lands. So in very early Colonial times or before both forms of control existed: by single villages (as is the tradition and now the law in the Chan Kom area) and by groups or alliances of villages, as in east central Quintana Roo today (Roys, 1939, esp. p. 39).

9. Fruit trees are owned separately from the land in Chan Kom too. The writer regrets that he did not inquire into the existence and extent of this conception in Dzitas. Hansen found no evidence that ownership of fruit trees separate from the land is recognized in Merida.

10. There is some evidence that the making of mortgages was commoner before the Revolution; nowadays foreclosures on home sites are not easy to secure.

Among the lower classes in Merida it is probably commoner to deposit the document of title informally with the money-lender than to make a formal mortgage.

11. CK, p. 78.

12. Durkheim, 1932; also Hughes, *American Journal of Sociology*, 33:757.

13. Hughes, *American Journal of Sociology*, 33:757, and *ibid.*, 43:404–13.

14. Tönnies, 1935; Sombart, 1937.

CHAPTER VIII

1. Landa (Gates's trans.; 2d ed.), 1937, pp. 41–42; also Beals, *American Anthropologist*, 32:467–75.

2. Eggan, *American Anthropologist*, 36:188–202. The alternative possibility suggested by the Motul dictionary terms (which Eggan also noted), that the ancient Maya marriage was a system of brother-sister exchange, has been recently made to appear slightly more probable by appearance of the fact that the present-day Chorti, a Mayan people, forbid cousin marriage but practice a systematic sibling exchange and have a system of kinship terminology that is consistent with this form of marriage. See Wisdom, 1940.

3. Unless the companies are to be regarded as vestiges of an ancient unilinear kinship group.

4. Soustelle, *Maya Research*, 2:325–44.

5. Redfield and Villa, 1939.

6. The census of 1930 reported four divorced persons in the municipio of Cuncunul to which Chan Kom then belonged. During the study of Chan Kom one inhabitant took steps toward securing a divorce.

7. Unpublished data compiled directly from the archives of the Civil Register in Merida give the following number of divorced persons per 1,000 at the time of the study: the entire state, 5.2; municipio of Dzitas, 4.3; municipio of Merida, 6.9; city of Merida, 7.4. Divorce of Yucatecans in Yucatan, most frequent at the time of the Revolution, declined sharply in frequence in the years that followed.

8. CK, p. 300.

9. Eggan, *op. cit.*

10. Villa's materials do not securely establish the extension of the terms to these affinal relatives; they strongly indicate it. But the point should be verified.

11. QR, chap. xiv.

12. Landa (chap. xxv, Book I) tells us the custom existed then.

13. Eggan, *op. cit.*, p. 194.

14. *Ƶob* (*sob*) should probably be added to this list as a probable corruption of *sobrino*. The word does not occur in the Motul dictionary.

15. "Hase de advertir si los que vienen a casar vienen de su voluntad o los traen por fuerza sus padres o parientes o unos viejos casamenteros que suele haber en algunos pueblos" (Bishop Toral's diocesan instructions [*ca.* 1565]).

16. Confirmation of the formal, familial, and sacred character of marriages among the Quintana Roo is to be found in Adrian, *Ƶeitschrift der Gesellschaft für Erdkunde*, 1924–25, pp. 241–43.

17. CK, pp. 195–98.

18. As among the Yaqui of Arizona (Spicer, 1940, pp. 91–116).

19. CK, pp. 188–90. 22. CK, pp. 184–86.

20. QR, chap. xiv. 23. CK, pp. 186–88.

21. QR, chap. xiv. 24. QR, chap. xiv.

CHAPTER IX

1. CK, pp. 134–36.

2. CK, pp. 339–56. 5. CK, pp. 143–44.

3. CK, pp. 119–21; QR, chap. x. 6. CK, pp. 175–76.

4. CK, p. 128. 7. CK, p. 175.

8. This and the succeeding five paragraphs were prepared by A. T. Hansen after discussion with R. Redfield.

9. CK, p. 108; QR, chap. x.

10. QR, chap. xi.

11. CK, p. 148.

12. This and the succeeding seven paragraphs were prepared by A. T. Hansen.

CHAPTER X

1. Doll, Master's thesis, University of Chicago, 1939.

2. QR, chap. xii.

3. Landa (Gates's trans.; 2d ed.), 1937, p. 70, says: "To do this with the greater solemnity, on this day they renewed all the service things they used, as plates, vases, benches, mats and old garments, and the mantles around the idols. They swept their houses, and threw the sweepings and all these old utensils outside the city on the rubbish heap, where no one dared touch them, whatever his need."

4. Redfield, *Maya Research*, 3:231–43.

5. QR, chap. xi.

6. As will appear more fully in connection with the account of the festal organization as it exists in Dzitas, it is in many cases customary for this first meeting, held soon after the festival, to be followed later in the year by another meeting, at which the organization is reviewed and perfected. Villa did not determine whether such is the case in X-Cacal. That such a second meeting is customary in that area is indicated by the account of Pacheco Cruz (1934, pp. 47–50) relative to the village of Xiatil, not far from the X-Cacal group of settlements. He says that the meeting, called *chumuc-haab* ("middle of the year") is accompanied by praying and the distribution of corn-husk cigarettes.

7. Villa (QR, chap. xii) suggests that this chair is an imitation of the Bishop's Seat, the empty chair which used to be placed beside the bishop's throne in the cathedral in Merida (and probably of St. Peter's Throne, which stands above the Pope's throne in St. Peter's in Rome). It is also possible that the Holy Seat of X-Cacal has been influenced by the seat or bench as a symbol of ruling power among the ancient Maya.

8. QR, chap. xii.   9. CK, pp. 153–55.   10. Redfield, *op. cit.*

11. Apparently this is a vestige of another custom which to some degree is preserved in Dzitas. John L. Stephens (1843, p. 101), describing the annual festival in Ticul, says: "The báyle de dia was intended to give a picture of life at a hacienda, and there were two prominent personages, who did not appear the evening before, called fiscales, being the officers attendant upon the ancient caciques, and representing them in their authority over the Indians. These wore long, loose, dirty camisas hanging off one shoulder, and with sleeves below the hands; calzoncillos, or drawers, to match, held up by a long cotton sash, the ends of which dangled below the knees; sandals, slouching straw hats, with brims ten or twelve inches wide, and long locks of horse hair hanging behind their ears. One of them wore awry over his shoulder a mantle of faded blue cotton cloth, said to be an heirloom descended from an ancient cacique, and each flourished a leather whip with eight or ten lashes. These were the managers and masters of ceremonies, with absolute and unlimited authority over the whole company, and, as they boasted, they had a right to whip the Mestizas if they pleased.

"As each Mestiza arrived they quietly put aside the gentleman escorting her and conducted the lady to her seat. If the gentleman did not give way readily, they took him by the shoulders, and walked him to the other end of the floor. A crowd followed wherever they moved, and all the time the company was assembling they threw everything into laughter and confusion by their whimsical efforts to preserve order."

CHAPTER XI

1. CK, pp. 31–49; QR, chap. vi.
2. CK, pp. 164–68; QR, chap. xiii; DDZ, pp. 61–63.
3. CK, pp. 168–69; QR, chap. xiii; DDZ, pp. 63–64.
4. CK, pp. 161–64; QR, chap. xiii; DDZ, pp. 63–65.
5. The item of belief mentioned in this sentence is the only one of this group which does not appear in Hansen's materials from the city. Hansen thinks it likely that the idea is nevertheless present there, and on the general question of the participation of the lower-class Meridano in the folk culture he says: "I think it often happens that a Yucatecan who has occasion to travel in the peninsula or to converse with visitors from other communities often hears of details of thought and practice that he has not met in his contacts with his neighbors and friends at home. When this takes place, he tends to accept the new items or, at least, not to be surprised by them. They are consistent with what he already knows. My point is that the participation of Yucatecans in the Yucatecan folk culture goes beyond the sharing of particular items of knowledge. There are common general conceptions, and, as long as the local variations seem to square with these general conceptions, a Yucatecan feels more or less 'at home.' This is one of the reasons there are no subcommunities of rural migrants in the capital, as I thought there might be at one time. The Yucatecan folk culture is abundantly represented in the city. It is falling to pieces, but many of the pieces are familiar or are similar to and consistent with that which is familiar."

6. CK, pp. 177, 304.

7. QR, chap. viii.

8. CK, p. 177.

9. CK, pp. 252–53.

10. DDZ, p. 78.

11. DDZ, p. 78.

12. CK, chap. viii.

13. DDZ, p. 56.

14. The cases from Dzitas that have been published (DDZ, pp. 58–60) are not directly comparable with those collected by Hansen in Merida because each case of the former is a record made by a single patient to a single practitioner, and the patient might have been consulting other practitioners before, after, or during consultation with Aurelia. But good cases of sickness, reporting the treatment of the case, from whatever sources, were recorded in Dzitas.

15. Hansen, 1934*b*.

16. *Ibid.*

17. *Ibid.*

18. *Ibid.*

19. The abhorrence in which the Quintana Roo Indians hold the idea of witchcraft is also noted by Gann (1918, pp. 35–36). Thompson's materials (1930, pp. 74–75) suggest that cases of imputed witchcraft are less uncommon in British Honduras than they are in Quintana Roo. A myth Thompson collected in Socotz explains the existence of sickness because of the failure of people in the ancient times completely to destroy the magical equipment of a legendary sorcerer (*ibid.*, pp. 166–67).

20. CK, p. 177.

21. CK, pp. 226–29.

22. CK, Appen. B.

23. DDZ, pp. 75–77.

24. DDZ, p. 79.

25. CK, pp. 87, 95, 192.

26. Hansen, 1934*b*.

27. According to a recent census, the numbers of males for each 100 females in three age groups are: twenty to twenty-nine, 75.5; thirty to thirty-nine, 86.2; forty to fifty-nine, 91.4. The disproportion is thus greatest in the early age of adulthood, when the interest in sex is strong.

28. DDZ, pp. 75–77.

CHAPTER XII

1. T. E. Jones compared the results of questionnaires given residents in certain Japanese rural communities differing as to the degree to which they had been affected by modern urban influences (Jones, Doctor's thesis, Columbia University, 1926).

2. Redfield, *American Anthropologist*, 36:57–69.

3. Recent work has indicated the possibilities of a combination of ethnological and documentary historical method in reaching conclusions as to the historic trend of change with respect to kinship terminology and institutions. Eggan (*American Anthropologist*, 39:34–52) reached the conclusion that a once widespread Crow type of kinship structure has in the cases of several tribes in the North American Southwest been progressively modified in the same direction as in degrees of change closely correlated with the degree of general change brought about in the Indian societies through contact with white civilization. Eggan compared societies differing as to the relative degree of change undergone, but he made his conclusion possible by reference also to documentary records of the

state of kinship terms and practices of certain of the tribes at periods beyond recall of informants. Spicer (1940, pp. 86–88) indicates the possibilities of reporting recent changes in kinship terminologies by comparing current practice of younger people with more conservative usage of older people. An important application of mixed documentary-historical and ethnological methods to these same problems of changes in kinship institutions has been made by Han Yi Feng in his monograph on "The Chinese Kinship System" (*Harvard Journal of Asiatic Studies*, Vol. II, No. 2 [1937]).

4. Redfield, *op. cit.*, p. 68.

5. A discussion of the city as a type of society characterized by large, dense, permanent settlements of heterogeneous people, in which appear other characteristics consistent, on the whole, with that "type" as opposed to that of the folk, including impersonal relations and disorganization of culture, and the weakening of the bonds of kinship, occurs in Louis Wirth's paper, "Urbanism as a Way of Life," *American Journal of Sociology*, 44:1–24.

6. Hook, *Encyclopaedia of the Social Sciences*, 3:114.

7. In this connection I have been helped—but probably not enough—by Dr. Leo Srole.

8. Redfield, *op. cit.*, p. 69.

9. Linton, 1936, p. 275.

10. *Ibid.*, p. 273.

11. *Ibid.*, p. 275.

12. *Ibid.*, p. 283.

13. *Ibid.*, pp. 283–84.

14. The word "disjunction" may be more suitable than "disorganization."

15. For some readers the suggestions contained in these pages may be made more acceptable if "integration" or "configuration" should be substituted for "organization." If such a substitution be made, it should be noted that "integration" has had recent important use in connection especially with the social relationships making up societies, and also that what is discussed in the present pages is not what Benedict (1934), for example, is chiefly concerned with in dealing with configuration. She also recognizes cultures as more than the sums of their parts, but while she is particularly interested in distinguishing and perhaps classifying the cultures, so seen as wholes, in terms of aspects of their particular custom or content—what kinds of behavior they emphasize—the present writer is concerned with the phenomena of organization (or configuration) themselves. Thus the Zuñi culture and that of the Northwest Coast are by Benedict sharply distinguished in that the former emphasizes quite other virtues and ideals than does the latter. But it might appear that, with respect to the four characteristics of organization enumerated on a foregoing page of this chapter, the Zuñi and the Kwakiutl cultures are closely alike.

16. Durkheim (trans. G. W. Swain), 1915, pp. 38 ff.

17. CK, pp. 175–77.

18. This is substantially the understanding of secularization given by Walter Bagehot (1890, pp. 156 ff.), who has argued that the discussion of principles is a means to the breakdown of sacred custom.

19. *Ibid.*, pp. 409 ff.

20. For example, the relative sacredness of two collections of tales and myths might be determined somewhat more precisely than would result from the expression of the investigator's general impression if each story were considered

with reference to such questions as: Does the story refer back to remembered action or forward to anticipated action? If it does, what is the role of that action in custom and belief? Are there recognized limitations on the time or place of telling the story or as to who may tell it? What is the response if the story is mocked or treated lightly?

21. Thomas and Znaniecki, 1920, 4:2–3.

22. Tax, *Scientific Monthly*, 48:463–67.

23. *Ibid.*, p. 467.

24. Tax, *American Anthropologist*, 39:423–44; also Tax, *ibid.*, 40:27–42.

25. Blom, 1932, pp. 533–56.

26. In a personal communication Ralph L. Roys suggests that in the century before the Conquest the communities may have reverted to a more independent, self-sufficient condition. He writes: "Just now I am occupied with the idea that this condition was the result of an attempt at social revolution of a sort in 1441, when the age of the real cities ended, that the big cities were ruled by a warrior-trader caste, but after the fall of Mayapan, the agriculturalist got the upper hand. Although I admit this was not the case everywhere, I think it was so in the Cupul area at least. I don't know whether I will ever be able to convincingly show this, but I am trying to construct a foundation for it." If this should be proved to be the fact, the version in eastern Yucatan toward a more sacred society with few impersonal sanctions might have begun before the Conquest.

GLOSSARY OF SPANISH AND MAYA
WORDS USED IN THE TEXT

[Spanish words are printed in italics; Maya words, in roman. Words borrowed from one language and used in the other in an altered form or with a changed meaning are regarded, so far as this list is concerned, as in the borrowing language (e.g., *cenote*, caliz, oxdias). Where a phrase contains elements from the other language, even if the elements are unchanged, the entire phrase is regarded as in the language in which it appears (e.g., Hahal Dios).

Standard Spanish words, used with their usual dictionary meanings and plainly translated in the text where they occur, are not included in this list. But even words that have been adopted into English are included in this glossary if they are used in the text of this book in a special local sense.

In the text Maya words have been freely treated in making plurals. When the word seemed to the writer to lend itself easily to anglicization, it has been (but not always) given an English plural (e.g., h-mens, *but* kuilob-kaaxob).]

ALAKOB, n.—Domestic animals; applied to wild animals under patronage of deities.

ALBORADA MISA, n.—A mass held at dawn, initiating certain festivals in the remote villages.

ALCALDE, n.—Title of chief Indian civil functionary in the older traditional town government, now supplanted by the *municipio* government.

ALUXOB, n.—Small, goblin-like supernatural beings associated with the ancient ruins and pottery made by the ancient Maya.

AREPA, n.—Festal breads made of maize, lard, and honey.

ATOLE, n.—Maize gruel.

AUDIENCIA, n.—In earlier times, the place of public meeting for civil purposes of the Indians of a community, where Indians were recognized as a distinct group.

BAILE, n.—The usual word for a dance; used especially in contradistinction to *jarana* to designate an occasion where modern European dances are danced.

BALAMOB (BALAMS), n.—The supernatural guardians of men, villages, and cornfields.

BALCHE, n.—A beer or mead made of the fermented bark of the *Lonchocarpus* tree and honey; used in the pagan ceremonies and in festivals.

BARRIO, n.—Originally a community of the lower class, dependent on and peripheral to the center of cities and towns where lived the élite; nowadays, a traditional neighborhood of town or city.

BATAB, n.—The chieftain of an Indian village; an old term now almost extinct.

BOOY, n.—Shade.

BOX UINICOB, n.—Term applied to negroes by the Quintana Roo Maya.

CAANCHE, n.—A hollowed log, raised on posts and filled with earth and used to grow herbs and vegetables.

CABECERA, n.—The principal settlement and seat of municipal government of a *municipio*.

CACICAZGO, n.—A subtribe of the Quintana Roo Maya.

CACIQUE, n.—The master of ceremonies at a festival.

CALIZ, n.—A sacred liquor, made of honey and water, used in the ceremonies held in Quintana Roo.

CARGA, n.—(1) The responsibility to carry on the annual festival of the patron saint and the men who carry it on. Equivalent to "cuch." (2) A measure of harvested maize; about 42 kilos.

CARGADOR, n.—The one who assumes the principal authority for the *carga*.

CASAMENTERO, n.—Functionary who arranges marriages as the intermediary between the boy's family and the girl's.

CATRÍN, n.—A localism for one wearing European dress rather than Yucatecan folk costume.

CENOTE, n.—Natural well or deep water hole resulting, in Yucatan, from erosion of the limestone down to the ground water.

CHAACOB (CHAACS), n.—The rain-gods.

CHA-CHAAC, n.—The rain ceremony, communal in the villages.

CHANCLETAS, n.—Soft, heelless slippers worn by *mestiza* women.

CHEN REZAR, n.—The name given in Quintana Roo to the ceremony performed to appease the souls of the dead.

CHIC ("COATI"), n.—A buffoon at certain festivals.

CHUC HEL ("seek successor"), n.—A meeting in Holy Week at which the organization for festival of the patron saint is effected.

CHUMUC-HAAB ("middle of the year"), n.—A meeting of members of a cuch to complete the organization for the festival of the patron saint.

CICHCELUM YUM, n.—Jesus Christ.

COMISARIO, n.—The elected chief officer of the civil government of a *municipio*.

COMPADRE, COMADRE, n.—Man (or woman) related to you by the fact that he or she has acted as sponsor of your child in baptism, hetzmek, or marriage, or by the reciprocal fact that you have so acted in the case of his or her child.

CORREDOR (aside from other meanings of the term), n.—In Quintana Roo, the public building at X-Cacal in which secular activities of the subtribe are held.

CORRIDA, n.—A bullfight.

CUARTEL, n.—Building used for purposes of secular government in the villages; in X-Cacal, Quintana Roo, one of a number of such buildings, each used by one of the companies making up the *cacicazgo*.

CUCH, n.—In the villages the organization of the festival of the patron saint; also the responsibility or duty of maintaining the festival. Same as *carga*.

CURANDERA, n.—A (woman) professional who treats illness with herbal and other medical or magical means.

CUTZ-CAL-TZO, n.—A ritual strangling of turkeys during the fiesta of the patron at Dzitas.

DE VESTIDO, adj.—Said of one who wears European dress rather than the folk costume.

DEVOTO, n.—One agreeing to take a share (usually a night of prayer) in a *novenario*.

DIPUTACIÓN, n.—A group of functionaries at a festival headed by a *diputado*

DIPUTADO, n.—A word used in some communities for the principal members of the organization of men charged with carrying on the festival of the patron saint.

DUEÑOS DEL MONTE, DUEÑOS DEL CERRO, n.—A city man's, or town-man's, phrases for the supernatural beings of bush and field.

DZA AKAB, n.—A ritual wherein the young men participating in the festal bullfight spend a night of vigil under supervision of the shaman-priest.

DZULOB, n.—Term used by Indians for white townspeople (see chap. iii).

EDZCUNAH GRACIA, n.—A ceremony addressed to the crosses, performed in Quintana Roo at any time of need.

EJIDOS, n.—The legally recognized, collectively owned agricultural and pasture lands of a village.

ENCOMENDERO, n.—In Colonial times, a Spaniard to whom Indian settlements were handed over for protection and exploitation.

ENRAMADA, n.—A bower, or roofed dancing floor, constructed to serve at festivals.

ESCABECHE, n.—Turkey cooked in spices and served sliced with a spiced sauce.

ESPOSO, ESPOSA, n.—Husband, wife. Also used for the partners in well-established informal unions.

EVANGÉLICO, n.—Local word for Protestant.

FAGINA, n.—Compulsory labor at public improvements.

FINCA, n.—An agricultural estate or large farm.

GENTE DE CATEGORÍA, n.—Same as *gente decente*.

GENTE DECENTE, n.—The upper class, chiefly white people, in Colonial Merida; today the term is also used in the towns for the upper class, even though the amount of white blood is small.

GLORIA, n.—Heaven; celestial abode of God and the saints.

GRACIA, n.—(1) Maize, when growing in the milpa; (2) the spiritual essence of food offerings made to the gods.

GREMIO, n.—A group organized to carry on certain aspects of the ritual centering around the patron saint of a commodity.

GUARDIA, n.—Compulsory attendance and performance of police, sentry, and messenger duties for the villages.

HAAN-CAB, n.—The custom whereby a man, on marrying, lives temporarily with his wife's parents and works for them to earn his wife.

HADZ PACH, n.—A ritual whereby the girls who dance in the festival are cleansed of evil winds.

HAHAL DIOS, n.—The supreme deity.

HANAL PIXAN, n.—"Dinner of the souls." The ritual observances on All Saints' Day and All Souls' Day.

HEK, n.—Broth of fowl thickened with corn meal.

HERMANO, HERMANITO, n.—Older brother, younger brother.

HETZMEK, n.—The ceremony wherein an infant is for the first time carried astride the hip and a sponsor puts in its hands articles symbolizing the sought-for, sound development of the child's abilities.

H-MENS (Maya plural, H-MENOB), n.—The shaman-priests of the Yucatan Maya.

HOL-CHE, n.—First-fruit ceremony.

HOLHUNTAZMUYAL, n.—The doorway in the clouds through which the rain-gods emerge.

HUACHOB, n.—Term applied by the Quintana Roo Maya to the Mexicans (i.e., those from outside the peninsula of Yucatan). The term is used with the same meaning and with a Spanish plural in colloquial Spanish in Merida and elsewhere in Yucatan.

HUIPIL, n.—The woman's exterior garment, a loose blouse, constituting part of the folk costume.

INDIO, n.—Indian; a person with a Maya surname (see chap. iii).

IXIM, n.—Maize, when not growing in the field.

JARANA, n.—The folk dance of Yucatan.

JÍCAMA, n.—A starchy edible root (*Pachyrhizus erosus* [L.] H.B.K.).

JOTA, n.—A folk dance of Spain.

JUZGADO, n.—A word for the building used for village or municipal administration.

KAH IK ("notification"), n.—A meeting held Christmas Eve of the men making up the organization to carry on the festival of the patron saint.

KAT ZIPIL ("ask pardon"), n.—A ritual of penance wherein devotees approach an altar on their knees.

KAXCHE, n.—Word used in the villages for the rustic bull ring built there for a bullfight.

KAZ-DZUL, n.—Term used by Indians for persons intermediate between the Indian groups and the white urban group (see chap. iii).

KEX, n.—A therapeutic ceremony wherein the sickness or evil is conveyed out of the body to something which it occupies in place of the afflicted person.

KOL, n.—Broth of fowl.

KUB-MESA, n.—Functionary appointed to direct the men who prepare offerings for the *santo* at a festival.

KUILOB-KAAXOB, n.—The supernatural beings who protect the forest.

KUNKU-CHAAC, n.—Chief of the rain-gods.

LA ENCAMISADA, n.—A personage of certain festivals: a man, dressed as a woman, who dances with a rattle.

LADINO, n.—In Guatemala, a person of Spanish language and culture, as contrasted with one who follows Indian ways of life.

LIGA, or *LIGA DE RESISTENCIA*, n.—A local or occupational union affiliated with the governmental political party; in the villages, a city-fostered organization of all adult males.

LOH, n.—A ceremony of lustration from the evil winds.

MAESTROS CANTORES, n.—Those village professionals whose function it is to recite Catholic prayers at certain religious rites.

MALDAD, n.—Bewitchment; evil done by magic.

MATAN DZOC, n.—Term applied in Quintana Roo to a mass held on Palm Sunday.

MAYORDOMÍA, n.—A word used in Mexico but not much in Yucatan (see cuch and *carga*) for the organization which maintains the cult of the patron saint, especially for the principal office in that organization.

MAZEHUALOB, n.—The principal term applied by the Indians to themselves (see chap. iii).

MECATE, n.—A measure of land; about one twenty-fifth of a hectare.

MERIDANO, n.—A native, or resident, of Merida.

MESTIZO, n.—Primarily an Indian-Spanish mixed-blood, but, as the term is more commonly used in Yucatan, one who wears the folk costume and not European dress (see chap. iii).

METNAL, n.—The underworld of the sinful dead; hell.

MILPERÍO, n.—A group of neighboring cornfields, made out in the bush.

MILPERO, n.—One who makes milpa; an independent maize farmer.

MONTE, n.—Wild or uncultivated land, especially forested land.

MUHUL, n.—The bride-gift, consisting in the villages of a *terno*, certain food, and usually a gold chain.

MULATA, n.—Half-blood.

MUNICIPIO, n.—The smallest administrative subdivision of the state; a rural area including one or more villages or other settlements.

NAKUL, n.—Subordinate of a *cargador*.

NOCHERO, n.—At least in the city and the town, the leaders of one of the nights of prayer making up a *novenario*.

NOHOCH DZUL ("great dzul"), n.—Term applied by the Indians to a respected white or urban person.

NOHOCH TATA ("Great Father"), n.—The title of the priestly supreme functionary of the Quintana Roo Maya.

NONA, n.—A parade performed after a *jarana* and just before dawn at a festival.

NOOX, n.—A person, or object, used to support another.

NOVENA, n.—A ritual recitation of Catholic prayer, in church or house, on one night or on a series of nights.

NOVENA DE PROMESA, n.—A *novena* held in compliance with a special promise to do so in response to a special need, as distinguished from *novenas* held on the name day of a saint.

NOVENARIO, n.—A series of nine consecutive nights of (Catholic) prayer.

OJO-IK, n.—A group of disease-bearing evil winds.

OKOT-BATAM, n.—Term used in Quintana Roo for the principal rain ceremony.

OKOZTAH POL ("dance of the head"), n.—Ritual dance with a decorated pig's head performed at the culmination of the festival of the patron saint.

OXDIAS, n.—A ritual bread of maize used in ceremonies in Quintana Roo.

PADRINOS, n.—The sponsors of a child at baptism, or at hetzmek, or at marriage.

PARTIDO, n.—One of sixteen large administrative districts into which the state of Yucatan was formerly divided.

PAYALCHI, n.—The six basic Catholic prayers, knowledge of which is expected of everyone among the Quintana Roo Maya.

PIBIL-NAL, n.—Ceremony of first-fruit offering of new maize ears.

PINOLE, n.—A seasoned drink or gruel of toasted corn.

PISOTE, n.—The coati, or coatimundi.

POBLANO, n.—A resident of the small towns or villages, in contrast to the Meridano.

POC-KAB, n.—A ceremony in which, by ritually washing the hands of their *compadres*, the parents of a baptized child show the thanks and respect they extend to their *compadres*.

PROMESA, n.—A vow, or sacred promise.

PUC KEYEM ("dissolve pozole"), n.—A ceremonial making of a maize beverage and of a sweetmeat of squash seeds and chaya leaves at festivals of the patron saint.

PUEBLO, n.—A category of municipal settlement, legally recognized, provided with a municipal government including a *comisario* and other officers.

PUESTOS, n.—Locations for booths at festivals or fairs; also the booths themselves.

RAMILLETE, n.—A pole, provided with suspended hoops, and decorated with cigarettes, *arepas*, and other ritual objects.

REBOZO, n.—Head scarf making up part of the folk costume of the woman.

RELACIÓN, n.—In Colonial times, an account of some happening reduced to document.

RELLENO, n.—Turkey stuffed with meat and seasonings and boiled whole.

REZADORA, n.—A woman recognized for her ability to recite the Catholic prayers used in novenas and other ceremonies.

REZO, n.—As used in Chan Kom and in Quintana Roo, a prayer offered to the souls of the dead.

ROSARIO, n.—In Chan Kom this word is sometimes used to designate a simple (Catholic) prayer ritual at which a rosary is recited. In Merida it is used as is *rezo* in Chan Kom (i.e., a whole evening of prayers devoted to the dead by a gathering of relatives and friends is called a *rosario*).

SANTIGUAR, n.—A therapeutic ceremony by which the evil or sickness of the patient is stroked or washed away from him.

SANTO, n.—A saint, and especially the image of a saint.

SUBLEVADOS, n.—Term applied to those Indians of Quintana Roo who rebelled in the War of the Castes and to their descendants.

SUPLENTE, n.—The second officer in the municipal government; next in authority to the *comisario*.

TAMAN, n.—A word meaning "piety" or "good conduct."

TANCAZCHE, n.—A tree (*Zanthoxylum fagara* [L.] Sarg.) the wood of which is used as a magical preventive of sickness.

TERNO, n.—A *huipil* of fine material and adornment.

THUP, n.—A word applied to the least, or youngest, of a series.

TUNKUL, n.—The ancient drum, made of a hollow log, now almost extinct in Yucatan.

TUP-KAK, n.—An annual agricultural ceremony performed in Quintana Roo.

TZAHBIL KEKEN, n.—A seasoned pork dish served at village festivals.

TZICIL, n.—A ceremony in which the parents of a baptized child express the respect they have for their *compadres*.

UAXIN, n.—A tree, *Leucena glauca*.

UAY-CHUP, n.—A sorcerer in animal form that is believed to have sexual intercourse with sleeping persons.

U-HANLI-COL, n.—A periodic ceremony carried on by the individual agriculturalist to assure him good crops.

UINIC, n.—The usual Yucatec Maya word for "man," "person"; applied contemptuously to outsiders by Quintana Roo Indians.

U LUUM CEH YETEL CUTZ ("the land of the deer and the curassow"), n.—A traditional poetic phrase for Yucatan.

U LUUM MAZEHUALOB ("the land of the Indians"), n.—A phrase used by Indians of Quintana Roo for the territory they inhabit and regard as theirs.

U TZICIL IGLESIA ("the offering of the church"), n.—A ritual meal concluding the annual festival at X-Cacal.

VAQUERAS, n.—The girls who take part in a *vaquería*.

VAQUERÍA, n.—A *jarana* when forming a part of the activities of the festival, including a bullfight.

VAQUEROS, n.—The male participants in a bullfight and in a *jarana* at a festival.

VECINO, n.—A term, going out of use, for persons of European ancestry, as evidenced by Spanish rather than Indian surname. (The word has more general meaning as "neighbor" and as "enjoyer of civic rights.")

VESTIDO, adj.—See *de vestido*.

X-KAX-BAAC, n.—A woman who treats sprains and dislocations.

X-MUUCH, n.—Ritual objects made of dyed corn husks, attached to ramilletes.

X-TABAI, n.—A supernatural being in woman's form who may entice men to their death.

X-THUP-NAL, n.—A quick-maturing variety of maize.

XUNAN, n.—Word for white woman or for any married woman.

YERBATERO, n.—A word used in Spanish for the shaman-priest (h-men); more generally, an herbal curer. In the latter sense, the curer may be a woman, in which case the term is *yerbatera*.

YUM, n.—Respectful title used toward Indians as equivalent to *don* (literally, "lord").

YUNTZILOB, n.—"The Lords," a collective term for the pagan gods of the bush, milpa, rain, and village.

ZACA, n.—Corn meal, prepared without lime and stirred into water; used as an offering.

ZARAPE, n.—Blanket worn as a garment by men.

ZAZTUN, n.—The piece of glass or crystal used by the shaman-priest in divination.

ZIP, n.—Supernatural protectors of the deer.

ZIPCHE, n.—A plant (*Bunchosia glandulosa* [Cav.] D.C.) of which ritual use is made by the h-men.

ZUCUUN, n.—A term for elder brother, or for certain other elder male relatives of the speaker's own generation.

ZUHUY, adj.—A word meaning "pure," "uncontaminated."

REFERENCES

ADRIAN, H. 1924–25. "Eineges über die Maya-Indianer von Quintana Roo," *Zeitschrift der Gesellschaft für Erdkunde*, pp. 241–43.

BAGEHOT, WALTER. 1890. *Physics and Politics*. New York: D. Appleton & Co.

BEALS, RALPH. 1933. "Unilateral Organizations in Mexico," *American Anthropologist*, 32:467–75.

BENEDICT, RUTH. 1934. *Patterns of Culture*. New York: Houghton Mifflin Co.

———. 1937. Book reviews in *American Anthropologist*, 39:342.

BLOM, FRANS. 1932. *Commerce, Trade and Monetary Units of the Maya*. "Middle American Papers: Middle American Research Series," Pub. 4. New Orleans: Tulane University of Louisiana.

BLUMER, HERBERT. 1935. "Moulding of Mass Behavior through the Motion Picture," *Publications of the American Sociological Society*, 29:115–27.

CARR, MALCOLM. 1937. "The Concept of Evil or Dangerous Wind in Middle America." Master's thesis (on file with the Department of Anthropology), University of Chicago.

CRUZ. *See* Pacheco Cruz, S.

Discurso sobre la constitución de las provincias de Yucatán y Campeche. ("Documentos para la historia de Yucatán," Vol. III.) Merida, Yucatan, Mexico, 1938.

DOLL, EUGENE. 1939. "The Stewardship of the Saint in Mexico and Guatemala." Master's thesis, University of Chicago.

DURKHEIM, EMILE. 1915. *The Elementary Forms of the Religious Life*. Trans. G. W. SWAIN. London: G. Allen & Unwin, Ltd.; New York: Macmillan Co.

———. 1932. *De la division du travail social*. Paris: F. Alcan.

EGGAN, FRED. 1934. "The Maya Kinship System and Cross-Cousin Marriage," *American Anthropologist*, 36:188–202.

———. 1937. "Historical Changes in the Choctaw Kinship System," *ibid.*, 39:34–52.

FÊNG, HAN-YI. 1937. "The Chinese Kinship System," *Harvard Journal of Asiatic Studies*, Vol. II, No. 2.

GANN, THOMAS W. F. 1918. *The Maya Indians of Southern Yucatan and Northern British Honduras*. Smithsonian Institution, Bureau of American Ethnology, Bull. 64. Washington.

HANSEN, ASAEL T. 1934a. "The Ecology of a Latin-American City," pp. 124–42 in *Race and Culture Contacts*, ed. E. B. REUTER. New York: McGraw-Hill Book Co., Inc.

———. 1934b. "Magic in Urban Yucatan." Paper read at the annual meeting of the American Anthropological Association, Pittsburgh.

HOOK, SIDNEY. 1937. "Determinism." *Encyclopaedia of the Social Sciences*, 3:114. New York: Macmillan Co.

HUGHES, EVERETT C. 1928. "Personality Types and the Division of Labor," *American Journal of Sociology*, 33:757.

———. 1937. "Institutional Office and the Person," *ibid.*, 43:404–13.

JONES, THOMAS E. 1926. "Mountain Folk in Japan." Doctor's thesis, Columbia University.

LANDA, DIEGO DE. 1937. *Yucatan before and after the Conquest*. Trans., with notes, WILLIAM GATES. 2d ed. Baltimore: Maya Society.

LINTON, RALPH. 1936. *The Study of Man*. New York: D. Appleton–Century Co.

MARTINEZ HERNANDEZ, JUAN (ed.). 1929. *Diccionario de Motul, Maya-Español*. Merida, Yucatan, Mexico.

MENDIBURU M., RAFAEL, and GÓNGORA R. DE LA GALA, PEDRO. 1934. *Indicador informativo*. Merida, Yucatan: Propagandas-Cía. Editora.

MOTUL DICTIONARY. *See* Martinez Hernandez, Juan (ed.).

PACHECO CRUZ, S. 1934. *Estudio etnográfico de los Mayas del ex-territorio Quintana Roo*. Merida, Yucatan, Mexico.

PARSONS, ELSIE CLEWS. 1927. "Witchcraft among the Pueblos, Indian or Spanish?" *Man*, 27:106–12, 125–28.

———. 1936. *Mitla: Town of the Souls*. Chicago: University of Chicago Press.

RADCLIFFE-BROWN, A. R. 1939. *Taboo*. "Frazer Lecture." Cambridge: Cambridge University Press.

REDFIELD, MARGARET PARK. 1935. *The Folk Literature of a Yucatecan Town*. "Carnegie Institution of Washington Contributions to American Archaeology," No. 13. Washington.

REDFIELD, ROBERT. 1934. "Culture Changes in Yucatan," *American Anthropologist*, 36:57–59.

———. 1936. "The Coati and the Ceiba," *Maya Research* (New Orleans), 3:231–43.

———. 1938. "Race and Class in Yucatan," pp. 511–32 in Carnegie Institution of Washington Pub. 501: *Cooperation in Research*. Washington.

REDFIELD, ROBERT, and REDFIELD, MARGARET PARK. 1940. *Disease and Its Treatment in Dzitas, Yucatan*. Carnegie Institution of Washington Pub.

523. "Contributions to American Anthropology and History," Vol. VI, No. 32. Washington. [Referred to briefly in the notes as "DDZ."]

REDFIELD, ROBERT, and VILLA, ALFONSO. 1934. *Chan Kom: A Maya Village.* Carnegie Institution of Washington Pub. 448. Washington. [Referred to briefly in the notes as "CK."]

———. 1939. *Notes on the Ethnography of Tzeltal Communities of Chiapas.* Carnegie Institution of Washington Pub. 509. Washington.

———. 1942. *The Maya of East Central Quintana Roo.* Washington: Carnegie Institution of Washington. [Referred to briefly in the notes as "QR."]

ROYS, R. L. (ed. and trans.). 1933. *The Book of Chilam Balam of Chumayel.* Washington: Carnegie Institution of Washington.

———. 1939. *The Titles of Ebtun.* Carnegie Institution of Washington Pub. 505. Washington.

ROYS, R. L.; SCHOLES, FRANCE V.; and ADAMS, ELEANOR B. 1940. *Report and Census of the Indians of Cozumel, 1570.* "Carnegie Institution of Washington Contributions to American Anthropology and History," Vol. VI, No. 30. Washington.

SHATTUCK, GEORGE. 1933. *The Peninsula of Yucatan.* Carnegie Institution of Washington Pub. 431. Washington.

SOMBART, WERNER. 1937. *A New Social Philosophy.* Princeton, N.J.: Princeton University Press.

SOUSTELLE, JACQUES. 1935. *Le Totémisme des Lacandons, Maya Research,* 2:325–44.

SPICER, EDWARD H. 1940. *Pascua: A Yaqui Village in Arizona.* Chicago: University of Chicago Press.

STEPHENS, JOHN L. 1843. *Incidents of Travel in Yucatan,* Vol. II. New York: Harper & Bros.

SUMNER, W. G. 1907. *Folkways.* Boston: Ginn & Co.

TAX, SOL. 1939. "Culture and Civilization in Guatemalan Societies," *Scientific Monthly,* 48:467.

———. 1941. "World View and Social Relations in Guatemala," *American Anthropologist,* 43:27–42.

THOMAS, WILLIAM I., and ZNANIECKI, FLORIAN. 1920. *The Polish Peasant in Europe and America.* Chicago: University of Chicago Press.

THOMPSON, J. ERIC. 1930. *Ethnology of the Mayas of Southern and Central British Honduras.* "Field Museum of Natural History: Anthropology Series," Vol. XVII, No. 2. Chicago.

TIZIMÍN, CHILAM BALAM DE. Quarto manuscript, 52 pages (Gates's reproduction).

TÖNNIES, FERDINAND. 1935. *Gemeinschaft und Gesellschaft: Grundbegriffe der reinen Soziologie.* Leipzig.

TORAL (BISHOP). *ca.* 1565. "Diocesan Instructions." Mexico City: Archivo general de Indias, n.d.

TORQUEMADA, F. JUAN DE. 1723. *Segunda parte de los veinte i un libros rituales i monarchia indiana, etc.* Madrid: N. Rodriguez Franco.

WAUCHOPE, ROBERT. 1938. *Modern Maya Houses.* Carnegie Institution of Washington, Pub. 502. Washington.

WIRTH, LOUIS. 1938. "Urbanism as a Way of Life," *American Journal of Sociology*, 44:1–24.

WISDOM, CHARLES. 1940. *The Chorti Indians of Guatemala.* Chicago: University of Chicago Press.

INDEX

Acknowledgments, made to persons assisting the author, xii, xiii

Adrian, H., 382

Adultery, 189; not a cause for breaking up marriage, 190

"Aggregation" versus "organization," 113, 132

Agrarian committee, in Chan Kom, 46

Agricultural techniques, historical origin of, 88

Agriculture: in Chan Kom, 44; in Dzitas, 38; in Merida, 21, 22; in Quintana Roo, 51

Alakob, 118

Alcalde, 68

All Saints' Day, 249

All Souls' Day, 145, 249; ceremonies in connection with, 126

Almanac, source for baptismal names, 226

Alphabetic writing, 92

Altars: flowers used on, 106; in Quintana Roo, 107, 285, 289; oriented, 96; table, 95

"Alternatives," 111, 347; associated with interdependence of elements of a culture, 350

Alux (*aluxob*), 116, 148; confused with *yuntzilob*, in Dzitas, 232; connected with witchcraft, 239; cult not dependent upon shaman-priests, 236–37

Americans, 311; at Chichen Itza, 49; sympathetically regarded in Quintana Roo, 53

Amulets, 307

Angelus, the, 101

Animal husbandry, 90

Animals, domestic, of the gods, 118

Arabic, spoken, 24

Architecture, of the folk, 89

Aristocracy: of city, compared with primitive village, 188; in Merida, 73; race purity of, 23; social position of, 24

Ash Wednesday, in Quintana Roo, 100, 103

Assimilation, 154

Atole, as offering, 106, 285

"Attacks," 317

Auction, 298

Audiencia, 68

Automobile road, to Chichen Itza, 43

Automobile roads, 37

Avoidance, brother-sister, 94

Bagehot, Walter, 386

Balche; see Bark beer

Banking, 156

Baptism, 124; decline of importance of, 221; local differences in, 219–23; mythological sanction for, 220; in relation to *hetzmek*, 124; rituals in connection with, 223–26; simplification of rituals of, 223–24, 225

Bargaining, 159, 161

Bark beer, 96, 106, 107, 121, 275, 296

Barrios: business in, 30; disorganization of, 31; in old-time Merida, 26 ff.; organization of, 28; versus center, in the city, 27, 28

Barter, 164

Baseball, 99

Batab, 68, 154

Bathing, therapeutic, 307

Beals, Ralph, 382

Bee cult, 136; absent in Dzitas, 148

Bee-gods, dwelling to the east, 120

Beehives: ceremonies at opening of, 97; construction of, 89

Bees, ceremonies attendant on, 96

Belize, 164; amount of rainfall at, 5

Bell-ringing, 91

Benedict, Ruth, 370, 386

Bible, 144–45

Bilinguals, 42; in Chan Kom, 46; in Merida, 23

401

Chancah, shrine village, 51

Chanter, 106; in Chan Kom, 46; as godparents, 221; role of, 106; as sacred professional, 81; in the villages, always a man, 253; woman as, 174

Chen rezar, 249

Chichen Itza, 14, 45, 158, 308, 311

Chicle, 11; boom in, 184; commercial exportation of, 163; exported, 162; gatherers of, in Quintana Roo, 11; marketing of, 51; an open resource, 165; in world-economy, 156

Chicleros, 60

Chicxulub, festival of, 300–302

Children, discipline of, 193

Chinese, 374; in Quintana Roo, 54; spoken, 24; in Yucatan, 3

Chocolate, 89

Choice of spouse, general attitudes with respect to, 92

Christ, birthplace of, in East, 120; story of, 91, 103

Church: in Chan Kom, 48; a formal institution in the city, 255; as an interest group, 258; in Tusik, 56; in X-Cacal, 56

Cities, principal, of Yucatan, 19

Citrus fruit, 90

City: commercialism of, 160; maker of trade, 156; summarized briefly, 34; as a type of society, 386

City influence, in Dzitas, 152–53

Clans, 189

Class: changes in, in Merida, 74; middle, 301; upper, religion of, 256

Class and race, history of, 58 ff.

Class system, disintegration of, in Merida, 28

Classes: breakdown of, 70, in Dzitas, 67; conclusions as to, summarized, 59; in Dzitas, 64–66, 150, 377; in old Dzitas, 70; in present-day Merida, 74; relatively absent in the village, 166; tabular summary of, 375

Classificatory terms, 94

Climate, of peninsula, 4–5

Clowns, sacred, 294

Coati-impersonator, 96, 279, 294

Coffee, 91

Collective labor, secularization of, 179

Colors, associated with four directions, 95

Comisario, 46

Commerce: differences among communities as to, 155 ff.; in Dzitas, 40–41; effect of, in Guatemalan highlands, 365–66; and secularization of society, 185

Commercialism: of city, 160; of four communities, 183

Commercialization: of festival of patron, 297–302; of healing functions, 325–26

Communications, in Quintana Roo, 52

Communion, 95, 100, 140, 285; a widespread element, 91

Communism, 227

Communities: on haciendas, 370; size of, 371–72; studied, reasons for choice, 14

Community: defined, 15; the isolated, characterized, 343; two contrasting types of, 343

Compadre: as a general word of respect, 222; choice of, 221; general attitudes with respect to, 92

Companies: of Quintana Roo tribes, 53–54, 178; of subtribe, in festival organization, 281–82

Conclusions: final summary, 368–69; general, of this work, 338–39; generalizing, of this work, 341 ff.; of study, stated in advance, 18

"Configuration," 386

Conflict: within family, 192; between folk and modern medicine, 316–17; interpersonal, in connection with sickness, 330–31; with respect to class system, 150

Connotations, 112

Conservatism, 188

Contacts, in relation to cultural disorganization, 134

Continence, ceremonial, 96

Copal, 94

Corn; *see* Maize

Corredor, in X-Cacal, 56

Cosmological ideas, increasing vagueness of, 148

Cosmos, quadrilateral, 95, 119

Costume: in Chan Kom, 48; changes

Property, 166 ff.; family, 191; in land, 170–72

Protestantism: in Chan Kom, 144–46; effect of, on baptism, 221; of little influence on the pagan cult, 235; patron saint challenged by, 244; in relation to sectarian differences, 195

Protestants: in Dzitas, 149, 151; self-consciousness of Catholics at appearance of, 266

Public works, 178

Publications, other, of this project, xi

Puc keyem, 280, 285, 294, 298

Punishment: after death, 91; of children, 193; for moral wrongs, 190

"Pure" versus "impure," 354

Purification, 128; of fowl scarificed, 96

Purity, ritual for, 121

Quarrels, 151; within the family, 190; present in Chan Kom, 328

Quintana Roo: density of population in, 7; depopulation of, 9; family in, 188–90, 194; festival of the patron, in, 278–86; history of, 57; isolation of, 7, 14; kinship terms in, 204–7; Maya of, 11; race and class in, 80 ff.; *santos* in, 241–42; social change in, 57; tribal organization of, 50–51

Rabbit stories, 99

Race: in Chan Kom, 47; mythological, 144; in Quintana Roo, 54; role of, in Merida, 75

"Race," as used in this work, 374

Race and class, history of, 58 ff.

Racial intermixture, 67; in Dzitas, 64, 66

Radcliffe-Brown, A. R., 371

Railroad, as an industrial development in Dzitas, 40

Railroads, centering in Merida, 9

Rain ceremonies: as combination of cults, 106–7; comparison of, in Chan Kom and Quintana Roo, 95, 107; connection of, with Catholic rite, 248; differences of, in the four communities, 237; mentioned, 71; in old-time Dzitas, 154; as performed in Dzitas, 233; Protestant participation in, 145

Rain forest, 6; as hiding-place for rebel Indians, 9

Rainfall: regional differences in, 5; seasonal differences in, 5

Rainfall gradient, 5–6

Rain-gods, 95, 122; animals of, 117; appearing in the first rains, 5; connected with sacrifice of animals, 96; impersonated, 96, 120; St. Michael as chief of, 140; as thought of in Dzitas, 232

Ramillete: in Chan Kom area, 288; in Quintana Roo, 286

Rationalization, 231; in connection with reasons for festival of patron, 302; of stories about *santos*, 261–62

Rebozo, 91

Reciprocal terms, 94

Reciprocity, between gods and men, 115

"Red men," 144

Redfield, Margaret Park, 370

Reform, 150

Religion: becoming magic, summarized, 264–65; Catholic, 140, in Chan Kom, 101, as in interest group, 267, two distinct cults in the city, 256; Christian, adjustment to in peripheral communities, 101–7, in Merida, 254–62, secularization of, 240–44, survival of, in peripheral communities, 99–100; Christian and Indian elements in, 91–92; in connection with the marketing of maize, 63; in connection with morals, 309; in connection with morals apparent at death rites, 307; European, distribution of, 99; Indian elements in, 95; integrated with conceptions of disease, 309–10; local differences, summarized, 258–59; not intensely personal, 230, 311; not often connected with sickness in Merida, 324; pagan, becoming folklore, 240, causes of decline in, 235–36, decline of generalized, 230, disappearance of, 266–67, in Dzitas, 98, 231, in Merida, 238–39, secret character of, 105, survival of, 96–97; pagan and Christian connected, 139; relating to morality, 130; separation of Catholic and pagan elements, 266; separation of Spanish and Indian elements, 35; tending to become magic, 234–35; of upper class, 256

cult upon, 236; function of, in festival of patron, 290, in Quintana Roo, 55; lustrative ceremony for, 182, lustrative retreat of, 96; medical and religious knowledge of, 310; practically absent in Merida, 239; in Quintana Roo, 105; in relation to chanter, 106; without rivals in the village, 329; skepticism toward, 311; as treater of disease, 309

Share-croppers, 37

Shattuck, George, 373

Shrine village, 53

Shrines, 88, 94

Sickness; see Disease

Simplicity, of Yucatan, 1 ff.

Sin, 126; in connection with maize, 127; in connection with witchcraft, 333

Sisal; see Henequen

Skepticism, 164; in Dzitas, 98; relative absence of, in Quintana Roo, 101; with regard to magic, 337; with regard to pagan religion, 231, 235; with regard to shaman-priest, 311

Smallpox, 97

Smoking, ritual, 219

Social gradient, 13

Social relations, definition of, 15

"Social segment" versus "social organ," x

Socialist party, 20

Societas versus *civitas*, x

Society: consideration of Yucatan as a single, 58; definition of, 15; isolated, characterized by secular and impersonal features, 358; in transition, 154

Sombart, Werner, 382

Son-in-law service, 205, 214

Sophistication, 72, 110

Sorcery; see Witchcraft

Soul of the dead: in connection with sickness, 309–10; after death, 126; peace of, dependent upon conditions of balance, 128

Soustelle, Jacques, 382

Spanish language: prestige of, 62; role of, in social life, 23; use of, in Chan Kom, 46, in Dzitas, 42, in Merida, 23, in Quintana Roo, 54

Spicer, Edward H., 383, 386

Spices, 91

Spiritualism, 151, 244; in connection with disease, 312 ff.

Sponsors, of marriage, 219

Sponsorship, Indian custom of, 220

Sport, 24

Srole, Leo, 386

Status, 67; in connection with the city, 313; diagrams of, 81, 82, 83, 84; in Dzitas, 38, 39, 63 ff.; history of, summarized, 83, 84; history of, in Yucatan, summarized, 58; history of changes in, summarized, 79; inferior, of Indians, 61; influence of occupation on, in Quintana Roo, 165; in Merida, 24, 25, 72 ff.; in old Dzitas, 68, 69; in Quintana Roo, 55; in relation to choice of godparents, 222; of shaman-priests, 181; summary as to, 58, 59; summary restated, 75, 76; symbols of, 71; terms for gradual differences in, 76; in town and village, summarized, 63, 64

Status groups, common definition of, 59

Status terms, functional character of, 78; regional differences in, 78

Stephens, John L., 384

Stores, 155–56, 157

"Strain of consistency," 141

Strangers, attitude toward, 62

Structure, in connection with culture, 112

Subcultures, 349–50

Sublevados, 11

Subtribes, in Quintana Roo, 13, 51

Sugar, 91; nonproduction of, in Dzitas, 36; production regions of, 22

Suicide, 119

Sumner, W. G., 141

Surnames: change of, 69; Maya, social significance of, 25; and social classes, in Merida, 73; Spanish, 66, 67; and status, 66; unimportance of, in present-day Merida, 74

"Survivals," 138; of ancient customs, 278–79, 294–95, 304

Symbols: of fertility, 279; of status, 64

Syrians, 23, 25, 72, 222; in Dzitas, 40; residential concentration of, 32; in Yucatan, 3